CW00404782

The Organization of
African Unity

The Organization of African Unity

An Analysis of its Role

Second Edition

Gino J. Naldi

MANSELL

LONDON AND NEW YORK

Mansell Publishing Limited, *A Cassell imprint*
Wellington House, 125 Strand, London WC2R 0BB
370 Lexington Avenue, New York, NY 10017–6550

First published 1989. Second edition 1999

© Gino J. Naldi 1989, 1999

All rights reserved. No part of this publication may be reproduced or
transmitted in any form or by any means, electronic or mechanical, including
photocopying, recording or any information storage or retrieval system, without
prior permission in writing from the publishers or their appointed agents.

British Library Cataloguing-in-Publication Data
A catalogue record for this book is available from the British Library.

ISBN 0-7201-2243-0

Library of Congress Cataloging-in-Publication Data
Naldi, Gino J.
     The Organization of African Unity : an analysis of its role/Gino
J. Naldi.—2nd ed.
        p.   cm.
     Includes index.
     ISBN 0-7201-2243-0
     1. Organization of African Unity,   2. African cooperation.
     3. Africa—Foreign relations—1960–   I. Title.
     KQE721.N35   2000
     351.24'9—dc21   99-15336
                                                                                                          CIP

Typeset by Ensystems, Saffron Walden, Essex
Printed and bound in Great Britain by Bookcraft (Bath) Ltd.

Contents

Preface vii

Abbreviations ix

Table of Cases xiii

1. The Organization of African Unity 1

2. The Question of the Western Sahara 52

3. Refugees 78

4. The African Charter on Human and Peoples' Rights 109

5. Protection of the Environment 213

6. The African Economic Community 240

Index 259

Preface

The developments that have occurred in Africa since the publication of the first edition of this book in 1989 justify the appearance of a new edition. Progress has been made across various fronts, white domination has crumbled, autocrats have been toppled, democratic regimes are taking office across much of Africa, human rights are being strengthened, political and economic reforms are showing some signs of bearing fruit, so much so that there is talk of an African renaissance. However, there is no room for complacency as the dreadful events in the Great Lakes region of Central Africa demonstrate. In addition, the roots of democracy are sometimes shallow and the forces of reaction, such as in Sierra Leone, have demonstrated that they are still dangerous. The UN has been driven to despair on occasion, as in Angola. Despite the wars, human rights abuses and famine that seem to characterize postcolonial Africa, it would be wrong to dismiss the whole of Africa as a hopeless mess, and the OAU as an inconsequential forum. Are Yugoslavia, or Georgia, or Cyprus representative of Europe? Africa is a continent of variety, with many differences but also with some common problems. It has been the intention to accentuate both the positive and negative features of modern Africa as addressed by the OAU.

This book reflects the preoccupations of the OAU. There is a new chapter, on environmental law, while the chapter on economic law has been rewritten to focus exclusively on the African Economic Community. The chapter on human rights has been extensively expanded and account has been taken of domestic developments as illustrative points. The other chapters have been revised and updated. It may be that the Western Sahara dispute discussed in Chapter 2 will be resolved in the very near future. The referendum is scheduled for 2000. However, there have already been so many postponements that it should not surprise us if the millennium comes and goes without any further progress being made. The chapter on Chad has been dropped since it had lost its topicality although information still of relevance to a broader study of the OAU has been incorporated into Chapter 1. The objective of the second edition remains the same, that is, to undertake a critical analysis, from a legal perspective, of the principal issues relating to the endeavours of the OAU.

I owe a debt of gratitude to all those who contributed, in whatever way, to this book. In particular, I would like to thank Dr. Frank Wooldridge, Dr. Konstantinos Magliveras, Professor Rosemary Pattenden, Mark Stallworthy for their helpful suggestions, and Jenny Deadman, who typed part of the manuscript. I am grateful to UEA for the period of study leave which allowed me to bring this edition to completion within a reasonable time. I am especially grateful to Veronica Higgs and Dominic Shryane of Mansell for their patience and for their advice on all matters of publication.

Special thanks are due to Angela for sharing the burden of this work. Her support and encouragement were instrumental in its completion.

I have endeavoured to state the law as it stood on 31 December 1998.

Gino J. Naldi
School of Law
University of East Anglia

Abbreviations

AC	Appeal Cases
ACHR	American Convention on Human Rights
ACP	African-Caribbean-Pacific Community
ADB	African Development Bank
AEC	African Economic Community
AIR	All India Reports
AJIL	*American Journal of International Law*
All ER	All England Law Reports
ALR	Australian Law Reports
APPER	Africa's Priority Programme for Economic Recovery
ASICL Proc.	*Proceedings of the African Society of International and Comparative Law*
BCLR	Butterworths Constitutional Law Reports
BPEAR	Bureau for the Placement and Education of African Refugees
BYIL	*British Yearbook of International Law*
CC	Constitutional Court of South Africa
CLB	*Commonwealth Law Bulletin*
CMLR	Common Market Law Reports
CMLRev	*Common Market Law Review*
COMESA	Common Market for Eastern and Southern Africa
EC	European Community
ECA	United Nations Economic Commission for Africa
ECHR	European Convention on Human Rights
ECJ	European Court of Justice
ECOMOG	ECOWAS Cease-fire Monitoring Group
ECOSOC	United Nations Economic and Social Council
ECOWAS	Economic Community of West African States
ECR	European Court Reports
EHRR	European Human Rights Reports

ELRev	*European Law Review*
F 2d	Federal Reporter 2d series
FRELIMO	Front for the Liberation of Mozambique
HRC	Human Rights Committee
HRLJ	*Human Rights Law Journal*
IACHR	Inter-American Court of Human Rights
ICARA	International Conference on Assistance to Refugees in Africa
ICCPR	International Covenant on Civil and Political Rights
ICES	International Covenant on Economic, Social and Cultural Rights
ICJ	International Court of Justice
ICLQ	*International and Comparative Law Quarterly*
IHRR	*International Human Rights Reports*
IJIL	Indian Journal of International Law
ILC	International Law Commission
ILM	*International Legal Materials*
ILO	International Labour Organization
IMF	International Monetary Fund
IMO	International Maritime Organization
JAL	*Journal of African Law*
Keesing's	*Keesing's Contemporary Archives/Record of World Events*
LesCA	Court of Appeal of Lesotho
LRC	Law Reports of the Commonwealth
MINURCA	United Nations Mission in the Central African Republic
MINURSO	United Nations Mission for the Referendum in Western Sahara
MISAB	Inter-African Mission to Monitor the Implementation of the Bangui Agreements
MONUA	United Nations Observer Mission in Angola
MR	Mauritius Reports
Naldi	*Documents of the Organization of African Unity* (1992)
NGO	Non Governmental Organization
NIEO	New International Economic Order
NILR	*Netherlands International Law Review*
NmH	High Court of Namibia
NmS	Supreme Court of Namibia
OAS	Organization of American States
OAU	Organization of African Unity
OECD	Organization for Economic Co-operation and Development

UNOMOZ	United Nations Operation in Mozambique
PCIJ	Permanent Court of International Justice
QB	Queen's Bench Division
RADIC	*African Journal of International and Comparative Law*
RENAMO	Mozambique National Resistance Movement
RGDIP	*Revue Générale de Droit International Public*
RIAA	Reports of International Arbitral Awards
RPF	Rwandan Patriotic Front
SA	South African Law Reports
SADC	Southern African Development Community
SADR	Saharan Arab Democratic Republic
SARRED	International Conference on the Plight of Refugees, Returnees and Displaced Persons in Southern Africa
S.Ct.	United States Supreme Court Reports
UDHR	Universal Declaration on Human Rights
UN	United Nations
UNAMIR	United Nations Assistance Mission for Rwanda
UNAVEM	United Nations Angola Verification Mission
UNCED	United Nations Conference on Environment and Development
UNEP	United Nations Environment Programme
UNESCO	United Nations Educational, Scientific and Cultural Organization
UNHCR	United Nations High Commission for Refugees
UNITA	National Union for the Total Independence of Angola
UNITAF	Unified Task Force
UNOMIL	United Nations Observer Mission in Liberia
UNOSOM	United Nations Operation in Somalia
UN PAAERD	United Nations Programme of Action for African Economic Recovery and Development
UNTS	United Nations Treaty Series
WLR	Weekly Law Reports
YEL	*Yearbook of European Law*
ZH	High Court of Zimbabwe
ZLR	Zimbabwe Law Reports
ZS	Supreme Court of Zimbabwe

Table of Cases

AFRICAN COMMISSION ON HUMAN AND PEOPLE'S RIGHTS

Account of the Internal Legislation of Nigeria and the Disposition of the African Charter on Human and Peoples' Rights (Communication No. 129/94) **207**

Achutan, Khrischna (on behalf of Aleke Banda) *v.* Malawi (Communication No. 64/92) 3 IHRR (1996) 134 **168**

Amnesty International (on behalf of Orton and Vera Chirwa) *v.* Malawi (Communication Nos. 68/92, 78/92) 3 IHRR (1996) 134 **120, 168**

Amnesty International *v.* Tunisia (Communication No. 69/92) **207**

Badjogoume, Hilaire *v.* Benin (Communication No. 17/88) **207**

Baes, Maria *v.* Zaire (Communication No. 31/89) **206**

Buyingo *v.* Uganda (Communication No. 8/88) **207**

Capitao, Alberto *v.* Tanzania (Communication No. 53/91) 3 IHRR (1996) 123 **207**

Centre for Independence of Judges and Lawyers *v.* Algeria (Communication Nos. 104/94, 109–126/94) **206**

Civil Liberties Organization (in respect of Nigerian Bar Association) *v.* Nigeria (Communication No. 101/93) **124, 182**

Civil Liberties Organization *v.* Nigeria (Communication No. 129/94) 18 HRLJ (1997) 35 **162, 180**

Commission Nationale des Droits de l'Homme et des Libertés *v.* Chad (Communication No. 74/92) 18 HRLJ (1997) 34 **159, 160–1, 167, 175, 179, 208**

Constitutional Rights Project (in respect of Wahab Akamu, G. Adega and Others) *v.* Nigeria (Communication No. 60/91) 3 IHRR (1996) 132 **168, 180**

Constitutional Rights Project (in respect of Zamani Lakwot) *v.* Nigeria (Communication No. 87/93) 3 IHRR (1996) 137 **122, 168, 170, 180**

Co-ordinating Secretary of the Free Citizens Convention *v.* Ghana (Communication No. 4/88) **206**

Courson *v.* Zimbabwe (Communication No. 136/94) 3 IHRR (1996)
129   **197**

Degli, Jean Yaovi (au nom du Caporal N. Bikagni), Union Interafricaine des
Droits de l'Homme, Commission Internationale de Juristes *v.* Togo
(Communication Nos. 83/92, 88/93, 91/93) 3 IHRR (1996) 125   **208**
Diawara, El Had Boubacare *v.* Benin (Communication Nos. 18/88, 16/88,
17/88) 3 IHRR (1996) 122   **207**
Dioumessi, Kande, Kaba *v.* Guinea (Communication No. 70/92) 4 IHRR
(1997) 85   **206**
Dumbuya, Sana *v.* The Gambia (Communication No. 127/94) 3 IHRR (1996)
129   **207**

Free Legal Assistance Group, Lawyers Committee for Human Rights, Union
Interafricaine des Droits de l'Homme, and Les Témoins de Jéhovahs *v.*
Zaire (Communication Nos. 25/89, 47/90, 56/91, 100/93)   **168, 175,**
177, 179, 184, 194, 195, 207, 208

Haye, Paul S. *v.* The Gambia (Communication No. 90/93) 3 IHRR (1996)
126   **207**

International Pen (in respect of Kemal al-Jazouli) *v.* Sudan (Communication
No. 92/93) 3 IHRR (1996) 127   **207**

Katangese Peoples' Congress *v.* Zaire (Communication No. 75/92) 3 IHRR
(1996) 136   **44, 133, 206**
Kenya Human Rights Commission *v.* Kenya (Communication No. 135/94) 4
IHRR (1997) 86   **207**

Lawyers' Committee for Human Rights *v.* Zaire (Communication No. 47/
90) 18 HRLJ (1997) 32   **179**

Njoka *v.* Kenya (Communication No. 142/94) 3 IHRR (1996) 130   **206**

ARBITRAL AWARDS

Arbitral Award of 31 July 1989 (Guinea-Bissau *v.* Senegal) 83 ILR 1   **44**

Colombia/Venezuela Boundary Arbitration (1922)   **43**
Conference on Yugoslavia Arbitration Commission No. 1 92 ILR 162   **76**
Conference on Yugoslavia Arbitration Commission No. 2 92 ILR 167   **44**
Conference on Yugoslavia Arbitration Commission No. 3 31 ILM 1499
(1992)   **43, 44**
Conference on Yugoslavia Arbitration Commission No. 8 92 ILR 199
45, 76

Guinea/Guinea-Bissau Arbitration 25 ILM 251 (1986)   **46**

Island of Palmas Case 2 RIAA 829 (1928)   **44**

Texaco *v.* Libya 17 ILM 1 (1978)   **192, 202**
Trial Smelter Arbitration (1938 and 1941) 3 RIAA 1905; 9 ILR 315   **204, 234**

AUSTRALIA

Commonwealth of Australia *v.* Tasmania (1983) 46 ALR 625   **204**

Gerhardy *v.* Brown (1985) 57 ALR 472   **163**

Koowarta *v.* Bjelke-Petersen (1982) 39 ALR 417   **163**

BOTSWANA

Dow, Unity *v.* Attorney-General [1992] LRC (Const) 623   **160, 165, 177**

State *v.* Ntesang [1995] 2 LRC 338   **176**
State *v.* Petrus [1985] LRC (Const) 699   **175**

CANADA

Reference re Secession of Quebec 37 ILM 1340 (1998)   **44, 201**

COLOMBIA

Fundepublico *v.* Mayor of Bugalagrande and Others (1992)   **234**

EUROPEAN COMMISSION ON HUMAN RIGHTS

Arrowsmith *v.* United Kingdom (1981) 3 EHRR 218   **185**

Cyprus *v.* Turkey (1976) 4 EHRR 482   **198**

East African Asians *v.* United Kingdom (1981) 3 EHRR 76   **106, 163, 164, 189**

Gay News Ltd *v.* Lemon (1983) 5 EHRR 123   **185**

Paton *v.* United Kingdom (1981) 3 EHRR 408   **170**

EUROPEAN COURT OF HUMAN RIGHTS

Abdulaziz, Cabales and Balkandali *v.* United Kingdom Series A, Vol. 94 (1985)   **163, 164, 196, 197**
Airey *v.* Ireland Series A, Vol. 32 (1979)   **181**
Aksoy *v.* Turkey, Reports 1996– VI   **173**
Aydin *v.* Turkey, Reports 1997– VI   **173, 198**

Barbera, Messegue and Jabardo *v.* Spain Series A, Vol. 146 (1988)   **180, 182**
Belgian Linguistic Case Series A, Vol. 6 (1968)   **162, 195**
Belilos *v.* Switzerland Series A, Vol. 132 (1988)   **181**
Bonisch *v.* Austria Series A, Vol. 92 (1985)   **182**
Bouamar *v.* Belgium Series A, Vol. 129 (1988)   **177**
Boyle and Rice *v.* United Kingdom Series A, Vol. 131 (1988)   **162**
Brannigan and McBride *v.* United Kingdom Series A, Vol. 258-B (1993)   **159**
Brogan *v.* United Kingdom Series A, Vol. 145-B (1988)   **159, 178**

Campbell *v.* United Kingdom Series A, Vol. 233 (1993)   **160**
Campbell and Cosans *v.* United Kingdom Series A, Vol. 48 (1982)   **196**
Campbell and Fell *v.* United Kingdom Series A, Vol. 80 (1984)   **182**
Castells *v.* Spain Series A, Vol. 236 (1992)   **186**
Colozza and Rubinat *v.* Italy Series A, Vol. 89 (1985)   **182**
Cossey *v.* United Kingdom Series A, Vol. 184 (1990)   **196, 197**
Cruz-Varas *v.* Sweden Series A, Vol. 201 (1991)   **102**

De Jong, Baljet and Van den Brink *v.* The Netherlands Series A, Vol. 77
    (1984)   **178**
Dudgeon *v.* United Kingdom Series A, Vol. 45 (1981)   **160, 197**

Engel *v.* The Netherlands Series A, Vol. 22 (1976)   **188**
Ezelin *v.* France Series A, Vol. 202 (1991)   **188**

F *v.* Switzerland Series A, Vol. 128 (1987)   **197**
Findlay *v.* United Kingdom Reports 1997–I   **179**
Fox, Campbell and Hartley *v.* United Kingdom Series A, Vol. 182
    (1990)   **177**
Funke *v.* France Series A, Vol. 256-A (1993)   **180**

Gaskin *v.* United Kingdom Series A, Vol. 160 (1989)   **238**
Glasenapp *v.* Germany Series A, Vol. 104 (1986)   **190**
Goddi *v.* Italy Series A, Vol. 76 (1984)   **182**
Golder *v.* United Kingdom Series A, Vol. 18 (1975)   **180**
Granger *v.* United Kingdom Series A, Vol. 174 (1990)   **181**
Guerra and Others *v.* Italy Reports 1998–I   **235, 236**

Handyside *v.* United Kingdom Series A, Vol. 24 (1976)   **160, 185, 187**
Herczegfalvy *v.* Austria Series A, Vol. 244 (1992)   **178**
Hoffmann *v.* Austria Series A, Vol. 255-C (1993)   **165**
Huber *v.* Switzerland Series A, Vol. 188 (1990)   **178**

Inze *v.* Austria Series A, Vol. 126 (1987)   **165, 199**
Ireland *v.* United Kingdom Series A, Vol. 25 (1978)   **119, 159**

James *v.* United Kingdom Series A, Vol. 98 (1986)   **191**
Jersild *v.* Denmark Series A, Vol. 298 (1994)   **186**
Johnston *v.* Ireland Series A, Vol. 112 (1987)   **165, 197**

Kjeldsen, Busk Madsen and Pedersen *v.* Denmark Series A, Vol. 23 (1976)   **196**

Klass *v.* Germany Series A, Vol. 28 (1979)   **162**

Kokkinakis *v.* Greece Series A, Vol. 260-A (1993)   **182, 184**

Kosiek *v.* Germany Series A, Vol. 105 (1986)   **190**

Laskey, Jaggard and Brown *v.* United Kingdom Reports 1997 I   **177**

Lawless *v.* Ireland Series A, Vol. 3 (1961)   **159**

Leander *v.* Sweden Series A, Vol. 116 (1987)   **238**

Lingens *v.* Austria Series A, Vol. 103 (1986)   **185, 186, 187**

Lithgow *v.* United Kingdom Series A, Vol. 102 (1986)   **160, 192, 202**

Loizidou *v.* Turkey Report 1996–V   **206**

López Ostra *v.* Spain Series A, Vol. 303-C (1994)   **235, 236**

Luedicke, Belkacem and Koç *v.* Germany Series A, Vol. 29 (1978)   **183**

McCann, Farrell and Savage *v.* United Kingdom Series A, Vol. 324 (1995)   **167, 168**

Marckx *v.* Belgium Series A, Vol. 31 (1979)   **165, 191, 199**

Mathieu-Mohin and Clerfayt *v.* Belgium Series A, Vol. 113 (1987)   **190**

Mueller *v.* Switzerland Series A, Vol. 133 (1988)   **160, 187**

National Union of Belgian Police *v.* Belgium Series A, Vol. 19 (1975)   **188**

O, H, W, B and R *v.* United Kingdom Series A, Vols. 120 and 121 (1987)   **211**

Oberschlick *v.* Austria Series A, Vol. 204 (1991)   **186**

Observer, The and The Guardian *v.* United Kingdom Series A, Vol. 216 (1991)   **186**

Olsson *v.* Sweden Series A, Vol. 130 (1988)   **160**

Otto-Preminger-Institut *v.* Austria Series A, Vol. 295 (1994)   **184**

Pine Valley Developments *v.* Ireland Series A, Vol. 222 (1991)   **236**

Plattform 'Artze für das Leben' *v.* Austria Series A, Vol. 139 (1988)   **188**

Poitrimol *v.* France Series A, Vol. 277-A (1993)   **181**

Pretto *v.* Italy Series A, Vol. 71 (1983)   **182**

Quaranta *v.* Switzerland Series A, Vol. 205 (1991)   **181**

Rasmussen *v.* Denmark Series A, Vol. 87 (1984)   **162**

Rees *v.* United Kingdom Series A, Vol. 106 (1986)   **197**

Schiesser *v.* Switzerland Series A, Vol. 34 (1979)   **177**

Schmidt and Dahlstrom *v.* Sweden Series A, Vol. 21 (1976)   **187, 188**

Soering *v.* United Kingdom Series A, Vol. 161 (1989)   **162, 176, 206**

Stogmuller *v.* Austria Series A, Vol. 9 (1969)   **181**

Swedish Engine Drivers Union *v.* Sweden Series A, Vol. 20 (1976)   **187**

Tomasi *v.* France Series A, Vol. 241-A (1992) **171**
Tre Traktorer Aktiebolag *v.* Sweden Series A, Vol. 159 (1989) **191**
Tyrer *v.* United Kingdom Series A, Vol. 26 (1978) **160, 175**

Van der Mussele *v.* Belgium Series A, Vol. 70 (1983) **176**
Van Droogenbroeck *v.* Belgium Series A, Vol. 50 (1982) **176**
Van Marle *v.* The Netherlands Series A, Vol. 101 (1986) **183, 191**
Vilvarajah *v.* United Kingdom Series A, vol. 215 (1991) **100, 101, 102**

Welch *v.* United Kingdom Series A, Vol. 307-A (1995) **182**
Wemhoff *v.* Germany Series A, Vol. 7 (1968) **160, 178, 181, 209**

Young, James and Webster *v.* United Kingdom Series A, Vol. 44 (1981) **188**

EUROPEAN COURT OF JUSTICE

Amministrazione delle Finanze dello Stato *v.* Simmenthal SpA (Case 106/
77) [1978] ECR 629 **257**

Barber *v.* Guardian Royal Exchange Assurance Group (Case C-262/88)
[1990] ECR I-1889 **193**
Bilka-Kaufhaus GmbH *v.* Weber von Hartz (Case 170/84) [1986] ECR
1607 **162, 193**

Comitato di Coordinamento per la Difesa della Cava *v.* Regione Lombardia
(Case C-236/92) [1994] ECR I-483 **235**
Commission *v.* Belgium (Case 149/79) [1980] ECR 3881 **190**
Commission *v.* Belgium: Re Imports of Waste (Case C-2/90) [1993] 1 CMLR
365 **227, 235**
Commission *v.* Council (ERTA) (Case 22/70) [1971] ECR 274 **254, 256**
Commission *v.* Denmark: Re Disposable Beer Cans (Case 302/86) [1988]
ECR 4607 **234, 235**
Commission *v.* Germany [1991] ECR 2567 **237**
Commission *v.* Germany [1991] ECR I-4983 **237**
Commission *v.* Italy (Case 225/85) [1987] ECR 2625 **190**
Commission *v.* Spain [1993] ECR I-4221 **235**
Commission *v.* United Kingdom: Re Equal Treatment for Men and Women
(Case 165/82) [1983] ECR 3431 **162**
Costa *v.* ENEL (Case 6/64) [1964] ECR 585 **256**

Dekker *v.* Stichting Vormingscentrum Voor Jong Volwassenen (Case C-177/
88) [1990] ECR I-3941 **193**
Defrenne *v.* SABENA (No. 2) (Case 43/75) [1976] ECR 455 **193**
Defrenne *v.* SABENA (No. 3) (Case 149/77) [1978] ECR 1365 **164**

Enderby *v.* Frenchay Area Health Authority (Case C-127/92) [1993] ECR I-
5535 **193**

European Parliament *v.* Commission (Case C-156/93) [1995] ECR I-2019 **254**

European Parliament *v.* Council (Chernobyl) (Case C-70/88) [1990] ECR 2041 **255**

European Parliament *v.* Council (Comitology) (Case 302/87) [1988] ECR 5616 **255**

Faccini Dori *v.* Recreb (Case C-91/92) [1994] ECR I-3235 **256**

Firma Foto-Frost *v.* Hauptzollamt Lübeck-Ost (Case 314/85) [1987] ECR 4199 **257**

Firma A. Racke *v.* Hauptzollamt Mainz (Case 98/78) ECR 69 **256**

Garland *v.* British Rail Engineering Ltd (Case 12/81) [1982] ECR 359 **193**

Grant *v.* South West Trains Ltd (Case C-249/96) [1998] All ER (EC) 193 **162, 166**

Grimaldi *v.* Fonds des Maladies Professionelles (Case C-322/88) [1989] ECR 4407 **256**

Internationale Handelsgesellschaft GmbH *v.* EVGF (Case 11/70) [1970] ECR 1125 **209, 257**

Jenkins *v.* Kingsgate (Clothing Productions) Ltd (Case 96/80) [1981] ECR 911 **193**

Kalanke *v.* Freie Hansestadt Bremen (Case C-450/93) [19996] All ER (EC) 66 **165**

Lachmuller *v.* Commission (Case 43/59) [1960] ECR 463 **253**

Levin *v.* Staatssecretaris van Justitie (Case 53/81) [1982] ECR 1035 **258**

Marleasing SA *v.* La Comercial Internacional de Alimentacion SA (Case C-106/89) [1992] ECR I-4135 **256, 257**

Marschall *v.* Land Nordrhein-Westfalen (Case C-409/95) [1998] I CMLR 547 **165**

Marshall *v.* Southampton and South West Area Health Authority (Teaching) (No. 1) (Case 152/84) [1986] ECR 723 **164**

Mulder *v.* Minister van Landbouw en Visserij (Case 120/86) [1988] ECR 2321 **256**

P *v.* S and Cornwall County Council (Case C-13/94) [1996] ECR I-2143 **164**

Pecastaing *v.* Belgium (Case 98/79) [1980] ECR 691 **182**

R *v.* Henn and Darby (Case 34/79) [1978] ECR 3795 **160**

R *v.* Kirk (Case 63/83) [1984] ECR 2689 **256**

R *v.* Minister for Agriculture, Fisheries and Food, ex parte Fedesa (Case C-331/88) [1990] ECR 4023 **256**

R *v.* Secretary of State for Transport ex parte Factortame Ltd No. 2 (Case C-213/89) [1990] ECR I-2433 **255, 257**

Rinner-Kuhn *v.* FWW Spezial Gebaudereinigung GmbH (Case 171/88) [1989] ECR 2743 **162, 193**

Roquette Frères *v.* Council (Case 138/79) [1980] ECR 3333 **254**

Stichting Greenpeace Council *v.* Commission (Case C-321/95 P) [1998] All ER (EC) 620 **235**

Torfaen Borough Council *v.* B & Q plc (Case 145/88) [1989] ECR 3851 **257**

Van Gend en Loos *v.* Nederlandse Administratie der Belastingen (Case 26/62) [1963] ECR 1 **256**

Von Colson and Kamann *v.* Land Nordrhein-Westfalen (Case 14/83) [1984] ECR 1891 **256**

COURT OF FIRST INSTANCE

WWF UK (World Wide Fund for Nature) (Sweden intervening) *v.* Commission (France and United Kingdom intervening) (Case T-105/95) [1997] 2 CMLR 55 **238**

GERMANY

Brunner *v.* The European Union Treaty [1994] 1 CMLR 57 **257**

HUMAN RIGHTS COMMITTEE

Ackla *v.* Togo (Communication No. 505/92) **189**

Aduayom *et al. v.* Togo (Communications Nos. 422–424/1990) **185, 186, 190**

Aumeeruddy-Cziffra *v.* Mauritius 4 HRLJ (1983) 139 **162, 164, 196**

Bahamonde, Oló *v.* Equatorial Guinea (Communication No. 468/1991) **167, 177, 178, 180, 181, 189**

Birhashwirwa and Mulumba *v.* Zaire (Communication Nos. 241 and 242/1987) **175, 177, 178, 189**

Bozize *v.* Central African Republic (Communication No. 428/1990) **174–5, 178**

Bwalya *v.* Zambia (Communication No. 314/1988) **177**

Camargo *v.* Colombia (Communication No. 46/1979) **168**

EHP *v.* Canada (Communication No. 67/1980) **236–7**

El-Megreisi *v.* Libya (Communication No. 440/1990) **175, 177, 178**

J.R.T. and the W.G. Party *v.* Canada (Communication No. 104/81) **187**

Kanana, Isidore *v.* Zaire (Communication No. 458/1991) **120, 177**

Koné *v.* Senegal (Communication No. 386/1989) **177, 178**

Lovelace *v*. Canada 2 HRLJ (1981) 158   **162**
Lubuto *v*. Zambia (Communication No. 390/90)   **169, 181**

Marais *v*. Madagascar (Communication No. 49/1979)   **175, 181**
Mbenge *v*. Zaire (Communication No. 16/1977)   **170**
Miango *v*. Zaire (Communication No. 194/1985)   **167**
Mika Miha *v*. Equatorial Guinea (Communication No. 414/1990)   **157, 161, 175, 177, 178**
Mukong *v*. Cameroon (Communication No. 458/1991)   **119**

Ominayak, Bernard, Chief of the Lubicon Lake Band *v*. Canada (Communication No. 167/1984)   **162**

Pratt and Morgan *v*. Jamaica (Communications Nos. 210/1986 and 225/1987)   **176**

Tshishimbi *v*. Zaire (Communication No. 542/1993)   **168, 177**
Toonen *v*. Australia (Communication No. 488/1992)   **162, 166, 197**

INDIA

Indian Council of Enviro-Legal Action *v*. Union of India [1996] 2 LRC 226   **234–5, 237**

Mehta *v*. Union of India AIR 1988 p. 1037   **234, 238**

Rural Litigation and Entitlement Kendra and Others *v*. State of Uttar Pradesh and Others AIR 1987 p. 359   **234**

INTER-AMERICAN COMMISSION ON HUMAN RIGHTS

Baby Boy Case 2 HRLJ (1981) 110   **170**

INTER-AMERICAN COURT OF HUMAN RIGHTS

Aloeboetoe *v*. Suriname (Reparations) 14 HRLJ (1993) 425   **212**

Colotenango *v*. Guatemala (Provisional Measures) 2 IHRR (1995) 414   **211, 212**
Compulsory Membership in an Association Prescribed by Law for the Practice of Journalism 25 ILM 123 (1986)   **160, 186, 209, 211**

Effect of Reservations on the Entry into Force of the American Convention 3 HRLJ 153   **208**

Godinez Cruz *v*. Honduras (Preliminary Objections) Series C, No. 3 (1987)   **211**
Government of Costa Rica (In the Matter of Viviana Gallardo) 2 HRLJ (1981) 328   **210**

Habeas Corpus in Emergency Situations 9 HRLJ (1988) 204 **178, 211**

International Responsibility for the Promulgation and Enforcement of Laws in Violation of the Convention 16 HRLJ (1995) 9 **169, 210, 212**
Interpretation of the Meaning of 'Other Treaties' Subject to the Consultative Jurisdiction of the Court 3 HRLJ (1982) 140 **209, 210**

Proposed Amendments to the Naturalization Provisions of the Constitution of Costa Rica 5 HRLJ (1984) 161 **164, 210**

Restrictions of the Rights and Freedoms of the American Convention – The Word 'Laws' in Article 30 7 HRLJ (1986) 231 **211**
Restrictions to the Death Penalty Case 4 HRLJ (1983) 339 **169, 210**

Velasquez Rodriguez *v.* Honduras 9 HRLJ (1988) 212 **161, 168, 175**

INTERNATIONAL COURT OF JUSTICE

Anglo-Norwegian Fisheries Case (United Kingdom *v.* Norway) ICJ Reports 1951, p. 116 **75**
Application of the Convention on the Prevention and Punishment of the Crime of Genocide Case (Bosnia and Herzegovina *v.* Yugoslavia (Serbia and Montenegro)) ICJ Reports 1993, p. 3 **205**
Application of the Convention on the Prevention and Punishment of the Crime of Genocide Case (Bosnia and Herzegovina *v.* Yugoslavia (Serbia and Montenegro), Preliminary Objections, ICJ Reports 1996, p. 595 **51**
Asylum Case (Colombia *v.* Peru) ICJ Reports 1950, p. 266 **44, 80, 190**

Barcelona Traction, Light and Power Co. Case (Belgium *v.* Spain), Second Phase, ICJ Reports 1970, p. 3 **163, 171, 205, 211**

Certain Expenses of the United Nations Case ICJ Reports 1962, p. 151 **31, 49, 256**
Certain Phosphate Lands in Nauru Case (Nauru *v.* Australia), Preliminary Objections, ICJ Reports 1992, p. 240 **202, 237**
Conditions of Admission of a State to Membership in the United Nations Case ICJ Reports 1948, p. 57 **35, 76, 77**
Continental Shelf Case (Libya/Malta) ICJ Reports 1985, p. 13 **46**
Continental Shelf Case (Libya/Tunisia) ICJ Reports 1982, p. 18 **46**

East Timor Case (Portugal *v.* Australia) ICJ Reports 1995, p. 90 **46, 48, 75, 200, 201, 202, 237**

Frontier Dispute Case (Burkina Faso/Mali) ICJ Reports 1986, p. 554 **38, 43, 44, 46, 47, 75, 200, 201**

Gabčíkovo-Nagymaros Project Case (Hungary/Slovakia) ICJ Reports 1997, p. 7. **225, 232, 233, 235–6, 238**

Interhandel Case (Switzerland *v.* United States of America) ICJ Reports 1959, p. 6   **207**

Kasikili/Sedudu Island Case (Botswana/Namibia) (pending)   **46**

Land and Maritime Boundary Case (Cameroon *v.* Nigeria), Jurisdiction and Admissibility, (pending)   **46**
Land and Maritime Boundary Case (Cameroon *v.* Nigeria) (Preliminary Objections) ICJ, General List No. 94 1998   **46, 49**
Land, Island and Maritime Frontier Dispute Case (El Salvador/Honduras, Nicaragua Intervening) ICJ Reports 1992, p. 351   **43**
Legal Consequences for States of the Continued Presence of South Africa in Namibia (South West Africa) Notwithstanding Security Council Resolution 276 (1970) ICJ Reports 1971, p. 16   **163, 200**
Legality of the Threat or Use of Nuclear Weapons Case ICJ Reports 1996, p. 226   **47, 49, 225, 227, 234, 235**

Military and Paramilitary Activities in and Against Nicaragua (Nicaragua *v.* United States of America), Jurisdiction and Admissibility, ICJ Reports 1984, p. 392   **46**
Military and Paramilitary Activities In and Against Nicaragua (Nicaragua *v.* United States of America) ICJ Reports 1986, p. 14   **39, 42, 47, 49, 74, 202**

Norwegian Loans Case (France *v.* Norway) ICJ Reports 1957, p. 9   **210**
Nottebohm Case (Liechtenstein *v.* Guatemala) ICJ Reports 1955, p. 4   **51**
Nuclear Test Cases (Australia *v.* France) ICJ Reports 1974, p. 253   **49, 76**

Questions of Interpretation and Application of the 1971 Montreal Convention arising from the Aerial Incident at Lockerbie (Libya *v.* United States of America), Jurisdiction and Admissibility, (pending)   **46**

Reparation for Injuries Suffered in the Service of the United Nations Case ICJ Reports 1949, p. 174   **48, 256**
Request for an Examination of the Situation in Accordance with Paragraph 63 of the Court's Judgment in the 1974 Nuclear Tests Case ICJ Reports 1995, p. 288   **225, 232, 233**
Reservations to the Convention on Genocide Case ICJ Reports 1951, p. 15   **57, 160**

South West Africa Cases (Second Phase) ICJ Reports 1966, p. 6   **15, 163**

Territorial Dispute Case (Libya/Chad) ICJ Reports 1994, p. 6   **43, 44, 46**

United States Diplomatic and Consular Staff in Tehran Case (United States of America *v.* Iran) ICJ Reports 1980, p. 3   **157**

Western Sahara Case ICJ Reports 1975, p. 12   **46, 54, 74, 200**

INTERNATIONAL CRIMINAL TRIBUNAL FOR THE FORMER YUGOSLAVIA

Prosecutor *v.* Furundzija 38 ILM 317 (1999) **173, 198**

INTERNATIONAL CRIMINAL TRIBUNAL FOR RWANDA

Prosecutor *v.* Akayesu 37 ILM 1399 (1998) **100**
Prosecutor *v.* Kambanda 37 ILM 1411 (1998) **100**
Prosecutor *v.* Kanyabishi, Decision on Jurisdiction 92 AJIL (1998) 66 **204**

LESOTHO

Director of Public Prosecutions and Another *v.* Lebona 1998 (5) BCLR 618
(LesCA) **178**

Seeiso *v.* Minister of Home Affairs and Others 1998 (6) BCLR 765
(LesCA) **188, 189**

MAURITIUS

Amasimbi *v.* State (1992) MR 227 **176**
Andony *v.* State (1992) MR 249 **182**
Aumeer *v.* L'Assemblée de Dieu (1988) MR 229 **184**

Bacha, Kowlessur & Barbeau *v.* Boodhoo (1989) MR 51 **182**
Bhewa *v.* Government of Mauritius (1990) MR 79 **184, 197**
Bizlall *v.* Commissioner of Police (1993) MR 213 **189**

DPP *v.* 101B & Shanto (1989) MR 110 **178**
Duval *v.* District Magistrate of Flacq (1990) MR 36 **182**

Hossen *v.* District Magistrate of Port Louis (1993) MR 9 **178**

Pelladoah *v.* Development Bank of Mauritius (1992) MR 5 **179**

R. *v.* Boodhoo and another (1990) MR 191 **187**

Sheriff *v.* District Magistrate of Port Louis (1989) MR 260 **177**

NAMIBIA (SOUTH WEST AFRICA)

Ex Parte Attorney-General, Namibia: In re Corporal Punishment by Organs
of State 1991 (3) SA 76 (NmS) **160, 175, 176**

Free Press of Namibia (Pty) Ltd. *v.* Cabinet for the Interim Government of
South West Africa 1987 (1) SA 614 (SWA) **186**

Government of the Republic of Namibia *v.* Cultura 2000 1994 (1) SA 407
(NmS) **160**

Kauesa *v.* Minister of Home Affairs 1994 (3) BCLR 1 (NmH) **164, 187**

Minister of Defence, Namibia *v.* Mwandinghi 1992 (2) SA 355 (NmS) **160**

S *v.* Heidenreich [1996] 2 LRC 115 **178**
S *v.* Heita and Another 1992 (3) SA 785 (Nm) **181**
S *v.* Namseb 1991 (1) SACR 223 (SWA) **195**
S *v.* Shikunga 1997 (9) BCLR 1321 (NmS) **180**
S *v.* Strowitski and Another 1995 (1) BCLR 12 (Nm) **178**
S *v.* Tcoeib 1996 (7) BCLR 996 (NmS) **167**
S *v.* Van Wyk 1992 (1) SACR 147 (NmS) **164**

NIGERIA

Nemi and Others *v.* The State [1994] 1 LRC 376 **161, 170**

PERMANENT COURT OF INTERNATIONAL JUSTICE

Certain German Interests in Polish Upper Silesia PCIJ Reports Ser. A, No. 7
(1926) **191**

Mavrommatis Palestine Concessions Case PCIJ Reports Ser. A, No. 2
(1924) **48**

Tunis-Morocco Nationality Decrees Case PCIJ Reports Ser. B, No. 4
(1923) **40**

Wimbledon Case PCIJ Reports Ser. A, No. 1 (1923) **210**

PHILIPPINES

Minors Oposa *v.* Factoran 33 ILM 173 (1994) **234**

SOUTH AFRICA

Azanian Peoples Organization (AZAPO) and Others *v.* President of the
Republic of South Africa and Others 1996 (8) BCLR 1015 (CC) **167**

Bernstein and Others *v.* Bester NO and Others 1996 (4) BCLR 449 (CC) **177**

Christian Lawyers Association of SA and Others *v.* Minister of Health and
Others 1998 (11) BCLR 1434 (T) **170**
City Council of Pretoria *v.* Walker 1998 (3) BCLR 257 (CC) **163**

Democratic Party *v.* Minister of Home Affairs and another (1999,
unreported) (CC) **164**

Ferreira *v*. Levin and Others 1996 (1) BCLR 1 (CC) **180**

Fraser *v*. Children's Court, Pretoria North 1997 (2) BCLR 153 (CC) **166, 167**

Harksen *v*. Lane NO and Others 1997 (11) BCLR 1489 (CC) **163**

National Coalition for Gay and Lesbian Equality and Others *v*. Minister of Justice and Others 1998 (12) BCLR 1517 (CC) **162**

Nel *v*. Le Roux NO and Others 1996 (4) BCLR 592 (CC) **180**

New National Party of South Africa *v*. Government of the Republic of South Africa and others (1999, unreported) (CC) **190**

Parbhoo and Others *v*. Getz NO and Another 1997 (10) BCLR 1337 (CC) **180**

President of the Republic of South Africa and Another *v*. Hugo 1997 (6) BCLR 708 (CC) **163**

Prinsloo *v*. Van der Linde and Another 1997 (3) SA 1012 (CC) **163**

S *v*. Bhulwana 1996 (1) SA 388 (CC) **180**

S *v*. Coetzee and Others 1997 (4) BCLR 437 (CC) **180**

S *v*. Lawrence; S *v*. Negal; S *v*. Solberg 1997 (10) BCLR 1348 (CC) **183, 184**

S *v*. Makwanyane and Mchunu 1995 (3) SA 391 (CC) **160, 168, 176**

S *v*. Mhlungu and Others 1995 (7) BCLR 793 (CC) **164**

S *v*. Ntuli 1996 (1) BCLR 141 (CC) **163**

S *v*. Williams and Others 1995 (7) BCLR 861 (CC) **171, 173–4, 176**

S *v*. Zuma and Others 1995 (2) SA 642 (CC) **160, 180**

Sanderson *v*. Attorney-General, Eastern Cape 1997 (12) BCLR 1675 (CC) **178**

Shabalala and Others *v*. Attorney-General of the Transvaal and Another 1995 (12) BCLR 1593 (CC) **164**

South African National Defence Force Union *v*. Minister of Defence and another (1999, unreported) (CC) **186, 188**

Wild and Another *v*. Hoffert NO and Others 1998 (6) BCLR 656 (CC) **178**

TANZANIA

Akonaay and Another *v*. Attorney-General [1994] 2 LRC 399 **180, 191**

Ephrahim *v*. Pastory [1990] LRC (Const) 757 **165**

Mbushuu *v*. Republic [1995] 1 LRC 216 **168, 176**

UNITED KINGDOM (including the Judicial Committee of the Privy Council)

Attorney-General *v*. Guardian Newspapers Ltd and others [1987] 3 All ER 316 **185**

Attorney-General of the Gambia *v*. Mamodun Jobe [1984] AC 689 **160**

Cambridge Water Co. *v.* Eastern Counties Leather plc [1994] 2 WLR 53   **234**

Musisi, In Re [1987] AC 514   **102**

R *v.* Immigration Appeal Tribunal, ex parte Miller, *The Times*, 25 February
    1988   **102**
R *v.* Ministry of Defence, ex parte Smith [1996] QB 517   **166**
R *v.* Secretary of State for the Home Department, ex parte Adan [1998] 2
    WLR 702   **100**
R *v.* Secretary of State for the Home Department, ex parte Bugdaycay [1987]
    AC 514   **102**
R *v.* Secretary of State for the Home Department, ex parte H, *The Times*, 24
    March 1988   **102, 104**
R *v.* Secretary of State for the Home Department, ex parte Mendis, *The
    Times*, 18 June 1988   **102**
R *v.* Secretary of State for the Home Department, ex parte Sivakumaran *et
    al.* [1987] 3 WLR 1047, CA; [1988] 2 WLR 92, HL   **81, 100**

Société United Docks and Others *v.* The Government of Mauritius [1985] 1
    AC 585   **160**

UNITED STATES OF AMERICA

Filartiga *v.* Peña-Irala (1980) 630 F.2d 876   **119**

Gregg *v.* Georgia (1976) S. Ct. 2909   **176**

Immigration and Naturalization Service *v.* Cardoza-Fonseca (1987) 107 S.
    Ct. 1207   **81, 100**

Sale, Acting Commissioner, INS *v.* Haitian Centers Council (1993) 113 S. Ct.
    2549   **101**

William H. Webster, Director of Central Intelligence, Petitioner *v.* John Doe
    (1988) 108 S. Ct. 2047   **166**

ZAMBIA

Attorney-General and Another *v.* Kasonde and Others [1994] 3 LRC
    144   **160**

Nyirongo *v.* Attorney-General of Zambia [1993] 3 LRC 256   **189**

ZIMBABWE

Catholic Commission for Justice and Peace in Zimbabwe *v.* Attorney-
    General, Zimbabwe 1993 (4) SA 239 (ZS)   **160, 176**
Chikweche, In re 1995 (4) BCLR 533 (ZS)   **183, 184**

Chinamora v. Angwa Furnishers (Pvt) Limited (Attorney-General intervening) 1997 (2) BCLR 189 (ZS) **179**

Conjwayo v. Minister of Justice, Legal and Parliamentary Affairs 1992 (2) SA 56 (ZS) **175**

Corbett v. The State [1990] LRC (Crim) 30 **181**

Davies v. Minister of Land, Agriculture and Water Development 1995 (1) BCLR 83 (ZH); 1996 (9) BCLR 1209 (ZS) **191**

Dongo, Margaret v. Vivian Mwashita and Registrar-General of Elections and Chairman, Electoral Supervisory Commission and Chairman Election Directorate (unreported) **190**

Hewlett v. Minister of Finance 1981 ZLR 571 **191**

Holland and Others v. Minister of the Public Service, Labour and Social Welfare 1997 (6) BCLR 809 (ZS) **179**

Mhunhumeso, Davison and Others, In re 1994 (1) ZLR 49 **188**

Mlambo, In re 1991 (2) ZLR 339; 1992 (4) SA 144 (ZS) **178, 179**

Mlauzi v. Attorney-General 1992 (1) ZLR 260; 1993 (1) SA 207 (ZS) **178, 183**

Mutasa v. Makombe NO 1997 (6) BCLR 841 (ZS) **179**

Nkomo v. Attorney-General, Zimbabwe 1994 (1) SACR 302 (ZS) **176**

Paweni v. Minister of State Security 1984 (1) ZLR 236 **181**

Rattigan and Others v. The Chief Immigration Officer and Others 1994 (2) ZLR 54 **189, 198**

Retrofit (Pvt) Limited v. Minister of Information, Posts and Telecommunications 1996 (3) BCLR 394 (ZS) **185–6**

S v. Chogugudza 1996 (3) BCLR 427 (ZS) **180**

S v. Juvenile 1990 (4) SA 151 (ZS) **176**

S v. Kalize 18 CLB (1992) 50 **182**

S v. Ketose (No. 64/90) **176**

S v. Mcgown 1995 (1) ZLR 4 **170**

S v. Masitere 1991 (1) SA 821 (ZS) **175**

S v. Ncube 1988 (2) SA 702 (ZS) **160, 175**

Salem, Patricia Ann v. Chief Immigration Officer and Another 1994 (2) ZLR 287 **189**

Smith v. Mutasa NO and Another 1990 (3) SA 756 (ZS) **179**

Smyth v. Ushewokunze and Another 1998 (2) BCLR 170 (ZS) **178, 182**

United Parties v. Minister of Justice, Legal and Parliamentary Affairs and Others 1998 (2) BCLR 224 (ZS) **186**

Woods and Others v. Minister of Justice, Legal and Parliamentary Affairs and Others 1995 (1) BCLR 56 (ZS) **186**

To Angela

1

The Organization of African Unity

On 25 May 1963 the independent States of the African continent brought to a close the Conference of Heads of State and Government meeting in Addis Ababa, Ethiopia, by adopting the constituent charter of a new international body, the Organization of African Unity (OAU). The conception of a pan-African organization may be said to have been the culmination of a series of ministerial conferences held throughout 1961 and 1962.[1] Various factors were responsible for the creation of the OAU. The decolonization of Africa in the post-war period, which gathered pace in the 1960s, literally multiplied tenfold the number of sovereign States. Indeed, in 1945 there were only four independent States in Africa: Egypt, Ethiopia, Liberia and the Union of South Africa. The transition to independence was not always peaceful and the fear of foreign intervention, as confirmed by the Congo crisis in 1960, was strong. The multiplicity of independent nations in its turn gave rise to regional political and economic groupings, but no lasting political unions existed. Moreover, the concept of pan-Africanism or African unity was a highly motivating factor towards the eventual founding of the OAU.

The quest for African unity is rooted in history. Pan-Africanism has its origins in nineteenth-century America where the American Colonization Society for the Establishment of Free Men of Color of the United States was formed in 1816 in response to the alienation and exploitation of the Afro-Americans with the purpose of repatriating freed slaves.[2] This led to the founding of Liberia in West Africa as a free and sovereign State in 1847. Nevertheless, the pan-African movement, which gathered momentum at the turn of the century, continued to struggle for the end of the colonial system in Africa and called for the dismantling of the colonial boundaries agreed upon at the Congress of Berlin 1885, and the creation of a united Africa. But it was the post-Second World War era that provided the impetus for self-determination in Africa. The demand for political, economic and cultural self-determination became a flood that the colonial powers could not dam. The independence of Ghana on 6 March 1957 marked the beginning of a new dawn in Africa.

The intellectual energy of the President of Ghana, Kwame Nkrumah, was the prime motivating force behind the quest for African solidarity at this time. Numerous conferences were held with a view to liberating the colonies and forging closer links among the independent African States.[3] These meetings clearly highlighted common concerns about colonialism, apartheid, and tribalism. Furthermore, anxiety was expressed that decolonization should not, either deliberately or unconsciously, lead to the 'balkanization' of Africa, an opinion that eventually was to find expression in a rule of international law.[4] They were agreed on the need to forge a genuine identity from among disparate communities.

The rapidly increasing number of independent African States from 1960 onwards soon brought divisions, based either on ideological grounds or personal antagonism, to the pan-African movement. A clear difference of opinion emerged as to the ends to be achieved and the means to be adopted. This state of affairs was reflected by the emergence of rival groups, in particular the moderate Brazzaville Group and the radical Casablanca Group.[5] The former represented a gradualist approach to African unity and it advocated a loose association of States. It in turn led to the formation of the Monrovia Group which included seven other States not in the Casablanca group.[6] The Monrovia Group rejected political integration but stressed the sovereignty of States and non-interference in the internal affairs of States. It sought unity of aspirations and of action based on African social solidarity and political identity, and it particularly urged co-operation in the economic, cultural, scientific and technical fields. The Casablanca Group, led by President Nkrumah, sought a political union and the creation of a United States of Africa along federal lines under a High Command. Despite the wide gulf of opinion between these groups, shared interests on colonialism, apartheid and other issues effected a *rapprochement* which led to the summit conference in Addis Ababa in May 1963 which founded the OAU.

Thirty States were represented at the constituent assembly when the arguments for and against federalism were again advanced. However, the Monrovia Group's vision of African unity, based on close co-operation among sovereign States, ultimately prevailed.[7] The OAU Charter thus emphasizes the sovereign nature of the Member States. Nevertheless, the Casablanca Group was not wholly out-manoeuvred as the OAU Charter reflects its views on colonialism, apartheid and racialism, and the establishment of the Liberation Committee – responsible for providing aid to national liberation movements – was a direct result of its persistence. The OAU Charter is thus a product of compromise but the aims of the Monrovia Group predominated.

Objectives

The Charter of the OAU was signed originally by thirty-two States;[8] its present membership is fifty-three.[9] All independent, sovereign African States, including island States in the proximity of Africa, are eligible for membership, although this provision has been questioned in view of the admission of the SADR in 1984 and Morocco's consequent withdrawal, which has presented the OAU with one of its most serious political crises to date.[10] The underlying philosophy was to promote inter-African co-operation in the fields of economics, culture, science and technology. The idea of a loose confederation based on an eventual political union was rejected. On this issue, as has been seen, the view of the Monrovia Group prevailed so that sovereignty and non-interference in the internal affairs of States was accentuated. Indeed, the OAU Charter places great emphasis on the principles of territorial integrity and political independence of African States.

The OAU Charter consists of a preamble, an operative section of thirty-two articles and a protocol.[11] The preamble lists some of the general objectives and fundamental beliefs of the OAU, and as such is characteristic of the constituent documents of other international organizations. The most significant tenets are its commitment to the inalienable right of all people to self-determination and to freedom, equality, justice and dignity; the desire and need to promote greater understanding among their people, and co-operation among their respective States; the establishment and maintenance of international peace and security, in particular founded upon the UN Charter and the UDHR, and now complemented by the African (Banjul) Charter on Human and Peoples' Rights. Respect for 'the hard-won independence as well as the sovereignty and territorial integrity of our States' is accorded and the need 'to resist neo-colonialism in all its forms' is stressed.

The preamble contains some distinctive features. It promotes the unity and solidarity of Africa. Thus, although the integrationists were defeated at Addis Ababa the quest for eventual unity was not abandoned. Although to a large extent this exhortation remains merely rhetorical, developments in the economic sphere may well bring about integration in some fields over the longer term. But perhaps more importantly, this ideal also signified an undertaking to overcome their differences free from external manipulation. However, and somewhat paradoxically, unity is interrelated with the defence of sovereignty, independence and territorial integrity. This is not only an attempt at bolstering the fragile unity of many African States but constitutes an affirmation of the principle of *uti possidetis*, or the permanence of inherited colonial frontiers, and a rejection of irredentist claims of other African States. The OAU has made clear in various disputes its support for the principle of territorial integrity and its opposition to secession, a current example being the non-recognition of the breakaway Republic of Somaliland. Additionally this provision seeks to preclude external intervention in African affairs. This aim is linked to the goal of eradicating all forms of colonialism and neo-colonialism from Africa, which has almost been achieved.[12] This was a reference not only to the racist regimes of Southern Africa, which undermined the security and well-being of the Front-Line States in particular and the continent as a whole, but also to the policies by which external powers indirectly maintained or extended their influence over African countries. The eradication of colonialism in all its forms was therefore regarded as a necessary prerequisite to the attainment of the OAU's goals.

The preamble also records the adherence of the Member States to the principles enshrined in the UN Charter and the UDHR, a commitment now complemented by the African (Banjul) Charter on Human and Peoples' Rights. In this fashion the African States emphasized the OAU's compatibility with the aims and purposes of the UN and its adherence to general international law and fundamental human rights.

The principles proclaimed in the preamble do not constitute binding legal norms in themselves but serve as a reaffirmation of existing rules and a statement of objectives to be achieved. They therefore put the substantive principles of the OAU Charter in context.

The aims of the OAU, which are set out in Article 2(1), are:

a. To promote the unity and solidarity of the African States;

b. To co-ordinate and intensify their co-operation and efforts to achieve a better life for the peoples of Africa;

c. To defend their sovereignty, their territorial integrity and independence;

d. To eradicate all forms of colonialism from Africa; and

e. To promote international co-operation, having due regard to the Charter of United Nations and the Universal Declaration of Human Rights.

To an extent these principles reassert the objectives enunciated in the preamble. They are a mixture of political desiderata, legal principles and practical goals. Sub-paragraph (e) clearly indicates that the OAU is perceived to be a regional body coming within the ambit of Article 52(1) of the UN Charter.[13]

Towards achieving the ends enumerated in Article 2(1), the Member States must, according to Article 2(2), co-ordinate and harmonize their general policies, particularly in the fields of:

a. Political and diplomatic co-operation;

b. Economic co-operation, including transport and communications;

c. Educational and cultural co-operation;

d. Health, sanitation, and nutritional co-operation;

e. Scientific and technical co-operation; and

f. Co-operation for defence and security.

Article 2(2) thus lists some of the major areas for co-operation among the Member States and provides the OAU with its *raison d'être*. The emphasis is clearly on the social and economic fields rather than the political or military. Indeed, it is noticeable that political unity and military integration are hardly alluded to among the purposes of the OAU, although significant developments in these fields have occurred. Proposals for a Political Security Council, modelled on the UN Security Council, have, for example, never gained the necessary support. This difference in emphasis has also been reflected in practice where progress in the social and economic fields, particularly in co-operation with other international bodies, has led to some concrete achievements.[14] However, the military aspect has not been entirely ignored, although an African Defence Force, called for by Nkrumah, has never materialized. Peace-keeping by African forces under the auspices of the OAU became a major consideration as it sought to adopt local solutions to solve African conflicts and finally came to fruition in 1993 under the Mechanism for Conflict Prevention, Management and Resolution. However, as will be seen, the steps taken have been tentative and the initiative still lies with the UN.

The principles of the OAU are contained in Article 3, according to which the Member States adhere to the following tenets:

1. The sovereign equality of all Member States;
2. Non-interference in the internal affairs of States;
3. Respect for the sovereignty and territorial integrity of each State and for its inalienable right to independent existence;
4. Peaceful settlement of disputes by negotiation, mediation, conciliation, or arbitration;
5. Unreserved condemnation, in all its forms, of political assassination as well as subversive activities on the part of neighbouring States or any State;
6. Absolute dedication to the total emancipation of the African territories which are still dependent;
7. Affirmation of a policy of non-alignment with regard to all blocs.

These are the guiding principles of the OAU. Paragraph 1 reflects Article 2(1) of the UN Charter, and in turn a general principle of international law, and refers to equality in law and is not based on other considerations such as political or economic influence.[15] This provision was deemed necessary to allay the fears of the smaller States about the motives of their larger neighbours. Paragraph 1 is supplemented by Article 5 which declares that all Member States shall enjoy equal rights and have equal duties. Representation in the two main organs of the OAU is guaranteed on the basis of equality with equal voting capacity. All the Member States participate collectively in the decision-making process thereby preventing the domination of the small by the mighty.[16] It also seeks to ensure that the policies of no one State or group of States predominate although in practice some States prove to be more influential than others.

The second principle, that of non-interference in the internal affairs of

States, which reflects in part the domestic jurisdiction clause contained in Article 2(7) of the UN Charter, is a corollary of the independence and equality of States and of the right of self-determination. States are under an obligation not to interfere in the internal and external affairs of other States. This is a fundamental principle of international law which has found expression in numerous documents.[17] African States have traditionally insisted on absolute compliance with this principle and have, for instance, viewed international concern for human rights and democratic governance as pretexts for undermining their sovereignty. However, the self-interest of States has meant that on occasions this proscription has itself been ignored by African States.[18] Thus, the Rwandese Patriotic Front (RPF) was helped to power by Uganda. Mobutu's regime in Zaïre was overthrown in a civil war by forces with discreet backing from Rwanda, Uganda and, to a lesser extent, Burundi.[19] However, Mobutu's successor, Laurent Kabila, is embroiled in a civil war with rebels assisted by Rwanda and Uganda while his regime is bolstered by the military intervention of Angola, Namibia and Zimbabwe. Angolan government forces assisted in the coup that overthrew the legitimate government of President Lissouba of the Congo in October 1997, which had been providing support to the former Angolan rebel movement, UNITA.[20] Zaïre provided considerable support to UNITA, allowing its territory to be used for the transport of mercenaries, weapons, equipment, medicines and food, on clandestine night-time flights to Angolan territory under UNITA control, and providing UNITA forces with safe havens. In September 1998, South African forces, supported by troops from Botswana, invaded Lesotho to secure the ruling party's hold on power. Eritrea and Sudan, and Sudan and Uganda are mutually providing assistance to rebel forces fighting the central governments.

The principle of domestic jurisdiction is nevertheless a relative one and as international law has evolved, particularly in the field of human rights, its scope and extent has been restricted accordingly.[21] Thus the African States never accepted the argument of the colonial powers that questions relating to non-self-governing territories were purely matters within their domestic jurisdiction. Neither did similar considerations deter them from their efforts to eradicate apartheid. By the same token, however, African States have been compelled to accept international scrutiny of their own human rights records.[22]

Indeed, intolerance of human rights abuses, mismanagement, bad governance, malpractice and maladministration, breakdowns in civil society, and coups d'états,[23] sometimes determined to amount to threats to international peace and security,[24] have led in recent years to pressure for reform being brought to bear on certain regimes by African States and/or the international community. For example, the political and economic transition to constitutionalism which has taken place in Malawi and Zambia in the 1990s would arguably not have transpired without such pressure.[25] The military coups in Lesotho that deposed King Moshoeshoe II brought about the involvement of Botswana, South Africa and Zimbabwe which mediated a compromise agreement initiating constitutional change leading to the restoration of the King in January 1995 as a constitutional monarch.[26] Nigeria's membership of the Commonwealth was suspended in 1995 as a result of human rights abuses. The UN Security Council imposed sanctions on Sierra Leone, and authorized ECOWAS to enforce them, to force the military junta to restore power to the legitimate government.[27] Burundi's neighbours, at the initiative of former President Nyerere of Tanzania, have imposed economic and political sanctions against the regime of Major Buyoya following his assumption of power in a coup in July 1996. These sanctions have been endorsed by the OAU in an effort to encourage negotiations between the warring ethnic groups in Burundi leading to a peaceful solution of the crisis.[28]

Indeed, the conflicts in Africa have forced the UN in particular to expand its efforts at preventive diplomacy. The UN has deployed a number of multidimensional operations of a peacekeeping, peacebuilding or peace-making nature with or without the consent of affected States which provide useful illustrations of the weakening of the principles of domestic jurisdiction and non-interference and the readiness of the UN to intervene for humanitarian purposes under the authority of Chapter VII of the UN Charter.[29]

The recent history of Rwanda is one such example. Since independence the conflict between the Hutu majority (85% of the population) and the Tutsi minority (14% of the population) has resulted in numerous human rights abuses and massacres. In the early 1990s war between the regime of President Juvenal Habyarimana and the insurgents of the RPF had reached a stage when victory for the RPF seemed assured. International pressure brought about an attempted reconciliation, the Arusha Agreement of 1993, according to which a transitional government was to be established and the army reformed. A UN operation known as UNAMIR (UN Assistance Mission for Rwanda) was deployed inside Rwanda pursuant to Security Council Resolution 872 (1993) to assist in the implementation of the Arusha Agreement. However, the Agreement collapsed with President Habyarimana's assassination in April 1994 triggering organized and systematic massacres against the Tutsi minority and moderate Hutus by Hutu extremists. In a matter of months some one million persons were slaughtered in a preplanned genocide. The RPF terminated the cease-fire and invaded from neighbouring Uganda. Under Security Council Resolution 912 (1994) UNAMIR was authorized to work with the parties to the conflict on a cease-fire agreement and to resume relief operations. Continuing bloodshed led the Security Council to determine under Resolution 918 that the situation in Rwanda constituted a threat to international peace and security and imposed an arms embargo on Rwanda. UNAMIR's mandate was extended, to include the protection of civilians, by force if necessary, and its troop strength expanded but their deployment did not prove possible. France unsuccessfully attempted to deny the RPF victory and relied on the massacre of civilians by the incumbent authorities and the mass exodus of refugees to mount a humanitarian intervention, *Operation turquoise*, establishing a so-called 'humanitarian protection zone', that the UN Security Council supported only reluctantly but which the OAU did not endorse.[30] Responsibility for the 'safe-zone', controlled by the French army from June to August 1994, when many of the Hutus involved in genocide were seemingly protected, was transferred to UNAMIR with units from African States. The war ended in July 1994 when the RPF took control of the country and put a halt to the genocide. The RPF government has since faced the immense challenge of rebuilding the country. However, the situation has not stabilized as Hutu militants given sanctuary in the neighbouring Democratic Republic of the Congo continue to terrorize civilians living near the border regions.

The case of Somalia provides another good example of humanitarian intervention by the international community. The fall of President Barré in January 1991 resulted in a power struggle and clashes between clans in many parts of Somalia, including intense fighting in Mogadishu. The State collapsed and anarchy resulted. Millions of lives were at risk from malnutrition and, in the absence of any central authority, it was decided in these exceptional circumstances that the UN should secure the delivery of humanitarian aid. Accordingly, the Security Council in Resolution 794 (1992) endorsed action under Chapter VII of the UN Charter in order to establish a secure environment for humanitarian relief operations and to help restore peace and public order.[31] Hence UNITAF (the United Nations Task Force), led by the United States, was deployed in Mogadishu in December 1992. Under Resolution 814 (1993) the Security Council established UNOSOM II which was authorized to provide humanitarian and other assistance to the people of Somalia in rehabilitating their political institutions and economy and promoting political settlement and national reconciliation. In addition, UNOSOM II had the crucial task of disarming the armed gangs that terrorized the people and obstructed humanitarian activities. Violence resulted. In Resolution 837 (1993) the Security Council condemned the attacks on UNOSOM forces and reaffirmed the UN's authority to take all necessary measures against those responsible. The precarious security situation prompted a number of countries, including the United States, to withdraw their troop contingents. The phase-out of UNOSOM II began in November 1994 and was completed by 2 March 1995. Insufficient co-operation from the Somali factions over security issues undermined the UN operation in Somalia which, nevertheless, had been successful in its humanitarian objectives.[32] However, the UN continued to promote national reconciliation and in December 1997 the Somali factions adopted the Cairo Declaration on Somalia accepting a political settlement.[33]

The UN has also been intimately involved in finding peaceful solutions to the internal conflicts in Mozambique and Angola. The recent histories of these States have much in common. Both are former Portuguese colonies which became independent in 1975 after long and bitter wars of liberation.

Marxist governments assumed power soon after independence, FRELIMO in Mozambique and the MPLA in Angola. Both were plunged into civil war as RENAMO and UNITA respectively, with external support, took up arms against the authorities. The pragmatic policies of President Chissano of Mozambique set the peace process in motion and in October 1992 a peace agreement was signed in Rome between the government of Mozambique and RENAMO, which required the UN, *inter alia*, to supervise the cease-fire, monitor disarmament and demobilization programmes, and provide assistance and verification for national elections. Under Resolution 797 (1992) the UN Security Council mandated ONUMOZ (United Nations Operation in Mozambique) to, *inter alia*, verify and monitor the peace agreement. Free and fair elections held in October 1994 led to a narrow victory for FRELIMO and the election of President Chissano. ONUMOZ successfully completed its peace-building mandate and was withdrawn in 1995.[34] The government of Mozambique continues to pursue a policy of reconciliation, democracy and development and the strengthening of peace and stability.

Peace in Angola has proved more elusive. UNAVEM II (United Nations Angola Verification Mission II) was established in 1991 with the task of ensuring that the warring parties maintained the UN negotiated cease-fire and verifying the elections as accepted under the terms of the Lisbon peace agreement of May 1991. UNITA rejected the results of the general elections held in September 1992, regarded as free and fair by international observers. The cease-fire did not hold as UNITA took up arms again and under Resolution 864 (1993) the Security Council, pursuant to Chapter VII, established an arms embargo against UNITA. Protracted negotiations eventually paved the way for the signing of the Lusaka Protocol in November 1994 and UNAVEM III was established under Security Council Resolution 976 (1995) to facilitate its implementation. The main features of UNAVEM's mandate included the provision of good offices and mediation to the parties; supervision, verification, and monitoring of the cease-fire; verification and monitoring of the withdrawal, quartering and demobilization of UNITA forces; verification of the movement of Angolan government forces to barracks; and verification and monitoring of the formation of a new armed force. In July 1997, pursuant to Security Council resolution 1118, MONUA (United Nations Observer Mission in Angola) assumed responsibility in assisting the parties in consolidating peace and national reconciliation. However, the pace of implementation of the Lusaka Protocol has been delayed by UNITA's lack of co-operation, especially in disarming its units and integrating them into the national army and in resisting the extension of State administration into occupied territories; and in October 1997 the UN Security Council imposed sanctions against UNITA.[35] The UN Security Council has made its position clear that it holds UNITA responsible for the lack of progress in finalizing a political settlement.[36]

The UN has also been involved in efforts to restore peace to the Central African Republic following an army rebellion in 1996. The opposing parties accepted the need for national reconciliation under the Bangui Agreements which provided for wide-ranging reforms leading to free and fair elections. UN Security Council resolution 1125 (1997), adopted under Chapter VII, authorized an African force, MISAB (Inter-African Mission to Monitor the Implementation of the Bangui Agreements), to supervise the implementation of the Bangui Agreements, although this force was replaced by a UN force in April 1998.[37]

It should not be overlooked that the UN participated in the transition to democracy in South Africa. The UN Observer Mission in South Africa (UNOMSA) monitored the transition process and by virtue of resolution 894 (1994) the Security Council decided to provide a team of observers to monitor the electoral process.[38]

The civil war in Liberia is a particularly interesting case because of the role of ECOWAS which pioneered new ground for an African regional organization by dispatching a peace-keeping force to the troubled land. The war erupted in December 1989 when the rebel forces of Charles Taylor's National Patriotic Front of Liberia (NPLF) took up arms to overthrow the authoritarian government of Samuel Doe. Social order collapsed and the disorder spread to neighbouring States, particularly Sierra Leone which has been destabilized. The internationalization of the Liberian conflict has been manifested by the involvement of ECOWAS which has maintained a military force, ECOMOG, in the country since 1990, endorsed by the UN Security Council.[39] A peace agreement signed in Cotonou, Benin, in July 1993 established a cease-fire and required the disarmament and demobilization of the opposing factions under international supervision. Under Resolution 866 (1993) the Security Council set up UNOMIL (UN Observer Mission in Liberia) to oversee this process jointly with ECOMOG. ECOMOG and UNOMIL appear to have successfully overseen a transitional period leading to elections in 1997 and UNOMIL has now concluded operations.[40]

The international community has also become involved in the civil unrest in Sierra Leone, destabilized by the civil war in neighbouring Liberia. In May 1997 the elected government of President Kabbah was overthrown by a military junta. However, the international community actively pursued the restoration of the legitimate government which led to the Conakry peace plan between the junta and ECOWAS providing for, *inter alia*, the reinstatement of the Kabbah government by April 1998. The junta's unwillingness to abide by the agreement, in addition to the harassment of ECOMOG forces, led the UN Security Council in October 1997 to impose a sanctions regime under resolution 1132 (1997) against Sierra Leone and finally led ECOMOG to use force to oust the junta in February 1998 and reinstate the legitimate government of President Kabbah. The war continues, however.

In the light of all these events it is difficult to argue with the conclusion of the then UN Secretary-General, Boutros Boutros-Ghali that 'the time of absolute and exclusive sovereignty' has passed.[41]

The principle of non-interference is supplemented by Article 3(5) which condemns political assassinations and subversive activities. The inclusion of this provision was motivated by the assassination of the then President of Togo and the accusation by certain Member States that their neighbours were attempting to destabilize their regimes. In 1965 the OAU adopted a Declaration on the Problem of Subversion under which the Member States undertook not to tolerate any subversion against the OAU or its Member States.[42] Nevertheless, such accusations still surface regularly. For example, it was alleged that Zaïre had links with Colonel Bob Denard, a French national, who led a group of mercenaries which engineered a coup d'état in the Comoros in 1989 during which the President, Ahmed Abdallah Abderemane, was assassinated.[43] The deaths of President Ndadaye of Burundi and President Habyarimana of Rwanda in a plane crash in 1994 may have been caused in an attempt to destabilize further the precarious situation in the Great Lakes region. In 1995 an attempt was made on President Mubarak's life by terrorists allegedly backed by Sudan as he was attending an OAU meeting in Addis Ababa, leading to the imposition of sanctions against Sudan under UN Security Council resolution 1054 (1996).

The concern of the OAU for the threats to the sovereignty, independence, security and territorial integrity of its members posed by mercenarism led it to adopt in 1977 the Convention for the Elimination of Mercenarism in Africa.[44] According to the terms of the Convention mercenarism, whether committed by individuals or sponsored by a State, is condemned as an international crime punishable by the severest penalties under domestic law, including capital punishment.[45] Mercenaries are denied the status of combatants and are not entitled to prisoner-of-war status.[46] State parties undertake, *inter alia*, to prohibit on their territory any activities promoting mercenarism or using mercenaries against any OAU Member State or African people engaged in a liberation struggle; to prohibit the recruitment, training, financing and equipping of mercenaries; to prevent their nationals or foreigners on their territory from engaging in mercenarism; and to prevent the entry and passage through their territory of mercenaries or their equipment. The use of mercenaries has been an established feature of many African conflicts, often aimed at thwarting the right of self-determination and destabilizing constitutional governments in southern Africa. In recent years UNITA has been accused of recruiting mercenaries to fight alonside its forces, and African and European mercenaries were reported serving alongside the Zaïrian army in its struggle against the Tutsi Banyamulenge of eastern Zaïre in 1996 as the Mobutu regime collapsed.[47]

Article 3(3), a logical extension of the two preceding paragraphs, provides that the sovereignty and territorial integrity of each Member State be respected. This provision appears to go further than the corresponding provision in the UN Charter in that it tacitly prohibits *any* action which might undermine the sovereignty and territorial integrity of a State whereas the UN Charter is primarily concerned with the threat or use of force. However, as has been illustrated, these apparently absolute principles have been considerably weakened in recent years. Article 3(3) has nevertheless proved to be controversial because it gives implied recognition to the principle of *uti possidetis*, that is, 'securing respect for the territorial boundaries at the moment when independence is achieved'.[48] This principle first emerged in Latin America in the early nineteenth century as a consequence of the independence of the ex-Spanish colonies. It sought to avoid, somewhat unsuccessfully, disputes among the successor States by preserving the *status quo* upon independence. It sought to ensure that no territory in the continent was to be considered as *terra nullius* and thus potentially open to further colonization.[49]

The African States meeting in Addis Ababa thus faced a dilemma. Should they adopt the principle of *uti possidetis*, thus endorsing a legacy of the colonial era, or ignore the question entirely and thereby increase the risk of border disputes? The result, Article 3(3), was a compromise. It would seem that the initial reluctance to incorporate explicitly the principle of *uti possidetis* may have been attributable to the influence of the pan-African movement and an anxiety that any approval of the principle should not be construed as an endorsement of colonialism.[50] However, even this compromise did not receive unanimous approval as Morocco and Somalia, irredentist claims to neighbouring territories outstanding, reserved their positions. They argued that the OAU Charter did not have retroactive effect and did not apply to existing disputes but that the *status quo* as ordained by the OAU Charter prevailed only insofar as future disputes were concerned. Clearly the situation was unsatisfactory for the majority of States and it was considered necessary to emphasize the principle explicitly and in 1964 the OAU adopted the Resolution on the Intangibility of Frontiers according to which the Member States reaffirmed Article 3(3) and pledged themselves to respect the frontiers existing on their achievement of national independence.[51] Given that the delimitation of Africa's political boundaries, particularly by the Congress of Berlin in 1885, took no account of ethnic and tribal considerations it is hardly surprising that modern African States chose to apply it. As the ICJ recognized, preserving the stability of new States was an imperative consideration for Africa, and justified it in the following terms, 'Its obvious purpose is to prevent the independence and stability of new States being endangered by fratricidal struggles provoked by the challenging of frontiers following the withdrawal of the administering power'.[52] Nevertheless, border incidents have been numerous.[53]

The principle of *uti possidetis* was discussed in detail by the ICJ in the *Frontier Dispute Case* where the ICJ had to delimit the common frontier between the African States of Burkina Faso and Mali.[54] Both parties specifically requested the ICJ to take account of the principle of the intangibility of frontiers inherited from colonial times in determining their common frontier. In view of its importance to the parties and to African States as a whole, the ICJ considered it necessary to emphasize the general scope of the principle of *uti possidetis*, declaring that this 'principle of a general kind' had become one of universal application.[55] It was adopted by the newly emancipated African States which gave it implied recognition in Article 3(3) of the OAU Charter and subsequently affirmed it expressly in the Resolution on the Intangibility of Frontiers. However, the principle has been reinterpreted in one major respect; in Africa the principle of *uti possidetis* encompasses the principle of territorial integrity.[56] This is apparent from, *inter alia*, the aforementioned documents and state practice with respect to the purported secessions of Katanga and Biafra. It was thus the opinion of the ICJ that African States have recognized and confirmed the important legal principle of *uti possidetis*.[57]

The ICJ found that the principle of *uti possidetis* was applicable in the case of Burkina Faso and Mali despite the fact that when they achieved independence in 1960 the OAU did not yet exist and the Resolution on the Intangibility of Frontiers dates only from 1964. This conclusion would appear to be acceptable if it can be established that the principle of *uti possidetis* was a customary rule of international law at that time. Given state practice it is not unreasonable to assert that this may have been the case; however, if this were so, the ICJ's statement would appear to take little account of the rule of intertemporal law which requires that the situation be determined by the rules of international law as they existed at that time, and not by contemporary standards.[58] Nevertheless, it can safely be asserted that by 1963 the majority of African States had accepted the frontiers imposed by the colonial powers as being legally valid, although notable exceptions remain.

The ICJ went on to state that an apparent conflict existed between the principles of *uti possidetis* and self-determination but that African States have however decided that maintenance of the territorial *status quo* is the wisest policy. In interpreting the principle of self-determination account has always been taken of the principle of *uti possidetis*.[59] The ICJ thus appears to be suggesting that the right of self-determination is qualified in Africa. Regrettably the ICJ did not elaborate further saying that, for the purposes of the case, there was no need to show that *uti possidetis* is a firmly established principle of international law where decolonization is concerned.[60] It is perhaps unfortunate that the ICJ did not grasp the opportunity to clarify the relationship between these two principles which has long been a source of controversy.[61] However, the ministerial conference that adopted the Banjul Charter did make it clear that the right to self-determination did not encompass a right to secession.

One of the legacies of the partition of Africa has been the threat of secession.[62] As has been observed, the OAU has placed emphasis on the principle of territorial integrity both as a principle of general application and in concrete cases. Thus, when Biafra purported to secede from Nigeria in 1967 the approach of the OAU was supportive of the federal cause.[63] The Republic of Somaliland, which declared its independence in January 1991, corresponding to the territory of the former British Somaliland, which in 1960 joined with the former Italian Somaliland to form Somalia, remains unrecognized by the international community notwithstanding the fact that it seems to fulfil the criteria of statehood, something which the collapsed State of Somalia does not appear to do.[64] The OAU is attempting to mediate in the Comoros between the federal government and the separatists controlling the islands of Anjouan and Moheli which, prompted by economic decline, seceded in August 1997.[65] But of particular interest is the case of Eritrea, not least because it is the only successful example of a seceding entity in Africa achieving statehood and thereby establishing what may be an unhelpful precedent. In what has been described as an example of 'African imperialism',[66] Eritrea fought for thirty years to establish its independence from Ethiopia. Eritrea was originally an Italian colony which was federated with Ethiopia after the Second World War in accordance with UN guidelines. However, in 1962 Ethiopia effectively annexed Eritrea giving rise to a war of independence/secession. Independence was largely accomplished through the force of arms by 1991 but the creation of the new State was legitimized by a referendum in April 1993 which overwhelmingly endorsed Eritrean independence.[67] It is interesting to observe that recent developments suggest that some States are accepting the need for accommodation on this issue.[68]

Article 3(4) provides for the peaceful settlement of disputes by negotiation, mediation, conciliation or arbitration and is analogous to Article 2(2) and Article 33(1) of the UN Charter.[69] This provision is further supplemented by Article 19, which establishes a Commission of Mediation, Conciliation and Arbitration, and the Protocol on the Commission of Mediation, Conciliation and Arbitration.[70] These means have now been effectively superseded by the Mechanism for Conflict Prevention, Management and Resolution.[71] The commitment to the principle of peaceful settlement of disputes was perceived to be an indispensible condition to the development of Africa and it was an important consideration in view of the prevailing instability, particularly regarding frontier disputes.

For many years resort to informal procedures was the preferred mode of dispute settlement by the OAU. International mediation, conciliation or the use of good offices of African statesmen were regular features.[72] Ad hoc committees were often appointed to help settle disputes. The resolution of the Algerian–Moroccan border dispute in the 1960s was visibly facilitated by the work of an ad hoc commission.[73] In many other instances, however, such as the Somali–Ethiopian conflict over the Ogaden region in the 1960s and 1970s,[74] the civil war in Chad,[75] and the Western Sahara dispute,[76] their efforts were unsuccessful. Common factors in all these cases appear to have been persuasion rather than dictation, pragmatism rather than legalism, and the suggestion of political solutions in conformity with the fundamental principles of the OAU rather than the imposition of legal settlements.[77] However, it must be observed that such efforts still have an important role to play as acknowledged by the UN.[78] Mention might be made of the mediation efforts of Julius Nyerere with respect to Burundi, Togo in relation to the dispute between Cameroon and Nigeria over the Bakassi Peninsula, and Rwanda concerning the border dispute between Eritrea and Ethiopia. Of special significance appears to be the appointment in 1997 of a joint UN/ OAU Special Representative for the Great Lakes region.[79]

Article 3(4) does not require the compulsory settlement of disputes although under Article 19 Member States pledge themselves to settle *all* their disputes peacefully. Under international law States must refrain from the use or threat of force in settling their disputes. The consent of the parties to a dispute is a condition precedent to its settlement. Article 3(4) does not establish a hierarchy of methods but it does not exclude other possibilities.[80] Nevertheless, notable by its absence is any reference to international judicial settlement. No mention is made of the ICJ despite the fact that all the OAU Member States (with the exception of the SADR) as members of the UN, are parties to the Statute of the ICJ.[81] Proposals at the Addis Ababa conference for the establishment of an African International Court were abandoned. There are a number of reasons for this omission. First, there is a general reluctance among the international community to submit to binding judicial settlement where States have no control over the outcome of the case. Thus States prefer to resort to various diplomatic processes where the possibility of salvaging something is far greater. This appears to be particularly true of the African States where, as has already been observed, recourse to informal consideration by *ad hoc* committees has been preferred. Secondly, the ICJ's controversial decision in the *South West Africa Cases* (Second Phase) in 1966[82] led the African States to shun this forum for many years. Thirdly, African States view judicial settlement as alien to their culture. This, apparently, was a major factor why no Court of Human Rights was originally established under the Banjul Charter on Human and Peoples' Rights.[83] However, recent litigation before the ICJ suggests that in future they may be more willing to resort to this mode of dispute settlement.[84] In addition, support for the view that opposition to third party adjudication among African States is weakening considerably may be evidenced by developments within the OAU itself. Thus, the Court of Justice established under the AEC Treaty may be given extensive jurisdiction by virtue of Article 18(4) thereof. Furthermore, the African Court on Human and Peoples' Rights is given jurisdiction over, *inter alia*, African human rights instruments. Arguably, this description could include the OAU Charter itself since it makes reference to human rights.

Article 3(6) commits the Member States and the OAU to the total emancipation of dependent African territories and complements the undertaking in the preamble 'to fight neo-colonialism in all its forms'. Africa was a classic victim of colonialism which established a relationship of subordination and exploitation. Colonization damaged the social, cultural, political and economic structures of the colonized peoples and dispossessed them of their land, wealth and possessions. Decolonization was no panacea as neo-colonialism simply perpetuated this system of domination and exploitation.

Demands for a new economic order are thus explicable against this background.

This provision nevertheless reflects the right of self-determination in its external sense, a norm of international law applicable to the decolonization of non-self-governing territories according to which their inhabitants can freely determine their political status.[85] It is arguable, as has been alluded to earlier, that in Africa the right of self-determination has been constrained by the principle of *uti possidetis*.[86] However, Article 3(6) was not restricted solely to non-self-governing territories but its application extended to victims of apartheid in South Africa and the occupied territory of Namibia. In this regard the OAU and the Front-Line States took some practical steps. The Liberation Committee, now dissolved, was created in 1963 as one of the specialized agencies of the OAU with responsibility for co-ordinating the provision of aid to national liberation movements fighting for the independence of their homelands and freedom from racial oppression.[87] The OAU has obviously played a prominent role in the struggle against apartheid.[88] It presented a united front, making international public opinion aware of the threat South Africa posed to Africa as a whole. The OAU sponsored the World Conference for Action against Apartheid in 1977, which adopted the Lagos Declaration for Action against Apartheid, condemning that system. The Conference also recognized the legitimate aspirations of the peoples of South Africa and committed governments to provide support for the liberation movements recognized by the OAU. The OAU prompted the Front-Line States to organize and create secure bases for action by the liberation movements in their struggle against apartheid, providing them with moral and material support. In 1979 the OAU proposed a solution in the Lusaka Manifesto, where it acknowledged that a smooth handover of power could not happen overnight but would require transitional arrangements. It created an *ad hoc* Committee on southern Africa to mobilize diplomatic and other action against the pariah regimes.[89] With the demise of institutionalized racism signalled by the independence of Zimbabwe and Namibia, and the transition to a multiracial democratic society in South Africa in 1994, the OAU lost what has probably been its major motivational and unifying cause. Colonialism in its classic form has now been eradicated from continental Africa, but the status of certain Indian Ocean islands are still in dispute. The Comoros and Madagascar claim the French territories of Mayotte and the Malagasy Islands, respectively, while Mauritius claims the British Indian Ocean Territory dominated by Diego Garcia.[90] Without this unifying theme the demise of the OAU has been predicted, but exaggerated, as the OAU must redouble its efforts to resolve Africa's longstanding problems, namely, peace and security and economic development and integration.

Article 3(6) does not specify how the emancipation of the dependent nations was to be achieved and indeed the OAU Charter is silent on this point. It has been seen that the OAU established the Liberation or Decolonization Committee entrusted with providing aid to liberation movements.

This begs the question as to what type of assistance was considered permissible. The type and level of assistance seemed dependent on the status of the struggle, in particular whether it satisfied the definition of a war of national liberation. A war of national liberation has been defined as 'armed conflicts in which peoples are fighting against colonial domination and alien occupation and against racist regimes in the exercise of their right to self-determination'.[91] The view has also been expressed that wars of national liberation refer to the organized struggle of oppressed peoples for total independence and against all forms of 'imperialism, colonialism and neo-colonialism'.[92] A war of national liberation may also be defined by reference to its goal: the implementation of the right of self-determination. There has been considerable support for the view that wars of national liberation had the status of international armed conflicts, which would make the international norms relating to the use of force, including the concept of self-defence, applicable thereto,[93] but Western opposition to such classification has been significant. Assistance to national liberation movements seems to have taken three distinct forms: political and moral support; indirect material assistance; and direct military intervention. A general consensus of opinion exists that assistance confined to humanitarian and economic aid was acceptable but a divergence of views exists as to whether military or material aid was allowable. The Western position has generally sought to exclude military and material assistance whereas Third World States adopted the opposite view.[94] In view of the substantial opposition it cannot be asserted that a customary norm of international law emerged to the effect that national liberation movements were entitled to receive material and military aid. In fact, the OAU usually confined itself to providing moral, political and financial aid, but it did recognize the legitimacy of the armed struggle. Thus in the Dar-es-Salaam Declaration of 1975 it stated:

> The liberation of those areas under colonial and racist domination can
> be achieved either by peaceful means or by armed struggle . . . we
> would prefer to achieve our objectives by peaceful means if that were
> possible. But whether the solution takes the form of intensified military
> confrontation or negotiations would entirely depend on the response of
> the racist and colonialist regimes.[95]

With the exception of the Polisario Front's struggle in the Western Sahara, it would seem that this issue now has little practical relevance for the States of Africa.

Article 3(7) affirms a policy of non-alignment with regard to all blocs, a rare victory for the Casablanca Group, but which now seems obsolete as a relic of Cold War rhetoric. There were various reasons for the adoption of such a policy. First, an unwillingness, rooted in the colonial past, to compromise their hard-won independence and sovereignty. Secondly, a reluctance, more observed in the breach, to become embroiled in superpower rivalry.

And thirdly, the freedom to accept aid from whatever source. Many African States thus became prominent in the Non-Aligned Movement which was also a vehicle for condemning white domination and neo-colonialism. Nevertheless, despite the fact that the African States were not formal parties to any alliance during the Cold War many had close political, commercial and military links to one or other superpower and it appears true to say that superpowers actively supported their allies, destabilized others, and fought wars by proxy, Angola being a prime example.[96] The collapse of the Soviet Union has led to a more detached interest towards Africa by foreign powers, with radical consequences, however. Politically, African States have committed themselves to pluralism, good governance and human rights, and southern Africa achieved peace and democracy, while economically the role of the market has become pre-eminent. Nevertheless, the commitment to non-alignment should not be airily dismissed, as a concrete manifestation of this policy has been the adoption in 1996 of the African Nuclear-Weapon-Free Zone Treaty (Treaty of Pelindaba).[97]

The importance of these guiding principles to the OAU and its Member States can be ascertained from the fact that under Article 6 the Member States pledge themselves to observe scrupulously the principles enumerated in Article 3. It is doubtful whether this article adds anything of substance since the Member States have already solemnly affirmed and declared their adherence to those principles. Nevertheless, it emphasizes their commitment and it appears to create a binding legal obligation, a violation of which could be regarded as a material breach of a treaty.

It will become apparent during the course of this work that these principles have not always been observed. The question therefore arises as to the binding nature of the obligations which the OAU Charter imposes upon the signatories. The OAU Charter is a multilateral convention and according to the principle *pacta sunt servanda* it is binding upon the parties to it,[98] although it should be noted that a number of signatories have entered reservations. Nevertheless, certain OAU Charter provisions, and in particular the preamble, contain statements of policy to be achieved or political desiderata. As such, violations thereof, albeit undesirable, may not necessarily infringe international law. However, as has been stated, Article 3 reaffirms many fundamental principles of international law and UN Charter provisions which are *a priori* binding upon the African States as members of the international community.[99] Violations of the OAU Charter may therefore constitute violations of general international law and vice versa.

Institutional Structure

The OAU is an organization possessing international personality, i.e., it is a body with rights and duties under international law.[100] To enable it to perform its functions various institutions have been created under the

Charter. Article 7 enumerates the principal institutions of the OAU. These are: the Assembly of Heads of State and Government; the Council of Ministers; the General Secretariat; and the Commission of Mediation, Conciliation and Arbitration. It is important to note that, in addition, the AEC, the Treaty and Protocols, form integral parts of the OAU.[101]

Assembly of Heads of State and Government

According to Article 8 the Assembly is 'the supreme organ of the Organization' which discusses matters of 'common concern to Africa with a view to co-ordinating and harmonising the general policy of the Organization'. It may also 'review the structure, functions, and acts of all the organs' and specialized agencies and according to Article 3 of the Rules of Procedure it may establish any specialized agencies it deems necessary. The Assembly is the competent body to interpret and amend the OAU Charter.[102] Article 9 states that the Assembly is composed of, as its full name indicates, the Heads of African States and Governments, and meets once a year and, when approved by a majority, in extraordinary session. Under Article 10 each Member State has one vote, and resolutions, except on procedural matters, require a two-thirds majority for adoption. The resolutions have no binding force; the OAU operates by consensus. The OAU was designed to act only when assured of widespread support. It is submitted that this fact undermines the effectiveness of the OAU. Two-thirds of the total membership of the OAU forms a quorum.

Certain practices that are not provided for in the OAU Charter have become institutionalized in practice. Thus the Assembly meets in a different State capital each year. In addition, the host Head of State becomes the chairman of the OAU until the subsequent summit. This position is simply titular and is devoid of any executive authority but is nevertheless of considerable prestige. This has led to problems on occasions. Hence there was substantial opposition to the chairmanship of Idi Amin in 1975 and Colonel Gadaffi in 1982. In order to avoid such political embarrassment, and as a cost-cutting exercise, it has been suggested that the Assembly should, like the Secretariat, be permanently based in Addis Ababa. A proposal to endow the OAU Chairman with some executive powers under the Banjul Charter on Human and Peoples' Rights did not come to fruition.

The Assembly has various roles to play under the Banjul Charter, which came into force in October 1986, most of which are of a procedural nature but some are substantive.[103] The Assembly is ultimately responsible for the composition of the African Commission on Human and Peoples' Rights whose task it is to promote human and peoples' rights and ensure their protection in Africa. Thus under Article 33 of the Banjul Charter the Assembly elects the members of the Commission by secret ballot from a list of persons nominated by the State parties. In case of the death or resignation of a member of the Commission the Assembly has the task under Article 39(3) of replacing that member for the remainder of his or her term.

The Assembly also has a supervisory role, not dissimilar to the one performed by the Committee of Ministers of the Council of Europe under the ECHR. Thus, under Article 54 of the Banjul Charter the Commission must submit an annual report on its activities to the Assembly. But more significantly the Assembly is involved, albeit to a limited extent, in the complaints mechanism relating to alleged violations of human rights. Therefore, according to Article 52 of the Banjul Charter, the Commission communicates to the Assembly its report on any alleged violation and pursuant to Article 53 of the Banjul Charter it may make to the Assembly such recommendations as it deems useful. Furthermore, if the Commission unveils the existence of a series of serious or massive violations of human and peoples' rights it is empowered under Article 58 of the Banjul Charter to bring these cases to the Assembly's attention. The Assembly may then request the Commission to undertake an in-depth study of these cases and present a factual report. In addition, the Commission may submit an emergency case to the Chairman of the Assembly who may then request an in-depth study.

The Assembly is ultimately responsible for taking whatever action appears necessary. However, a considerable weakness exists in that the OAU Charter does not currently make any provision for enforcement machinery and history regrettably suggests that the Assembly, by its very nature, may not be able to be emphatic enough in the protection of fundamental rights and freedoms. Nevertheless, the Banjul Charter does provide the Assembly with some leverage in that Article 45(4) empowers it to delegate to the Commission any task it deems necessary. In addition, the Assembly may exercise some political pressure upon errant States by making public any measures taken under the Banjul Charter and by publishing the Commission's reports pursuant to Article 59. It should also be observed that the Assembly will have certain funtions under the Nouakchott Protocol on the African Court on Human and Peoples' Rights.[104] The Assembly will, *inter alia*, elect the Court, it, or any other OAU organ, will be empowered to request an advisory opinion from the Court, and it will monitor the Court's judgments. It is important to note that the Assembly has a significant role to play in the AEC.[105]

The Council of Ministers

The functions and duties of the Council of Ministers are set out in Articles 12–15 of the Charter. It is composed of the Foreign Ministers, or other designated ministers, of the Member States and meets at least twice a year and when requested and approved by two-thirds of its members, in special session. Its functions and duties include the 'responsibility of preparing conferences of the Assembly' and it is entrusted with the power to implement the decisions of the Assembly. It must also consider any matter referred to it by the Assembly. The Council also 'co-ordinates inter-African co-operation with the instructions of the Assembly and in conformity with Article 2(2)'. The AEC Treaty allocates major functions to the Council[106] and the Council will effectively monitor the execution of the Court's judgments on the Assembly's behalf under the Nouakchott Protocol.[107]

A quorum of not less than two-thirds of the total membership of the Council is necessary for any meeting. Each Member State has one vote but, unlike the Assembly, resolutions are adopted by a simple majority. The reason appears to be that Council resolutions are merely recommendations to the Assembly which is the organ competent to take final decisions.

The Council plays a significant role in the adoption of the budget. The Secretary-General submits the draft budget to the Council which then scrutinizes and adopts the budget. This takes place during its first annual meeting in February.[108]

The General Secretariat

A permanent secretariat is a *sine qua non* of any international organization and the OAU Charter makes provision for this in Articles 16 to 18. Article 16 establishes the post of an Administrative Secretary-General, appointed by the Assembly, to direct the affairs of the Secretariat. The Assembly may also appoint Assistant Secretaries-General to this end. The Secretary-General is appointed for a four year term and may be re-elected. No account must be taken of nationality or regional origin. The Secretary-General must be an impartial and neutral official and must be independent of any government. However, the Secretary-General is subordinate to the Organization and in particular the Council to which, according to Article 7 of the Rules of the Secretariat, he is directly responsible for the proper execution of his duties. In the performance of his functions the Secretary-General enjoys certain diplomatic privileges and immunities.

The functions of the Secretary-General are listed in Article 11 of the Rules of the Secretariat, the most important of which are:

- To submit to the Member States a month in advance of the Summit Meeting the budget and the minutes of the Council of Ministers and specialized commissions;
- To communicate a copy of the notification of accession or adhesion to the Charter to Member States, in accordance with Article 28 of the Charter;
- To receive a written notification from any State wishing to renounce its membership, in accordance with Article 32;
- To receive a written request from any Member State for the amendment or revision of the Charter and to notify all the Member States, in accordance with Article 33;

- To accept on behalf of the OAU gifts, bequests and other donations after approval by the Council of Ministers, in accordance with Article 30;
- To call ordinary and extraordinary sessions of the Council of Ministers and of the Assembly;
- To draft the provisional agenda and to communicate it to the Member States;
- To prepare and submit the OAU's annual budget for the approval of the Council of Ministers; and
- To create or abolish, subject to the approval of the Council of Ministers, any administrative or technical offices or sections which he deems necessary for the proper functioning of the General Secretariat.

The use of the adjective 'administrative' is significant since it denotes the role that the founding fathers had reserved for the Secretary-General. Not for them a politically active Secretary-General in the Hammarskjöld mould; simply an apolitical administrator who would implement decisions but not take them.[109] Nevertheless, these attempts at a politically neutered Secretary-General did not diminish the capacity for controversy.

The decision of the then Secretary-General, Edem Kodjo, in 1982 to admit the SADR to the OAU presented the Organization with arguably its greatest crisis to date and threatened it with dissolution. Kodjo argued throughout that his action was purely an administrative one in conformity with Article 28(2) and Article 11(3) of the Rules of the Secretariat, and however politically naive his decision may have seemed, it appears to have been strictly legal.[110]

The current Secretary-General, Salim Ahmed Salim of Tanzania, has, however, adopted a more proactive approach and prepared the ground for the eventual establishment of the Mechanism for Conflict Prevention, Management and Resolution. Under that machinery the Secretary-General has been accorded certain executive powers authorizing him to take initiatives to resolve disputes.

The General Secretariat is the OAU's civil service and acts as such for the Assembly, the Council of Ministers, the specialized commissions and any other organs of the OAU, including the AEC. The specific duties of the General Secretariat are set out in its Rules of Procedure which, according to Article 1 thereof, include not only the functions ascribed to it under the OAU Charter as defined by the Rules, but also any other duties as agreed by the Member States in any other treaty. According to Article 2 of the Rules of Procedure the Secretariat supervises the drafting of the Council of Ministers' decisions on economic, social, legal and cultural matters affecting Member States and in particular:

- It acts as an archive and depository of documents from the meetings of all OAU organs;

- It puts all its administrative and technical services at the disposal of the specialized commissions;
- It is a depository of all the instruments of ratification of treaties concluded between Member States;
- It drafts an annual report on the activities of the OAU;
- It drafts a report, for submission to the Council, on the activities of the specialized commissions; and
- It drafts the budget of the OAU which is submitted to the Council of Ministers for approval.

All the servants of the OAU enjoy diplomatic immunity in accordance with the General Convention on the Privileges and Immunities of the OAU 1965 and Additional Protocol 1980.[111]

The Secretary-General has also assumed various functions under the Banjul Charter.[112] First, he is involved in the composition of the Commission. Thus, according to Article 35 he must invite State parties to nominate candidates for the Commission at least four months before the election. He must then draft an alphabetical list of the persons thus nominated and communicate it to the Assembly at least one month before the election. Furthermore, under Article 39, in case of death or resignation of a member of the Commission, the Chairman of the Commission must immediately inform the Secretary-General who must declare the seat vacant. According to Article 41 the Secretary-General has the task of appointing the Secretary to the Commission. He must also provide the staff and services necessary for the effective discharge of the Commission's duties. Article 42(5) allows the Secretary-General to attend the Commission's meetings but he must neither participate in the deliberations nor does he have a vote, although he may be invited to speak by the Commission's Chairman.

Secondly, the Secretary-General is involved in the procedural work of the Commission. Thus, under Article 46, the Commission may hear from the Secretary-General in the course of its investigations. Furthermore, under Article 47, the Secretary-General must also receive a communication from any State party that has accused another State party of violating the Banjul Charter. If a State party wishes to refer the alleged violation directly to the Commission under Article 49, the Secretary-General must also receive a communication to that effect.

Finally, the Secretary-General has a purely administrative role to fulfil. Thus, under Article 63(1) the instruments of ratification or adherence to the Banjul Charter must be deposited with the Secretary-General who, according to Article 67, must infom the OAU Member States of the deposit of each such instrument. In addition, any State party that wishes to make an amendment to the Banjul Charter must submit a written request to that effect to the Secretary-General, and if the amendment has been duly implemented it will come into effect for those States in favour three months after the Secretary-General has received notice of the acceptance.

Commission of Mediation, Conciliation and Arbitration

The final principal institution listed in the OAU Charter is the Commission of Mediation, Conciliation and Arbitration.[113] The Commission was established by Article 19 of the OAU Charter and its duties and functions are defined in an additional protocol, the Protocol of the Commission of Mediation, Conciliation and Arbitration which was signed by thirty-three States in 1964.[114] By virtue of Article 19 of the OAU Charter and Article 32 of the Protocol, the said document forms an integral part of the Charter. Every Member State is *ipso facto* a party to the Protocol and no reservations are permissible. The Commission has yet to become operational, however.

The mandate of the Commission is to hear and settle disputes between Member States by peaceful means. A dispute in this particular text appears to refer not only to justiciable disputes, i.e., matters that raise legal questions and that can be settled by the application of international law, but encompasses political issues or other extra-legal considerations.[115] While the Commission is not a judicial organ, in case of a dispute Article 19 of the Protocol offers three, seemingly alternative, modes of settlement: mediation, conciliation and arbitration. These terms have technical meanings.[116] Mediation and conciliation are non-adjudicatory and informal procedures, the former involving official third party involvement seeking to reconcile the claims of the parties or offering advice or advancing proposals for a possible solution which nevertheless are non-binding.[117] According to Article 21(1) of the Protocol the mediator must confine his role to reconciling the views and claims of the parties. If accepted the proposals will become the basis of a protocol of agreement between the parties. The parties do not appear to be compelled to accept the proposals although the duty to settle the dispute peacefully would still be operative. Moreover, in such a situation it would seem that the mediator is not empowered to propose a further solution. By contrast, the latter procedure refers to an impartial examination of the subject matter of the dispute and a search for an acceptable settlement. According to Article 24(1) of the Protocol conciliation entails objective evaluation and clarification of the issues in dispute and the endeavour to bring about an agreement between the parties upon mutually acceptable terms.[118] Under Article 22 of the Protocol a petition for conciliation, which must include a summary of the facts, must be submitted to the President of the Commission by at least one of the parties. Prior written notice must have been given to the other party. Again, if the other party refuses to accept the procedure of conciliation, the matter is referred to the Council of Ministers. It should be observed that a settlement reached through mediation or conciliation does not have to be based on international law. The Commission is entrusted with finding peaceful solutions to disputes and it can therefore take account of extra-legal considerations.

Arbitration, on the other hand, differs considerably from the other modes of dispute settlement. It describes a judicial method of dispute settlement which entails the delivery of a binding decision based on law by a tribunal whose composition is determined by the parties.[119] It is therefore a compulsory means of dispute settlement and submission to arbitration is therefore dependent upon prior agreement between the parties. This definition finds expression in Articles 27 and 29 of the Protocol.

Article 29 of the Protocol stipulates that the parties must conclude a *compromis* specifying the undertaking of the parties to go to arbitration and accepting the decision of the tribunal as legally binding; the subject matter of the dispute; and the seat of the Tribunal. In addition, the *compromis* may specify the law to be applied by the Tribunal or, if the parties agree, they can confer upon the Tribunal the power to adjudicate *ex aequo et bono*. The *compromis* is binding upon the Tribunal and affords its basis for jurisdiction. The opportunity provided to the parties to specify the applicable law is a feature characteristic of arbitration.[120] However, in the absence of any reference to the applicable law in the *compromis*, Article 30 of the Protocol states that the Tribunal must decide the dispute according to treaties concluded between the parties; international law; the OAU Charter; the UN Charter; and, if the parties agree, *ex aequo et bono*. This provision gives rise to a number of points. It would appear that it attempts to create a hierarchy of sources which the Tribunal should consider in a systematic fashion.[121] No express reference is made to Article 38(1) of the Statute of the ICJ, which states that in deciding disputes the ICJ will apply international conventions, international custom, general principles of law, and judicial decisions and the teachings of highly qualified publicists. However, since the Tribunal is empowered to apply international law it is submitted that by definition this must include the sources enumerated in Article 38 of the Statute of the ICJ. Furthermore, there would appear to be considerable overlap between the clauses relating to international law and subsequently to the UN Charter, since the UN Charter forms part of the *corpus* of international law *qua* treaty and is also responsible for generating customary law. Since the term 'international law' is not defined by the Protocol it is submitted that, in applying international law, the Tribunal could not ignore a document as fundamental as the UN Charter, thereby bringing into question the notion of hierarchy of sources. It should be noted that international law may not apply automatically, since in this hierarchical system preference should be given where possible to treaties concluded between the parties. These treaties would have to be in conformity with the concept of *jus cogens*.[122]

A further problem that arises from the concept of hierarchy of sources concerns the relationship between the OAU and the UN Charters. In a hierarchical system the OAU Charter would take precedence but this would be incompatible with Article 103 of the UN Charter which states that in the event of a conflict between the obligations of the Member States under the UN Charter and their obligations under any other international agreement, their UN obligations shall prevail.[123] This suggests therefore, that the Tribunal should give prior consideration to the UN Charter. Nevertheless, this approach assumes that the OAU and the UN Charters may be inconsistent but it could be argued that no such inconsistency exists. The OAU is a regional organization as envisaged by Article 52(1) of the UN Charter and in its Charter the OAU reaffirms its commitment to the principles of the UN. The OAU Charter does not appear to contain any provision that is inconsistent with the UN Charter. Furthermore, all Member States of the OAU, except for the SADR, are members of the UN. It could therefore be said that the two organisations are mutually compatible and that in applying the OAU Charter first, a possibility that is not prohibited by the UN Charter, no conflict need arise.

Alternative arguments have been advanced to prove that even in a hierarchical system no discrepancy need exist.[124] First, and following from the above submission, since many of the principles of the UN Charter form part of general international law the Tribunal would be obliged to apply these principles before considering the OAU Charter. Secondly, and in a similar vein, the UN Charter is a multilateral treaty to which all but one of the OAU Member States are parties. Article 30 of the Protocol lists treaties concluded between the parties as the first applicable law to be considered. Hence the UN Charter would again have priority over the OAU Charter. All these arguments accentuate a fundamental flaw in the draftsmanship of the provision. If these submissions are correct the view that Article 30 of the Protocol enumerates a hierarchy of applicable law is rendered meaningless. What would be the point of listing the UN Charter as a distinct source in fourth position if it forms part of sources one and two and thus takes priority over source three? Listing the UN Charter as a separate source thus seems pointless. Either the UN Charter does not form part of sources one and two and should be considered only when the preceding three have been discounted, or no hierarchy exists. The better view would appear to be that no hierarchical system can be presumed, and this conclusion is strengthened by analogy to Article 38 of the Statute of the ICJ which most jurists agree has no substantive hierarchical structure.[125] The Tribunal would thereby have the added advantage of flexibility in considering the applicable law.

Finally, Article 30 of the Protocol, in addition to Article 29(2), empowers the parties to instruct the Tribunal to decide the case *ex aequo et bono*. This enables the parties to authorize the Tribunal to adjudicate *ex aequo et bono* once the proceedings have been instituted. The power to adjudicate *ex aequo et bono* is commonplace in international adjudication although little use has been made of this procedure. Thus Article 38(2) of the Statute of the ICJ, which empowers the Court to decide a case *ex aequo et bono*, has never been invoked. Nevertheless the *ex aequo et bono* procedures have certain advantages in that they endow the Tribunal with greater flexibility in choosing the basis for resolution, including in particular extra-legal considerations.

It is noteworthy that the Protocol does not provide for other modes of dispute, such as negotiation,[126] or, more importantly, judicial settlement. Recourse to these or other modes of settlement does not appear, however, to be precluded by the Protocol.[127] However, it should be observed that the Commission is endowed with powers of investigation and inquiry with regard to disputes submitted to it.[128]

The Commission is to consist of twenty-one members, of which no two members shall be the nationals of the same State, elected by the Assembly from a list of candidates nominated by the Member States and prepared by the Secretary-General, for a renewable term of five years. The Members of the Commission must be suitably qualified professionally which, with the exception of the members of the Arbitral Tribunal, does not necessarily entail having legal qualifications. In this respect political or diplomatic experience would presumably suffice. Members of the Commission cannot be removed from office except by a two-thirds majority decision of the total membership of the Assembly on the grounds of inability to perform their duties or of proved misconduct.[129] This provision seeks to guarantee their independence.

The Commission does not possess compulsory jurisdiction; consent by a party in some form is necessary for the Commission to assume jurisdiction. Article 14 of the Protocol states that consent to submit to the jurisdiction of the Commission may be evidenced by: (a) a prior written undertaking; (b) reference of a dispute to the Commission; and (c) submission to the jurisdiction in respect of a dispute referred to the Commission by another State, by the Council of Ministers, or by the Assembly. Where a party refuses to submit to the jurisdiction of the Commission, Article 13(2) states that the Bureau must refer the matter to the Council of Ministers for consideration. The Commission has, according to Article 12 of the Protocol, jurisdiction over inter-state disputes but then only when empowered jointly by the parties concerned, by a party to the dispute, by the Assembly or by the Council of Ministers. Thus disputes involving individuals, international organizations or corporate bodies are beyond the scope of the Commission.[130] The Protocol does not make it clear whether only State parties to the OAU may have recourse to the Commission or whether a dispute between a Member State and a non-Member State may be referred to the Commission. Given the regional character of the OAU it appears safe to conclude that only disputes between Member States are envisaged.

The lack of compulsory jurisdiction on an unconditional basis may be perceived as undermining the efficacy of the Commission, should it become operational, but it would be unrealistic to expect States, especially those, such as African States, that are particularly jealous of their sovereignty, to accept such an extensive obligation. This would be unusual in international affairs because traditionally some form of prior consent is deemed necessary. Nevertheless there are some positive features. Thus the Commission may exercise jurisdiction upon a unilateral application by a party to the dispute. This is comparable to Article 36(2) of the Statute of the ICJ, the so-called Optional Clause. However, the other party to the dispute must subsequently accept the Commission's jurisdiction, failing which the question is referred to the Council of Ministers. The Protocol does not elaborate further on this issue and the only sanction that appears available to the Council is that of political pressure. Also to be welcomed is the fact that, subject to a State's *ex post facto* consent, the Council of Ministers or the Assembly may refer a dispute to the Commission.[131] However, a serious limitation would appear to be the fact that there is no provision for submissions by third States, only interested States and the OAU's political organs have *locus standi*. These provisions must be read in the context of Article 19 of the Charter which places an absolute stipulation on the Member States to settle *all* their disputes by peaceful means. This obligation appears to go beyond what is required by customary international law, which prohibits the use of force except in self-defence, and even Article 2(3) of the UN Charter.[132]

The Protocol does impose other general obligations upon the Member States. Thus Article 15 thereof requires Member States to refrain from any act or omission that is likely to aggravate a situation which has been referred to the Commission. This obligation extends to *all* Member States and not solely to the parties to a dispute and is therefore a more stringent condition than that imposed by Article 41(1) of the Statute of the ICJ which applies only to the parties to the dispute. Article 28 requires that parties resorting to arbitration submit in good faith to the award of the Arbitral Tribunal. It is peculiar that this obligation applies only to arbitration and not to the other modes of dispute settlement but it is submitted that the principle of good faith is a norm of customary international law which Member States must therefore observe.[133] Finally, under Article 18 of the Protocol, where, in the course of dispute settlement, it appears necessary to conduct an investigation or inquiry for the purpose of elucidating relevant facts or circumstances, the parties concerned and all other Member States must extend their fullest co-operation in the conduct of such investigations.

As has been stated, the Commission has not yet become operational. The reason is not due to a lack of ratifications since no provision exists requiring such formal adoption. According to Article 32 of the Protocol all that is necessary for the Protocol to become an integral part of the OAU Charter is the approval of the Assembly, approval that was given during the course of the first Assembly in July 1964. Technically, the Protocol is in force, and binding upon Member States, and the Commission still officially exists. But no Member State has yet felt it necessary to invoke its provisions and it could be said that the Commission has fallen into disuse and that its functions are being performed by a number of *ad hoc* bodies[134] and the Mechanism for Conflict Prevention, Management and Resolution. The reason for this appears to be a mistrust of formal dispute settlement and yet, paradoxically, African States have not been averse to the establishment of numerous *ad hoc* bodies under the auspices of the OAU and the involvement of the UN to settle their disputes.

Specialized Commissions

Article 20 of the OAU Charter makes provision for the establishment of specialized commissions by the Assembly, corresponding largely to the fields of co-operation listed in Article 2(2) of the OAU Charter.[135] According to Article 21 of the OAU Charter each specialized commission is composed of the Ministers concerned with the relevant area or other Ministers or Pleni-potentiaries designated by the Member States. Their constitutional basis lies in Article 22 of the OAU Charter which states that the Council of Ministers shall approve regulations governing the performance of their functions. Indeed, the Council approved these measures at its second ordinary session in February 1964 and provided that each commission operates as part of the General Secretariat.[136] However, many of the commissions have, to a greater or lesser extent, fallen into disuse to be superseded by the Assembly or specialized ministerial conferences. Nevertheless, questions of economic co-operation and defence have loomed large on the agenda of the OAU.

The OAU has been particularly active in the economic area. It has a close working relationship within the UN's ECA; it has established the African Development Bank (ADB) which makes concessionary loans to African States; it is influential within the so-called 'Group of Seventy-Seven' of Developing States in the UN and other international fora; it has adopted an African Maritime Transport Charter to promote foreign trade and econ-omic development;[137] and the overwhelming majority of African States are parties to the Fourth Lomé Convention 1989 between the EC and ACP States and which provides for aid and investment by the EC in developing countries. But particularly significant has been the recent adoption of the treaty providing for an African common market, the AEC Treaty, which is considered in greater detail subsequently in Chapter 6.

The OAU Charter is largely silent on the question of defence simply stating in Article 2(2)(f) that Member States should co-operate in the areas of defence and security, with the assistance of the Defence Commission. The Defence Commission defined its role as acting primarily as an 'organ of consultation, preparation, and recommendation for the collective and/or individual self-defence of the OAU Member States against any act or threat of aggression'.[138] Thus Nkrumah's suggestions for an African Defence Force under a High Command to pursue a common defence policy have never been implemented. The Defence Commission has effectively fallen into desuetude and its remit has been assumed by other bodies.

As has been stated the OAU Charter makes no provision for an OAU standing army or peace-keeping force, nor does it provide for collective security in the sense that Member States are legally bound to come to the assistance of other Member States in the event of an armed attack. The African States, as members of the UN, have a right of collective self-defence under Article 51 of the UN Charter, and in any event the right of collective self-defence in customary international law is still available.[139] Furthermore, Article 52(1) of the UN Charter permits the creation of regional agencies designed to uphold international peace and security,[140] while Article 3(4) of the OAU Assembly's Rules of Procedure in particular appears to provide the constitutional basis for such a force in that it empowers the Assembly to create any specialized body it deems necessary for the purposes of Articles 8 and/or 20 of the OAU Charter. Moreover, it is submitted that the establishment of an African force lies within the implied powers of the OAU by analogy, *mutatis mutandis*, to the UN which the ICJ has recognized as possessing the implied powers necessary for the fulfilment of its purposes, including carrying out peace-keeping operations.[141] It thus seems clear that the OAU is constitutionally competent to establish an African force.

On various different occasions the Assembly mooted the possibility of an African force, such as creating a standing army or a rapid intervention force, or resorting to national units on an *ad hoc* basis, but it was only in 1978 that the Council of Ministers gave it serious consideration. Plans were elaborated further the following year and welcomed by the then Secretary-General, Edem Kodjo. It was explained that the proposed force would not be based upon a standing army but would involve a procedure whereby threatened States could call upon troop contingents from other Member States. At its Eighteenth Session held in Nairobi in June 1981 the Assembly approved in principle the establishment of a pan-African defence force.[142]

The civil conflict in Chad provided the OAU with its first opportunity to create a force and involve itself in peace-keeping operations.[143] Pursuant to resolution 102 (XVIII) Rev. 1, the Assembly created an OAU peace-keeping force destined for Chad. The then Chairman of the OAU, President Moi of Kenya, required that two preconditions be satisfied before the OAU force be sent to Chad: first, and in conformity with established UN practice, the force had to be invited by the incumbent Chadian Government;[144] and second, Libyan troops, which had been present in the country since 1980 at the invitation of the then Head of State, President Goukouni, had to be withdrawn. These requirements were complied with and by 16 November 1981 all Libyan troops had left Chad.

The OAU force in Chad was bedevilled with problems from the outset. First, the precise mandate of the force was unclear. According to its constituent resolution, the function of the force was to 'ensure the defence and security of the country whilst awaiting the integration of Government Forces'. President Moi felt that its proper role was to enable the people of Chad to decide on a national government of their choice through free and fair elections supervised by the OAU with the help of an African peace-keeping force. Alternatively the OAU Standing Committee on Chad clarified the role of the peace-keeping force as being to assist the government to maintain peace and create a united, integrated, national force. Nevertheless, in performing these functions the force would continue to remain neutral and would not involve itself in the internal affairs of Chad. Thus, the OAU properly envisaged a neutral role for the force, assisting the establishment of negotiations between the warring parties. President Goukouni of Chad, however, appeared to view the OAU force as nothing more than another army with which to continue the fighting, a role manifestly beyond the scope of an international peace-keeping force.

Secondly, the OAU lacked the necessary mechanism to deal with such an operation. Logistic and financial difficulties were encountered. Originally, six States had volunteered to provide troops for the force: Nigeria, Senegal, Benin, Togo, Guinea, and Zaïre. The initial number of troops was to total over 10,000 but, after Benin, Guinea and Togo withdrew their offer of troops, only 3,265 eventually arrived in Chad. The OAU force was by then already receiving substantial financial aid. The Senegalese contingent was financed by France, and the USA contributed $12,000,000 towards the costs incurred by Nigeria and Zaïre. The OAU force cost £87,000,000 a year and consequently the UN was approached for financial assistance since only £270,000 was raised by the OAU Member States towards the cost of the force. The UN Security Council accordingly adopted Resolution 502 (1982) which called on the UN Secretary-General 'to establish a fund for assistance to the peace-keeping force of the OAU in Chad, to be supplied by voluntary contributions'. At its Nineteenth Session held in Addis Ababa in 1983, the Assembly decided that Member States would meet their share of the costs incurred by the participating States.[145] This decision seems only logical and fair and it is interesting to note that in the *Certain Expenses of the United Nations* Case the ICJ found that expenditure relating to peace-keeping operations constituted 'expenses of the Organization' which Member States had to meet as determined by the General Assembly.[146]

The reticence of the rival Chadian forces to negotiate created further problems for the OAU force. Since no political solution was foreseeable and the war showed no signs of abating, Nigeria withdrew half its contingent, 1,000 men. Moreover, the peace-keeping force was becoming embroiled in hostilities and President Goukouni accused it of worsening the situation. When the capital N'Djamena fell to the forces of President Goukouni's rival, President Habré, on 7 June 1982, the OAU Chairman ordered the withdrawal of the OAU force by the end of the month.[147]

It appears correct to conclude that the activities of the OAU peace-keeping force in Chad resulted in abject failure. The establishment of the force was a costly venture that achieved little of merit and which gave rise to grave disappointment. Some States, particularly Cameroon and Gabon, were opposed to the idea of an OAU force and alternatively advocated UN involvement. But another unwelcome outcome of this fiasco was that the OAU was unwilling or unable to contemplate peace-keeping operations for a number of years.[148] Nevertheless, as will be seen below, it seems that a pan-African force is an idea whose time has come.

The Mechanism for Conflict Prevention, Management and Resolution

A singularly important development in recent times has been the establishment of a Mechanism for Conflict Prevention, Management and Resolution.[149] As has already been observed, the OAU has traditionally relied on *ad hoc* arrangements to deal with disputes among Member States. However, the deficiency of this flexible system has been that it is remedial and reactive rather than preventive and proactive. Consequently, in 1990 the OAU adopted the Declaration on the Political and Socio-Economic Situation in Africa and the Fundamental Changes Taking Place in the World according to which the OAU committed itself to work toward the peaceful and speedy resolution of all conflicts in Africa, including internal ones. The Secretary-General thus set in motion the process on consultation on the establishment of a permanent mechanism for conflict management and in 1992 submitted his report on Proposals for an OAU Mechanism for Conflict Prevention and Resolution to the Twenty-Eighth Assembly meeting in Dakar.[150] The report explored a number of radical options, including the creation of an African Security Council within the OAU, that the Bureau of the Assembly assume responsibility for dealing with intra-state and inter-state disputes at the diplomatic and political level, that the Court of Justice of the AEC be generally available for judicial settlement of disputes, and that the OAU Member States earmark units within their armed forces for an African peace-keeping force. However, many of these proposals proved too extreme for the majority of Member States but nevertheless the fundamental proposition of a special mechanism for conflict prevention, management and resolution was accepted in principle and formally endorsed by the Cairo Summit the following year.

The Mechanism operates subject to the fundamental principles of the OAU, especially in respect of the sovereignty and territorial integrity of Member States, non-interference in the internal affairs of States, and the inviolability of inherited borders. The consent and co-operation of the parties to a conflict is a prerequisite.[151]

The Mechanism's primary objective is the anticipation and prevention of conflicts, with emphasis on anticipatory and preventive measures.[152] It is mandated with undertaking confidence-building measures in order to resolve conflicts. The expectation is that prompt and decisive action will prevent the emergence of conflicts, prevent them from degenerating and obviating the need to resort to complex and demanding peace-keeping operations.[153]

The Mechanism is based on the Central Organ composed of the States members of the Bureau of the Assembly that are elected annually. It assumes the overall direction and co-ordination of the activities of the Mechanism and functions at the level of the Heads of State and Government as well as that of Ministers and Ambassadors accredited to the OAU.[154] It meets at least monthly and its decisions are taken by consensus.

The Secretary-General of the OAU is the chief executive of the Central Organ and, under its authority, and in consultation with the parties involved in the conflict, has the task of deploying efforts and taking all appropriate initiatives to prevent, manage and resolve conflicts. The Secretary-General and the Central Organ may resort to various aspects of conflict resolution in the performance of their functions.[155]

The OAU must co-ordinate its activities with African regional and sub-regional organizations, and co-operate, where appropriate, with neighbouring countries. Similarly, it must liaise with the UN with regard to peace-making and peace-keeping activities, and when necesssary, call upon the UN to provide financial, logistic and military support for the OAU's efforts in conflict management.[156]

The Mechanism has already become operational and in the space of a few short years has been active.[157] It has mediated in internal conflicts in Rwanda, the Congo, Somalia, Angola, amongst others. In Burundi, military and civilian forces have been deployed as a confidence-building measure. A delegation is attempting to reverse the secession of Anjouan from the Comoros. Elections have been monitored in various countries, including South Africa. In Liberia and Sierra Leone the OAU has been supportive of the ECOWAS intervention. At the inter-state level it has mediated in the dispute between Cameroon and Nigeria over the Bakassi Peninsula, and the war between Ethiopia and Eritrea. It is especially interesting to note that the Mechanism is preparing the ground for peace-keeping forces.[158]

The creation of the Mechanism is undoubtedly significant. At a practical level, it must enhance the OAU's capacity to deal with conflicts.[159] Endowing it with a preventive role is especially welcome. However, peace-making, as can be seen from the UN involvement in Somalia and the former Yugoslavia, is fraught with difficulties and strongly suggests that only where the warring factions are interested in a peaceful resolution can outside intervention succeed in contributing to the outcome without resorting to forceful measures. Nevertheless, recent events provide cause for optimism, but the political will of Africa to resolve its own problems has to be a condition precedent. At a conceptual level, the Mechanism appears revolutionary in that it calls for a rethinking of the rigid adherence of African States to the principles of sovereignty and non-interference. Their erosion, already under way, seems implicit.[160]

The Budget

According to Article 23 of the OAU Charter the budget is provided by contributions from Member States. However, the burden is not shared equally but is apportioned on the basis of the scale of UN assessment, which is based on national incomes, and no Member State is assessed for an amount exceeding 20 per cent of the OAU's yearly regular budget. Therefore, while not proving equal, it seeks to be equitable.[161] Like other international organizations, the OAU has been bedevilled by the problem of debt arrears, not surprising perhaps in the world's poorest continent.[162] Financial restraint has been adopted and the sanctions for defaulting States have been increased.[163]

Membership

Membership of the OAU is governed by a number of separate Charter provisions and subsidiary clauses. Article 4 of the OAU Charter provides that each independent sovereign African State is entitled to membership, while Article 24(1) states that the OAU Charter is open for signature to all independent sovereign African States. According to Article 28 an independent sovereign African State may at any time notify the Administrative Secretary-General of its intention to adhere or accede to the OAU Charter but admission is dependent on a simple majority vote of the Member States. The Secretary-General must communicate a copy of the notification to adhere or accede to all Member States which in turn must convey their decision to the Secretary-General who then communicates the final decision to the applicant State.[164]

These provisions give rise to a number of points. It would appear that the assumption was that every independent sovereign African State would seek membership of the OAU, which indeed has been the case.[165]

The definition of the words 'independent' and 'sovereign' has been brought into question as a result of the admission of the SADR in 1984.[166] Morocco contended that the SADR was not eligible for membership because it did not fulfil the requirements of Article 4, namely, that the SADR was not an independent sovereign State since it did not satisfy the criteria for statehood. Nevertheless, in 1980 twenty-six Member States out of fifty, a majority in accordance with Article 28(2), voted to admit the SADR to the OAU. However, because of the furore that this decision caused, the SADR's membership was postponed *sine die*. But in 1982 the Secretary-General in effect admitted the SADR, subject to the Assembly's ratification which was obtained in 1984. The Secretary-General defended his action by saying that the question of the SADR's admission was purely an administrative matter within the framework of Article 28(2) of the OAU Charter and Article 11(3) of the Rules of the Secretariat since a majority of the Member States had already voted for the SADR's admission. In his view the Secretary-General bore sole responsibility for the final decision on the question of admission, a statement that did not meet with unanimous approval. The SADR's opponents alleged that the question of admission was properly a procedural matter that required a two-thirds majority vote. This claim is clearly erroneous not only in the light of Article 28(2) but also in view of Article 10(3) which plainly states that the Assembly will decide questions of procedure by a simple majority.[167]

Despite the fact that the statehood of the SADR was then, and still is, a matter of considerable debate the majority of the Member States were of the view that the SADR was eligible for membership. The reasons for this view are numerous and include geopolitical, ideological and legal considerations. In the last context it should be noted that a considerable body of opinion supports the view that the right of self-determination compensates for the lack of the formal criteria of statehood.[168] The admission to the UN of Guinea-Bissau in 1974 before it had entirely liberated itself from Portuguese rule provides a precedent.[169] However, it should be observed that, in the absence of a resolution to the dispute, support for the continued membership of the SADR appears to be ebbing.

Where an organization's constitution does not define a 'State' for purposes of admission, as is the case here, the organ competent to determine questions of admission must decide whether the entity seeking admission is a 'State'.[170] Thus in the *Conditions of Admission of a State to Membership in the United Nations* Case, the ICJ stated that conditions for admission are subject to the judgment of the Organization and, in the final analysis, that of its Members.[171] Lauterpacht suggests that admission ought to constitute 'sufficient proof of the existence of the requirements of statehood or of governmental capacity' while Brownlie states that membership of an international organization may constitute *prima facie* evidence of statehood.[172] Therefore, it may be argued that the Members of the OAU, acting through the appropriate organ, the Assembly, possess the capacity necessary to recognize a political entity as a State for the purposes of that organization.

The question therefore arises whether the OAU adheres to a policy of collective recognition. It is interesting to note that a former UN Secretary-General, Trygve Lie, stated that it was constitutionally impossible for the UN to pursue a policy of collective recognition[173] but it appears to follow from certain provisions of the UN Charter and the practice of the UN organs that the UN does have the capacity to recognize States when considering substantive and procedural questions.[174] *Mutatis mutandis* this argument could be applicable to the OAU by analogy. However, such determination of statehood would seem to be binding within the particular and functional context of the respective Charters, and whether or not it is valid for general purposes must depend on the relevance to general international law of the particular criteria employed.

However, it would seem that admission does not imply general recognition *vis-à-vis* other Member States.[175] The SADR's admission to the OAU would not have compelled Moroccan recognition so that Morocco could therefore have continued to refuse to recognize the SADR although it may have been obliged to deal with it with regard to matters pertaining to the OAU.

It is interesting to note that the OAU has traditionally adhered to a policy of non-recognition of governments. This expression of the Estrada Doctrine is based on the principle of non-interference in the internal affairs of States, but the OAU has not avoided problems because of this. The OAU has attracted considerable criticism, even from within its own ranks, because of its general support for incumbent governments, however undemocratic, and apparent tolerance of repressive regimes which this approach has generated. President Museveni of Uganda, for instance, has been scathing in his denunciation of a policy which has often proved unhelpful to insurgents seeking to overthrow repressive regimes. The Burundian Government of Major Buyoya claims that it seized power to put an end to inter-ethnic massacres and is attempting to address the appalling human rights situation that existed but has encountered considerable hostility from neighbouring States which imposed OAU endorsed sanctions. However, the combined effect of the 1990 Declaration on Fundamental Changes in the World and the 1993 Cairo Declaration may force a reappraisal of a hitherto inflexible policy but the practice of the OAU still seems somewhat erratic and confused.[176]

Cessation of membership is governed by Article 32 of the OAU Charter which stipulates that any State that wishes to renounce its membership must give a year's notice by submitting a written notification to the Secretary General.[177] The notification may be withdrawn within that time. To date only one State, Morocco, has availed itself of this provision which submitted its withdrawal in November 1984, with effect from November 1985, in protest at the formal admission of the SADR.[178] There have been recent calls for the readmission of this influential State.

No provision for the expulsion of Member States exists in the OAU Charter. However, it would appear that in the absence of an express provision to the contrary, an organization such as the OAU possesses an implied power of suspension or expulsion.[179] It would seem that if the activities of a Member State were to prove incompatible with the principles or aims and purposes of the Charter of an organization, it is arguable that that State would no longer satisfy the criteria on which the organization is based and that its membership could therefore be revoked, even in the absence of an express provision for expulsion. Furthermore, it could be argued that an errant State is in material breach of the treaty. Although the Vienna Convention on the Law of Treaties 1969 is inapplicable to the constitution of an international organization, it may be that the principle enshrined in Article 60(3)(b) thereof can be applied by way of analogy. This text states that a material breach consists of, *inter alia*, the violation of a provision essential to the accomplishment of the object or purpose of a treaty, and consequently justifies suspension or termination of the treaty between the defaulting State and the parties not in breach thereof.[180] It is submitted that such a power is vested in the OAU and that the Assembly would be the organ competent to take such a decision.

However, there are cogent reasons, primarily political, why the OAU would be unlikely to resort to such drastic measures. The OAU usually avoids confrontation and promotes reconciliation through negotiation. Greater persuasion may be brought upon a Member State than a non-Member State. And finally past history suggests that, despite just cause having been provided on a number of occasions, the OAU has not resorted to expulsion and there is no reason to believe that the OAU would behave otherwise in the future.

The continued membership of the SADR is open to doubt. Some Member States which previously recognized it have subsequently withdrawn their recognition and have called for its expulsion. This possibility, as well as that of cessation of membership, might have to be addressed given the additional fact that the result of the UN sponsored referendum may well endorse the Moroccan position.

Conclusion

The principal task of the OAU is to advance the development of African States in a variety of fields and this it seeks to do by promoting co-operation and urging collaboration among its Members. It is also committed to the resolution of disputes. Any international body which encourages greater co-operation among its Members and which is also motivated by humanitarian ideals and the rule of law is to be welcomed. It has forged a closer sense of identity amongst the African States, in particular between the Arab north and sub-Saharan Africa. However, as may be apparent, its degree of success varies and in many areas has been modest. The OAU operates by consensus but progress is often handicapped by its very lack of mandatory powers. In general the decisions of the Assembly are only recommendatory in nature. No provision is made for powers analogous to those available to the UN Security Council under Chapter VII of the UN Charter. No organ having disciplinary powers exists and there is little that the OAU can do in the form of punishment for errant members other than mobilize public opinion. Its slavish adherence to the principle of domestic jurisdiction, long abandoned by the UN, has generated a negative image which is only now being modestly addressed. Furthermore, progress across many fields has been thwarted by the profileration of conflicts, seemingly endemic, and a catalogue of natural disasters and their catastrophic socio-economic consequences.

The OAU was established in a sea of idealism and expectations of its achievements may have been unrealistically inflated. It cannot be denied that the OAU has disappointed, often reflecting inter-State divisions and demonstrating impotence in the face of internal repression and human rights abuses. Yet a regional organization for Africa appears to be a necessity and it cannot be denied that the OAU has achieved considerable success in certain areas, such as the development of refugee law, its contribution to the struggle against apartheid and continuing progress in the fields of human rights and democracy. There are grounds for believing that economic performance may be improving. These are achievements that must be encouraged. The establishment of machinery for conflict resolution, long overdue, is a welcome development. Although too early properly to assess its contribution to the peaceful settlement of disputes in Africa grounds for optimism exist. If successful, socio-economic development may follow. Success in this field is imperative, and the creation of an African common market seems a salient step in this direction. The OAU therefore continues to have an important role to play and it is to be hoped that its Members allow it to do so to the full.

Notes

1. C.O.C. Amate, *Inside the OAU: Pan-Africanism in Practice* (1986) Chapter 1; M. Wolfers, *Politics in the Organisation of African Unity* (1976).
2. Amate, note 1 *supra*, pp. 34–9; T. O. Elias, *Government and Politics in Africa* (1961); I. Geiss, *The Pan-African Movement* (1974); C. Legum, *Pan-Africanism: A Short Political Guide* (1962); D. K. Orwa, The Search for African Unity, in J.C.B.O. Ojo, D.K. Orwa, and C.M.B. Utete, *African International Relations* (1985) Chapter 5.
3. Amate, note 1 *supra*, pp. 40–6; B. Boutros-Ghali, 'The Addis Ababa Charter – A Commentary', 546 *International Conciliation* (1964) pp. 6–7.
4. See, e.g., Article 6 of General Assembly Resolution 1514 (XV) 1960 Declaration on the Granting of Independence to Colonial Countries and Peoples which states that, 'Any attempt at the partial or total disruption of the national unity and the territorial integrity of a country is incompatible with the Purposes and Principles of the United Nations'. Note also the relevance to Africa of the principle of *uti possidetis, Frontier Disputes Case* (Burkina Faso/Mali) ICJ Reports 1986, p. 554. See also M. Shaw, *Title to Territory in Africa* (1986) pp. 180–87; and further *supra* pp. 12–14.
5. The Brazzaville Group was composed of Cameroon, Central African Republic, Chad, Congo (Brazzaville), Côte d'Ivoire, Dahomey (now Benin), Gabon, Mauritania, Madagascar, Niger, Senegal and Upper Volta (now Burkina Faso). The Casablanca Group was composed of Ghana, Guinea, Mali, Morocco, United Arab Republic (now Egypt) and the Provisional Government of Algeria. See Amate, note 1 *supra*, pp. 46–50; I.LL. Griffiths, *The Atlas of African Affairs* (2nd edn 1994) pp. 76–7.
6. These were Liberia, Togo, Ethiopia, Libya, Nigeria, Sierra Leone and Somalia.
7. Boutros-Ghali, note 3 *supra*, pp. 9–23.
8. In fact thirty States were present at the conference: Algeria, Burundi, Cameroon,

Central African Republic, Chad, Congo (Brazzaville), Congo (Leopoldville) (subsequently Zaïre, now Democratic Republic of the Congo), Côte d'Ivoire, Dahomey (now Benin), Ethiopia, Gabon, Ghana, Guinea, Liberia, Libya, Madagascar, Mali, Mauritania, Niger, Nigeria, Rwanda, Senegal, Sierra Leone, Somalia, Sudan, Tanganyika (now Tanzania), Tunisia and Burkina Faso. Absent were Morocco, in protest at the presence of Mauritania to which it had a territorial claim, and Togo, following a *coup d'état*.

9. Algeria, Angola, Benin, Botswana, Burkina Faso, Burundi, Cameroon, Cape Verde, Central African Republic, Chad, Comoros, Congo, Democratic Republic of the Congo, Djibouti, Egypt, Equatorial Guinea, Eritrea, Ethiopia, Gabon, Gambia, Ghana, Guinea, Guinea-Bissau, Côte d'Ivoire, Kenya, Lesotho, Liberia, Libya, Madagascar, Malawi, Mali, Mauritania, Mauritius, Mozambique, Namibia, Niger, Nigeria, Rwanda, SADR, São Tomé e Principe, Senegal, Seychelles, Sierra Leone, Somalia, South Africa, Sudan, Swaziland, Tanzania, Togo, Tunisia, Uganda, Zambia and Zimbabwe. The breakaway Republic of Somaliland and Anjouan remain unrecognized. Morocco formally withdrew in 1985 in protest at the admission of the SADR.

10. See Article 4 of the OAU Charter, and further *supra* pp. 34–6. On the Western Sahara dispute generally, see Chapter 2.

11. For text, see *Naldi*, pp. 3–10, 32–7. For commentary, see generally, Boutros Ghali, note 3 *supra*; T.O. Elias, 'The Charter of the Organization of African Unity', 59 *AJIL* (1965) 243.

12. The remaining non-self-governing territories are the British Indian Ocean Territory, otherwise the Chagos Archipelago claimed by Mauritius, which British governments have undertaken to cede to Mauritius when the military base at Diego Garcia is no longer needed, and the Malagasy Islands, under French tutelage and claimed by the Comoros and Madagascar, see Shaw, note 4 *supra*, pp. 130–4; Griffiths, note 5 *supra*, p. 209.

13. Relations between the OAU and the UN have been on an institutional footing since 1965, see the United Nations–Organization of African Unity Co-operation Agreement of 15 November 1965, 548 UNTS 316. See further, United Nations, Report of the Secretary-General on: The Causes of Conflict and the Promotion of Durable Peace and Sustainable Development in Africa, 10 *RADIC* (1998) 549, para. 20, on co-operation between the UN and OAU in the sphere of peacemaking.

14. On developments in the fields of refugees and economics, see Chapters 3 and 6 respectively. On attempts to tackle environmental degradation see Chapter 5. On cultural affairs note, e.g., the Convention on a Cultural Charter for Africa 1976, in force 1990, ratified by thirty-three States, which deals with the right of peoples to practise and expand their cultural life.

15. See, e.g., General Assembly Resolution 2625 (XXV) 1970 Declaration on Friendly Relations and Co-operation Among States in Accordance with the Charter of the United Nations; I. Brownlie, *Principles of Public International Law* (5th edn 1998) pp. 289–90. For facts on African States, see I.LL Griffiths, *The African Inheritance* (1995) Chapters 7–10.

16. Amate, note 1 *supra*, pp. 64–5. Unlike the UN Security Council or the EC Council of Ministers.

17. See, e.g., Declaration on Friendly Relations and Co-operation among States; General Assembly Resolution 2131 (XX) 1965 Declaration on the Inadmissibility of Intervention in the Internal Affairs of States; and further, *Military and Paramilitary Activities In and Against Nicaragua* (*Nicaragua* v. *United States of America*) ICJ Reports 1986, p. 14 at pp. 108–11. See A. Bolaji Akinyomi, 'The Organization of African Unity and the Concept of Non-Interference in the Internal Affairs of Member States', 46 *BYIL* (1972–73) 393. France in particular

has often been closely involved in the internal politics of many African States, thus consorting with some of the continent's most unsavoury characters, such as Bokassa and Mobutu, and the genocidal regime in Rwanda in 1994, see C. Clapham, *Africa and the International System* (1996) pp. 77–98.

18. Report of the Secretary-General on: The Causes of Conflict and the Promotion of Durable Peace and Sustainable Development in Africa, note 13 *supra*, paras. 7–15. However, an unsuccessful attempt at providing stability was the Arusha Accords of 1993 according to which Burundi, Tanzania, Uganda and Zaïre agreed to the non-use of their territories as bases for destabilizing Rwanda.

19. UN Press Release SC/6465, 9 January 1998.

20. In a statement issued on 16 October 1997, the Security Council condemned all external interference in the Congo and called for the immediate withdrawal of all foreign forces, *ibid.* See further, UN Doc. E/CN.4/1998/31, paras. 43–6.

21. Brownlie, note 15 *supra*, pp. 294–7; M. Shaw, *International Law* (4th edn 1997) pp. 454–5. In *Tunis-Morocco Nationality Decrees Case* PCIJ, Ser. B, No. 4 (1923) at p. 24, the PCIJ stated that the 'question whether a certain matter is or is not solely within the jurisdiction of a State is an essentially relative question; it depends upon the development of international relations.'

22. Under the extensive UN system, see generally A.H. Robertson, and J.G. Merrills, *Human Rights in the World* (4th edn 1996) Chapters 2 and 3. On 18 December 1992 the UN General Assembly adopted resolution 47/142 on the situation in Sudan, expressing deep concern at serious human rights violations and called on the Sudanese government to respect fully human rights and to comply with its international obligations. The UN has appointed Special Rapporteurs to examine allegations of serious abuses of human rights in, *inter alia*, Burundi, pursuant to resolution 1996/1 of the Commission on Human Rights, and see further, UN Doc. E/CN.4/1997/12, Equatorial Guinea, pursuant to resolution 1996/66 of the Commission on Human Rights, and see further, UN Doc. E/ CN.4/1997/54, Nigeria, pursuant to resolution 1996/79 of the Commission on Human Rights, and see further, UN Doc. E/CN.4.1997/62, Rwanda, pursuant to General Assembly resolution 50/200, and see further, UN Doc. E/CN.4/ 1996/111, Sudan, pursuant to resolution 1996/73 of the Commission on Human Rights, and see further, UN Doc. E/CN.4/1997/58, and Zaïre, pursuant to resolution 1996/77 of the Commission on Human Rights, and see further, UN Doc. E/CN.4/1997/6. Pursuant to resolution 935 (1994) the UN Security Council established a Commission of Experts to examine the grave violations of international humanitarian law in Rwanda. In 1997, the UN authorized the establishment of an investigative team to look into human rights abuses in the Democratic Republic of the Congo, UN Press Release SC/6465, 9 January 1998. Particularly noteworthy has been the establishment under Chapter VII of the UN Charter, as a subsidiary organ of the Security Council, of the International Criminal Tribunal on Rwanda to try the crimes committed there during the ethnic conflict of the early 1990s, see UN Security Council resolution 955 (1994), 33 *ILM* 1602 (1994). Since independence, African countries have gradually established an international system which would respect human rights, making due allowance for their own history and values, the Banjul Charter on Human and Peoples' Rights; see Chapter 4.

23. See, e.g., the Harare Commonwealth Declaration 1991, 18 *CLB* (1992) pp. 347–9; Report of the Secretary-General on: The Causes of Conflict and the Promotion of Durable Peace and Sustainable Development in Africa, note 13 *supra*, paras. 71–7. It is interesting to observe that it has been suggested that there is an embryonic right to democratic governance, T.M. Franck, 'The Emerging Right to Democratic Governance', 86 *AJIL* (1992) 46. See further, D.M. Ayine, 'Ballots as Bullets?: Compliance with Rules and Norms Providing for the Right to

Democratic Governance, an African Perspective', 10 *RADIC* (1998) 709. It is instructive to note that the question of the promotion and protection of human rights through the promotion of a democratic society is being studied by the UN, see UN Doc. E/CN.4/Sub.2/1997/30.

24. In a special meeting held in 1992, the Security Council stated that the 'non-military sources of instability in the economic, social, humanitarian and ecological fields have become threats to peace and security', 31 *ILM* 759 (1992) at p. 761. At a Ministerial Meeting on Africa on 25 September 1997, the UN Security Council expressed its grave concern at the number and intensity of conflicts in Africa, UN Press Release SC/6465.

25. See further, M. Sinjela, 'Constitutionalism in Africa: Emerging Trends', No. 60 *The Review* (International Commission of Jurists) (1998) 23.

26. UN Doc. CERD/C/SR.1166 (14 August 1996) pp. 3–4.

27. UN Security Council resolution 1132 (1997). It should be noted further that the OAU authorized ECOMOG to remove the military junta in Sierra Leone, *Keesing's* Vol. 43, 1997, p. 41674. Sanctions were lifted in 1998, Security Council resolution 1181, on the restoration of the legitimate government.

28. UN Doc. CERD/C/SR.1175, pp. 5–9; UN Doc. E/CN.4/1997/12, paras. 18, 22; *Keesing's* Vol. 42, 1996, p. 41179. Security Council resolution 1072 A (1996) expressed 'strong support for the efforts of the regional leaders'. The sanctions were lifted in early 1999.

29. Report of the Secretary-General on: The Causes of Conflict and the Promotion of Durable Peace and Sustainable Development in Africa, note 13 *supra*, paras. 29–70.

30. J. Quigley, 'The "Privatization" of Security Council Enforcement Action: A Threat to Unilateralism', 17 *Michigan Journal of International Law* (1996) 249 at pp. 271 et seq.; M. Mubiala, 'La mission des Nations Unies pour l'assistance au Rwanda (1993–1996)', 8 *RADIC* (1996) 393; A. Parsons, *From Cold War to Hot Peace: UN Interventions 1947–1995* (1995) pp. 213–14. For an account of the massacres, see the Report on the situation of human rights in Rwanda submitted by Special Rapporteur René Degni-Ségui, UN Doc. E/CN.4/1995/71.

31. It should be observed that the African Group at the UN fully endorsed the UN action, UN Doc. E/CN.4/1993/35, para. 192. The Security Council had imposed an arms embargo under resolution 733 (1992). For an account of the UN operation in Somalia, see Parsons, note 30 *supra*, Chapter 16.

32. For an assessment of the negative implications of the UN failures in Somalia, see Report of the Secretary-General on: The Causes of Conflict and the Promotion of Durable Peace and Sustainable Development in Africa, note 13 *supra*, paras. 31–2.

33. 37 *ILM* 780 (1998). According to the terms of the Declaration the Somali factions agreed to adopt a federal system of government with regional autonomy and to form a transitional government of national unity.

34. See generally, Parsons, note 30 *supra*, Chapter 10.

35. Resolution 1135 (1997). See generally, Parsons, note 30 *supra*, Chapter 9.

36. Under resolution 1173 (1998) the UN Security Council, *inter alia*, condemned UNITA and held it responsible for its failure to abide by its obligations in the Lusaka Protocol and relevant Security Council resolutions. Under resolution 1173 B (1998) an international freeze of UNITA's financial assets, as well as other economic sanctions, were imposed.

37. MINURCA (United Nations Mission in the Central African Republic), established under Security Council resolution 1159 (1998), acting Chapter VII of the UN Charter. See further, Security Council resolution 1182 (1998).

38. Parsons, note 30 *supra*, pp. 102–3. See also, Report on the mission to South

Africa by Special Rapporteur Ms. Judith Sefi Attah, UN Doc. E/CN.4/Sub.2/1993/11/Add.1.

39. See, e.g., resolution 788 (1992), which imposed an arms embargo, reinforced by resolutions 1083 (1996) and 1116 (1997), and 856, establishing a partnership between UNOMIL and ECOMOG under Chapter VIII of the UN Charter; and see Report of the Secretary-General on: The Causes of Conflict and the Promotion of Durable Peace and Sustainable Development in Africa, note 13 *supra*, paras. 43–4. See further, Parsons, note 30 *supra*, pp. 215–19; M. Weller, (ed.) *Regional Peace-Keeping and International Enforcement: The Liberian Crisis* (1994); K.O. Kufuor, 'The Legality of the Intervention in the Liberian Civil War by the Economic Community of West African States', 5 *RADIC* (1993) 525.

40. UN Press Release SC/6465.

41. Report of the Secretary-General on an Agenda for Peace, 31 *ILM* 953 (1992) para 17.

42. The text of this Declaration can be found in *Naldi*, p. 57. This prohibition was reaffirmed by Article 3 of the OAU Convention on Refugee Problems in Africa 1969, according to which Member States must not permit refugees residing in their territories to conduct subversive activities against any OAU Member State. It is interesting to note that the UN Declaration on the Inadmissibility of Intervention in the Domestic Affairs of States and the Declaration on Principles of International Law Concerning Friendly Relations and Co-operation Among States prohibit States from organizing, assisting, fomenting, financing, inciting or tolerating subversive, terrorist or armed activities directed towards the violent overthrow of any other regime.

43. UN Docs. E/CN.4/1992/12, pp. 7–8; E/CN.4/1996/27, pp. 18–22.

44. In force 1985. Text in *Naldi*, pp. 58–62. At the time of writing the Convention has been ratified by the following States: Benin, Burkina Faso, Cameroon, Congo, Democratic Republic of the Congo, Egypt, Ethiopia, Ghana, Lesotho, Liberia, Mali, Niger, Nigeria, Rwanda, Senegal, Seychelles, Sudan, Tanzania, Togo, Tunisia, Zambia and Zimbabwe. It has been signed by Algeria, Angola, Guinea, and Morocco.

45. By resolution 44/34 of 4 December 1989, the UN General Assembly adopted the International Convention against the Recruitment, Use, Financing and Training of Mercenaries (not yet in force). It has been ratified by only sixteen States, including Cameroon, Mauritania, Seychelles and Togo, and signed by a further ten, including Angola, Congo, Morocco, Nigeria and the Democratic Republic of the Congo. It is unclear whether mercenarism is prohibited by general international law since the laws of most countries do not make mercenary activities a criminal offence but, according to the Declaration on Friendly Relations and Co-operation Among States, States are under a duty to prevent mercenarism. In the *Nicaragua Case* ICJ Reports 1986, at p. 103, the ICJ found that, *inter alia*, the sending of mercenaries to carry out acts of armed force against another State amounted to an armed attack as defined in Article 3(a) Definition of Aggression, General Assembly Resolution 3314 (XXIX) 1974, which the ICJ stated reflected customary international law. The UN has identified lacunae in treaty law, such as the inadequacy of existing legislation to define the legal status of the mercenary and the classification of mercenary activities, and has expressed concern about governments, such as that of Angola and Sierra Leone, hiring private companies providing military advice and training, UN Doc. E/CN.4/1997/24, pp. 26–34. See further, UN Doc. E/CN.4/1998/31, pp. 19–22. UN General Assembly resolution 52/112 has called for a clearer definition of mercenaries.

46. See also Article 47 of Protocol I Additional to the Geneva Conventions of 12 August 1949, and Relating to the Protection of Victims of International Armed

Conflicts 1977 which denies mercenaries the status of combatant or prisoner of war. However, according to Hague Convention IV Respecting the Laws and Customs of War on Land 1907 and the Geneva Conventions 1949 mercenaries and other volunteers are to be treated as any other combatant provided they observe the laws and customs of war.

47. See UN Docs. E/CN.4/1994/23, pp. 18–19, and E/CN.4/1997/24, para. 24. Historically, the Front-Line States in particular suffered heavily from mercenary activities, UN Docs. E/CN.4/1992/12, pp. 15–37; E/CN.4/1994/23, pp. 16–23. African countries that have recently experienced the activities of mercenaries include Sudan, the Comoros, the Democratic Republic of the Congo, the Congo and Sierra Leone, UN Docs. E/CN.4/1996/27, pp. 17–23, E/CN.4/1998/31, pp. 12–16. For a general perspective on mercenary activities in African countries, see UN Doc. E/CN.4/1998/31, pp. 10–12.

48. *Frontier Dispute Case* ICJ Reports 1986, at p. 566; *Land, Island and Maritime Frontier Dispute Case* (El Salvador/Honduras, Nicaragua Intervening) ICJ Reports 1992, p. 351 at pp. 386 and 388; and Conference on Yugoslavia Arbitration Commission, Opinion No. 3, 31 *ILM* 1499 (1992) at p. 1500. See further, M.N. Shaw, 'The Heritage of States: The Principle of *Uti Possidetis Iuris* Today', 67 *BYIL* (1996) 75 at pp. 97–8, 125–8. Application of the principle results in the former, often colonial, boundaries, whether administrative or international, being transformed into international frontiers upon independence, *Frontier Dispute Case* ICJ Reports 1986, pp. 566, 568; Conference on Yugoslavia Arbitration Commission, Opinion No. 3, ibid.; Shaw, above, pp. 111–19.

49. *Colombia/Venezuela Boundary Arbitration* (1922), in G.H. Hackworth, *Digest of International Law* (1940) Vol. I, pp. 733–6. See further, *Land, Island and Maritime Frontier Dispute Case* ICJ Reports 1992, pp. 386–7; *Territorial Dispute Case* (Libyan Arab Jamahirija/Chad) ICJ Reports 1994, p. 6 at p. 86, per Judge Ajibola, Separate Opinion; Shaw, note 48 *supra*, pp. 98–100; J. Klabbers, and R. Lefeber, 'Africa: Lost Between Self-Determination and *Uti Possidetis*', in C. Brölmann, et al. (eds.) *Peoples and Minorities in International Law* (1993) p. 37 at pp. 54–6; and S.R. Ratner, 'Drawing a Better Line: *Uti Possidetis* and the Borders of New States', 90 *AJIL* (1996) 590 at pp. 593–5.

50. Shaw, *Title to Territory in Africa*, note 4 *supra*, p. 183. There are numerous border disputes in Africa, see I. Brownlie, *African Boundaries: A Legal and Diplomatic Encyclopaedia* (1979); A.J. Day, *Border and Territorial Disputes* (1982); Shaw, above, Chapter 6; S. Touval, *The Boundary Politics of Independent Africa* (1972); Griffiths, *The African Inheritance*, note 15 *supra* Chapters 8, 12, 13. See also Z. Cervenka, 'The Settlement of Disputes Among Members of the Organisation of African Unity', 7 *Verfassungund Recht in Ubersee* (1974) 117; V.D. Degan, 'The OAU Charter and the Settlement of Territorial Disputes', 17 *Jugoslovenska Reviza za Medunorodno* (1970) 284. The Nigerian poet and writer, Wole Soyinka has argued that the real key to peace and stability in Africa is to rip up the colonial legacy, return to the drawing board, and redraw the map of Africa on the basis of geographical, ethnic and tribal borders. His suggestion is unlikely to be viewed as a serious proposition by African leaders.

51. For text, see *Naldi*, p. 49. This commitment has been reinforced by the Cairo Declaration on the OAU Mechanism for Conflict Prevention, Management and Resolution, 6 *RADIC* (1994) 158, para. 14, which lists the 'inviolability of borders inherited from colonialism' as one of the 'objectives and principles of the OAU Charter'.

52. *Frontier Dispute Case*, ICJ Reports 1986, pp. 565, 568. See further, *Territorial Dispute Case*, ICJ Reports 1994, pp. 87–8, per Judge Ajibola, Separate Opinion. See also, Report of the Secretary-General on: The Causes of Conflict and the

Promotion of Durable Peace and Sustainable Development in Africa, note 13 *supra*, para. 8.

53. Most recently, in 1998 hostilities broke out over a border dispute between Ethiopia and Eritrea. Under resolution 1177 (1998) the UN Security Council condemned the use of force, demanded that the parties cease hostilities, and urged them to achieve a peaceful settlement of their dispute.

54. ICJ Reports 1986, p. 554. See further, G.J. Naldi, 'The Case Concerning the Frontier Dispute (Burkina Faso/Mali): *Uti Possidetis* in an African Perspective', 36 *ICLQ* (1987) 893.

55. ICJ Reports 1986, p. 565. The Arbitration Commission of the European Conference on Yugoslavia reaffirmed that *uti possidetis* is a general principle of international law, Opinion No. 3, 31 *ILM* 1499 (1992). See also *Arbitral Award of 31 July 1989 (Guinea-Bissau v. Senegal)* 83 ILR 1, at pp. 37–8. In his Separate Opinion in the *Territorial Dispute Case*, ICJ Reports 1994, p. 89, Judge Ajibola expressed the view that *uti possidetis* is a principle of customary international law. See further, Shaw, 'The Heritage of States', note 48 *supra*, pp. 106–9; and Klabbers and Lefeber, note 49 *supra*, at 59–65, who are critical of lacunae in the ICJ's reasoning. It would appear that originally the principle of *uti possidetis* was in the nature of a regional custom, see the *Asylum Case* ICJ Reports 1950, p. 266. See further, Naldi, 'The Case Concerning the Frontier Dispute', note 54 *supra*, pp. 897–98; Ratner, note 49 *supra*, p. 599, although in the *Frontier Dispute Case* the ICJ was clearly of the view that it was applying a pre-existing custom, ICJ Report 1986, p. 566.

56. See Shaw, *Title to Territory in Africa*, note 4 *supra*, pp. 186–7, who cautions against equating the two principles which, although related, are distinct; Shaw, 'The Heritage of States', note 48 *supra*, pp. 124–5.

57. ICJ Reports 1986, pp. 566–7. See also *Arbitral Award of 31 July 1989*, pp. 37–8.

58. On intertemporal law, see *Island of Palmas Case* (1928) 2 RIAA 829 at pp. 845–6; T.O. Elias, 'The Doctrine of Intertemporal Law', 74 *AJIL* (1980) 285.

59. ICJ Reports 1986, p. 567.

60. ICJ Reports 1986, p. 565.

61. The Arbitration Commission of the European Conference on Yugoslavia has stated that 'it is well established that, whatever the circumstances, the right to self-determination must not involve changes to existing frontiers at the time of independence (*uti possidetis iuris*)', Opinion No. 2, 92 ILR 167 at p. 168. In *Katangese Peoples' Congress* v. *Zaïre* 3 *IHRR* (1996) 136, the African Commission on Human and Peoples' Rights held that the exercise of self-determination must be compatible with the sovereignty and territorial integrity of States.

62. Griffiths, *The African Inheritance*, note 15 *supra*, Chapter 11. It should be observed that secession is not *per se* contrary to international law. International law maintains a neutral attitude towards secession but will accept a seceding entity as a member of the international community if it fulfils the criteria of statehood, especially the capacity to defend its independence, P. Malanczuk, *Akehurst's Modern Introduction to International Law* (7th edn 1997) pp. 78, 336. The principle of self-determination does not normally apply to cases of secession unless there is oppression of minorities, or denial of minority rights, A. Cassese, *Self-Determination of Peoples* (1995) pp. 122–4, 251–3; *Reference re Secession of Quebec* 37 *ILM* 1340 (1998). See also *Katangese Peoples' Congress* v. *Zaire* 3 *IHRR* (1996) 136. According to the Vienna Declaration and Programme of Action, adopted by the UN World Conference on Human Rights in 1993, UN Doc. A/CONF.157/23, Part I, para. 2(3), the right of self-determination must not undermine the territorial integrity of States 'conducting themselves in compliance with the principle of equal rights . . . and thus possessed of a Government

representing the whole people belonging to the territory without distinction of any kind'.

63. See, e.g, resolution AHG/Res.51(IV) whereby the OAU condemned secession in any Member State, declared its support for the principle of territorial integrity and pronounced the right of self-determination inapplicable to such cases; and resolution AHG/Res.58(VI) which called for the unity of Nigeria in the overriding interest of Africa.

64. Clapham, note 17 *supra*, pp. 158–220. Thus, for the better part of a decade there has been no legitimate effective governmental authority but rival clans in many parts of Somalia engaged in violence and banditry, and rival militias vying for control of the capital, Mogadishu. However, as has been explained in note 33 *supra*, recent developments provide hope for national reconciliation. Whereas the extinction of a State cannot be presumed lightly under international law, see Conference on Yugoslavia Arbitration Commission, Opinion No. 8, 92 ILR 199, para. 2; Shaw, *International Law*, note 21 *supra*, pp. 147–9, the collapsed nature of the Somali State has been such that its very continuation as a member of the international community must have been open to question. By contrast, the Republic of Somaliland, led by President Mohammed Egal, whose authority is established in this north-west region, has a legal system based on the Somali Penal Code of 1962, including a Supreme Court.

65. *Keesing's* Vol. 43, 1997, pp. 41762–3, 41852, 41901; Vol. 44, 1998, p. 42110. The OAU has described the secession as 'totally unacceptable' and has refused to recognize the legitimacy of the self-proclaimed government of Anjouan.

66. Griffiths, *The Atlas of African Affairs*, note 5 *supra*, Chapter 37.

67. A compelling legal case for Eritrean independence is put by E. Gayyim, *The Eritrean Question: The Conflict Between the Right of Self-Determination and the Interests of States* (1993). See also, H. Minasse, 'Legality of the Secession: The Case of Eritrea', 8 *Emory International Law Review* (1994) 479.

68. Thus the new Ethiopian Constitution, reflecting the struggles in the region, provides for a right to secession, Article 39. In an attempt to resolve the enduring civil war in Sudan between the Islamic north and the Christian and animist African south, the Sudanese government concluded peace agreements with most of the warring factions in April 1997 which, *inter alia*, granted the right to self-determination to the people of the south, UN Doc. E/CN.4/1998/SR.48, paras. 21, 64. For criticism of the OAU's rigid approach to the question of secession, see C. Anyangwe, 'Obligations of States Parties to the African Charter on Human and Peoples' Rights', 10 *RADIC* (1998) 625 at pp. 655–6.

69. Under general international law States are not obliged to resolve their disputes, but note that under Article 2(3) of the UN Charter Member States must settle their disputes by peaceful means so that international peace and security are not endangered. See also the Declaration on Friendly Relations and Co-operation Among States and General Assembly Resolution 37/590 (1982) Manila Declaration on the Peaceful Settlement of Disputes. In addition, States are prohibited from resorting to the use or threat of force as a means of dispute settlement, see Article 2(4) of the UN Charter. See T. Maluwa, 'The Peaceful Settlement of Disputes Among African States, 1963–1983: Some Conceptual Issues and Practical Trends', 38 *ICLQ* (1989) 299 at p. 301, who states that 'the principle of the peaceful settlement of international disputes has been recognised and accepted as a binding principle of international law by African States'.

70. See *supra*, pp. 24–9.

71. See *supra*, pp. 32–3.

72. Amate, note 1 *supra*, pp. 162–8; Maluwa, note 69 *supra*, pp. 307–13; M. Shaw, 'Dispute Settlement in Africa', 37 *The Yearbook of World Affairs* (1983) 149.

73. Amate, note 1 *supra*, pp. 405–8; Brownlie, *African Boundaries*, note 50 *supra*,

pp. 55–83; Shaw, 'Dispute Settlement in Africa', note 72 *supra*, pp. 152–3; P.B. Wild, 'The Organization of African Unity and the Algerian—Moroccan Border Conflict: A Study of New Machinery for Peacekeeping and for the Peaceful Settlement of Disputes Among African States', 20 *International Organization* (1966) 18; A.O. Cukwurah, 'The Organisation of African Unity and African Territorial and Boundary Problems: 1963–1973', 13 *IJIL* (1973) 176 at pp. 185–91; Touval, note 50 *supra*, pp. 255–62.

74.   Amate, note 1 *supra* pp. 408–19; Day, note 50 *supra*, pp. 116–19, 132–7; Shaw, *Title to Territory in Africa*, note 4 *supra*, pp. 197–201, 249–50; Shaw, 'Dispute Settlement in Africa', note 72 *supra*, pp. 153–6; Cukwurah, note 73 *supra* pp. 193–201; Touval, note 50 *supra*, pp. 111–19.

75.   Amate, note 1 *supra*, pp. 181–8, 451–8.

76.   See *infra*, Chapter 2, pp. 61–5.

77.   Amate, note 1 *supra*, pp. 167–8.

78.   Report of the Secretary-General on: The Causes of Conflict and the Promotion of Durable Peace and Sustainable Development in Africa, note 13 *supra*, para. 21.

79.   Ibid., para. 23. Another example is the contribution of neighbouring countries to the peace effort leading to the, failed, peace-agreement of November 1996 in Sierra Leone between the government of President Kabbah and rebel military forces, UN Doc. E/CN.4/1998/31, para. 30.

80.   It could be said that a practice has evolved in Africa whereby resort should initially be had to regional agencies for the peaceful resolution of local disputes which, however, does not exclude the possibility of bringing disputes before other fora, *Military and Paramilitary Activities in and Against Nicaragua*, Jurisdiction and Admissibility, ICJ Reports 1984, p. 392 at p. 440; *Land and Maritime Boundary Between Cameroon and Nigeria (Cameroon v. Nigeria)* (Preliminary Objections), ICJ, General List No. 94 1998, paras. 48–60.

81.   The following African States have accepted the compulsory jurisdiction of the ICJ under Article 36(2) of its Statute: Botswana, Cameroon, Democratic Republic of the Congo, Egypt, Gambia, Guinea, Guinea-Bissau, Kenya, Liberia, Madagascar, Malawi, Mauritius, Nigeria, Senegal, Somalia, Sudan, Swaziland, Togo, Uganda.

82.   ICJ Reports 1966, p. 6.

83.   See further, Chapter 4 *infra*.

84.   In recent years African States have resorted to judicial settlement on numerous occasions, see, e.g., *Libya/Tunisia Continental Shelf Case*, ICJ Reports 1982, p. 18; *Libya/Malta Continental Shelf Case*; ICJ Reports 1985, p. 13; *Guinea/Guinea Bissau Arbitration* 25 *ILM* (1986) 251; *Frontier Dispute Case* (Burkina Faso/Mali) ICJ Reports 1986, p. 554; *Territorial Dispute Case* (Libya/Chad) ICJ Reports 1994; and currently pending before the ICJ, *Questions of Interpretation and Application of the 1971 Montreal Convention arising from the Aerial incident at Lockerbie (Libya v United States of America)*, Jurisdiction and Admissibility; *Land and Maritime Boundary Case (Cameroon v Nigeria)*, Jurisdiction and Admissibility; *Kasikili/ Sedudu Island Case* (Botswana/Namibia). In a speech to the UN General Assembly, Judge Stephen Schwebel, President of the ICJ, observed that Africa ranked 'high as a source of cases', ICJ Communiqué No. 98/33.

85.   See, e.g., Resolution 1514 (XV) 1960 Declaration on the Granting of Independence to Colonial Countries and Peoples, Resolution 1541 (XV) 1960, Declaration on Friendly Relations and Co-operation Among States, *Western Sahara Case*, ICJ Reports 1975, p. 12, *East Timor Case*, ICJ Report 1995, p. 90, General Comment XXI adopted by the Committee on the Elimination of Racial Discrimination, HRI/GEN/1/Rev.3, p. 114, paras. 8, 9. It should be observed that the commitment in the OAU Charter is supplemented by Article 20(3) of the Banjul Charter. But cf. Anyangwe, note 68 *supra*, p. 654, who argues that the right of

self-determination as understood by the OAU is not restricted to the colonial context.

86. *Frontier Dispute Case*, ICJ Reports 1986, p. 554. However, this would not be the case if, as Brownlie argues, self-determination is a norm of *jus cogens*, see *Principles of Public International Law*, note 15 *supra*, pp. 515, 517.

87. Amate, note 1 *supra*, Chapters 8 and 10; O. Aluko, 'The OAU Liberation Committee After a Decade: An Appraisal', 8 *Quarterly Journal of Administration* (1973) 59.

88. On the UN and South Africa, see Parsons, note 30 *supra*, Chapters 6 to 8. For an account of the effect of sanctions on South Africa, see UN Doc. E/CN.4/Sub.2/1992/12. The Commonwealth Heads of Government agreed in the Harare Declaration in 1991 to the gradual lifting of sanctions as soon as real progress was made towards the abolition of apartheid. UN General Assembly resolution 48/1 (1993) lifted all economic sanctions and the oil embargo whereas Security Council Resolution 919 (1994) terminated the mandatory arms embargo.

89. See, e.g., the Abuja Statement on Southern Africa 1991, UN Doc. E/CN.4/Sub.2/1991/57.

90. See note 12 *supra*.

91. Article 1(4) of Protocol I Additional to the 1949 Geneva Conventions 1977. On wars of national liberation, see G. Abi Saab, 'Wars of National Liberation and the Laws of War', 3 *Annales d'études Internationales* (1972) 93; N. Ronzitti, 'Wars of National Liberation – A Legal Definition', 1 *Italian Yearbook of International Law* (1975) 192; H.A. Wilson, *International Law and the Use of Force by National Liberation Movements* (1988).

92. K. Ginther, 'Liberation Movements', in R. Bernhardt (ed.), *Encyclopaedia of Public International Law* (1983) Vol. III, pp. 245–9.

93. Paragraph 3 of General Assembly Resolution 3103 (XXVIII) 1973 Basic Principles of the Legal Status of Combatants Struggling Against Colonial and Alien Domination and Racist Regimes; Article 1(4) of Protocol I Additional to the 1949 Geneva Conventions 1977; International Convention on the Taking of Hostages 1979.

94. General Assembly Resolutions 2105 (XX) 1965 and 2908 (XXVII) 1973 invited Member States to provide moral and material assistance to national liberation movements. Whereas Resolutions 2131 (XX) 1965, 2625 (XXV) 1970 and 3314 (XXIX) 1974 Definition of Aggression called upon Member States to support the struggle for self-determination. Western States have never accepted the argument that the latter extends to material aid. See also J. Crawford, *The Creation of States in International Law* (1979), pp. 108–18. See *contra*, C.J.R. Dugard, 'The Organisation of African Unity and Colonialism: An Inquiry into the Plea of Self-Defence as a Justification for the Use of Force in the Eradication of Colonialism', 16 *ICLQ* (1967) 157. It is interesting to note that in the *Nicaragua Case*, ICJ Reports 1986, paras. 206, 209, the ICJ, while making it clear that the question of decolonization was not at issue in the case, observed as a general rule that no right of intervention in support of an opposition within another State exists in contemporary international law.

95. Amate, note 1 *supra*, pp. 300–1.

96. Report of the Secretary-General on: The Causes of Conflict and the Promotion of Durable Peace and Sustainable Development in Africa, note 13 *supra*, para. 10.

97. 8 *RADIC* (1996) 456. It should be observed that the mere possession of nuclear weapons does not of itself constitute a threat contrary to Article 2(4) of the UN Charter, *Legality of the Threat or Use of Nuclear Weapons Case*, ICJ Reports 1996, p. 226.

98. See Article 26 of the Vienna Convention on the Law of Treaties 1969.

99. See Articles 38 of the Vienna Convention on the Law of Treaties 1969 and the Vienna Convention on the Law of Treaties between States and International Organizations 1986.

100. On the question of international bodies possessing international personality, see *Reparation for Injuries Case*, ICJ Reports 1949, p. 174 at p. 179.

101. See Articles 98, 99 of the AEC Treaty, in force 1994, and see further Chapter 6 *infra*, p. 253, note 9.

102. Article 33 of the OAU Charter; Article 3(5) of the Rules of Procedure. See generally, Elias, 'The Charter of the OAU', note 11 *supra*, pp. 255–6.

103. On the Banjul Charter, see further Chapter 4 *infra*.

104. See Chapter 4 *infra*, pp. 154–6.

105. See Chapter 6 *infra*, pp. 243–5.

106. See Chapter 6 *infra*, p. 243.

107. See Chapter 4, p. 156.

108. Elias, 'The Charter of the OAU', note 11 *supra*, pp. 256–60.

109. Amate, note 1 *supra*, Chapter 3; Elias, 'The Charter of the OAU', note 11 *supra*, pp. 260–63; B.D. Meyers, 'The OAU's Administrative Secretary-General', 30 *International Organization* (1976) 569.

110. See Chapter 2 *infra*, pp. 66–7.

111. The text of the General Convention is in *Naldi*, p. 38, and has been ratified by thirty-three States. The Additional Protocol, which governs the Specialized Agencies, has been ratified by three States only.

112. See Chapter 4 *infra*, pp. 140, 142–3.

113. Amate, note 1 *supra*, Chapter 5; V.D. Degan, 'Commission of Mediation, Conciliation and Arbitration of the OAU', 20 *Revue Egyptienne de Droit International* (1964) 53; T.O. Elias, 'The Commission of Mediation, Conciliation and Arbitration of the OAU', 40 *BYIL* (1964) 336; C. Legum, 'The Specialised Commissions of the Organisation of African Unity', 2 *Journal of Modern African Studies* (1964) 587.

114. Text in *Naldi*, pp. 32–7.

115. *Mavrommatis Palestine Concessions Case* PCIJ, Ser. A, No. 2 (1924) at p. 11; *East Timor Case (Portugal* v. *Australia)* ICJ Reports 1995, 90 at pp. 99–100.

116. See generally, J.G. Merrills, *International Dispute Settlement* (3rd edn 1998).

117. Merrills, note 116 *supra*, Chapter 2. Mediation seems to share common characteristics with good offices so that the two may be indistinguishable in practice. In the latter case, a third party, whether on its own initiative or at the request of one or more parties to the dispute, and subject to acceptance by all the parties to the dispute, may offer his good offices to facilitate efforts towards a peaceful settlement.

118. Merrills, note 116 *supra*, Chapter 4. See also Article 26 of the Protocol.

119. Merrills, note 116 *supra*, Chapter 5. See also Article 27 of the Protocol.

120. J.L. Simpson, and H. Fox, *International Arbitration* (1959) pp. 140–2. See also Article 2(2)(1) of the ILC Model Rules in Arbitral Procedure 1958. Cf. Article 38(2) Statute of the ICJ.

121. Degan, note 113 *supra*, p. 67. Cf. Article 38(1) Statute of the ICJ.

122. On *jus cogens*, see Articles 53 and 64 Vienna Convention on the Law of Treaties 1969 and Vienna Convention on the Law of Treaties between States and International Organizations 1986; G. Schwarzenberger, 'International *Jus Cogens*?', 43 *Texas Law Review* (1965) 455.

123. See also Articles 30(6) of the Vienna Convention on the Law of Treaties 1969 and Vienna Convention on the Law of Treaties between States and International Organizations 1986.

124. Degan, note 113, *supra* pp. 68, 69.

125. Brownlie, *Principles of Public International Law*, note 15 *supra* p. 4; M. Akehurst, 'The Hierarchy of the Sources of International Law', 47 *BYIL* (1974–75) 273.

126. Negotiation describes a flexible means of dispute settlement which only involves the parties to the dispute, which can therefore conduct the process in the way they deem most appropriate, Merrills, note 116 *supra*, Chapter 1.

127. The ICJ has observed that there is nothing in the UN Charter nor in general international law that requires the exhaustion of diplomatic negotiations as a precondition for a dispute to be referred to the ICJ. Furthermore, the existence of procedures for regional negotiation, whatever their nature, cannot prevent the ICJ from exercising its judicial function, *Land and Maritime Boundary between Cameroon and Nigeria Case*, ICJ, General List No. 94, 1998, paras. 48–73.

128. Article 18 of the Protocol. These describe impartial third-party procedures for fact-finding and elucidation of facts where they are in dispute. They also suggest appropriate remedies, Merrills, note 116 *supra*, Chapter 3.

129. Articles 2–4 of the Protocol.

130. Article 12 of the Protocol. Cf. Article 34 of the Statute of the ICJ. But cf. Articles 226 (ex Art. 169), 230 (ex Art. 173) and 232 (ex Art. 175) of the EC Treaty, as amended by the Treaty of Amsterdam 1997, 37 *ILM* 56 (1998).

131. Article 13(1) of the Protocol.

132. See note 69 *supra*.

133. Article 2(2) of the UN Charter; Articles 26 of the Vienna Convention on the Law of Treaties 1969 and Vienna Convention on the Law of Treaties between States and International Organizations 1986; *Nuclear Test Cases*, ICJ Reports 1974, p. 253 at p. 268; J.F. O'Connor, *Good Faith in International Law* (1991).

134. Letter to the author from Adwoa Coleman Tommy, Legal Officer, OAU.

135. The Economic and Social Commission, the Educational and Cultural Commission, the Health, Sanitation, and Nutrition Commission, the Defence Commission, and the Scientific, Technical and Research Commission; see Elias, 'The Charter of the OAU', note 11 *supra*, pp. 264–6. It should be observed that the OAU has adopted a number of treaties on technical issues, e.g., the African Civil Aviation Commission Constitution 1969, the Inter-African Convention Establishing an African Technical Co-operation Programme 1975, and the Convention for the Establishment of the African Centre for Fertiliser Development.

136. Article 15 of the Rules of Procedure of the General Secretariat.

137. 10 *RADIC* (1998) 367.

138. Amate, note 1 *supra*, Chapter 6; Legum, note 2 *supra*, pp. 587–8.

139. *Nicaragua Case*, ICJ Reports 1986, p. 14; *Legality of the Threat or Use of Nuclear Weapons Case*, ICJ Reports 1996, p. 226.

140. Thus, the intervention by ECOWAS in the civil war in Liberia was approved by the UN Security Council, see resolutions 788 (1992), 813 (1993) and 950 (1994). Under resolution 866 (1993) the Security Council noted that with the establishment of the UN Observer Mission in Liberia, 'this would be the first peace-keeping mission undertaken by the United Nations in co-operation with a peace-keeping mission already set up by another organization', see further *supra*. p. 10.

141. *Certain Expenses of the UN Case*, ICJ Reports 1962, p. 151 at p. 168.

142. *Keesing's* Vol. 28, 1982, pp. 31677–80.

143. On Chad, see M.P. Kelley, *A State in Disarray: Condition of Chad's Survival* (1986).

144. On this practice, see D.W. Bowett, *United Nations Forces* (1964) pp. 428–67.

145. *Keesing's* Vol. 29, 1983, p. 32420.

146. ICJ Reports 1962, p. 151.

147. *Keesing's* Vol. 28, 1982, p. 31677.

148. It should be observed that African States acting individually have contributed military units to UN peace-keeping operations, e.g., UNAMIR in Rwanda.

149. 6 *RADIC* (1994) 158.

150. 4 *RADIC* (1992) 1072.

151. Para. 14 of the Cairo Declaration; B.G. Ramcharan, 'The Evolving Doctrine of Democratic Legitimacy', No. 60 *The Review* (International Commission of Jurists) (1998) 179 at pp. 184–5. A comprehensive conceptual framework underpinning the OAU's revised approach to the principles of sovereignty and non-interference has been called for, see M.A. Hefny, 'Enhancing the Capabilities of the OAU Mechanism for Conflict Prevention, Management and Resolution: An Immediate Agenda for Action', *ASICL Proc.* 7 (1995) 176 at p. 180.

152. Para. 15 of the Cairo Declaration. See also Ramcharan, note 151 *supra*, pp. 182, 184; S.B.O. Gutto, 'The OAU's New Mechanism for Conflict Prevention, Management and Resolution and the Controversial Concept of Humanitarian Intervention in International Law' *ASICL Proc.* 7 (1995) 348 at p. 349. Overall responsibility for maintaining international peace and security still lies with the UN Security Council under Article 24(1) of the UN Charter.

153. As Hefny points out, the success of the Mechanism is ultimately dependent on adequate financing and the political willingness of Member States to support it, note 151 *supra*, pp. 181–3. Note the Special Fund set up to support exclusively OAU operational activities, para. 23 of the Cairo Declaration. The UN Secretary-General has emphasized the need of the UN to support regional initiatives at dispute settlement in Africa, Report of the Secretary-General on: The Causes of Conflict and the Promotion of Durable Peace and Sustainable Development in Africa, note 13 *supra*, paras. 41–5.

154. Paras. 17–20 of the Cairo Declaration; Ramcharan, note 151 *supra*, p. 183.

155. Paras. 19, 22 of the Cairo Declaration.

156. Paras. 24, 25 of the Cairo Declaration. The UN Secretary-General has stressed the need to reinforce the capacity of African countries to participate in peace-keeping operations. Joint peace-keeping exercises, enhanced training assistance, greater African participation in UN standby arrangements, and partnerships between donor countries and those that require logistical support, are among the recommendations made, Report of the Secretary-General on: The Causes of Conflict and the Promotion of Durable Peace and Sustainable Development in Africa, note 13 *supra*, para. 45.

157. Hefny, note 151 *supra*, pp. 178–9; Ramcharan, note 151 *supra*, pp. 184–8.

158. Ramcharan, note 151 *supra*, p. 187.

159. A.S. Osman, 'The Organisation of African Unity, the United Nations and Resolution of Conflicts: Need for Strengthening Cooperation and Partnership', *ASICL Proc.* 7 (1995) 171 at pp. 174. It has been noted that the UN Secretary-General has emphasized the need of the UN to support regional initiatives at dispute settlement in Africa, Report of the Secretary-General on: The Causes of Conflict and the Promotion of Durable Peace and Sustainable Development in Africa, note 13 *supra*, para. 41.

160. See *supra*, pp. 6–10.

161. Cf. Article 17 of the UN Charter.

162. See Article 2 (a)-(b) of the Resolution on Arrears of Contribution, in *Naldi*, pp. 45–6. By the end of 1996 the OAU was owed US$53 million in arrears, *Keesing's*, Vol. 42, 1996, p. 41179.

163. Under Article 97 of the Financial Rules and Regulations Member States can be deprived of their right to participate or vote on OAU decisions but the Resolution on Arrears of Contribution further deprived them of the right to speak at OAU meetings and the right to present candidates for OAU posts or bodies (Article 2(d)).

164. See also Article 11(3) of the Rules of Procedure of the Secretary-General.
165. See *supra*, pp. 2–3.
166. On the Western Sahara dispute, see further Chapter 2 *infra*; G.J. Naldi, 'The Statehood of the Saharan Arab Democratic Republic', 25 *IJIL* (1985) 448.
167. Article 27, which states that any question concerning the interpretation of the OAU Charter will be decided by a vote of two-thirds of the Assembly, was not invoked.
168. Crawford, note 94 *supra*, pp. 102–6.
169. Ibid., pp. 260–1.
170. E. Osieke, 'Admission to Membership in International Organisations: The Case of Namibia', 51 *BYIL* (1980) 220; F. Morgenstern, *Legal Problems of International Organizations* (1986) pp. 46–54.
171. ICJ Reports 1948, p. 62.
172. Sir Hersch Lauterpacht, *Recognition in International Law* (1948) pp. 402–403; Brownlie, note 15 *supra*, p. 95.
173. SCOR, Supp. 5 (January-May 1950) 20 UN Doc. 3/1466 (1950).
174. This would appear to emerge from a number of UN Charter provisions, in particular Articles 4, 11(2), 32, 35(2), 93 and 102. Note that under Article 34 of the Statute of the ICJ the ICJ has the capacity to determine for its purposes whether a party to a dispute is a State, see *Nottebohm Case (Liechtenstein* v. *Guatemala)* ICJ Reports 1955, p. 4; *Application of the Genocide Convention Case (Bosnia and Herzegovina* v. *Yugoslavia)* ICJ Reports 1996, p. 595 at paras. 17–24. See generally, J. Dugard, *Recognition and the United Nations* (1987).
175. Brownlie, note 15 *supra*, p. 95.
176. Notwithstanding the OAU's adherence to the principles of national sovereignty and non-interference the Mechanism has voiced its support for democratic legitimacy, Ramcharan, note 151 *supra*, pp. 186–7. On the representation of rival authorities, see Morgenstern, note 170 *supra*, pp. 54–62. On the Estrada doctrine, see 25 *AJIL* (1931) Supp. 203.
177. See also Article 11(4) of the Rules of Procedure of the Secretary-General.
178. *Keesing's* Vol. 31, 1985, pp. 33324–5.
179. F.L. Kirgis, *International Organizations in Their Legal Setting* (1977) p. 533; H. Schermers, *International Institutional Law* (1980) pp. 121–2. Support for this view may be evidenced by the practice of the Commonwealth which, as has been seen, assumed the power to suspend Nigeria's membership despite the fact that the Commonwealth has no constitution. Cf. *contra*, B.W. Bowett, *The Law of International Institutions* (1975) pp. 349–51.
180. Article 60(2)(a)(i) of the Vienna Convention on the Law of Treaties 1969. See also Article 60(2) of the unratified Vienna Convention on the Law of Treaties between States and International Organizations 1986, which will not have retroactive effect. See further, L.B. Sohn, 'Expulsion or Forced Withdrawal from an International Organization', 77 *Harvard Law Review* (1963–64) 1381 at pp. 1417–18.

2
The Question of the Western Sahara

The Western Sahara dispute has presented the OAU with one of its most intractable problems that has undermined the stability of the OAU. Over twenty years after the end of colonial rule, the status of the Western Sahara remains unresolved and the dispute continues to elude the good offices of the international community. Prior to a detailed discussion of the troubled relationship between the OAU and the Western Sahara it is necessary to present an account in historical perspective.

Origins of the Dispute

The Western Sahara conflict concerns disputed claims to sovereignty over that territory.[1] The Western Sahara is a former Spanish colony along the Atlantic coast of northwest Africa with a land area of some 266,000 square kilometres (approximately the same size as Britain). It experiences an extreme desert climate and is sparsely populated, the main habitation being the capital El Aauin. The Western Sahara is rich in minerals, especially phosphates.[2] Traditionally three distinct ethnic and cultural groups inhabit the Western Sahara. These are the Tekna in the northern part of Seguia el Hamra; the Reguibat, mainly in the centre of the country and the southern region of Rio de Oro; and the Ulad Delim who inhabit the southern coastal region. By tradition the Sahrawis are nomadic. Ethnically, they are of Moorish or mixed Arab-Berber descent and speak Hassaniya, an Arab dialect that is closely related to classical Arabic.

The Western Sahara was colonized by Spain in 1884 through a series of treaties with local rulers. Spain then proceeded to govern it with a policy of absent-minded neglect. The Spanish presence did meet with resistance and it was not until 1934 that its authority was finally established throughout the territory.[3]

The question of disputed sovereignty first arose upon Morocco's independence from France in 1956. Morocco maintained that the Western Sahara had formed an integral part of its kingdom prior to colonization and that it should therefore be reintegrated on the basis of historic title.[4] Mauritania, which became independent in 1960, also lodged a territorial claim to the Western Sahara asserting that in the pre-colonial era the people of the region owed tribal and religious allegiance to each other in a loose confederation known as the Bilad Shinguitti, the predecessor to the state of Mauritania.[5]

The question of the decolonization of the Western Sahara has been kept under constant review by the UN since 1963 when the General Assembly mandated the Special Committee with regard to the Implementation of the Declaration on the Granting of Independence to Colonial Countries and Peoples to seek suitable means for the immediate and full implementation of Resolution 1514 (XV) in all non-self-governing territories. In 1965 the General Assembly adopted its first resolution on the Western Sahara calling on Spain to implement the right of the Sahrawis to self-determination but without specifying how this was to be achieved. At this time Spain had adopted the position that the question of its African possessions, as integral parts of the metropolis, was a domestic issue under Article 2(7) of the UN Charter and thus outside the competence of the General Assembly. However, the General Assembly has long established the fact that questions relating to non-self-governing territories are a matter of international concern.[6] In 1966 the General Assembly expressed the view, which it has consistently maintained, that Sahrawi self-determination be expressed through a referendum. International pressure thus led Spain to accept the applicability of the principle of self-determination to the Western Sahara in 1967 but it procrastinated in the organization of a referendum in the evident hope of perpetuating its presence. Nevertheless, Spain made token efforts at developing self-rule in the Western Sahara and founded an indigenous assembly, the Yema'a, whose powers were merely advisory.[7]

Spanish intentions were to be partially frustrated by the emergence of Sahrawi nationalism, which in 1973 culminated in the founding of the Polisario Front, a national liberation movement committed to the creation of an independent Islamic republic.[8] Sporadic guerrilla warfare and deteriorating diplomatic relations with its north African neighbours were to convince the Spanish government that its continued presence in the Western Sahara was no longer tenable and in August 1974 it announced its intention to organize a referendum under the auspices of the UN the following year. The referendum was widely expected to result in an overwhelming call for independence. This probability prompted Morocco to adopt an overtly annexationist policy which the Spanish government, in disarray as a result of Franco's terminal illness, was unable to withstand.

Pursuant to the decolonization of the Western Sahara the General Assembly sent a Visiting Mission on a fact-finding tour in 1974. In an eminently sensible report the Mission noted that the population as a whole was categorically in favour of independence and rejected the territorial claims of Morocco and Mauritania. Furthermore, the Mission noted that the population showed, through demonstrations and statements, that it supported the objectives of the Polisario Front, which appeared to them as the dominant political force. The Mission therefore concluded that the Sahrawis were entitled to exercise their right to self-determination in accordance with Resolution 1541 (XV) under the aegis of the UN.[9]

Although Spain was now committed to the decolonization of the Western Sahara the General Assembly, consequent to intense lobbying by Morocco and Mauritania, requested an advisory opinion from the ICJ on whether the Western Sahara had been *terra nullius* at the time of colonization by Spain, and if not, what ties had existed between the Western Sahara and Morocco and the Western Sahara and the Mauritania entity (the Bilad Shinguitti).[10] The General Assembly considered that the ICJ's opinion would assist it in the decolonization of the Western Sahara but in the circumstances the recourse to the ICJ would appear to have been superfluous. It appears that Morocco confidently expected the ICJ to reinforce its claim to the Western Sahara by finding the existence of ties of sovereignty between Morocco and the Western Sahara prior to colonization by Spain. However, the Court's conclusion that no legal ties amounting to ties of sovereignty which could prejudice the right of the Sahrawi people to self-determination had ever existed seems to have removed the last vestiges of credibility from the Moroccan claim.[11]

In October 1975, following immediately upon the delivery of the ICJ's advisory opinion, King Hassan of Morocco announced the 'Green March' by 350,000 unarmed civilians on the Western Sahara which adopted the character of a holy crusade to liberate the Sahrawis from colonialism and restore Morocco's national unity. Although the UN Security Council met to consider this potentially explosive situation it failed to prevent the march from taking place or to take any action against Morocco. These events secured Spain's capitulation.[12]

On 14 November 1975, a tripartite agreement, known as the Madrid Accord, was signed by Spain, Morocco and Mauritania.[13] Under the terms of this agreement Spain transferred administration over the Western Sahara jointly to Morocco and Mauritania and undertook to withdraw completely from the territory by 28 February 1976. Morocco took the lion's share, acquiring over two-thirds of the territory, including the valuable phosphate mines at Bou Craa. The response of the Polisario Front was to make a unilateral declaration of independence on 27 February 1976 creating the Saharan Arab Democratic Republic (SADR).[14] The Polisario Front stated that the newly emergent state would be non-aligned, progressive and Islamic, and embarked immediately upon a double-pronged struggle – a war of national liberation and a diplomatic campaign to secure international recognition of the new State.

At the outset it appeared that the Polisario Front had embarked upon a hopeless task. It seemed overwhelmingly outnumbered and outgunned by superior forces and suffered some early reverses. However, with aid from Algeria primarily, the Polisario Front succeeded in turning the tide of the war for a time. Despite their apparent superiority, Morocco and Mauritania were proving unable to defeat the Polisario Front militarily. The Polisario guerrillas successfully employed hit-and-run tactics that struck deep into Morocco and Mauritania, inflicting heavy losses on its enemies and sabotaging the mine works at Bou Craa. The war quickly became an unsustainable drain on Mauritania's limited military and economic resources. Popular discontent with the deteriorating situation led to a bloodless *coup d'état* by the military in May 1978. Subsequently, a peace agreement was concluded with the Polisario Front on 5 August 1979, according to which Mauritania undertook to withdraw from the southern part of the Western Sahara which it had occupied since Spain's withdrawal in 1976. Under this 'definitive' peace agreement signed in Algiers, Mauritania recognized the Polisario Front as 'the sole legitimate representative of the people of the Western Sahara' and renounced all claims to the Western Sahara.[15] Thereafter Mauritania considered itself completely disengaged from the war and declared its 'total neutrality'. Morocco denounced the treaty as null and void and responded by occupying the 'liberated' territory.

With Mauritania's acknowledgement of defeat and its withdrawal from the conflict the Polisario Front was free to step up its campaign against Morocco. Polisario guerrilla units were involved in spectacular raids which penetrated southern Morocco. The demoralized Moroccan army suffered a number of military reverses that convinced the high command of the futility of attempting to patrol and control the whole region. The decision was therefore taken to consolidate the Moroccan presence behind a Maginot-type construction intended to protect the main habitations and the mineral-yielding areas, the so-called 'useful triangle'. The barrier, or berm, consists of a ditch behind an earthen mound bristling with barbed wire and mine-fields. Observation posts and fortified bases of operations have been built at various stages along this defensive line which has been reinforced with special radar equipment. The wall, which parallels the Algerian and Mauritanian borders, was completed in 1987 and is now some 1,500 miles long and covers virtually the whole territory.[16] The fortifications, though not impervious to Polisario attacks, proved highly effective and greatly reduced the efficacy and nuisance value of the guerrilla raids. The armed conflict ground to a stalemate. The focus of the action thus shifted to the diplomatic front.

The diplomatic struggle has been concerned essentially, on the one hand, with moves by the Polisario Front to gain international recognition of the SADR as an independent state and, on the other hand, with Morocco's attempts to neutralize the Polisario Front's efforts and to gain world-wide acceptance of the annexation of the Western Sahara. This campaign has been waged primarily before the OAU and the UN. Since the admission of the SADR to the OAU, the latter has yielded responsibility for procuring a settlement to the UN which has treated the issue of the Western Sahara as a question of decolonization.[17] The UN settlement plan is based on securing an exercise in self-determination acceptable to both parties.[18] It therefore rejects, albeit impliedly, the Moroccan annexation and the SADR's independence.

The end of the Cold War has, however, disadvantaged the Polisario Front, isolating it both militarily and diplomatically. Whilst the West remains a steadfast supporter of King Hassan, the Polisario Front has lost its closest allies. In February 1992 Morocco and Algeria entered into an agreement whereby Algeria undertook to cease its military support for the Polisario Front.[19] Moreover, consumed by its civil conflict with Islamic fundamentalism, Algeria is keen to promote relations with the West. Renewed military support for the Polisario Front is thus highly improbable.

It is submitted that the Moroccan occupation of the Western Sahara is incompatible with international law. Morocco appears to have violated the prohibition on the threat or use of force,[20] and may even have committed an act of aggression,[21] thereby rendering title to territory thus acquired invalid.[22] Furthermore, it has violated the right of self-determination.[23] It follows that the validity of the Tripartite Agreement must be questioned[24] given, in addition, that Spain seems to have been coerced into concluding the Agreement, a fact that would seem to render it null and void.[25] International support for the Polisario Front would thus appear to have some justification in law.

Whilst the UN had remained on the periphery of the dispute until 1988, the OAU had in the meantime had this matter under active consideration. The dispute tested the diplomatic skills of many African leaders, bringing the OAU itself perilously close to fragmentation on a number of occasions, especially over the issue of the admission of the SADR to the OAU when conservative and progressive States adopted mutually uncompromising positions. Nevertheless, the OAU engaged in significant work and advanced interesting proposals for a settlement which, unfortunately, ultimately came to nothing. With responsibility for negotiating a settlement now vested in the UN, the OAU appears to have adopted a policy of indifference towards the dispute.

Role of the Organization of African Unity

The OAU had been considering the problem of the Western Sahara since 1964 when it advocated its decolonization, an approach consistent with its struggle to free Africa from all forms of colonialism in accordance with Article 2(1)(d) of the OAU Charter. The OAU had not been pursuing an original line of action since the UN General Assembly had already recommended the decolonization of the Western Sahara; the OAU merely limited itself at first to endorsing these resolutions. Indeed, this was the position it maintained until 1976.

The question of the Western Sahara first received considered attention from the OAU in 1966 when it was seised of the issue of non-autonomous African territories. That October the political committee of the OAU, meeting in Addis Ababa, called for the independence of the Western Sahara. In the same restrained vein, the OAU appealed to Spain to participate in talks aimed at the decolonization of the territory at its Seventh Summit Conference held in Addis Ababa in September 1970. The intensive diplomatic pressure being exerted upon Spain by the UN General Assembly seemed more likely to succeed so the OAU contented itself with endorsing the relevant resolutions. It would also be true to say that the question of the Western Sahara was not considered to be a priority. The OAU's cautious stance on the Western Sahara question may be witnessed, for instance, by the Liberation Committee's unwillingness to list the Western Sahara as an African non-autonomous territory thus benefiting from its funds.

Morocco's increasing designs on the Western Sahara, however, projected this issue onto the forum of the OAU. Having relinquished its claim to Mauritania, Morocco intensified its campaign for the annexation of the Western Sahara. While couching its language in the traditional rhetoric of anti-colonialism, Morocco had ulterior motives. Upon accession to the OAU Morocco had expressly stated its reservation concerning the provisions on respect for sovereignty and territorial integrity of States as contained in Article 2(1) and Article 3(3) of the OAU Charter, stating that 'the signing of the Charter could not in any fashion be interpreted as either an explicit or implicit acknowledgement of these facts which Morocco refuses to recognize nor as renunciation of the pursuit of our rights by the legitimate means at our disposal'.[26] However, the inviolability of colonial frontiers is regarded as a sacrosanct principle by the OAU. One of its first acts was to adopt the Resolution on the Intangibility of African Boundaries confirming the permanent delimitation of inherited colonial frontiers, which, if non-binding, nevertheless reflects customary international law.[27] The question therefore arises as to whether the reservation entered by Morocco is valid under international law.

This question is governed by customary law which, as established by the dicta enunciated in the ICJ in its Advisory Opinion in the *Reservations to the Convention on Genocide Case*, maintains that to be valid a reservation has to be compatible with the object and purpose of the Convention.[28] It thus seems difficult to reconcile Morocco's reservation, which is based on its outstanding territorial claims, with the provisions of the OAU Charter declaring the permanence of inherited frontiers and the observance of the territorial integrity of Member States. While the validity of Morocco's reservation may therefore be open to question, the absence of any objection thereto suggests the OAU must be deemed to have consented to Morocco's reservation and would be estopped from challenging it in the future.[29] It is also doubtful whether Morocco is bound by the corresponding customary rule given its persistent objection.[30] As has already been stated, until 1976 the OAU had essentially confined itself to endorsing UN resolutions reaffirming the right of the Sahrawi people to self-determination. This had proved to be the case on a number of occasions; in the resolutions adopted by the Council of Ministers of November 1966, June 1972 and May 1973; and by the Summit in May 1973.[31] However, the OAU's position at this time was somewhat ambiguous given that at the Twenty-Fourth Session of the Council of Ministers held in Addis Ababa in February 1975, the Council resolved to support the Moroccan claim to the Spanish colony. Yet, at its subsequent session held in Kampala on 18 to 28 July 1975, the Council refused to endorse the Moroccan/Mauritanian plans for the partition of the territory in antici-pation of what it believed would be the ICJ's favourable judgment, although it did go as far as recommending official recognition of the Polisario Front. At the Twelfth Summit Conference the Assembly merely confined itself to appealing to Spain not to take any unilateral action pending the decision of the ICJ.[32]

The evolution of the conflict led the OAU to adopt a more prominent role however. In February 1976, the OAU Liberation Committee recom-mended that the Polisario Front be recognized as the legitimate representa-tive of the Sahrawi people. This led to Morocco and Mauritania issuing their first threats to withdraw from the OAU. The Liberation Committee further proposed the formation of a joint mediation committee with the Arab League, a suggestion that met with Morocco's approval.

No decision on the motion proposing the recognition of the Polisario Front was taken by the Council of Ministers at its meeting in Addis Ababa the following March. However, seventeen States out of the then forty-seven members declared themselves in favour of the OAU recognizing the Polisario Front. Owing to Moroccan and Mauritanian threats to renounce their membership of the OAU if such a decision were to be confirmed, a compromise resolution was adopted whereby each Member State was rendered free to grant or withhold recognition of the Polisario Front. Such discretion, however, is an inherent sovereign right and the resolution must therefore be interpreted as an admission by the OAU that a united policy could not be pursued on this question. Nevertheless, in a significant vic-tory for the Polisario Front, the conference noted that the Sahrawis had exercised their right to self-determination by creating the new republic, the SADR.[33]

The Twenty-Seventh Session of the OAU's Council of Ministers held in Port Louis, Mauritius on 24 June to 2 July 1976, proved to be a heated affair. Matters had not started propitiously when a Polisario Front delegation was refused entry by the Mauritian government, which considered the Polisario Front ineligible to participate in the conference. Since the Polisario Front delegation represented a nascent state unrecognized by Mauritius, and in view of the fact that neither the OAU Charter nor the Rules of Procedure address themselves to this question, it would appear that the Mauritian government may have acted *intra vires*. However, it is interesting to note that Article 82(1) of the unratified Vienna Convention on the Representation of States in Their Relations with International Organizations of a Universal Character 1975 states that:

> The rights and obligations of the host State and of the sending State under the present Convention shall be affected neither by the non-recognition of one of those States by the other State or of its government nor by the non-existence or the severance of diplomatic or consular relations between them.

It would appear that this provision is not reflective of international customary law nor has it generated customary law. Of further interest is paragraph 2 of the Resolution Relating to the Observer Status of National Liberation Movements Recognized by the Organization of African Unity and/or the League of Arab States, annexed to the Convention, which recommends:

> [T]he States concerned agree to accord to delegations of national liberation movements which are recognized by the Organization of African Unity and/or the League of Arab States in their respective regions and which have been granted observer status by the international organization concerned, the facilities, privileges and immunities necessary for the performance of their tasks and to be guided therein by the pertinent provisions of the Convention adopted by this Conference.

The Polisario Front was eventually admitted to the conference with observer status.

During the debate on the Western Sahara, the representatives of both Morocco and Mauritania walked out of the session in protest, arguing that the Saharan issue was not on the agenda and that a decision had already been reached at the Council's previous session. However, Article 20 of the Council's Rules of Procedure makes it clear that the Council may discuss a motion that is not on the agenda. Following a lengthy and heated debate the Council adopted a draft resolution by twenty-nine votes to two (Gabon and Senegal) with sixteen abstentions and with the delegations of Morocco and Mauritania absent. Two draft resolutions introduced by Mauritania directed against Algeria and the Polisario Front were defeated by large majorities. The adopted resolution reaffirmed the inalienable right of the Sahrawi people to self-determination and independence; requested the UN Secretary-General to ensure that the Sahrawi people 'exercise freely their right to self-determination'; expressed its unconditional support for their 'just struggle'; demanded the immediate withdrawal of 'all foreign occupation forces'; and requested that the territorial integrity of the Western Sahara be respected. The Council also noted that 'the decolonization process' had 'not been in conformity with the resolutions of the OAU and UN' and once again it was left to the discretion of individual states to grant or withhold recognition of the Polisario Front.[34]

Moroccan and Mauritanian opposition at the subsequent summit ensured that the Assembly did not ratify this resolution but adopted instead an alternative compromise resolution tabled by Nigeria which made an unsuccessful call to the interested parties, including the Sahrawis, to seek a peaceful settlement and additionally called for an extraordinary summit meeting which would be entrusted with seeking a just and lasting solution.[35] The year 1977 was characterized by Polisario attempts to obtain an OAU extraordinary summit meeting on the question of the Western Sahara, as provided for by Article 5 of the Assembly's Rules of Procedure. It emerged that no state was willing to host the meeting, either for political or financial reasons, and the two-thirds quorum necessary to convene the meeting could not be mustered. Morocco's uncompromising attitude in refusing to contemplate the participation of a Polisario delegation and disagreement over the proposed venue sealed the fate of this diplomatic initiative.

The question of the Western Sahara nevertheless continued to be disruptive. The government of Togo invited a Saharan delegation to attend the Twenty-Eighth Session of the Council of Ministers held in Lomé. Morocco and Mauritania boycotted the meeting as a result; indeed Morocco announced that it would withdraw temporarily from all OAU activities as a gesture of protest.

The subsequent Fourteenth Assembly of Heads of State and Government held in Libreville, Gabon, in July 1977 proved to be similarly disruptive. Gabon's President Bongo, acting Assembly Chairman and a loyal ally of Morocco, refused a Sahrawi delegation entry into the country. This move led to vehement protests on the part of Burundi and Madagascar, which refused to send senior delegates to the Assembly. The Polisario Front claimed that President Bongo had acted *ultra vires*, particularly given the fact that the Sahrawi cause was supported by a majority of African states.

The existing situation was patently unsatisfactory and in 1978 the OAU made a brave attempt to address itself effectively to the Western Sahara dispute. During the Fifteenth Assembly held in Khartoum in July 1978 the Assembly adopted resolution AHG/Res. 92 (XV) which introduced a significant development.[36] The Assembly, pursuant to Article 37 of its Rules of Procedure, established an ad hoc committee of at least five Heads of State and Government, under the chairmanship of President Numeri of Sudan, who was the acting OAU Chairman, entrusted with the task of seeking a solution to the dispute compatible with the right of self-determination. In addition, the resolution called upon the States of the region to abstain from any unilateral action that might hamper the search for a peaceful solution. Neither Algeria nor the Polisario Front were satisfied with this initiative since they were of the view that only the UN had sole jurisdiction with regard to questions of decolonization. However, this objection would not appear to take into account Article 53 of the UN Charter. Morocco and Mauritania, on the other hand, were prepared to accept the mediation of the

Ad Hoc Committee. The Committee was not charged with investigating the international legal issues relevant to the dispute.

Ad Hoc Committee

The Ad Hoc Committee, also known as the Committee of Wise Men, held its constitutive session on 1 December 1978 in Khartoum.[37] Besides Sudan's President Numeri the committee was also composed of President Nyerere of Tanzania, President Traoré of Mali, President Obasanjo of Nigeria, President Houphouët-Boigny of the Côte d'Ivoire and President Touré of Guinea.

Following a two-day meeting a sub-committee, consisting of Presidents Obasanjo and Traoré and accompanied by the OAU Secretary-General, was established with the mandate to visit the region and contact all the parties interested and concerned in the dispute, including the Saharan people, in order to implement the measures necessary for restoring peace and security. The warring parties were requested to observe an immediate ceasefire to enable the sub-committee to accomplish its duties.[38]

With the express purpose of ascertaining the attitudes of the interested parties the sub-committee conducted a tour of Algeria, Mauritania, Morocco and Spain. The sub-committee submitted its report in June 1979 which overall was favourable to the Sahrawi cause. The sub-committee expressed the view that all the interested parties, save Morocco, were of the opinion that the people of the Western Sahara had not exercised their right to self-determination and moreover, that the Tripartite Agreement had merely transferred administration of the territory to Morocco and Mauritania but not sovereignty. Consequently, it made certain recommendations concerning the exercise of the right of self-determination by the people of Western Sahara and the modalities of its exercise. The Ad Hoc Committee adopted these recommendations and submitted them to the OAU Assembly at its Sixteenth Ordinary Session held at Monrovia, Liberia, in July 1979 which subsequently adopted them as Resolution 114 (XVI). This resolution recommended, *inter alia*:

1. The preparation of a proper atmosphere for peace in the area through a general and immediate cease-fire supervised by an OAU peace-keeping force.

2. The withdrawal of all Moroccan troops from the Western Sahara.

3. The exercise of the right of self-determination by the people of Western Sahara in a general and free referendum which will enable them to choose one of the following options:
    a.   total independence; or
    b.   maintenance of the status quo.

4. The convening of a meeting of all the parties concerned, including the

representative of Western Sahara, to request their co-operation for the implementation of this decision.

5.   The establishment of a special committee of six Member States of the OAU, known as the Implementation Committee, to work out the modalities and to supervise the organization of a referendum with the co-operation of the UN on the basis of one person one vote.[39]

This resolution was significant in various respects. It no longer appeared necessary to delegate the Western Sahara dispute to an extraordinary summit conference. The recommendation also constituted a significant success for the Polisario Front since it recognized the right of the Sahrawi people to self-determination and called for the organization of a referendum under the auspices of the UN and the OAU. However, this recommendation was not entirely satisfactory for it made no explicit reference to the Polisario Front but merely talked of the representative of the people of Western Sahara; it did not require the withdrawal of Moroccan and Mauritanian troops from the territory, a *sine qua non* for the Polisario Front; and lastly, since the creation of the SADR in February 1976 the Polisario Front had considered a referendum largely superfluous, although in 1988 it did accept a UN plan for a referendum.

The work of the Ad Hoc Committee was rendered particularly difficult when in 1980 the SADR applied for membership of the OAU. The application met with considerable opposition and, in an attempt to prevent the OAU from disintegrating, the Secretary-General rejected the SADR's application.

The Ad Hoc Committee acknowledged the gravity of the situation and put forward a compromise resolution which, *inter alia*, requested the presence of a UN peace-keeping force to supervise the cease-fire and referendum. The Polisario Front expressed its willingness to abide by this decision if the Moroccan forces withdrew from the Western Sahara. Morocco, on the other hand, rejected the Committee's suggestions and in view of the Committee's failure to make reference to the Polisario Front, in addition to the SADR's failure to join the OAU, or to request the termination of the Moroccan presence in the territory, regarded the affair as a diplomatic victory.

The onus of finding a solution was to pass from the hands of the Ad Hoc Committee when in 1981 King Hassan of Morocco expressed his desire for a pacific solution and accepted in principle the notion of a referendum. The OAU Assembly consequently resolved to create an Implementation Committee entrusted with the task of enforcing the recommendations of the Ad Hoc Committee. The Implementation Committee was not limited to examining events and submitting propositions but it was empowered to take a proactive approach.

Implementation Committee

The Implementation Committee, composed of representatives from Guinea, Kenya, Mali, Nigeria, Sierra Leone, Sudan and Tanzania, was established under Resolution 103 (XVIII) 1981 with the purpose of working out, in collaboration with the parties to the conflict, the modalities and all other details relevant to the attainment of a cease-fire and the conduct and administration of a referendum; and its mandate was to participate with the UN in taking all necessary measures to guarantee the exercise by the people of Western Sahara of self-determination through a general and free referendum.[40]

Unfortunately, the Implementation Committee proved unable to reach an acceptable solution. Initially both Morocco and the Polisario Front appeared to agree on the principle of a referendum, at least in public, but irreconcilable differences existed between them as to how it ought to be achieved.[41] King Hassan told the Committee that Morocco was 'ready, when the OAU is ready, to organize a peaceful, honest and unequivocal referendum'. However, Morocco remained adamant that its troops would not withdraw from the territory before a referendum took place and it opposed the presence of a UN/OAU peace-keeping force in the territory. Furthermore, as far as Morocco was concerned, the referendum would ask only one question:

> Do you approve of the acts of allegiance which imply that you belong to the Kingdom of Morocco?

Morocco expressed the view that only those Sahrawis who were listed in the census carried out by Spain in 1974 (which was rejected at the time by Morocco who claimed that 30,000 to 40,000 Sahrawi refugees were living in Morocco) were entitled to vote.

The Polisario Front naturally rejected the Moroccan proposals. It expressed the hope that the referendum would take place in an environment free of any constraints imposed by the presence of Moroccan troops. It expressed itself in favour of a UN/OAU peace-keeping force to ensure stability and to guarantee free elections and, further, it considered an international neutral administration, such as that which was to oversee Namibia's transition to independence in 1989 and 1990, to be an absolute necessity. The Polisario Front suggested that the following question be asked at the referendum:

> Yes or no to independence?

Those entitled to vote would be all Sahrawis who had been scrutinized by the proposed neutral administration to ensure that they were indigenous to the territory.[42]

The consensus resolution arrived at by the Implementation Committee in August 1981 decided that the question to be asked at the referendum would be:

Independence or integration with Morocco?

The implementation of the cease-fire would be left to the parties to the conflict. In preparation for the free elections, the Committee considered it necessary that an impartial interim administration be established to collaborate with the existing Moroccan administration. The former body would be assisted by a joint UN/OAU peace-keeping force. The Moroccan administration would remain in office until the scrutiny of the eligible voters started, when the elections would be supervised by a team of observers who would subsequently submit a report on the validity of the exercise to the UN and OAU, based partially on the system used in Zimbabwe in 1980. The Committee suggested further that the troops belonging to the belligerents be confined to barracks or bases during the conduct of the referendum when law and order would be maintained by the peace-keeping force. Finally, on the controversial question of the franchise, the Committee suggested that the estimated size of the population of Western Sahara should be based on the figures of the Spanish census of 1974, account being taken of the relevant documents provided by the UNHCR and the rate of demographic growth of the population.[43]

In February 1982 the Implementation Committee submitted the following proposals on the organization of the referendum: (a) that an interim administration be appointed by the Implementation Committee vested with the legislative and administrative powers required for the organization and conduct of a referendum; (b) that a commissioner be appointed to head the interim administration 'at least one month before the cease-fire takes effect'; and (c) that a joint OAU/UN commission be sent to the Western Sahara at least one month prior to a cease-fire to make arrangements for the poll. In addition, the Implementation Committee drew up detailed provisions for the organization of the referendum. These recommendations provided, *inter alia*, that the people of Western Sahara express themselves freely and democratically by secret ballot on the basis of one person one vote without discrimination on the ground of sex, on whether they wanted independence or integration with Morocco; that the Commissioner be responsible for the drafting of voting regulations, including a register of electors, voting procedures, including the electoral boundaries, or districts, measures to prevent abuses and to ensure the security of voters and ballots, and penalties for any electoral abuses. In addition, in preparation for the referendum, a campaign of public information should be undertaken to familiarize voters with the significance of the referendum, the issues involved and the voting procedure. Consequently, the interim administration should take measures to guarantee freedom of expression, assembly, publication and movement.[44]

The Implementation Committee also adopted detailed provisions concerning a cease-fire in the Western Sahara. The recommendations included the stationing of a peace-keeping force and/or a military observer group, including a civilian police component having the necessary powers to supervise a cease-fire, including fixing the respective positions of each side's forces; the confinement of troops to bases or such areas where their presence would not constitute a psychological or other hindrance to the conduct of a free and fair referendum; and the exchange of prisoners of war at the direction of and under the supervision of the commander of the peace-keeping force.[45]

All the suggestions advanced by the various committees met with serious difficulties *ab initio*. Morocco and the Polisario Front adopted mutually irreconcilable positions which gave little hope for a peaceful solution.

The Polisario Front insisted that, prior to accepting the proposal for a referendum, Morocco must comply with the precondition that its forces withdraw completely from the territory. Morocco resisted this condition, and the Implementation Committee's failure to secure acceptance of the Polisario Front's requirement constituted an obvious impediment to any further negotiations. Morocco rejected the proposed participation of an OAU/UN peace-keeping force, which was considered necessary to maintain the peace and supervise free and fair elections. In addition, the SADR's admission as an OAU member at this time seriously undermined the prospect of further Moroccan co-operation with the Implementation Committee.[46]

Nevertheless, the OAU Assembly endorsed the Implementation Committee's endeavours. At its Nineteenth Ordinary Session held at Addis Ababa in June 1983 the Assembly called upon the Implementation Committee to secure a cease-fire and to make preparations for the referendum, scheduled for December 1983, and it called upon the UN, in conjunction with the OAU, to provide a peace-keeping force for the duration of the referendum. In addition, it called upon the parties to the conflict to enter into direct negotiations with a view to permitting the exercise of the referendum.[47]

Morocco subsequently refused to co-operate in the holding of the referendum by the specified date which led the OAU to seat the SADR at its Twentieth Ordinary Session held at Addis Ababa in November 1984. Morocco withdrew from the OAU in protest.[48]

Admission of the Saharan Arab Democratic Republic

One fundamental reason for the lack of success of the Ad Hoc and Implementation Committees was the admission of the SADR to the OAU in 1984 which not only pre-empted the findings of the Committees but, in face of considerable opposition, presented the OAU with a grave crisis. It is therefore necessary to consider the SADR's admission in some depth.[49] The

SADR's claim to membership of the OAU is based upon Article 28 of the OAU Charter, which states that:

1. Any independent sovereign African State may at any time notify the Administrative Secretary-General of its intention to adhere or accede to this Charter.

2. The Administrative Secretary-General shall, on receipt of such notification, communicate a copy of it to all the Member States. The decision of each Member State shall be transmitted to the Administrative Secretary-General, who shall, upon receipt of the required number of votes, communicate the decision to the State concerned.

The SADR first sought membership of the OAU at the Seventeenth Summit Conference held in Freetown, Sierra Leone, in 1980. This move followed a successful diplomatic campaign by the Polisario Front, which had led to the UN, the Non-Aligned Movement and the OAU's Ad Hoc Committee calling for the right of self-determination to be exercised in the disputed territory. Moreover, at that time the SADR had been recognized by thirty-five States.

When the question of the SADR's admission came before the Assembly, the SADR gained the necessary number of votes in accordance with Article 28(2) to be admitted – twenty-six out of fifty. Morocco, along with various other countries, reiterated its threat to withdraw from the OAU if such a decision was confirmed. Indeed, by adroitly managing to postpone the issue of the admission of the SADR, President Siaka Stevens remarked, 'Not everything that is legal is expedient, so we shelved it'.[50]

Morocco's objections to the admission of the SADR were both procedural and legal. First, Morocco alleged that the question of the Western Sahara dispute had been delegated at an earlier meeting to an extraordinary session of the OAU, whereas the meeting at Freetown which had decided to confer membership upon the SADR was merely an ordinary summit conference and consequently was not competent to handle the matter. However, there is nothing in the OAU Charter to suggest that the Assembly of Heads of State and Government cannot discuss any subject it pleases. Secondly, Morocco argued that the SADR could not fulfil the requirements of Article 4 of the OAU Charter. Article 4 states that:

Each independent sovereign African State shall be entitled to become a Member of the Organization.

Morocco's contention was that the SADR was not an independent sovereign State, since it did not satisfy the criteria for statehood.[51] Matters had come to a head when, at a meeting of the Council of Ministers in February 1982, the OAU Secretary-General, Edem Kodjo, invited the delegation of the SADR to join the proceedings. This move was tantamount to admission to the OAU, a decision which would nevertheless have had to be ratified by the subsequent summit conference of the Assembly of Heads of State and Government at Tripoli in August 1982. Edem Kodjo's decision was subject to criticism, but it appears that his act, however politically maladroit it may have appeared to some, was perfectly legal in accordance with Article 28(2) of the OAU Charter and Article 11(iii) of the Rules of the General Secretariat. It was alleged that the SADR's admission was a procedural matter which required a two-thirds majority vote. This contention is clearly mistaken, since Article 10(3) plainly states that the Assembly will decide questions of procedure by a simple majority. Whether or not a question is one of procedure is also determined by a simple majority vote. Similarly, Article 14(2) states that resolutions of the Council of Ministers must be determined by a simple majority. Edem Kodjo defended his action by saying that the question of the SADR's admission was purely an administrative matter since a majority of OAU Member States had voted for the admission of the SADR at the summit conference held at Freetown. Edem Kodjo added that he had worked within the framework of Article 28(2) which empowers the Secretary-General to collect the votes of Member States and communicate the decision to the State seeking admission. Furthermore, the Secretary-General bore the sole responsibility for the final decision on the admission of States. Edem Kodjo said that, although the Freetown Summit had certainly appeared to postpone indefinitely the question of the admission of the SADR, certain Member States had reminded him of his duties under the OAU Charter and he had acted accordingly.[52] If his interpretation of the OAU Charter was incorrect, it would then be possible that Article 27 be invoked. Article 27 states that any question concerning the interpretation of the OAU Charter will be decided by a vote of two-thirds of the Assembly of Heads of State and Government.

Consequences of the Admission of the Saharan Arab Democratic Republic

The violent disagreement over the admission of the SADR disrupted the proceedings of the OAU.[53] These events did not augur well for the Assembly scheduled for Tripoli, Libya, in August 1982. A number of States had decided to participate no further in OAU sessions until the SADR was expelled and at least a third of the membership was expected to boycott the Tripoli meeting. The OAU Chairman, President Moi of Kenya, did not underestimate the seriousness of the situation. He viewed the admission of the SADR as 'the most serious challenge to the survival of the OAU in its . . . history'.[54] Consequently, several unsuccessful attempts at a solution were sought. In April a special OAU committee convened to discuss the contentious issue of the SADR's membership but no specific remedies were proposed. The OAU Bureau issued an appeal to Member States to attend the Tripoli Summit. At its July session the Council of Ministers also attempted to find a solution.

The talks were handicapped from the outset when only a total of thirty-seven States attended. Although a majority of those present supported the SADR it was expected that at least a further six States would boycott the Assembly if the SADR attended, thereby depriving the session of the necessary thirty-four member quorum. Nigeria submitted a compromise solution according to which the SADR would keep away from the Summit Meeting in exchange for taking its seat at the Council's session. However, the proposal, which was merely a short-term solution, was rejected both by the SADR and its opponents. The Council of Ministers thus failed to draft an agenda for the Tripoli Summit and long-held fears about the possible disruption of the Summit Meeting appeared to materialize.

The Nineteenth Summit Assembly of Heads of State and Government at Tripoli in August 1982 was confronted with two intractable problems, either of which was capable of destroying the precarious relationship between the moderate and progressive States. One was the Western Sahara dispute; the other concerned the official representation of the government of Chad. Furthermore, many governments held reservations about Colonel Gadaffi becoming chairman of the OAU. In the event, nineteen States failed to appear, consequently depriving the session of its two-thirds quorum of thirty-four States. To ensure some modicum of constitutionality it was decided that the delegations from Chad and the SADR would not count towards determining the quorum. Those States that did attend were divided as to what ought to be done, some urging a postponement while others wanted to proceed regardless. In the immediate aftermath thirty so-called radical States arranged an informal meeting to devise a formula which would allow the Summit Conference to take place before the end of 1982. The rump summit adopted the Tripoli Declaration which reaffirmed, *inter alia*, support for the SADR.[55]

It was feared that this meeting could further split an already deeply divided Organization and a real danger existed that the African continent could have been polarized between 'moderate' and 'radical' States. Sub-Saharan Africa, which regards the Western Sahara dispute as primarily an Arab conflict and peripheral to the wider and more pressing problems of Africa, was deeply concerned at this turn of events and efforts to reconcile differences were intensified. However, a major crisis was averted when the SADR temporarily withdrew from a meeting of the Council of Ministers held in Tripoli in November. Subsequently, the Polisario Front declared that in future it would participate in all OAU meetings.[56]

The failure of the Tripoli summit led to successful calls by a number of African States for the reconvention of the Nineteenth Summit in Addis Ababa. This meeting would be held without preconditions, which would appear to have constituted an implied rejection of the demands of the moderate States that the SADR's membership be rescinded or suspended. However, continued opposition to the presence of the SADR meant that the future of the conference was still in doubt and the formal opening of the summit was consequently postponed. Pressure was therefore exerted upon the SADR to stay away and attempts at a compromise were made. Thus the SADR eventually agreed to suspend, without prejudice, its participation in the summit. The SADR's Foreign Minister, Mr Ibrahim Hakim, stated that, 'In the interests of African unity . . . the Saharan Arab Democratic Republic, as a member of the OAU, has decided voluntarily and temporarily not to participate in the 19th Summit of the OAU'.[57] This temporary success for Morocco and the eighteen other moderate States proved to be illusory. The resumption of OAU business after a fifteen-month paralysis caused by the admission of the SADR led to pressure being placed upon Morocco to withdraw its troops and administration from the Western Sahara and to initiate negotiations with the Polisario Front. In addition, the Assembly debate was dominated by calls urging Morocco and the Polisario Front to enter into direct negotiations.

In the final event, the Assembly adopted resolution AHG/Res. 104 (XIX) by consensus, which in itself constituted a defeat for Morocco which had unsuccessfully attempted to secure an adjournment, that, *inter alia*, called upon:

1. The parties to the conflict to undertake direct negotiations to secure a cease-fire and to create the necessary conditions for a referendum to be carried out without any administrative or military constraints under the auspices of the OAU and the UN;

2. The Implementation Committee to ensure the observance of the cease-fire and the organization of the referendum by the end of 1983;

3. The UN, in conjunction with the OAU, to provide a peace-keeping force to be stationed in the Western Sahara to ensure peace and security during the referendum process.[58]

This resolution is significant in that it officially recognized the Polisario Front as a party to the dispute. On the other hand, its exhortation to the Implementation Committee to work out the modalities of the referendum was superfluous in view of the fact that the Implementation Committee had already put forward an eminently sensible proposal in August 1982. Indeed, a further meeting of the Implementation Committee collapsed in September 1983 over the question of direct talks between the two parties.[59]

Morocco's procrastination over the proposed referendum led to Morocco's increasing diplomatic isolation as Mauritania and Nigeria recognized the SADR in response thereto. It also suggests that Morocco had not been acting in good faith contrary to international law.[60]

The Twentieth Assembly of Heads of State and Government held in Addis Ababa in November 1984 proved to be a watershed. The Western Sahara dispute had seriously disrupted four previous summits and in the view of the vast majority of the membership the ability of the OAU to confront Africa's many pressing problems was being undermined. Morocco's intransigence led to increased support for the SADR which was determined to take its seat. Indeed, the SADR went on formally to take its seat as the OAU's fifty-first member. Morocco fulfilled its threat by withdrawing from the OAU but interestingly it was supported only by Zaïre which boycotted that conference in protest.[61]

It is axiomatic that Morocco's gamble was unsuccessful in that the oft-threatened mass walk out by the moderate faction which would have permanently deprived the OAU of a quorum never materialized. If Morocco's intention was to split or paralyse the OAU it proved ineffectual. Morocco may have acted precipitately given that membership of an international organization does not necessarily imply general recognition *vis-à-vis* other Member States.[62] Morocco could therefore have remained in the OAU but simply declared that it would not recognize the SADR. Nevertheless, the SADR's admission obviously weakened Morocco's case but Morocco could have remained in the OAU without prejudice to its territorial claim, as is the case with many other members of both the OAU and UN, in a manner compatible with its OAU and UN Charter obligations. Ultimately, however, it must be acknowledged that Morocco does not appear to be suffering any disadvantages as a result of its withdrawal from the OAU. And it is instructive to note that this question still has the potential to cause ructions at the OAU. The Summit Assembly at Ouagadougou, Burkina Faso, in 1998, thus saw calls by various States for the expulsion of the SADR and the return of Morocco. However, any further action appears to have been postponed pending the result of the UN sponsored referendum.

The Role of the United Nations

Since the admission of the SADR to the OAU the UN has assumed the responsibility of finding and implementing a comprehensive peace settlement to the dispute.

As has been seen, for a time the UN delegated the responsibility for the resolution of the dispute to the OAU and restricted itself to merely supporting the OAU's attempts at a negotiated settlement. These resolutions called for the independence of the Western Sahara through the conduct of an impartial referendum and supported the struggle for independence waged by the Polisario Front. Although the General Assembly considered the Polisario Front a party to the dispute and envisaged its participation in any peace negotiations, the resolutions always fell short of recognizing the SADR as an independent State. However, when the OAU failed to secure a settlement the UN embarked on a proactive policy.[63]

The origins of the UN peace plan for the Western Sahara lie in a proposal made by the then UN Secretary-General, Javier Pérez de Cuéllar, to Moroccan and Polisario Front representatives in August 1988, which made provision for a transitional period during which a cease-fire would come into effect and peaceful conditions would be created for holding a referendum under UN supervision.[64] The principle of this Settlement Plan was endorsed by the Security Council in Resolution 658 (1990) which called for a cease-fire to take effect as from 6 September 1991, to be followed in January 1992 by a referendum held under UN auspices in which the Sahrawis would be able to vote for independence or integration with Morocco. The Settlement Plan itself was adopted by the Security Council in Resolution 690 (1991) which formally established a UN force known as MINURSO (UN Mission for the Referendum in Western Sahara) and which also provided for the implementation of a comprehensive cease-fire, which has generally held.[65] MINURSO was given the tasks of implementing and monitoring the cease-fire, supervising the withdrawal of half of the Moroccan occupying force, and restricting the movement of the remaining troops, supervising the return of Sahrawi refugees, overseeing the release of political detainees and prisoners of war, identifying and registering voters and organizing the poll. MINURSO became operational in September 1991. However, MINURSO soon encountered difficulties so that by the time of writing the referendum has yet to take place.

The principal obstacle has been over the electoral roll. According to the Security Council resolutions, which had been accepted by both parties, the census conducted by the Spanish administration in 1974, which listed a Sahrawi population of 74,000, was to form the basis of the electoral roll, which MINURSO was to update. However, this plan was then rejected by Morocco which presented MINURSO with a list of a further 120,000 people which it maintained should be eligible to vote on the ground that they are Sahrawi refugees who fled colonial rule in the 1950s. The Polisario Front saw this as an attempt to gerrymander the electoral roll by entering on it people who are not Sahrawi and who had been transplanted to the area since the Moroccan occupation.

In an attempt to break the deadlock, UN Secretary-General Pérez de Cuéllar suggested that the voting criteria be amended so that all those whose fathers had been born in the territory, in addition to those with intermittent residence over twelve years prior to December 1974, should be eligible to vote.[66] This plan would have added a further 30,000 people on to the electoral roll, most of them Moroccan nationals. The Secretary-General's report attracted fierce criticism from the OAU and the Polisario Front, which insisted on full compliance with the terms of resolution 658. The Security Council did not accept these recommendations but asked the incoming Secretary-General, Boutros Boutros-Ghali, to draft a fresh report.

The Secretary-General's report, presented to the Security Council in February 1992, was critical of Morocco which it identified as largely responsible for cease-fire violations. The Security Council took note of the report and expressed its support for the efforts of the Secretary-General and his representatives to secure the implementation of the peace plan.

In a further report, the Secretary-General identified the refusal of the

two parties to participate in direct negotiations, and the differing interpretations of the criteria for voter eligibility as the principal obstacles to the
implementation of the peace plan. This led the Security Council, in Resolution 809 (1993), to call upon the Secretary-General to consult with both sides
to find an acceptable solution to the problem of voter registration, and set
the end of 1993 as the deadline for the holding of the referendum. Hence, as
a result of the Secretary-General's mediation, the first ever direct talks
between Morocco and the Polisario Front took place in July 1993. This
encouraging development ultimately proved fruitless as neither party
expressed a willingness to accept the Secretary-General's compromise proposal on the voter identification plan.[67] Thus, in 1995, a frustrated Security
Council, in Resolution 973, stressed the urgency of holding the referendum
without further delay. However, because little progress was being achieved,
and in an attempt to concentrate minds, the Security Council began to
contemplate the withdrawal of MINURSO. In May 1996 the Secretary-
General reported that the parties were not providing MINURSO with the co-
operation necessary to complete the identification process. The Security
Council therefore acted on its threat by suspending the referendum process
and withdrawing the majority of the UN force under resolution 1056.

In March 1997 the former US Secretary of State, James Baker, was
appointed as UN Special Envoy to seek a way through the impasse. Under
his auspices agreement on the contentious issues between the parties was
finally possible as set out in the Houston Declaration of 16 September 1997,
according to which the parties accepted the UN's role in ensuring that the
necessary conditions existed for the holding of a free and fair referendum
and settled their differences over the identification process.[68] Pursuant to a
number of Security Council resolutions[69] the identification of eligible voters
resumed and a plan for the organization and conduct of the referendum,
now expected in 2000,[70] was finalized.

Conclusion

The Western Sahara dispute, the only significant neo-colonial struggle
remaining in Africa, posed the OAU, and thus Africa in general, a crisis of
not insignificant proportions that could easily have led to its collapse. The
OAU proved to be a prisoner of its own weaknesses. One of the fundamental
principles of the OAU is the promotion of collaboration and reconciliation
while avoiding confrontation, an approach that was patiently adopted in this
dispute but which nevertheless failed singularly. In adopting a pragmatic
approach the OAU did not wish to precipitate a crisis. However, the OAU's
task was made virtually impossible in view of the uncompromising attitudes
of the parties and given that it has no power to adopt legally binding
resolutions. A weakness of the OAU, particularly if compared with the UN,
is the lack of machinery to impose sanctions, economic or otherwise, upon

members that violate its Charter. In addition, no express power providing for expulsion of errant members exists. It can therefore be seen that the OAU was labouring under a considerable handicap if it should have wanted to resort to forceful measures to impose a settlement. Nevertheless the OAU must be seen to be upholding international law and resisting the use of, or threat of use of, force. In the African context it is imperative that the OAU and its members adhere to the principles of *uti possidetis* and self-determination. In admitting the SADR, notwithstanding grave reservations about its status, the OAU was upholding these principles and rejecting international lawlessness.

As a result of this decision the OAU was no longer in a position to try to reach an amicable settlment to the dispute. The admission of the SADR was a brave decision which rejected the Moroccan claims to sovereignty and its disregard for international law. Yet, in practical terms, little changed as Morocco continued to occupy the disputed territory. The international environment has meant that the international community has been reluctant to adopt forceful measures to deal with an errant, but favoured client State, Morocco. The intervention of the UN has finally presented a workable peace plan but to date a settlement is still to be secured and constant delays in its implementation and conclusion continue to arise, although it is to be hoped that the referendum will take place in 2000. Although the Security Council has consistently supported MINURSO's role and expressed its adherence to the principle of self-determination the observation must be made that it has indulged Morocco's obstructive policies.[71] How 'free' the referendum will be is open to question given Morocco's history of harassment of MINURSO. On the other hand, the UN successfully nursed Namibia to independence in not dissimilar circumstances. Much is at stake, however. Neither party can contemplate losing the referendum. It is not beyond the realm of possibility that the losing side may reject the result of the referendum. The very credibility of the UN, natural justice for the Sahrawi people and respect for the international rule of law are simultaneously on trial in this exercise.

Notes

1. On the Western Sahara dispute generally, see M. Barbier, *Le Conflit du Sahara Occidental* (1982); J. Damis, *Conflict in North West Africa: The Western Sahara Dispute* (1983); T. Hodges, *Western Sahara: the roots of a desert war* (1983); T.M. Franck, 'The Stealing of the Sahara', 70 *AJIL* (1976) 694. The best interdisciplinary account is J. Mercer, *Spanish Sahara* (1976).
2. See Mercer, note 1 *supra*, Chapters 1, 2, 8 and 9.
3. Mercer, note 1 *supra*, Chapter 7.
4. R. Lazrak, *Le Contentieux Territorial entre le Maroc et l'Espagne* (1974); T. Kabbaj, *L'Affaire du Sahara Occidental* (1981).
5. M. Shaw, *Title to Territory in Africa* (1986) pp. 52–5.

6. UN Doc. HRI/GEN/1/Rev. 3, pp. 13–14; I. Brownlie, *Principles of Public International Law* (5th edn 1998) p. 600.
7. The best analytical judgement on the Yema'a may be found in the Report of the Special Committee on the Situation with Regard to the Implementation of the Declaration on the Granting of Independence to Colonial Countries and Peoples GAOR, 30th Session, Supp No 23 (A/10023/Rev.1) Vol III, p. 44.
8. See A.-B. Miské, *Front Polisario – L'ame d'un Peuple* (1978).
9. See note 7 *supra*.
10. General Assembly resolution 3292 (XXIX) 1974.
11. *Western Sahara Case*, ICJ Reports 1975, p. 12. For analysis, see M. Shaw, 'The Western Sahara Case', 49 *BYIL* (1978) 49; F. Wooldridge, 'The Advisory Opinion of the International Court of Justice in the Western Sahara Case', 8 *Anglo-American Law Review* (1979) 88.
12. On the 'Green March' see Kabbaj, note 4 *supra*; A. Byman, 'The March on the Spanish Sahara: A Test of International Law', 6 *Denver Journal of International Law and Policy* (1976) 95.
13. The text of this agreement may be found in J. Gretton, *Western Sahara – The Fight for Self-determination* (1976) Appendix IV.
14. GAOR, 31st Session, Supp No 23 (A/31/23/Rev.1) pp. 218, 219.
15. For text see Damis, note 1 *supra*, Appendix B.
16. See *The Times*, 20 April 1987, p. 7, and 29 April 1987, p. 7; *The Guardian* 6 March 1987, p. 11 and 29 April 1987, p. 7.
17. According to resolutions 41/16 (1986) and 43/33 (1988) the General Assembly regards the Western Sahara dispute as a question of decolonization. This position is implicit in the approach of the Security Council, see further *supra*, pp. 70–2.
18. UN Doc. S/21360; UN Security Council resolution 690 (1991).
19. *Keesing's*, Vol. 39, 1993, R146.
20. This is a customary rule having the character of *jus cogens* enshrined in Article 2(4) of the UN Charter and reiterated in numerous General Assembly resolutions, the most important of which is resolution 2625 (XXV) 1970, Declaration on Principles of International Law Concerning Friendly Relations and Co-operation Among States in Accordance with the Charter of the United Nations. Note the interesting pronouncements by the ICJ in *Military and Paramilitary Activities Against Nicaragua (Nicaragua v United States of America)* ICJ Reports 1986, p. 14. It now seems clear that international law prohibits the use of force to deny the exercise of self-determination, A. Cassese, *Self-Determination of Peoples: A Legal Reappraisal* (1995) pp. 180–5, 194–7.
21. General Assembly resolution 3314 (XXIX) 1974, Definition of Aggression, which in parts appears to reflect customary law, see *Nicaragua Case*, ICJ Reports 1986, p. 103.
22. R.Y.Jennings, *The Acquisition of Territory in International Law* (1963) Chapter 4.
23. Numerous General Assembly resolutions indicate that the right of self-determination must not be frustrated; see resolution 2625 (XXV); Articles 3 and 6 of resolution 2131 (XX) 1965, Declaration on the Inadmissibility of Intervention in the Domestic Affairs of States and the Protection of their Independence and Sovereignty; Article 1(b) of resolution 2160 (XXI) 1966 on the Strict Observance of the Prohibition of the Threat or Use of Force in International Relations and of the Right of Peoples to Self-determination; and Article 2 of resolution 3103 (XXVIII) 1973 on Basic Principles of the Legal Status of the Combatants Struggling against Colonial and Alien Domination and Racist Regimes. In this context, it is clear that States are under an obligation to permit the free exercise of the right to self-determination, see the comment by the HRC, UN Doc. HRI/GEN/1/Rev.3, para. 6, and denial of that right amounts to a use of force, *Nicaragua Case*, ICJ Reports 1986, para. 191; a violation of human rights, Vienna Declaration

and Programme of Action, UN Doc. A/CONF.157/23, Part I, para. 2(2); and an international crime, see Article 19(3)(b) of the International Law Commission's Draft Convention on State Responsibility. Furthermore, the pronouncement by the ICJ that the principle of self-determination has an *erga omnes* character means that all States must facilitate realization of this right, *East Timor Case*, ICJ Reports 1995, p. 90, para. 29. According to Professor Brownlie, the right of self-determination is a norm of *jus cogens* which means that no derogation therefrom is permissible, see Brownlie, note 6 *supra*, pp. 515, 517.

24. See Articles 53 and 64 of the Vienna Convention on the Law of Treaties 1969 and the unratified Vienna Convention on the Law of Treaties between States and International Organizations 1986 which make it clear that a treaty in conflict with a norm of *jus cogens* is null and void.

25. Article 52 of the Vienna Convention on the Law of Treaties 1969 and Article 52 of the Vienna Convention on the Law of Treaties between States and International Organizations.

26. See R. Rezette, *The Western Sahara and the Frontier of Morocco* (1974).

27. See *Frontier Dispute Case*, ICJ Reports 1986, p. 554, and further Chapter 1 *supra*, pp. 12–13.

28. ICJ Reports 1951, p. 15 at pp. 24 and 29. This principle is now enshrined in Article 19(c) of the Vienna Convention on the Law of Treaties 1969 and the Vienna Convention on the Law of Treaties between States and International Organizations which declare that a State may, when signing, ratifying, accepting, approving or acceding to a treaty formulate a reservation unless the reservation is incompatible with the object and purpose of the treaty.

29. It is interesting to note that Article 20(3) of the Vienna Convention on the Law of Treaties 1969 and the Vienna Convention on the Law of Treaties between States and International Organizations 1986 provide that when a treaty is a constituent instrument of an international organization a reservation requires the acceptance of the competent organ of that organization.

30. *Anglo-Norwegian Fisheries Case*, ICJ Reports 1951, p. 116 at p. 131.

31. See resolutions CM/206 (XIII), CM/209 (XIV) and CM/234 (XV); Barbier, note 1 *supra*, p. 88.

32. *Keesing's*, Vol. 21, November 1975, p. 27417.

33. *Keesing's*, Vol. 22, May 1976, p. 27746.

34. *Keesing's*, Vol. 22, August 1976, p. 27884.

35. *Keesing's*, Vol. 22, August 1976, p. 27885.

36. GAOR 33rd Session, 1978, A/33/235, Annex II.

37. See G.J. Naldi, 'Peace Keeping Attempts by the Organization of African Unity' 34 *ICLQ* (1985) 593 at p. 596.

38. OAU Res AHG/93 (XVI), Report of the *Ad Hoc* Committee on Western Sahara, in GAOR, 34th Session, 1979, Supp. No. 23 (Doc A/34/23/Rev. 1).

39. OAU Res AHG/93 (XVI), Annex VII.

40. Naldi, note 37 *supra*, pp. 597–601.

41. A meeting of the Implementation Committee in September 1983 collapsed after Morocco refused to conduct direct negotiations with the Polisario Front. The Polisario Front, on the other hand, insisted on direct negotiations with Morocco as a precondition to a referendum; see *Keesing's*, Vol. 30, April 1984, p. 32822.

42. *The Guardian*, 26 August 1981, p. 5.

43. AHG/IMPC/WS/Dec 1(1).

44. AHG/IMPC/WS/Dec 2(II) Rev 2.

45. AHG/IMPC/WS/Dec 1(II) Rev 2.

46. With the progressive completion of the fortified walls that neutralized the fighting capacity of the Polisario Front, King Hassan adopted an intransigent position, declaring that the status of the Western Sahara was subject neither to

negotiation nor concession; see *The Guardian*, 9 March 1985, p. 5. Note Article 3(4) of the OAU Charter which requires Member States to settle disputes peacefully through negotiation, mediation, conciliation or arbitration.

47.   AHG/Res 104 (XIX).

48.   The compatibility of Morocco's actions with the principle of good faith enshrined in Article 2(2) of the UN Charter must be open to question, see *Nuclear Test Cases*, ICJ Reports 1974, p. 253 at p. 268.

49.   See further, G.J. Naldi, 'The Organization of African Unity and the Saharan Arab Democratic Republic', 26 *JAL* (1982) 152.

50.   *The Guardian*, 21 July 1980.

51.   For a more detailed discussion of this complex question, see G.J. Naldi, 'The Statehood of the Saharan Arab Democratic Republic', 25 *IJIL* (1985) 448. Whereas the SADR clearly did not fulfil the criteria of statehood as laid down in Article 1 of the Montevideo Convention on the Rights and Duties of States 1933 at this time, it did possess certain attributes of sovereignty and it now seems generally accepted that the right to self-determination compensates for the partial failure to satisfy these requirements in the cases of States *in statu nascendi*, Brownlie, note 6 *supra*, pp. 71, 602; J. Crawford, *The Creation of States in International Law* (1979) pp. 102, 103, 261, 262. It should also be noted that the SADR was recognized by some seventy States. However, developments since that time suggest that the benefit of the doubt initially given to the SADR may no longer be appropriate. Since the construction of the berm the Polisario Front has been virtually excluded from the territory of the Western Sahara and it now appears that the Polisario Front is in control of little, or nothing, of the Western Sahara. Certainly States can lose their personality gradually, see Arbitration Commission on Yugoslavia, Opinion No. 1, 92 ILR 162 at pp. 164, 165, and it is therefore not surprising that a number of African States, Equatorial Guinea, Guinea-Bissau, Togo, amongst others, have withdrawn their recognition of the SADR, which is permissible if the nascent State fails to meet the criteria of statehood, see P.M. Brown, 'The Legal Effects of Recognition', 44 *AJIL* (1950) 639; M. Whiteman, *Digest of International Law*, Vol. II (1963) pp. 27, 28. Furthermore, the Polisario Front's acceptance of the UN peace plan, even if without prejudice, must bring the status of the SADR into question since it is premised on completion of an unfinished exercise in self-determination (the proclamation of independence by the Polisario Front in 1976 may no longer be deemed to constitute a valid exercise of the right to self-determination). A vote for independence would provide the SADR with retrospective legitimacy; alternatively it could lead to the birth of a new State, such as happened in Namibia. Whereas a vote for integration with Morocco would inevitably result in recognition of Moroccan sovereignty and, assuming the SADR does have personality, its extinction, a possibility acknowledged by international law, such as the case of Yugoslavia, see Arbitration Commission on Yugoslavia, Opinion No. 8, 92 ILR 199; UN Security Council resolution 777 (1992). Can the statehood of the SADR be deemed to be suspended or in abeyance pending the outcome of the referendum? The precedent set by the Baltic States in terms of continuity of statehood suggests that independence and sovereignty can re-emerge after illegal occupation despite the passage of many years, see Cassese, note 20 *supra*, pp. 258–64.

52.   See E. Osieke, 'Admission to Membership in International Organisations: The Case of Namibia', 49 *BYIL* (1983) 189 at p. 221 who suggests that when the Charter of an international organization does not define a State for the purposes of admission the competent body must determine whether the applicant fulfils the requirements of the Organization. It is interesting to note that with regard to the UN the ICJ held in *Conditions of Admission of a State to Membership in the UN*, ICJ Reports 1948, p. 57 that the question of admission of an applicant State to the

UN could not be based on factors extraneous to Article 4 of the UN Charter. However, the question was subject to the judgement of the Organization and, ultimately, that of its members.

53. Thus a number of ministerial meetings were disrupted, *The Guardian*, 1 April 1982, p. 7; 6 April 1982, p. 8; and 23 April 1982, p. 8.

54. *The Guardian*, 24 April 1982, p. 7; *Keesing's*, Vol. 39 (1983), p. 31935.

55. *Keesing's*, Vol. 39 (1983), pp. 31935–6.

56. *Keesing's*, Vol. 39 (1983), pp. 31937–8.

57. *Keesing's*, Vol. 39 (1983), p. 32419.

58. Ibid.

59. *The Guardian*, 23 September 1983, p. 8.

60. See note 48 *supra*.

61. *Keesing's*, Vol. 31 (1985) pp. 33324–5.

62. Brownlie, note 6 *supra*, p. 95.

63. The UN assumed sole and exclusive responsibility for the organization of the referendum though the OAU was to have a role as observer, see General Assembly resolution 40/50 and UN Doc. S/21360.

64. UN Doc. S/21360.

65. C. Rucz, 'Un Referendum au Sahara Occidental?', 40 *Annuaire Française de Droit International* (1994) 243.

66. UN Doc. S/22464.

67. The proposal was endorsed by the Security Council in resolution 907 (1994), which set in motion the voter identification and registration process.

68. UN Doc. S/1997/742. The UN Secretary-General has since reported acceptance of the identification process by both parties, UN Doc. S/1999/307.

69. See, e.g., resolutions 1131 (1997), 1133 (1997), 1185 (1998) and 1204 (1998).

70. Security Council Resolution 1238 (1999). See also, Report of the Secretary-General on the Situation Concerning Western Sahara, UN Doc. S/1999/483, and Add. 1.

71. Franck's observation in 1976 that the 'disposition of the Sahara case by the United Nations has been monumentally mishandled, creating a precedent for future mischief out of all proportion to the importance of the territory', see Franck, note 1 *supra*, p. 694, is still apt.

3

Refugees

Perhaps one of the most overwhelming tragedies that Africa has faced over many years is massive human dislocation. Through a combination of external and internal conflicts, and the failure to find political solutions to such conflicts, ecological disasters, abuses of human rights,[1] maladministration, impoverishment, communal violence and social unrest, the African continent is confronted with perpetuated instability giving rise to a refugee problem of catastrophic proportions. Recent events which have contributed to large population displacements include the civil war in southern Sudan, the collapse of civil society in Somalia, the civil wars in Liberia and Sierra Leone, which in each country has uprooted some one million people, and the ethnic conflict in the Great Lakes region of Central Africa, especially Rwanda which gave rise to an exodus of some two million refugees and displaced persons to neighbouring countries. Present numbers fluctuate between six and seven million people,[2] and at this time, despite the efforts of governments, NGOs and voluntary organizations to relieve their suffering, the scale of the problem remains staggering. As the number of refugees has escalated in the past few decades and mass exoduses have taken place from countries such as Mozambique, Liberia and Rwanda, the reception of refugees has led to serious problems for host States which are concerned about the security and environmental repercussions of large population movements. Moreover, the refugee burden continues to be unevenly divided and the financial and material burden thus imposed on African States with limited resources is straining their infrastructure and generally stretching their ability to cope and is increasingly giving rise to 'compassion fatigue' and 'donor fatigue' on the part of the wider international community. Yet it is ironic that in the international legal sphere the African States have secured considerable achievements. The purpose of this Chapter is to examine the international legal protection of African refugees and, in addition, some of the more practical achievements will be briefly addressed. However, it is first necessary to determine who is entitled to refugee status.

Definition

What constitutes a refugee in international law? A refugee has been defined simply as a person seeking asylum in a foreign country and at the very least it would appear to refer to a person who is forced to cross an international border in the absence of protection in his country of origin.[3] A generally accepted definition did not exist prior to 1950 when the UN drafted various international instruments relating to refugees. Article 1 (a)(2) of the Geneva Convention Relating to the Status of Refugees 1951 states that a refugee is, *inter alia*, a person having a 'well-founded fear of being persecuted for reasons of race, religion, nationality, membership of a particular social group or political opinion, is outside the country of his nationality and is unable or, owing to such fear, is unwilling to avail himself of the protection of that country'.[4] War criminals, or perpetrators of genocide, or anyone who has been guilty of acts contrary to the purposes and principles of the UN, cannot avail themselves of refugee status, nor is extradition for serious non-political offences prohibited.[5]

This definition was intended primarily for the protection of the individual refugee and was dependent on the fear of persecution being individual in nature. It was not deemed applicable to mass exoduses but the OAU considered that such a narrow definition failed to take account of the particular difficulties facing Africa, such as wars of national liberation and environmental catastrophes, such as drought and famine, which had given rise to flight *en masse* and displaced whole populations. In fact, eight different categories of African refugees have been identified, including those fleeing international conflicts, civil wars and other civil disorders, or wars of secession, such as in Eritrea, fleeing gross human rights violations, such as in the Sudan, ethnic peoples fleeing communal violence, as in the Great Lakes region of Central Africa, and refugees fleeing natural disasters, such as in the Sahel and Ethiopia.[6]

The OAU Convention Governing the Specific Aspects of Refugee Problems in Africa 1969 incorporates the Geneva Convention definition in Article 1(1) but extends it in paragraph 2.[7] It states that:

> The term 'refugee' shall also apply to every person who, owing to external aggression, occupation, foreign domination or events seriously disturbing public order in either part or the whole of his country of origin or nationality, is compelled to leave his place of habitual residence in order to seek refuge in another place outside his country of origin or nationality.

This definition was therefore intended to cover mass exoduses brought about by the problems of colonialism and the ensuing wars of national liberation, and the struggle against apartheid and other minority regimes. Although mass migration as a result of famine or other natural disasters was perhaps not originally envisaged as coming within the scope of the definition, it is certainly accepted now. People uprooted in such circumstances are often referred to as displaced persons. This wider and more liberal regime was motivated, as stated in the preamble to the OAU Convention, by 'the need for an essentially humanitarian approach towards solving the problems of refugees' and was therefore a step that met with acclaim. However, in light of Article 2 of the Banjul Charter, and other international human rights instruments, the question arises whether the concept of 'refugee' should be extended to cover every person who fears being persecuted for reasons of belonging to an ethnic group, or for reasons of colour, sex, sexual orientation, social origin, fortune, birth or other status. The protection thus offered would be all-embracing.[8] The ethnic conflict in the Great Lakes region of Central Africa from 1994 to 1996 makes a compelling argument for the extension of this definition.

International Protection

In any discussion about refugees it is necessary to draw a distinction between the applicable law and the international institutions which are active in drafting international conventions, putting the law into practice and bringing actual relief to the refugees.

The Applicable Law – The United Nations Convention and Protocol

Refugee law is now chiefly governed by international treaties but for those few States that have not yet ratified these instruments customary international law is still relevant. The concept of a refugee is known to customary international law although its precise definition is still unclear but at the very minimum it would appear to refer to a person who is forced to move abroad in the absence of protection in his country of origin.[9] In addition, it seems that customary international law now recognizes the principle of *non-refoulement*, i.e., that no refugee can be forcibly repatriated.[10] This right of non-return in fact forms the very core of refugee protection. Some would suggest that a customary international obligation may have arisen requiring the grant of asylum, i.e., protection afforded to a foreign national against the exercise of jurisdiction by another State, but this seems doubtful given that the granting of asylum constitutes a derogation from sovereignty. Moreover in the *Asylum Case* the ICJ found that no such customary right existed.[11] State practice since that time suggests no change in the position of customary international law.[12]

However, as has been stated, refugee law is now principally governed by conventional law and customary international law has been largely codified into the UN and OAU Conventions where it has been further developed. The UN Convention was a watershed in the development of refugee law but it originally had a limited effect because, as a response to the Second World War, it was geographically and temporally limited to Europe and events prior to 1951. Given, however, that the global refugee problem persisted it was considered necessary to extend the scope and effect of the UN Convention.[13] This was achieved through the UN Protocol relating to the Status of Refugees 1967 which extends the application of the UN Convention without geographic or temporal restrictions. At the time of writing most OAU Member States have ratified or acceded to either or both of these treaties.[14]

Article 1 of the UN Convention and Protocol require the fulfilment of four criteria for the determination of refugee status: (1) that the individual is outside his or her country of origin or nationality; (2) that he or she is unwilling or unable to avail himself or herself of the protection of that country, or to return there; (3) that he or she has a well-founded fear of persecution; (4) the persecution feared is based on reasons of race, religion, nationality, membership of a particular social group, or political opinion. A refugee is protected by Article 3 of the UN Convention without discrimination as to race, religion or country of origin. However, refugee status is determined by the host State[15] and this can lead to a lack of uniformity in the application of the UN Convention. The problems associated with the existence of this discretion can be demonstrated by comparing the House of Lords' judgment in *R* v. *Secretary of State for the Home Department, ex parte Sivakumaran et al.* with the US Supreme Court's judgment in *Immigration and Naturalization Service* v. *Cardoza-Fonseca* as in the former case the House of Lords refused to be bound by, and rejected, the UNHCR's interpretation, while in the latter the US Supreme Court did take account of the interpretation of the UNHCR. In addition, the interpretation given to the concept 'well-founded fear' by the respective courts differed.[16]

However, once an applicant is determined to be a bona fide refugee and is granted refugee status certain rights accrue. Some rights must correspond generally to the most favourable treatment accorded to foreign nationals and these include rights to property, the freedom of association, the right to employment, including self-employment and the practice of liberal professions, and the right to housing.[17] With regard to other rights refugees must be accorded the same treatment as nationals and these include access to the courts, public education and labour legislation and social security.[18] The fact that Article 33 of the UN Convention enshrines the principle of *non-refoulement* is of added importance. Thus no refugee can be expelled to a country where his life or freedom would be jeopardised on account of his race, religion, nationality, membership of a particular social group or political opinion.[19]

Refugees are particularly vulnerable to human rights abuses. It is therefore worth emphasizing that a wide array of rights enshrined in the corpus of human rights law is applicable to refugees. These rights cover the minimum standards of human dignity as set out in the UDHR, the International Covenants and the Banjul Charter and, in addition to those rights listed above, include the right to physical integrity, food, basic health care, education, the freedom of movement and the integrity of the family as the most fundamental social unit. In fact, refugees are vulnerable to frequent arbitrary detentions and violations of the right to life.[20]

The Organization of African Unity Convention

While many African States have ratified the UN Convention and Protocol the enduring refugee problem in Africa has proved to be a severe strain on friendly relations among OAU Member States. The need was identified early on of tackling this issue in an African context in the spirit of the OAU Charter. The OAU Charter suggests that the refugee problem is of concern to it since one of its goals, expressed in Article 2 (1)(b), is to seek a 'better life for the peoples of Africa'. Thus in 1964 the Council of Ministers created an *ad hoc* commission with the express mandate of examining the refugee problem in Africa and recommending its solution.[21] It further invited the commission to draw up a draft convention covering all aspects of the refugee problem in Africa.[22] The work of the drafting committee was endorsed by the OAU Assembly at its Second Summit Meeting in Accra in 1965 and the Assembly further requested OAU Member States that had not already done so to ratify the UN Convention and in the interim to apply its provisions.[23] The OAU Convention Governing the Specific Aspects of Refugee Problems in Africa was adopted in 1969 and entered into force on 20 June 1974 after it had been ratified by one-third of the Member States.[24] By virtue of Article 8(2) the OAU Convention is declared to be the effective regional complement to the UN Convention and Protocol but it must be stressed that it contains some distinctive features. To date it has been ratified by forty-three Member States.[25] The OAU Convention recognizes in the preamble that the UN Convention and Protocol constitute the basic and universal instruments relating to the status of refugees and their treatment and thus reaffirms the substantive provisions of the UN Convention. The OAU Convention does not seek to exclude the operation of the UN Convention and Protocol from Africa; the substantive measures of protection provided for therein but not mentioned in the OAU Convention apply. Moreover, it calls upon those OAU Member States that have not already done so to accede to the UN Convention and Protocol. However, it seeks to solve the refugee problem in an African context.

As has been stated, the OAU Convention is innovative in a number of respects. The significant step in broadening the concept of the refugee by virtue of Article 1(2) to include individuals and large numbers of people fleeing public disorder has already been mentioned. The original intention appears to have been to protect people fleeing from the effects of colonialism and apartheid, including members of national liberation movements, but one of the greatest problems adding to the refugee burden in Africa has been natural disasters. Drought and famine over the last few years is such an example. Other problems that have arisen in recent years concern displacement as a result of mass abuses of human rights, forced evictions and inter-ethnic conflict, such as in Rwanda[26] and the Sudan.[27] While such refugees, or displaced persons, may not have been originally intended as coming within the scope of the definition it is now beyond question that they are protected by the OAU Convention. In all other respects the OAU Convention repeats verbatim the UN Convention definition but, as has been suggested, scope for widening the concept of the refugee still exists. It is interesting to note that among the categories of persons barred from acquiring refugee status are included persons guilty of acts contrary to the purposes and principles of the OAU.[28]

Article 2 departs radically from the UN Convention by enshrining a right to asylum, a right which is reinforced by Article 12(3) of the Banjul Charter.[29] Article 33 of the UN Convention by comparison simply prohibits States parties from returning an asylum seeker to a country to which he or she is unwilling to go owing to a well-founded fear of persecution which, as has been indicated, does not prevent the host State from sending that person elsewhere. As has been stated the right to asylum is a conventional right and not a customary right. However, the OAU Convention was not the first international instrument addressing itself to this question. Thus, Article 14(1) UDHR declares a right to seek and enjoy asylum. In addition, in 1967 the UN General Assembly unanimously adopted the Declaration on Territorial Asylum which, however, is without prejudice to the sovereignty of States. Therefore, States retain an absolute discretion in deciding whether to grant asylum. Nevertheless, because the plight of refugees is a matter of international concern, where a State has difficulty in granting asylum other States are required to consider, in the spirit of international solidarity, measures to lessen that burden. The principle of *non-refoulement* is recognized subject to exceptions in the interests of national security or incidents of international crime.[30] No other universal instruments on asylum have been adopted.[31]

The OAU Convention strengthens the concept of asylum by diminishing the doctrine of State sovereignty, although it must be stressed that there is no automatic right to asylum; ultimately the granting of asylum remains a prerogative of the State.[32] Thus it declares that the granting of asylum is a peaceful and humanitarian act which must not be regarded as an unfriendly gesture by other OAU Member States. Moreover, OAU Member States must use their best endeavours to receive refugees and to secure the settlement of those unwilling or unable to return to their country of origin. It is interesting to observe that Article 12(3) of the Banjul Charter appears to apply a more restrictive approach to the granting of asylum in that asylum seekers are required to have suffered actual persecution rather than simply having a well-founded fear of persecution.

The OAU Convention further emphasizes its humanitarian credentials by declaring the principle of *non-refoulement* without exception.[33] Unlike the UN Convention, no express reference is made in this context to national security or public order. It would therefore seem that a *bona fide* refugee can not be expelled.[34] However, this guarantee must be read in light of the general obligation contained in Article 1(4)(g) of the OAU Convention according to which a person may lose his refugee status where he has 'seriously infringed the purposes and objectives of this Convention'. Since according to Article 3(1) a refugee is under a duty to abide by the laws of the country of asylum, including measures taken for the maintenance of public order, any breach thereof may result in the loss of refugee status and expulsion may ensue.[35] Nevertheless, the obligation of *non-refoulement* is complemented by Article 12(4) of the Banjul Charter which states that an alien lawfully in the territory of a State may be expelled only in accordance with the due process of law. It is significant that the principle of *non-refoulement* must be observed even in cases of mass influx of displaced persons which is complemented by Article 12(5) of the Banjul Charter which prohibits the mass expulsion of aliens.[36] However, as recent events in the Great Lakes region of Central Africa have demonstrated, the reception of large numbers of refugees is a very real problem for many African States which are not always in a position to cope. In Burundi thousands did not have access to food and water, exposed to the elements and disease.[37] Moreover, ethnic tensions can be exacerbated by a mass influx, such as in what was Zaïre where violent incidents occurred between the local population and refugees from Rwanda.[38] In apparent defiance of the obligation contained in Article 2(3) borders were closed and more than one million Rwandan and Burundian refugees were forced to leave Zaïre and Tanzania and return to their country of origin to face an uncertain future.[39] In turn, the forcible closure of refugee camps in the Kibeho area by the Rwandan authorities forced thousands to flee to Burundi and Zaïre.[40] However, many of these incidents are explicable against a background of violence as the refugee camps were used by opponents of the regimes, many with complicity in genocide, to incite insecurity and tension and may therefore have not been incompatible with refugee law.[41]

Where a refugee has not received the right to reside in any country, that person *may* be granted temporary residence. Provision is also made for burden sharing if a State finds difficulty in continuing to grant asylum to refugees. A State may thus appeal directly to other States or through the OAU for appropriate measures to be taken in the spirit of African solidarity and international co-operation. It is interesting to note that States granting the right of asylum are, for reasons of security, under an obligation to settle refugees a reasonable distance from the frontier of their country of origin. This requirement would appear, *prima facie*, to be incompatible with Article

26 of the UN Convention and Article 12(1) of the Banjul Charter which states that every individual is to have the right of freedom of movement and residence within the borders of a State. However, the personal security of refugees often requires their settlement away from borders in times of political instability. The wisdom of this provision has been substantiated by events in the Great Lakes region of Central Africa during 1996, and subsequently, when refugees along the Rwanda/Zaïre border often fell victim to acts of atrocities committed by different parties.[42]

A further distinctive feature of the OAU Convention is, as mentioned, Article 3 which prohibits refugees from engaging in subversive activities. This principle is in keeping with Article 3(5) of the OAU Charter and the Declaration on the Problem of Subversion.[43] Accordingly a refugee is under a duty to abide by the laws of the country in which he or she finds himself or herself and to refrain from any subversive activities against any OAU Member State. By restricting the prohibition on subversive activities towards OAU Member States only, the struggle of national liberation movements against colonial and racist regimes was left unfettered. A problem of definition may nevertheless arise. If the host State adopts a restrictive approach legitimate political dissent or agitation in support of human rights could be suppressed, at variance with the freedom of expression enshrined in Article 9(2) of the Banjul Charter. However, restrictions may be understandable to prevent unrest, rabble-rousing and destabilization. A person who does not abide by such a prohibition could lose his refugee status in accordance with Article 1(4)-(5) and face expulsion. State parties are under a similar obligation to prohibit refugees residing in their territories from attacking, or engaging in any subversive activities against any OAU Member State. The political upheaval in the Great Lakes Region of Central Africa in recent years has highlighted some of the difficulties associated with such a scenario. Mass population movements which mingled genuine asylum seekers with individuals who had committed crimes against humanity, or armed gangs, as in the case of Rwanda, posed enormous challenges to receiving States. Hutu militants (Interahamwe), some of whom were implicated in the genocide, opposed to the Rwandan government fomented unrest in refugee camps and hindered repatriation by spreading rumours that returnees would be punished and killed by the RPF. Refugee camps were used as bases from which to launch attacks against Rwandan territory and forces. Furthermore, armed resistance was offered to the ultimately victorious rebel forces of Laurent Kabila in Zaïre which swiftly overwhelmed the corrupt Mobutu regime. As a result some refugee camps were attacked and refugees killed and dispersed.[44] Camps were therefore dismantled not only to normalize conditions but to expose the criminal elements hiding therein. The legitimate security concerns of the authorities must be addressed and their refusal to tolerate subversive activities seems understandable. In order to protect bona fide refugees from, *inter alia*, being refused refugee status in such dangerous circumstances it is imperative that refugee camps be effectively guarded to prevent infiltration by criminal elements and human rights abusers and that screening procedures be implemented to separate refugees from such elements. The UNHCR therefore reached agreement with the governments of the region on security measures to ensure the civilian nature of the camps. These measures included the selective and gradual closure of problem camps, increased security in and around the camps, policing the camps to root out subversive elements, and the establishment of separation camps for those suspected of human rights violations and thus *prima facie* ineligible for refugee status.[45]

Article 5 contains a further distinctive measure in providing for voluntary repatriation. Although the subject of numerous UN General Assembly resolutions this principle has not featured in internationally binding instruments although the OAU Convention is an exception.[46] It emphasizes the voluntary nature of repatriation and, in light of the principle of *non-refoulement*, declares that no refugee is to be repatriated against his or her will. Unfortunately, as has already been mentioned, because of the insecurity in the Great Lakes region thousands of Rwandan and Burundian refugees have been forcibly repatriated. If a refugee does wish to be repatriated the country of origin and the country of asylum are obliged to collaborate to ensure the refugee's safe return. In addition, refugees who freely decide to return to their homeland on their own initiative, or as the result of assurances, must have their return facilitated by the country of origin, the country of asylum, voluntary agencies, NGOs and international organizations. But what if the country of origin is not a party to the OAU Convention and reneges on an agreement? Article 5(4) seeks to protect returning refugees stating that they should not be penalized. The OAU Convention does not address this possibility but presumably an appeal could be made to the OAU or to the African Commission on Human and Peoples' Rights.[47]

It has been suggested that voluntary repatriation offers the best solution to the refugee crisis but it is axiomatic that, unless the situations that gave rise to the displacement in the first place are not remedied, voluntary repatriation will amount to nothing more than a pious hope. Confidence-building measures seem to be a prerequisite, including measures to reassure refugees of their safety. Repatriation must be carried out under safe conditions and must be sustainable. International monitoring of returnees must be effective. Measures must be in place to ensure that commitments given by countries of origin are kept. There must be logistical support for the return and reintegration of refugees. Refugees contemplating repatriation may sometimes find it impossible to return to their home communities because those communities have been damaged or destroyed or because of continued unrest. Insecurity and unsustainable economic conditions will not encourage voluntary returns. For example, the 100,000 Mozambicans remaining in South Africa seem unlikely to return until that country's war-torn economy begins to revive. Some 300,000 Eritrean refugees remain in Sudan, deterred by the devastation suffered by their country's long struggle for independence and their government's initial reluctance to encourage mass returns until an internationally financed rehabilitation programme had been established. Hence the freedom of choice of intended destinations added to the freedom of movement might encourage returnees. Moreover, voluntary repatriation can only be made more effective if human rights are protected and if the safety of returnees can be assured. Thus in Rwanda the human rights situation discourages the return of refugees. It is common knowledge that there have been numerous reports of killings of returning refugees by the army and rebel groups in Burundi. This general climate of insecurity and violence constitutes a major impediment to orderly repatriation. The empty homes and property of refugees frequently results in such property being illegally occupied by others. Efforts must be made for the restoration of such property or for the payment of fair compensation for any property that cannot be restored.[48] Safe havens, such as that established in Iraq pursuant to Security Council resolution 688 (1991), may facilitate the return of refugees to their areas of origin but it is imperative that safe havens provide minimum guarantees of security and sustainability. Ultimately, however, only comprehensive steps aimed at national reconciliation and rehabilitation offer a truly durable solution.

In addition, given the UNHCR's responsibility for the monitoring, rehabilitation and reintegration of returnees, it is imperative for the sake of bona fide refugees that screening procedures be put in place to ensure that criminal elements do not take advantage of repatriation programmes. Opponents of the RPF implicated in genocide were among those repatriated to Rwanda and proceeded to pursue a policy of destabilization by murder and pillage. The UNHCR has therefore initiated a policy that refugee status determination procedures be adopted by countries of asylum hosting Rwandan refugees.[49] In the absence of such procedures, governments are unlikely to co-operate in repatriation programmes.

Nevertheless, positive developments have occurred. With the end of apartheid large numbers of people uprooted in the 1970s and 1980s as a result of the destabilizing policies pursued by the racist regime in South Africa have begun to return to Namibia and South Africa itself. The peace process in Mozambique, ending a civil war which had exiled some two million people, has similarly led to the return of many refugees. In the Western Sahara, agreement between Morocco and the Polisario Front in 1997 on the holding of a referendum has allowed the UNHCR to embark on a repatriation programme of Sahrawi refugees residing in neighbouring countries with a view, *inter alia*, to registering for the referendum.[50]

There is, however, another aspect to the principle of voluntary repatriation which is linked to the international human rights norm that a person cannot be arbitrarily deprived of the right to return to his or her country. The OAU Convention does not address this issue but under general international law a national cannot be denied entry to his or her country of origin.[51] Furthermore, according to Article 12(2) of the Banjul Charter an individual has the right to leave any country and to return to his or her country subject to the law of public order and security.

The importance of the OAU Convention to international law lies principally in its extension of the definition of the concept of the refugee, the implementation of voluntary repatriation programmes and its provision for a right of asylum. Motivated in part by problems largely peculiar to Africa, these humanitarian developments have been nonetheless welcome. Despite the advances in the legal sphere, however, the situation in practice gave less reason for optimism as Africa was overwhelmed by a series of human tragedies, and in 1979 an international conference was convened to review African refugee problems.[52]

The Arusha Conference

A further significant development in the field of refugee law and policy in Africa was the Pan African Conference on the Situation on Refugees in Africa held at Arusha, Tanzania, in May 1979 (hereafter the Arusha Conference). The Arusha Conference was convened to review all the aspects of African refugee problems which came within the scope of the UN and OAU Conventions and to consider the causes of the refugee problems. The Arusha Conference was sponsored by the OAU, UNHCR, the ECA and a host of voluntary organizations. It was attended by thirty-eight Member States and national liberation movements recognized by the OAU. It adopted a number of recommendations on 'The Situation of Refugees in Africa and Prospective Solutions to the Problem in the 1980s'.[53]

The recommendations of the Arusha Conference can be divided into two categories, the first relating to legal and protective matters and the second concerning social, economic and administrative issues, which are considered below in greater detail. The legal and protection issues are of particular significance because they reflect the views of the African States on the interpretation, development and implementation of the UN and OAU Conventions.

The question of asylum in Africa was addressed by Recommendation 1. It was stressed that according to public international law an individual has no such right, since the State retains the discretion whether or not to grant asylum. However, it was recognized that the OAU Convention did constitute an improvement on the existing law and progress was being made on strengthening the individual's right to asylum which seemed to be gaining wider aceptance in Africa. OAU Member States were encouraged to incorporate the right of asylum into their domestic legal systems. The principle expressed in Article 2(2) of the OAU Convention that the granting of asylum is a peaceful and humanitarian act and should not be construed as an unfriendly gesture was reaffirmed. Observance of the principle of *non-*

refoulement was emphasized and it was recommended that the principle be incorporated into domestic law. Where the refugee status of a person was still to be determined it was declared that he or she should enjoy protection pending the final decision. To ensure that extradition did not become a disguised form of *refoulement*, it was declared that extradition requests be considered in accordance with the due process of law. The voluntary nature of repatriation, which the OAU Convention made clear beyond doubt, was also reaffirmed. The existence of a number of agreements between certain African States which provided for the forcible return of refugees to their country of origin was condemned as violating the principles of asylum and *non-refoulement*. It was recognized that the granting of asylum could place an unduly heavy burden on some African States and therefore the principle of burden-sharing was stressed. It was felt that an effective implementation of the principle of burden-sharing could substantially contribute to the solution of this problem. Voluntary repatriation was acknowledged as one of the fundamental objectives of African refugee policy and it was noted that various examples of voluntary repatriation had been achieved successfully. It was recognized that the granting of amnesty was a powerful factor in many cases of voluntary repatriation but it seemed that in some cases the terms of amnesties had not been respected. Consequently, it was considered necessary that the concept of amnesty be examined. Finally, atrocities committed against refugees were condemned as violations of international law, in particular the Geneva Conventions 1949 and the Additional Protocols 1977, and the international community was urged to prevent such violations and to ensure the protection and the provision of humanitarian aid to refugees.[54]

Recommendation 2 addressed the questions of the definition of a refugee and the determination of refugee status. No change was deemed necessary to the definition of the concept of the 'refugee' contained in Article 1(1), (2) of the OAU Convention since it was agreed unanimously that this definition was the basis for determining refugee status in Africa. In addition, it provided a role model for the rest of the world. However, establishing refugee status was more problematic, although in practical terms much more important, and consequently it was stressed that a refugee be identified as such in accordance with established procedures. With regard to individual appeals for asylum African States were urged to adopt the basic requirements specified by UNHCR in 1977, viz., that border officials be familiar with international refugee instruments and in particular that they act in accordance with the principle of *non-refoulement*; that the applicant receive the necessary guidance as to the procedures to be followed; that the applicant receive the necessary facilities for submitting his case to the authorities, and that he be allowed to contact a representative of UNHCR; that the applicant be given sufficient time to appeal against a decision to deny him refugee status; and that the applicant be allowed to remain in the host State pending a decision on his initial request.[55] With regard to the influx *en masse* of refugees special procedures were called for which at the very least included a right of appeal or review where refugee status was denied. As an added measure of protection, it was decided that where an application for refugee status was rejected, the UNHCR should ensure that applicant's protection until an appropriate solution was found. The applicability of the principle of *non-refoulement* to mass movements was emphasized.[56]

The third recommendation dealt with the issues of illegal entry, expulsion and prohibited immigrants. It was noted that according to the laws of certain States refugees were classified as 'prohibited immigrants'. It was felt that in view of their special circumstances refugees should not be categorized as such and neither should they be subject to penalties for illegal presence or entry. This appears to be an eminently sensible suggestion since the vast majority of refugees, by the very nature of their predicament, are not in a position to comply with all legal requirements. Such conditions would not be appropriate in times of war or natural disasters nor can it be reasonably expected that a person who is being persecuted will simply be able to arrange openly for emigration. In conclusion, it was emphasized that refugees lawfully in the territory of a State Party could only be expelled in accordance with Article 32 of the UN Convention.[57] However, it should be observed that international developments in recent years have been characterized by the adoption of retrograde measures. The following may be noted: the requirement for entry and exit visas, carrier sanctions, restrictive interpretations of the refugee definition, and third country of asylum practice.[58]

Subsequent recommendations were concerned with different aspects of the treatment of refugees. Specifically, the fourth recommendation related to the detention and imprisonment of refugees. Concern was expressed that in many instances measures of detention and imprisonment aimed at refugees were not subject to administrative or judicial review. Such measures were condemned and a call was made urging States to guarantee the basic rights of refugees. The Banjul Charter might provide a remedy, however.[59]

Recommendation 5 addressed the movement of refugees and it urged African States to facilitate their movement, particularly for the purposes of study, training or resettlement. Such a recommendation was based upon Article 28 of the UN Convention and Article 6 of the OAU Convention.[60]

Recommendation 6 was concerned with the rights and obligations of refugees and of the States of asylum, addressing in particular problems relating to gainful employment and public education. The right of refugees to gainful employment and access to education is provided for by Article 17 of the UN Convention and in order to facilitate their effective implementation opportunities of access ought to be guaranteed by harmonizing national law with international law. The right of refugee children to public education was especially emphasized with a call for them to be accorded the same treatment as nationals and having access to secondary and technical education.

The importance of voluntary repatriation as a solution to the refugee problem was recognized but where the prospects of return were negligible naturalization, in accordance with Article 34 of the UN Convention, was urged as an alternative. However, it was recognized that the naturalization of refugee children presented a difficult problem which to a large extent was dependent on whether citizenship law was based on *jus soli* or *jus sanguinis*. No recommendation was made on this question.[61]

The obligation upon refugees not to engage in subversive activities against OAU Member States was reaffirmed while OAU Member States were in turn reminded of their obligation to prohibit and prevent refugees from engaging in such activities, as well as their obligation to settle refugees at a distance from their frontiers in the interests of security.[62]

Recommendation 7 exhorted African States to incorporate into national law the rights defined in the UN and OAU Conventions. In addition, it called for the refugee problem to be viewed in the wider context of human rights, a call that was heeded by the Banjul Charter.[63]

It cannot be said that the Arusha Conference constituted a great stride forward in the evolution of refugee law as such. Its recommendations, though subsequently endorsed by the OAU and UN, have no binding legal force but have mere hortatory effect, although they may also be viewed as persuasive interpretations of the provisions of the OAU Convention. Nevertheless, the Arusha Conference, in urging OAU Member States to comply more effectively with their international obligations, constituted an important expression of the political will of OAU Member States to reaffirm their legal and humanitarian obligations in accordance with the UN and OAU Conventions.

International Conferences on Assistance to Refugees in Africa – ICARA

One of the most significant developments to emerge from UN/OAU co-operation in recent years has been the International Conferences on Assistance to Refugees in Africa, known as ICARA I and ICARA II.[64] ICARA I was convened in response to OAU Assembly and UN General Assembly resolutions[65] with the object of focusing public attention on the plight of refugees in Africa; of mobilizing additional resources for refugee programmes in Africa; and of assisting States, economically and infrastructurally, burdened by the presence of large numbers of refugees. UN Member States were invited, as were UN agencies and other voluntary agencies and NGOs and national liberation movements. In total ninety-nine States attended. A plea for funds to finance UNHCR programmes in Africa was launched which succeeded in raising $567 million. Besides this practical achievement ICARA I was the first conference of its kind which brought the plight of the African refugee problem to the international community as a whole. It was acknowledged that the underlying causes of the refugee problem, which was inextricably linked with human rights violations, had to be considered.

However, problems with regard to the money pledged at ICARA I soon emerged. Certain sums were unspecified while others were earmarked for certain UN and Red Cross programmes and it was therefore argued that some pledges were not new money. In either event, ICARA I had not been a complete success in that only half the total money aimed for had in fact been raised. The Council of Ministers therefore urged further assistance to African refugees and called for a follow-up conference to ICARA I. Consequently in 1982 the UN General Assembly convened ICARA II for July 1984 to review the results of ICARA I and plan future strategy.[66]

ICARA II was again designed to increase awareness of the plight of African refugees; to obtain further financial assistance for the relief, rehabilitation and resettlement of refugees and returnees; and to emphasize the need for assistance for the social and economic infrastructure of asylum States. A list of one hundred and twenty-eight projects, including improvement of transport and energy supplies, development of agricultural education and training, health, water supplies and social development, costing a total of $362 million, was presented to the Conference. ICARA II adopted a programme for long term strategy which was envisaged to cover a period of four years, 1985 to 1989, and by the end of the Conference over a third of the required sum had been pledged. Over one hundred and twelve States participated in ICARA II and to this end many governments pledged money to assist voluntary agencies with refugee-related projects. It was also recognized that governments had to create the legal and practical conditions to encourage returnees.[67]

International Conference on the Plight of Refugees, Returnees and Displaced Persons in Southern Africa – SARRED

In August 1988 an international conference, under UN/OAU auspices,[68] was held in Oslo to highlight the burden that displaced people in southern Africa were placing on the countries of that region, and in particular, the Front-Line States. The International Conference on the Plight of Refugees, Returnees and Displaced Persons in Southern Africa (SARRED) was attended by more than one hundred UN Member States, as well as national liberation movements and NGOs. Its objectives were:

1. To bring to the attention of the international community the plight of refugees, returnees and displaced persons in Southern Africa;

2. To ensure that the international community accept to a greater extent the principles of burden sharing and international solidarity;

3. To seek increased material assistance for countries of asylum and other affected States;

4. To draft a concerted plan of action for international humanitarian intervention in the countries of the region.[69]

At its close, SARRED adopted, by consensus, a Declaration and Plan of Action on the Plight of Refugees, Returnees and Displaced Persons in southern Africa. The main conclusions of the Oslo Declaration and Plan of Action are as follows.

The Oslo Declaration declared that a lasting solution to the problems of uprooted people in Southern Africa could not come about until apartheid was abolished, South Africa's illegal occupation of Namibia was terminated and South Africa's policy of destabilization was brought to an end. Peace and national independence would bring about improved economic and social conditions. Although the new South Africa is not without its share of problems there are reasons for believing that peace in the region will be rewarded by greater prosperity.

The Declaration stated that the condition of refugees, returnees and displaced persons was a global responsibility and to this end it reaffirmed the principles of burden sharing and solidarity. At a practical level, as far as humanitarian assistance was concerned, the Declaration called for additional resources to provide urgent relief assistance. However, pursuant to ICARA II the Declaration sought to reduce the burden imposed on host countries and countries of origin and therefore emphasized the need to link relief, recovery and development assistance in order to promote self-sufficiency.

The Declaration reaffirmed the humanitarian character of the granting of asylum which was reaffirmed as an international obligation which should not be considered an unfriendly gesture. The Declaration condemned armed attacks on refugees and civilians in Southern Africa.

The Plan of Action identified four main areas where the problems of refugees, returnees and displaced persons in Southern Africa could be addressed: emergency preparedness; needs assessment and delivery of assistance; recovery and development; and mobilization of resources. The Plan of Action urged relevant international organizations to give their full co-operation and assistance to the governments concerned and called upon the international community to complement the efforts of the countries of the region through emergency and long-term assistance.

The Addis Ababa Recommendations

Held in 1994 in commemoration of the OAU Convention under the auspices of the OAU and UNHCR to review the achievements and challenges facing the Convention, the Symposium sought to draw attention to the continuing refugee crises in Africa.[70]

The Symposium started by considering the root causes of the refugee and displacement crisis in Africa and recommended that the OAU and its Member States should draw up a Plan of Action for tackling these issues, in particular, problems relating to ethnic strife, respect for human rights, good governance, the arms trade, and economic and social development. The political leadership of Africa was urged to meet the challenges of responsible and accountable government, inclusive politics and popular participation in national affairs, and progress towards civil society. To that end, the Symposium called for greater support for the OAU's activities in conflict prevention, management and resolution and urged all parties involved in armed conflict to respect humanitarian law.

The Symposium praised the progressive nature of the OAU Convention and set it as a standard to be followed by the international community. It called for its domestic implementation without diluting the obligations and standards set in the Convention.

The Symposium acknowledged that despite the liberal laws and policies on refugees throughout the continent, the nature of the problem was overwhelming the countries' ability to cope. Furthermore, financial and material support from the international community was becoming less generous. Accordingly, the Symposium reminded African governments of their legal obligations and, in particular, asked them not to close their borders, nor to refuse refugees admission nor return refugees to territories where their lives would be endangered. The international community, including the UNHCR and NGOs, was asked to provide financial, material and technical assistance so as to (i) ensure that the social and economic structures and community services of the host State were not unduly stretched; (ii) provide timely and adequate good water, shelter, sanitation and medical services; (iii) determine the refugee status of asylum seekers; (iv) assist the authorities to uphold law and order in refugee-hosting areas by dealing with the criminal elements endangering the lives of innocent refugees and civilians, and humanitarian personnel; (v) deal with illegal weapons in refugee hosting areas; and (vi) develop and strengthen national institutions dealing with refugees, develop and train human resources, and develop and strengthen technical and logistic resources.

At the same time as the refugee burden on African countries was increasing, the Symposium took note of the fact that in many countries a more restrictive interpretation of the definition of the refugee had been devised, along with the imposition of stricter migratory controls, which could deter and even deny entry to genuine refugees. The Symposium was of the view that the refugee crisis could only be properly addressed in a global and comprehensive manner and appealed for international solidarity and burden-sharing to be re-established as the norm. It therefore endorsed efforts to promote appropriate legal institutional and

operational mechanisms for the better protection and assistance of dislo-
cated people.

International Refugee Organizations

Perhaps of more immediate concern to the refugee and the displaced person is the work done and the projects put into effect by governments, the
OAU and relief organizations. A detailed study of this area is beyond the
scope of this book but because of its relevance to the OAU and Africa
generally a brief description appears necessary.

The UNHCR

Perhaps the principal humanitarian organization involved in alleviating the
suffering of refugees is the UNHCR.[71] According to Article 35 of the UN
Convention State parties are under an obligation to co-operate with the
UNHCR, an obligation reaffirmed by Article 8 of the OAU Convention and
the Arusha Conference. Given that the UNHCR is actively involved with
African refugees it appears necessary to provide a brief summary of the
UNHCR and its work.

The UNHCR was established by the UN General Assembly in 1950 for
the purpose of providing 'the necessary legal protection for refugees' and
of seeking 'permanent solutions for the problem of refugees'.[72] It is responsible to the General Assembly through ECOSOC. The UNHCR is a non-
political organization and its functions are humanitarian and social,
delivered in an impartial manner so as to facilitate its mandate. It co-
ordinates its activities with other UN organs, most recently with the UN
High Commission for Human Rights as human rights concerns are given a
higher profile,[73] and regional organizations and also relies heavily on NGOs
and voluntary agencies, notably the Red Cross, to address the problems
resulting from mass human dislocation. Broadly its functions are to human-
ize existing refugee problems and find solutions to them, and to avert new
displacements. Under Article 8(a) of its Statute, the UNHCR supervises and
promotes the application of international instruments for refugee protection,
including field missions, and its other roles include advice, negotiation and
fund raising which often assume an international aspect. As has already
been observed, the UNHCR undertakes repatriation programmes, which
encompass substantial rehabilitation and reintegration activities.[74] In
addition, the High Commissioner for Refugees and her staff plead the cause
of refugees with governments and bring problems to the attention of the
UN. In recent years the UNHCR has adopted a more proactive and comprehensive approach, in common with other relief agencies, with a view to
promoting the protection of refugees. A significant development has been

work on an early warning and preventive system to improve the UNHCR's capacity to identify, and respond to, emergencies, thus enabling prevention of mass abuses of human rights giving rise to human displacement.[75] Preventive measures have also been prioritized.[76] The UNHCR is concerned about addressing and preventing the root causes of mass exoduses, rather than simply meeting the needs of refugees, important though that is.

Since 1957, pursuant to General Assembly Resolution 1167 (XII), the High Commissioner can use her 'good offices' on behalf of persons who do not qualify for refugee status under the UN Convention but are nevertheless in a refugee-like situation, for example, internally displaced persons, an issue of increasing concern in Africa, notably in Somalia and the Sudan. In 1993 the UNHCR adopted criteria clarifying its involvement with the internally displaced, declaring that it would assume 'primary responsibility' in situations where there existed a 'direct link' with its basic activities on behalf of refugees, in particular where returnees are mingled with internally displaced populations or where there was a 'significant risk' that the internally displaced would give rise to a refugee problem.[77] The UNHCR thus provides protection and assistance to 'de facto' refugees displaced by armed conflict, even if they do not meet the strict convention definition which requires individualized determinations of persecution. Developments have meant that in practice the UNHCR is actively involved in relief work with displaced persons, such as in Africa.

In recent years the persistent conflict in the Great Lakes region has presented the UNHCR with a set of complex problems, in particular those posed by the general insecurity and violence in the refugee camps. One of the UNHCR's primary functions became the identification of potential threats to the personal security of refugees and the adoption of measures of prevention and redress. Consequently, the UNHCR deployed military and police advisers to co-operate with the national authorities in confronting this problem, including the introduction of screening procedures and separation camps. The UNHCR's other activities included maintaining camps for thousands of Burundi refugees in Tanzania, creating conditions conducive for the return of these refugees, rehabilitating the areas in the Democratic Republic of the Congo and Tanzania affected by the presence of large numbers of refugees, and finding a solution for the thousands of Rwandan refugees refusing repatriation.[78] Regrettably the scale of the humanitarian and military-politico crises in the region undermined the effectiveness of the UNHCR strategies[79] and only a durable political settlement based on respect for human rights seems likely to bring this sorry saga to a peaceful conclusion.[80]

The OAU Commission for Refugees

The OAU's involvement in the search for solutions to refugee problems has led to the creation of a couple of subsidiary bodies. In 1964 the OAU nominated a Commission of Ten for Refugees, which with some alterations has become, as the Commission of Twenty, a permanent organ of the OAU, with the task of studying all aspects of refugee problems in Africa. It has become the main policy-making organ of the OAU on refugee matters. The Commission identified a number of problems at the outset, in particular the lack of mutual trust between governments, and suggested that the OAU become involved in the repatriation of refugees. Furthermore, the Commission recommended that the countries of origin of the refugees set up investigative teams to determine the causes of flight; that favourable conditions be created for the return of refugees; and that an amnesty be granted to refugees.[81] The Commission drafted the Convention on Refugees.

One of the principal roles of the Commission of Twenty involves fact-finding missions to OAU Member States with a view to identifying the root causes of refugees in order to suggest possible practical recommendations to the refugee problem.[82] For instance, pursuant to Resolutions CM/Res. 774(XXXIV) 1980 and CM/Res. 829 (XXXVI) 1983 the Council of Ministers requested the Commission to undertake missions to a number of OAU Member States with a view to promoting the principle of burden sharing. The Commission was to emphasize the magnitude of the refugee problem and to make on-the-spot assessments of the gravity of the situation. The Commission was empowered to discuss, draw conclusions and make recommendations on, *inter alia*, work permits for refugees, fees and scholarships for refugee students; naturalization; national refugee machineries; burden sharing; the enactment of amnesty laws; and the accession to and implementation of international refugee instruments.[83]

The Commission submits its recommendations to the Council of Ministers for adoption at its ordinary sessions for subsequent discussion by the Assembly. The Commission also holds regular sessions where it considers issues relating to the practical improvement of refugee protection and finding durable solutions to the refugee problem. To that end it considers reports and briefs, including those submitted by the UNHCR.

Given the magnitude of the internal displacement problem, it has been suggested that the Commission expand its mandate specifically to deal with the question of the protection of the internally displaced.[84]

The Bureau for Refugees

The Bureau for Refugees, known until 1980 as BPEAR, was founded in 1967 by the OAU General Secretariat. The Bureau for Refugees was initially entrusted with the mandate of dealing with resettlement cases and finding educational and employment opportunities for refugees outside their first country of origin. Its structure consisted of a permanent secretariat based in Addis Ababa, linked to a network of national correspondents across Africa who were the Bureau's contacts with the national authorities.

Since 1968 the Bureau has assumed promotional functions and organized seminars and conferences, undertaken research and acted as a clearing house for information on African refugee problems. In 1974 its mandate was again expanded to enable it to assist the OAU in formulating its policy on key refugee issues and in creating more effective links with the UNHCR, from which the Bureau received funds. A further expansion occurred in 1980, and its mandate was extended to cover the issues of protection of refugees from arbitrary arrest and expulsion by their country of asylum.[85] A further restructuring occurred in 1992 and the Bureau now concentrates on education and training, research and placement but also has, to a much lesser extent, a protective jurisdiction.[86] However, the work of the Bureau is hampered by a lack of funding and a lack of operational autonomy.[87]

As has already been mentioned the Arusha Conference also adopted practical programmes designed to help African refugees. In this respect it should be noted that recommendations were adopted concerning rural and urban refugees, the employment, education and training of refugees, counselling services and policy and administrative issues.[88]

Conclusion

The legal protection afforded by the OAU to African refugees and displaced persons must be praised in view of the fact that it goes further than the generally accepted international norms, and indeed serves as a humanitarian example to the rest of the international community. It is perhaps ironic that the region with the most progressive legal instrument relating to refugees should be faced with the most intractable of refugee problems but it seems that it is because of such experiences that the OAU has sponsored progressive developments in refugee law.

Nevertheless, the refugee problem appears to be worsening and in practical terms much still needs to be done. The continent of Africa is composed of many of the poorest States in the world and they lack the financial, logistical and human resources to cope with refugees on such a large scale. Recent events in central Africa have thus seen imposed onerous burdens on receiving States, which have on occasion acted in a manner incompatible with their legal obligations. The various international conferences organized under the auspices of the UN/OAU have been partially successful in raising additional funds from the international community but the fact remains that these moneys are still insufficient. Certain aspects of the refugee problem could therefore be alleviated by providing more funds for strengthening the infrastructure of the host States, by developing more projects and by educating and retraining refugees so that they can lead productive lives. However, these measures, while ameliorating the consequences of exoduses, will not solve the root causes of the refugee problem, which, as the UNHCR consistently maintains, is the fundamental issue that must be addressed by the international community. Some causes, such as drought and crop failures, may be remedied by long term environmental programmes. Economic and social development which raises the standard of living will discourage economic refugees. Good governance, respect for the rule of law and human rights and pluralistic politics leading to a civil society should lessen repression and alienation and encourage national reconciliation. Hopefully, the Banjul Charter will help inhibit the gross violations of human rights.[89] Confidence-building measures must be put in place. Preventive presence by international organizations, such as the UN in Burundi, may deter conflicts from escalating.[90] Negotiated settlements to conflicts, achieving national reconciliation leading to the social reintegration of displaced people, must be a priority.[91] But the conflicts that form a major part of the problem cannot be tackled by the African States alone. The international community has, in various ways, the influence and the power, to assist Africa in tackling the crisis afflicting civil societies. The UNHCR has therefore observed that international solidarity is necessary in respect of countries of origin in seeking sustainable solutions as well as preventing the recurrence of the causes of human dislocation.[92]

Notes

1. The UN has established links between human rights violations and mass exoduses, see, e.g., Vienna Declaration and Programme of Action, UN Doc. A/CONF.157/23, 32 *ILM* (1993) 1661, Part I, para. 23(2); Report of the Secretary General on Human Rights and Mass Exoduses, UN Doc. E/CN.4/1996/42, pp. 4–12, 25. Ethnic and other forms of intolerance have been condemned as one of the major causes of forced migratory movements, see General Assembly resolution 41/70 (1986). Furthermore, under resolutions 1996/51 and 1997/75 the UN Commission on Human Rights recognized that human rights violations cause 'mass exoduses of populations'. In 'An Agenda for Peace' the UN Secretary-General identified the protection of human rights as a fundamental element of international peace and security, UN Doc. A/47/277-S/24111. The UN High Commissioner for Refugees has emphasized the need for the protection of the human rights of refugees and displaced persons and is, *inter alia*, seeking to ensure an international human rights presence in countries with large refugee/displaced populations, especially in locations where there is concern for their safety, such as camps, UN Doc. A/50/36. The UN High Commissioner for Human Rights has been given the mandate of, *inter alia*, addressing human rights violations giving rise to mass exoduses, UN General Assembly resolution 48/141 (1993). On the efforts made to integrate human rights perspectives into responses to emergencies, see the 1997 report of the UN Secretary-General to the UN General Assembly, UN Doc. A/52/494.

2. *The State of the World's Refugees* (1995) Annex II, Table I.
3. R. Plender, *International Migration Law* (1972) p. 215; Prince Sadruddin Aga Khan, 'Legal Problems Relating to Refugees and Displaced Persons', 49 *Hague Recueil* (1976) 287 at pp. 295–300; G.S. Goodwin-Gill, *The Refugee in International Law* (2nd edn, 1996) Chapter 1.
4. This definition is based upon that found in Article 6A(ii) of the Statute of the Office of the UN High Commissioner for Refugees, General Assembly resolution 428 (V) 1950. See also, Goodwin-Gill, note 3 *supra*, ibid. It appears that four categories of refugees are covered by this definition, see *R. v. Secretary of State for the Home Department, ex parte Adan* [1998] 2 WLR 702, which proceeded to make it clear that the UN Convention extends to the persecution of groups and not just individuals. It is interesting to note that the definition of the term 'well-founded fear' has proved problematic. The United Kingdom's House of Lords in *R. v. Secretary of State for the Home Department, ex parte Sivakumaran et al.* [1988] 2 WLR 92 interpreted the phrase as having an objective meaning, in that the applicant for refugee status had to demonstrate a reasonable degree of likelihood of persecution and that the fear of persecution had to be objectively determined in the light of existing circumstances, thereby overruling the Court of Appeal which had interpreted the term subjectively, [1987] 3 WLR 1047. However, the US Supreme Court appears to have adopted a combination of both elements in a definition that corresponds with that of the UNHCR. In *Immigration and Naturalization Service v. Cardoza-Fonseca* (1987) 107 S. Ct. 1207 the Court stated that well-founded fear was demonstrated by proving actual fear and good reason for that fear, looking at the situation from the point of view of one of reasonable courage in like circumstances of the applicant for refugee status. See also paragraph 42 of the *Handbook on Procedures and Criteria for Determining Refugee Status* published by the UNHCR in 1979; Goodwin-Gill, note 3 *supra*, pp. 33, 34. See further Plender, note 3 *supra*, pp. 415–24. It must be noted that in recent years a more restrictive definition of the concept of the refugee has arisen. For instance, concepts such as 'safe countries of origin', 'temporary protection', 'safety zones', 'in-country processing' and 'safe return' have been developed, see, e.g., Dublin Convention Determining the State Responsible for Asylum Lodged in one of the Member States of the European Communities 1990; Goodwin-Gill, note 3 *supra*, pp. 336–44, Annexe 2.13.
5. Article 1F(a), (b) and (c); Goodwin-Gill, note 3 *supra*, pp. 59–66. It is interesting to note that the UNHCR has denied refugee status to Rwandans indicted by the International Tribunal for Rwanda, UN Doc. E/CN.4/1997/SR.30, para. 6. It should be observed that the Tribunal has found as established accusations of genocide and crimes against humanity, *The Prosecutor v. Akayesu* 37 *ILM* 1399 (1998); *The Prosecutor v. Kambanda* 37 *ILM* 1411 (1998).
6. L.-G. Eriksson, G. Melander, and P. Nobel, (eds.) *An Analysing Account of the Conference on the African Refugee Problem, Arusha, May 1979* (1981) p. 9; F. Hofman, 'Refugee Law in the African Context', 52 *ZaöRV* (1992) 318 at pp. 320–1. By way of contrast, it is common ground that under the UN Convention victims of war and other armed conflicts are not *per se* refugees, *R. v. Secretary of State, ex parte Adan* [1998] 2 WLR 702; *Handbook on Procedures and Criteria for Determining Refugee Status*, note 4 *supra*, para. 164; J. Hathaway, *The Law of Refugee Status* (1991) p. 185. See also, *Vilvarajah v. United Kingdom* Ser. A, Vol. 215 (1991) para. 105. An EU resolution adopted in 1995 states, 'Reference to a civil war or violent internal conflict and the dangers they present is not sufficient to justify recognition as a refugee', *The Guardian* (London), 25 November 1995, p. 15.
7. Text of the OAU Convention in *Naldi*, p. 101.
8. See R.M. D'Sa, 'The African Refugee Problem, Relevant International Conventions and Recent Activities of the Organization of African Unity', 31 *NILR* (1984)

378 at pp. 380–4. It is interesting to note that in the Cartagena Declaration 1984 the Latin American States referred to the necessity of broadening the concept of the refugee, Goodwin-Gill, note 3 *supra*, pp. 20, 21. Ethnicity and class appear to have been root causes of the conflicts in Burundi and Rwanda in the early 1990s when hundreds of thousands were massacred in frenzied bouts of 'ethnic cleansing', UN Doc. E/CN.4/1995/50/Add.2. It must be made clear that all these instruments are restricted to persons who have left their country of origin or nationality and do not apply to internally displaced persons who, although frequently forced to flee their homes for the same reasons as refugees, cannot qualify as bona fide 'refugees' because they remain within national frontiers. Internally displaced persons have been defined as, 'Persons who have been forced to flee their homes suddenly or unexpectedly in large numbers, as a result of armed conflict, internal strife, systematic violations of human rights or natural or man-made disasters; and who are within the territory of their own country', Analytical Report of the Secretary-General on internally displaced persons, UN Doc. E/CN.4/1992/23, para. 17. See further, Report of the Representative of the Secretary-General on internally displaced persons, UN Doc. E/CN.4/1999/79, para. 11. There are an estimated 10 million internally displaced persons in Africa alone, and the problem is particularly acute in Somalia, Sudan and Rwanda; Addis Ababa Document on Refugees and Forced Population Displacements in Africa, 8–10 September 1994, and Burundi, UN Doc. E/CN.4/1995/50/Add.2. Although the UN General Assembly has acknowledged that victims of natural disasters and similar emergency situations are of concern to the international community, see resolutions 43/131 and 46/182, there is no specific universal legal instrument providing for their protection, UN Commission on Human Rights, Report of the Representative of the Secretary-General Mr. Francis Deng, UN Doc. E/CN.4/1996/52/Add.2. See, further, F.M. Deng, 'The International Protection of the Internally Displaced', 7 *IJRL* (1995) 74. However, in 1998 Mr. Deng submitted a report drafting Guiding Principles on Internal Displacement identifying the rights and guarantees relevant to the protection of the internally displaced, UN Doc. E/CN.4/1998/53/Add.2 since widely adopted, UN Doc. E/CN.4/1999/79.

9. See note 2 *supra*.
10. Goodwin-Gill, note 3 *supra*, Chapter 4; Plender, note 3 *supra*, pp. 425–33. The scope of the principle of *non-refoulement* has been greatly limited by the decision of the US Supreme Court in *Sale, Acting Commissioner, INS* v *Haitian Centers Council* 113 S.Ct. 2549 (1993), which sanctioned the return of Haitian refugees found on the high seas. It is doubtful whether this highly criticized decision reflects good law.
11. ICJ Reports 1950, p. 266.
12. Goodwin-Gill, note 3 *supra*, Chapter 5; Plender, note 3 *supra*, pp. 394–415. See also *Vilvarajah* v. *United Kingdom* Ser. A, Vol. 215 (1991) para. 102. However, it should be observed that the Vienna Declaration and Programme of Action makes reference to the right to seek and enjoy asylum from persecution in other countries, Part I, para. 23.
13. General Assembly resolution 2198 (XXI) 1966.
14. Algeria, Angola, Benin, Botswana, Burkina Faso, Burundi, Cameroon, Cape Verde (Protocol only), Central African Republic, Chad, Congo, Democratic Republic of the Congo, Côte d'Ivoire, Djibouti, Egypt, Equatorial Guinea, Ethiopia, Gabon, Gambia, Ghana, Guinea, Guinea-Bissau, Kenya, Lesotho, Liberia, Madagascar (Convention only), Malawi, Mali, Mauritania, Mozambique, Namibia (Convention only), Niger, Nigeria, Rwanda, São Tomé e Príncipe, Senegal, Seychelles, Sierra Leone, Somalia, South Africa, Sudan, Swaziland (Pro-

tocol only), Tanzania, Togo, Tunisia, Uganda, Zambia and Zimbabwe. Note that Morocco is a party to both treaties.

15. In the United Kingdom the determination of refugee status falls within the jurisdiction of the Home Secretary and the decision cannot usually be challenged, see, e.g., *R. v. Secretary of State for the Home Department, ex parte Bugdaycay* [1987] AC 514; *R. v. Secretary of State for the Home Department, ex parte H, The Times*, 24 March 1988. However, in *In Re Musisi* [1987] AC 514 the House of Lords held that although the question whether a danger of persecution exists is a matter for the Home Secretary his decision can be reviewed by the courts if improper consideration has been given or he has acted irrationally or unlawfully. This situation was deemed acceptable by the European Court of Human Rights in *Vilvarajah* v. *United Kingdom* Ser. A, Vol. 215 (1991) para. 123.

16. See note 4 *supra*.

17. Articles 13, 15, 17, 18, 19 and 21 respectively of the UN Convention. See further, Prince Aga Khan, note 3 *supra*, pp. 322–7.

18. Articles 16, 22 and 24 respectively of the UN Convention.

19. Goodwin-Gill, note 3 *supra*, Chapter 4. In *R. v. Secretary of State for the Home Department, ex parte Mendis, The Times*, 18 June 1988, the English Court of Appeal rejected the view of the UNHCR that where it could reasonably be assumed that a person's opinions would sooner or later find expression and that as a result he would come into conflict with the authorities, he could be considered to have fear of persecution for reasons of political opinion. Balcombe LJ stated that a person was not at risk of being persecuted for his political opinions if no events which would attract persecution had yet taken place. If that were not so, a person could become a refugee as a matter of his own choice. Note, however, that this obligation does not appear to prohibit a State from deporting an asylum seeker to a third State offering refuge. In *R. v. Immigration Appeal Tribunal, ex parte Miller, The Times*, 25 February 1988, the English Court of Appeal upheld the denial of asylum to a Jewish South African whose opposition to apartheid had led him to become a conscientious objector, a criminal offence punishable by imprisonment in South Africa, because he could go to Israel, although he did not in fact wish to go there. See further, Article 3(5) of the Dublin Convention.

20. UN Docs. E/CN.4/1995/50/Add.2, E/CN.4/1996/42, para. 35. The jurisprudence of the European Court of Human Rights suggests a strict approach to the claims of asylum seekers, see *Cruz-Varas* v. *Sweden* Series A, Vol. 201 (1991); *Vilvarajah* v. *United Kingdom* Series A, Vol. 215 (1991); and further, Goodwin-Gill, note 3 *supra*, pp. 315–21. Humanitarian law might also be applicable so that those not participating directly in hostilities must be treated humanely, see Article 3 common to the Geneva Conventions 1949, UN Doc. E/CN.4/1996/52/Add.2, paras. 21–23.

21. CM/Res. 19(II); now the Commission of Twenty, see further *supra*, p. 97.

22. CM/Res. 36 (III).

23. AHG/Res. 26(II).

24. Article 11.

25. Algeria, Angola, Benin, Botswana, Burkina Faso, Burundi, Cameroon, Cape Verde, Central African Republic, Chad, Congo, Democratic Republic of the Congo, Egypt, Equatorial Guinea, Ethiopia, Gabon, Gambia, Ghana, Guinea, Guinea-Bissau, Kenya, Lesotho, Liberia, Libya, Malawi, Mali, Mauritania, Mozambique, Niger, Nigeria, Rwanda, Senegal, Seychelles, Sierra Leone, South Africa, Sudan, Swaziland, Tanzania, Togo, Tunisia, Uganda, Zambia and Zimbabwe. Côte d'Ivoire, Madagascar, Mauritius and Somalia have signed but not ratified the OAU Convention and are therefore under a duty to abstain from acting in a manner contrary to the Convention, see Article 18 Vienna Conven-

tion on the Law of Treaties. Note that Morocco has ratified the Convention and still appears to be a party to it although according to Article 10(3) only OAU Member States are eligible. Only the SADR has failed to sign an international refugee law convention. On the OAU Convention see further, A.A. Aiboni, *Protection of Refugees in Africa* (1978); E.O. Awuku, 'Refugee Movements in Africa and the OAU Convention on Refugees', 39 *JAL* (1995) 79; Office of the UNHCR, 'Issues and Challenges in International Protection in Africa', 7 *International Journal of Refugee Law* (1995) 55; Hofman, note 6 *supra*.

26. In 1994 the world witnessed one of the worst tragedies in recent times in Rwanda. Since independence Rwanda has been racked by ethnic conflict. The assassination of President Habyarimana on 6 April 1994 led to widespread and systematic human rights violations against the Tutsi minority and moderate Hutus by Hutu extremists (Interahamwe). Hundreds of thousands were killed in massacres amounting to genocide. Millions of Tutsis and Hutus were displaced, both within and outside the country. By October 1994 some 1.5 million refugees were camping in neighbouring countries such as Tanzania. Hutu civilians in turn faced revenge killings as the RPF invaded from Uganda and took control of the country. Although the RPF government established its authority throughout the country and human rights violations decreased substantially, the refugee problem persisted as fear of reprisals by the new government and manipulation by the former political elite impeded the return of many refugees. The apparent elimination of the Interahamwe threat, assisted in part by the demise of the corrupt Mobutu regime in Zaïre which was fatally undermined by the Rwandan conflict when a rebellion erupted in October 1996 as Zaïrean Tutsis (Banyamulenge) fought the Interahamwe in the refugee camps, is aiding a return to normality. See UN Doc. E/CN.4/1997/61; *The State of the World's Refugees*, note 2 *supra*, pp. 32, 3, 121–3. It should also be observed that the neighbouring country of Burundi also experienced inter-communal violence between Tutsis and Hutus at this time, leading to massacres and mass displacement, following an attempted *coup d'état* in October 1993 and the assassination of President Ndadaye in April 1994, UN Doc. E/CN.4/1995/50/Add.2. On the human rights situation in the Great Lakes region, including what was eastern Zaïre, see, e.g., UN Docs. E/CN.4/1996/66, E/CN.4/1996/69, A/52/505.

27. The ongoing civil war in Southern Sudan that has been waged for most years of Sudanese independence has intensified since the current government came to power following a military *coup d'état* in 1989. The country is divided between an Islamic, Arabist north and a Christian and animist black south. The latter claim to be fighting a war of self-determination. All parties to the conflict have been accused of gross violations of human rights, particularly the government which has resorted to the indiscriminate aerial bombardment of civilians. The UNHCR estimates that there are some 600,000 southern Sudanese refugees in the neighbouring countries of Uganda, Ethiopia, Kenya and the Democratic Republic of the Congo. There are also large numbers of internally displaced in camps around Khartoum. See UN Commission on Human Rights, Situation of Human Rights in the Sudan, Report of the Special Rapporteur, Mr. Gaspar Biro, UN Docs. E/CN.4/1996/62, E/CN.4/1997/58, E/CN.4/1988/66. See further, UN Docs. A/49/539, annex, A/52/510.

28. Article 1(5). This provision would presumably be applicable to those such as the criminal elements and the Hutu militants (Interahamwe) implicated in the genocide of the Tutsi minority and Hutu moderates in Rwanda in 1994 who infiltrated refugee camps within and without Rwanda to maintain a destabilizing climate of insecurity. In many cases camps were closed down. The International Tribunal on Rwanda is seeking the extradition of some of these

individuals for alleged complicity in massacres, such persons being automatically excluded from asylum by the UNHCR and national authorities, UN Doc.
E/CN.4/1997/61, pp. 38–40. See further note 5 *supra*.

29. Awuku, note 25 *supra*, pp. 82, 83; Hofman, note 6 *supra*, pp. 324–5. The preamble to the OAU Convention makes express reference to the UN Declaration on
Territorial Asylum 1967, General Assembly resolution 2312 (XXII). The text can
be found in Goodwin-Gill, note 3 *supra*, Annexe VI. See further note 12 *supra*.

30. Article 3(2). See also, Articles 32(2) and 33(2) of the UN Convention according
to which a refugee may be expelled on grounds of national security or public
order, see, e.g., *R. v. Secretary of State for the Home Department, ex parte H*, *The
Times*, 24 March 1988. See further, Goodwin-Gill, note 3 *supra*, Chapter 4. The
UN Commission on Human Rights has stated that the principle of *non-refoulement* is not subject to derogation, resolution 1997/75, preambular paragraph.
These provisions thus gave the UNHCR the legal authority to deny refugee
status to those implicated in human rights abuses in the Great Lakes region of
Central Africa, see notes 5 and 28 *supra*.

31. Note, however, the UN Draft Convention on Territorial Asylum, in Goodwin-
Gill, note 3 *supra*, Annexe 4.1. Latin America, however, has reached agreement
on the question of asylum and the outcome has been two treaties which confer
asylum on individuals who are persecuted in their States of origin for their
beliefs, opinions, or political affiliations, or for acts which may be considered as
political offences, and which recognize asylum granted on diplomatic premises,
see Caracas Convention on Territorial Asylum 1954 and Caracas Convention on
Diplomatic Asylum 1954. For texts, see Goodwin-Gill, note 3 *supra*, Annexes 2.3
and 2.4.

32. D'Sa, note 8 *supra*, p. 387; Goodwin-Gill, note 3 *supra*, Chapter 5; Prince Aga
Khan, note 3 *supra*, pp. 316–22.

33. D'Sa, note 8 *supra*, pp. 387–9; Goodwin-Gill, note 3 *supra*, Chapter 4; Hofman,
note 6 *supra*, ibid.

34. However, it has been suggested that this is not in fact the case, D'Sa, note 8
supra, p. 388.

35. See note 28 *supra*.

36. However, note the mass expulsion of Ghanaian citizens by Nigeria in 1983, see
Keesing's, Vol. 30 (1984) pp. 32609–11. It would appear that the mass expulsions
of migrant workers occurs frequently in Africa, UN Doc. A/50/476, annex,
para. 101. During the apartheid era in South Africa, entire racial groups would
be expelled, forcibly relocated in designated areas, usually the nominally independent homelands, and deprived of their nationality so as to prevent the
exercise of their right to return, UN Doc. E/CN.4/Sub.2/1993/17, para. 226.
More recently, ethnic confrontations in what was eastern Zaïre (now Democratic
Republic of the Congo) between indigenous ethnic groups and ethnic groups
originating from Rwanda who had settled there following several waves of
migration over many years caused the displacement of populations, UN Doc.
E/CN.4/1996/66.

37. UN Doc. E/CN.4/1996/16. The exodus of refugees towards inhospitable areas
with difficult access for humanitarian organizations also occurred elsewhere in
the region, UN Doc. E/CN.4/1997/61.

38. UN Doc. E/CN.4/1996/66. In addition, when refugees, internally displaced
persons and returnees crowd into the same area, competing for scarce
resources, conflicts sometimes erupt, as happened in northern Burundi, UN
Doc. E/CN.4/1995/50/Add.2.

39. UN Docs. E/CN.4/1996/7, E/CN.4/1997/SR.46, para. 57. One of the UNHCR's
objectives in its Great Lakes Operation has been to assist the Tanzanian government in meeting its responsibilities under international refugee law. However,

as has been seen, the Hutu extremists present in the camps fomenting unrest not only undermines their status as legitimate refugees but also presents the authorities with a security dilemma. It has therefore been pointed out that host States failing to curb the subversive activities of such gangs would be in breach of their international obligations towards their neighbours, see C. Anyangwe, 'Obligations of States Parties to the African Charter on Human and Peoples' Rights', 10 *RADIC* (1998) 625 at p. 651. The UNHCR has consequently been working with the authorities in the region to implement security measures in the camps to ensure their civilian nature, although not always very successfully, UN Doc. E/CN.4/1997/61, pp. 38–40.

40. UN Doc. E/CN.4/1996/7. Refugee camps in Burundi were similarly affected, UN Doc. E/CN.4/1995/50/Add.2.

41. UN Doc. E/CN/4/1997/61, pp. 34, 35. However, the UN Commission on Human Rights has expressed concern at the widespread violation of the principle of *non-refoulement* with refugees being expelled in highly dangerous situations, resolution 1997/75, preambular paragraph.

42. UN Docs. E/CN/4/1997/61, pp. 34, 35, E/CN.4/1997/SR.46, para. 56. The UN Security Council has condemned the massacre of refugees in the Great Lakes region, resolution 1161 (1998). Since situations giving rise to population displacements are likely to be governed by states of emergency or exception, reasonable restrictions may be placed on the freedom of movement and residence of refugees in the interests of public order, see, e.g., Articles 4 and 12(3) ICCPR.

43. Awuku, note 25 *supra*, pp. 83, 84. For text of the Declaration, see *Naldi*, p. 57. This obligation is reinforced by Article 23(2) of the Banjul Charter. See also Article 2 of the UN Convention. It has therefore been suggested that priority is given to peaceful co-existence over refugee rights, Anyangwe, note 39 *supra*, pp. 650, 651. Under the Arusha Accords, the Governments of Burundi, Tanzania, Uganda and Zaïre agreed to the non-use of territories of other States as bases for destabilizing Rwanda, UN Doc. E/CN.4/1995/50/Add.2, para. 42.

44. UN Doc. E/CN.4/1995/50/Add.4, p. 3. In resolution 1161 (1998) the UN Security Council acknowledged the threat to the stability of the region posed by malicious propaganda.

45. UN Doc. E/CN.4/1997/61, pp. 36–40.

46. It should be observed that the UNHCR operates, *inter alia*, subject to repatriation principles which emphasize facilitation and promotion of voluntary repatriation, see Goodwin-Gill, note 3 *supra*, pp. 270–5, 438; B.S. Chimni, 'The Meaning of Words and the Role of the UNCHR in Voluntary Repatriation', 5 *IJRL* (1993) 442; M. Zieck, *UNHCR and Voluntary Repatriation of Refugees: A Legal Analysis* (1997). It is interesting to note that the Vienna Declaration and Programme of Action reaffirms the right to return to one's country, Part I, para. 23.

47. It is interesting to note that it has been suggested that the internally displaced should have access to the African Commission on Human and Peoples' Rights for redress for violations of human rights, and that the African Commission should conduct site visits to the camps of the displaced, Seminar on the Protection of African Refugees and Internally Displaced Persons, African Commission on Human and Peoples' Rights, Harare, February 1994, UN Doc. E/CN.4/1995/50, p. 59.

48. See Article 14 of the Banjul Charter which guarantees the right to property, and further, Chapter 4 *infra*, pp. 126–7. See further, UN Doc. E/CN.4/1996/52/Add.2, paras. 270–83. There have been numerous reports of violations of property rights in Rwanda, UN Doc. E/CN.4/1997/61, pp. 20–2.

49. UN Doc. E/CN.4/1997/61, pp. 38–40.

50. See Chapter 2 *supra*, p. 72.

51. See, Article 13(2) UDHR; Article 12(2) ICCPR; *East African Asians* v. *United Kingdom* (1981) 3 EHRR 76. The Vienna Declaration and Programme of Action reaffirms the right to return to one's country, Part I, para. 23(3), (4). In resolution 1994/24, on 'The right to freedom of movement', the Sub-Commission on Prevention of Discrimination and Protection of Minorities reaffirmed the right of refugees to return to their country of origin in safety and dignity.
52. On refugee law in the domestic law of African States, see Refugees Studies Programme, Final Report: Implementation of the OAU/UN Conventions and Domestic Legislation Concerning the Rights and Obligations of Refugees in Africa 1–28 September 1986 (Queen Elizabeth House, Oxford University). Thus, Botswana, Lesotho, Ghana, Malawi, South Africa and Zimbabwe have enacted, or are in the process of enacting, legislation to implement the international conventions.
53. REF/AR/CONF/Rpt./rec. 1/1–16. See also Eriksson, Melander and Nobel, note 6 *supra*; D'Sa, note 8 *supra*, pp. 390–5. The Recommendations were endorsed by the OAU Assembly and the UN General Assembly, CM/Res. 727 (XXXIII), and Resolution 34/61 (1979) respectively.
54. REF/AR/CONF/CTTEE. A/Rpt./Dec. 2. See also Eriksson, Melander and Nobel, note 6 *supra*, pp. 17–21, 36, 47, 48.
55. See Eriksson, Melander and Nobel, note 6 *supra*, p. 49.
56. REF/AR/CONF/CTTEE. A/Rpt./Dec. 1; Eriksson, Melander and Nobel, note 6 *supra.*, pp. 21, 48, 49.
57. REF/AR/CONF/CTTEE. A/Rpt./Dec. 2; Eriksson, Melander and Nobel, note 6 *supra*, pp. 21, 49.
58. Goodwin-Gill, note 3 *supra*, *passim*. See also note 4 *supra*.
59. It is instructive to note that asylum does not appear to be considered a civil right for the purposes of the European Convention on Human Rights, Goodwin-Gill, note 3 *supra*, p. 321. See also note 20 *supra*.
60. REF/AR/CONF/CTTEE. A/Rpt./Dec. 4; Eriksson, Melander and Nobel, note 6 *supra*, ibid.
61. Eriksson, Melander and Nobel, note 6 *supra*, p. 25.
62. REF/AR/CONF/CTTEE. A/Rpt./Dec. 4; Eriksson, Melander and Nobel, note 6 *supra*, pp. 23, 24, 52. See further, *supra*, pp. 84–5.
63. REF/AR/CONF/CTTEE. A/Rpt./Dec. 6; Eriksson, Melander and Nobel, note 6 *supra*, pp. 24, 52.
64. D'Sa, note 8 *supra*, pp. 395, 396.
65. CM/Res. 814 (XXXV) 1980; resolution 35/42 (1980) respectively.
66. See resolution 37/197 (1982).
67. D'Sa, note 8 *supra*, pp. 395, 396.
68. See UN General Assembly resolution 42/106 (1987) which endorsed the OAU's decision to convene an international conference.
69. *Refugees*, No 55, July-August 1988 (published by UNHCR).
70. See note 2 *supra*. It should also be observed that the Recommendations urged governments to carry out their responsibilities to the internally displaced and called upon parties to conflicts to allow humanitarian organizations access to the displaced.
71. On the UNHCR see, Goodwin-Gill, note 3 *supra*, Chapter 6, para. 1; Prince Aga Khan, note 3 *supra*, pp. 334–50. See also, P. Macalister-Smith, *International Humanitarian Assistance: Disaster Relief Actions in International Law and Organization* (1985).
72. Statute of the Office of the UN High Commissioner for Refugees, General Assembly Resolution 428 (V) 1950. The UNHCR would appear to be a subsidiary organ of the UN in accordance with Article 22 of the UN Charter. Under resolution 47/105 (1992) the General Assembly has additionally authorized the

UNHCR to provide protection and assistance to internally displaced persons, especially where they live alongside refugees and returnees under the care of the UNHCR. For the UNHCR's criteria for involvement with internally displaced persons, see *UNHCR's Operational Experience with Internally Displaced Persons* (1994) Annex 1 and Guiding Principles, note 8 *supra*.

73. Under General Assembly resolution 48/141 (1993) the UN High Commissioner for Human Rights was mandated with, *inter alia*, co-operating with the UNHCR so as to pay particular attention to situations which could cause mass exoduses and to contribute to efforts to address such situations effectively through protection measures, emergency preparedness and response mechanisms. See also UN Commission on Human Rights, resolution 1997/75. Although humanitarian action and protection of human rights have become increasingly intertwined in recent years, particularly in Africa, the UN High Commissioner for Refugees has cautioned against a merging of functions as the perception of the UNHCR being actively involved in the investigation and prosecution of human rights violations could jeopardize the safety of humanitarian personnel, UN Doc. E/CN.4/1995/SR.13, p. 4. Nevertheless, the UN Secretary-General has emphasized that the protection and promotion of human rights must be further integrated into the work of relief agencies, UN Doc. E/CN.4/1996/42, para. 116.

74. UN Doc. E/CN.4/1997/43/Add.1, para. 68. The UNHCR has further stated that sustainable solutions can only come about through comprehensive and effective rehabilitation and reconstruction programmes, Note on International Protection, UN Doc. A/AC.96/850.

75. UN Doc. A/50/566. See also the view of the UN Secretary-General, UN Doc. E/CN.4/1996/42, para. 118. The UN High Commission for Human Rights has similarly emphasized the adoption of early warning measures to prevent mass exoduses as a result of human rights violations, UN Doc. E/CN.4/1998/51, pp. 10–12. One example has been Burundi, where in 1995 the High Commissioner for Refugees deployed human rights observers with the consent of the government, UN Doc. E/CN.4/1996/42, para. 92. In Rwanda HRFOR (Human Rights Field Operation in Rwanda) was established with a mandate to rebuild confidence with the aim of eventual national reconciliation. HRFOR was to investigate the genocide and other human rights abuses, establish field officers to monitor the human rights situation throughout the country, and initiate promotional activities in the field of human rights, including rebuilding the Rwandan administration of justice, UN Doc. E/CN.4/1996/111.

76. UN Doc. E/CN.4/1998/51, pp. 12–14. See also the view of the UN Secretary-General, UN Doc. E/CN.4/1996/42, para. 117.

77. UN Doc. E/CN.4/1995/50, para. 144, endorsed by General Assembly resolution 48/116 (1993).

78. UN Doc. E/CN.4/1997/61, pp. 38–40. One of the problems impeding voluntary repatriation to Rwanda has been the frequent arbitrary detention of returnees, UN Doc. E/CN.4/1996/68.

79. UN Doc. E/CN.4/1997/61, pp. 32–40. The parties to the conflict appear to have found a convenient scapegoat in the UNHCR, blaming it for many of the humanitarian disasters that have occurred, UN Doc. E/CN.4/1997/6/Add.2, p. 12. However, responsibility primarily lies with the principal States and rebel actors who have demonstrated an enduring unwillingness to put an end to the fighting. At the time of writing the conflict is ongoing.

80. UN Doc. E/CN.4/1997/61, paras. 193–5.

81. C.O.C. Amate, *Inside the OAU: Pan-Africanism in Practice* (1986) pp. 462, 463; J. Oloka-Onyango, 'The Place and Role of the OAU Bureau for Refugees in the African Refugee Crisis', 6 *IJRL* (1994) 34.

82. See, e.g., *African Refugees*, No. 7, 1985 (published by OAU); Oloka-Onyango, note 81 *supra*, 38, 39.

83. *African Refugees*, Nos. 3 and 4, 1983 (published by OAU).

84. Seminar on the Protection of African Refugees and Internally Displaced Persons, African Commission on Human and Peoples' Rights, Harare, February 1994, UN Doc. E/CN.4/1995/50, p. 59. There have been recent calls for the OAU to adopt, promote and disseminate the Guiding Principles on Internal Displacement, note 8 *supra*, UN Doc. E/CN.4/1999/79, pp. 6–7, 22–3.

85. CM/Res. 727 (XXXIII); REF/AR/CONF./Rpt. 1.

86. Oloka-Onyango, note 81 *supra*, pp. 43 et seq.

87. Ibid., pp. 46 et seq.

88. Eriksson, Melander and Nobel, note 6 *supra*, pp. 53–60.

89. It should be common ground that human rights and humanitarian law must be respected. The High Commissioner for Refugees has emphasized the need for the continued protection of the human rights of refugees, UN Doc. A/50/36. An aspect of this has been calls to reverse the effects of 'ethnic cleansing' and a return to pluralistic society, e.g., that neighbourhoods in the Burundian capital, Bujumbura, which were previously ethnically mixed, be rehabilitated, UN Doc. A/50/18. The African Commission on Human and Peoples' Rights has urged the recognition of the right of humanitarian assistance of victims of war and displaced persons, Seminar on the Protection of African Refugees and Internally Displaced Persons, African Commission on Human and Peoples' Rights, Harare, February 1994, UN Doc. E/CN.4/1995/50, paras. 112, 115.

90. UN Doc. E/CN.4/1996/42, pp. 20, 21. In resolution 1993/70 the UN Commission on Human Rights refers to preventive diplomacy in the areas of human rights and humanitarian assistance as a means of averting new massive flows of refugees and displaced persons. See also UN General Assembly resolution 48/135 (1993) which urged all States to ensure effective implementation of international human rights instruments as a means to such an end.

91. UNHCR, Note on International Protection, UN Doc. A/AC.96/850. See, for example, UN Security Council resolution 1097 (1997) which endorsed a peace plan for eastern Zaïre. It called for the immediate cessation of hostilities, withdrawal of external forces, reaffirmation of respect for the territorial integrity and national sovereignty of Zaïre and other States in the region, protection for all refugees and displaced persons, and peaceful settlement of the crisis through dialogue.

92. UNHCR, Note on International Protection, UN Doc. A/AC.96/850. See further the view of the Secretary-General, UN Doc. E/CN.4/1996/42, para. 120. See also the Vienna Declaration and Programme of Action which reaffirms the right to return to one's country, Part I, para. 23(3), (4).

4

The African Charter on Human and Peoples' Rights

In June 1981 the Assembly of Heads of States and Governments meeting in Nairobi unanimously adopted the African Charter on Human and Peoples' Rights, better known as the Banjul Charter. The Banjul Charter did not come into force for a further five years, until October 1986, which in terms of international relations should not be considered an inordinate length of time, indeed it indicates a remarkable degree of consensus among the African States. A human rights document for Africa had nevertheless been in gestation for some considerable time.

The post-war era witnessed a concerted effort being made in the area of the protection of human rights, in particular through the adoption of international documents such as the UN Charter and specifically the Universal Declaration of Human Rights 1948 of the UN, which although non-binding *qua* treaty may be said to have reflected and/or generated customary international law.[1] Since then, a number of legally binding documents, such as the Council of Europe's European Convention on Human Rights 1950 (in force 1953), the UN's International Covenants on Economic, Social and Cultural Rights, and Civil and Political Rights 1966 (in force 1976), and the OAS's American Convention on Human Rights 1969 (in force 1978), have been adopted and have had a measure of success in protecting and promoting human rights.

This progress was not, however, matched in Africa to the same extent. Decolonization was still in its infancy and the young States jealously guarded their independence. The international protection of human rights was seen by some as a legacy of imperialism, blind to cultural diversity, or simply an excuse by the West to interfere in their internal affairs.[2] Yet the need for the protection of human rights was self-evident. The atrocities perpertrated by Idi Amin in Uganda (1971 to 1979), Bokassa in the Central African Empire (1966 to 1979), and Nguema in Equatorial Guinea (1969 to 1979), and the repercussions of *apartheid* on Southern Africa, made the strengthening of fundamental rights imperative. In addition, in a region where one-party rule and even personal rule was often the norm and where military intervention in politics even now seems to occur all too frequently, it has often been the case that constitutionalism and the rule of law have not been observed.[3] Furthermore, many African States have been of the view that certain basic collective, or second generation, rights, such as health, housing, food and work, must take precedence over civil and political rights. These conflicting philosophies delayed agreement on the precise nature of the rights to be safeguarded but the question had been under consideration for many years.

In 1961 African jurists met at the Lagos Conference on the Rule of Law under the auspices of the International Commission of Jurists. The Conference drafted a resolution known as the Law of Lagos which relied on the traditional exposition of civil and political rights.[4] The idea of an African human rights institution was launched at this event. In its preamble the Law of Lagos declares:

> That in order to give full effect to the Universal Declaration of Human Rights of 1948, this conference invites the African Governments to study the possibility of adopting an African Convention on Human Rights in such a manner that the conclusions of this conference will be safeguarded by the creation of a court of appropriate jurisdiction and that the recourse thereto be available for all persons under the jurisdiction of the signatory states.

This proposal did not find much favour in this era of decolonization when the emphasis of the young States was on the principles of sovereignty and non-interference. Nonetheless the OAU Charter does make reference to human rights. In the preamble the African States reaffirm their adherence to the principles of the UN Charter and UDHR and declare that freedom, equality, justice and dignity are essential objectives for the achievement of the legitimate aspirations of the African peoples. The OAU Charter itself pays regard to the UN Charter and UDHR and it urges Member States to co-operate in the fields of, *inter alia*, economics, education and culture, and health, sanitation and nutrition. In addition, the OAU Charter endorses the principle of self-determination by condemning colonialism and seeking the emancipation of the dependent African territories.

In 1969 the OAU took a significant step towards the protection of human rights by adopting the Convention on Refugee Problems in Africa. While many African States were already parties to the Geneva Convention on the Status of Refugees 1951 and the 1967 Protocol, the OAU felt it necessary to draft a regional complement dealing with the particular problems of African refugees. In many ways the OAU Convention constitutes an improvement on the rights protected under the Geneva Convention and Protocol.[5]

Nevertheless, the search for a human rights document proper continued. In 1967, on a Nigerian initiative, the UN Commission on Human Rights took up the call for the creation of African human rights institutions, and specifically in Resolution 24 (XXXIV) of 8 March 1972 it invited the OAU to create a regional human rights commission, a call it repeated in 1978.

This development was followed by a number of important conferences held in various parts of Africa which contributed to an increasing awareness of human rights issues in Africa, in particular in Cairo (1969), Addis Ababa (1971) and Dar-es-Salaam (1973). But of special significance was a colloquium of African jurists held in Dakar in 1978 which succeeded in drafting concrete proposals for a human rights document. President Senghor of Senegal agreed to sponsor a draft resolution which would make provision for an African human rights commission at the next OAU Assembly meeting, and delegated Keba Mbaye, then President of the Supreme Court of Senegal, to work on a text on human rights. This document formed the basis of the Banjul Charter.

Under Resolution 115 (XVI) 1979 the Assembly, meeting in Monrovia, instructed the OAU's Secretary-General to appoint a committee of experts with a mandate to draw up 'a preliminary draft on an African Charter on Human and Peoples' Rights providing, *inter alia*, for the establishment of organs for the promotion and protection of human and peoples' rights'. This reference to human and peoples' rights already indicated the ideological split among the OAU Member States. The socialist States would not support a document protecting civil and political rights without it being balanced by the protection of social, cultural and economic rights. Neither could such a document be divorced from its African roots stressing collective rights. In exercising its mandate the committee of experts therefore had to bear in mind a number of considerations. In particular, it had:

- to be inspired by the traditions of African society and the principles upon which such traditions are based;

- to respect the political options of States and consequently to ensure a fair balance between the various doctrinal systems current in Africa;

- to avoid favouring in one way or another individual or collective rights, civil and political or economic, social and cultural rights;

- to give a content acceptable to all the peoples' rights;

- to ensure the protection and promotion of human rights declared and accepted as such through the activities of a commission, although reserving the powers of the Assembly which must be associated with the final decisions; and

- not to exceed that which African States were ready to accept in the field of the protection of human rights.

The limitations contained in the Banjul Charter are thus explicable against this background. The drafters of the Banjul Charter adopted a cautious approach because they were aware that many States would not support a document that imposed too many restrictions on their sovereignty or did not reflect their political philosophy in some way. Due allowance had to be made for the history of Africa. A treaty like the ECHR would simply have been unacceptable.

The committee of experts met in November and December 1979 and a draft was submitted to a ministerial meeting in June 1980, with a recommendation that it be put before the Assembly Summit in Freetown, Sierra Leone. However, the ministers were unable to reach agreement and it was not until January 1981 that a final draft was approved at a second meeting in Banjul, The Gambia.

The draft text underwent a number of substantive amendments at this juncture. The draft preamble dropped any reference to co-operation with non-African States in the field of human rights, thus emphasizing the regional character of the Banjul Charter, and asserted the virtues of African values on human and peoples' rights. With regard to the operative part of the Banjul Charter, a provision to the effect that the Banjul Charter would apply provisionally immediately upon its adoption by the OAU Assembly pending its entry into force was not retained. However, this did not mean that the African States were free to disregard international human rights law since it should be noted that States owe a duty of good faith under international law, that they must abide by their obligations under international law and in addition, according to Article 18 of the Vienna Convention on the Law of Treaties 1969, are under an obligation to refrain from acts which would defeat the object and purpose of a treaty once they have signed it. In any event, as members of the international community, African States would be bound by human rights norms accepted as rules of customary international law.

A provision empowering the OAU Assembly Chairman to take 'measures' in exceptional circumstances to protect 'human and peoples' rights' was also abandoned. This clause would have created extraordinary difficulties owing to the emphasis in the OAU Charter on the principle of non-interference in the internal affairs of States and given also the nature of the Chairman's office. Endowing the Chairman with such executive authority would not only have upset the jurisdictional balance of power between the OAU organs but would in all probability have required an amendment to the OAU Charter. It is nevertheless apparent that the Member States resisted the notion of endowing the Chairman with executive powers.

Two other alterations are worthy of mention. An unconditional commitment to the negative freedom of association, i.e., that no one may be compelled to join an association, was made subject to the 'duties of solidarity' of the individual which require compulsory membership of associations promoting social and national solidarity. These duties of solidarity are in fact so broad that the negative freedom of association is rendered virtually meaningless.[6] An unconditional prohibition on mass expulsion was similarly weakened. A prohibition to the effect that neither economic nor political reasons could justify the adoption of such measures was redefined to apply to expulsions 'aimed at national, racial, ethnic or religious groups'. This amendment appears totally to undermine the original intention since it seems that the expulsion of ethnic groups could be justified on economic grounds. Thus, the Nigerian expulsion of Ghanaians in 1984 would not appear, prima facie, to have been prohibited by the Banjul Charter.[7]

This final text was adopted by the Eighteenth Assembly of Heads of State and Governments at Nairobi in July 1981 as the African Charter on Human and Peoples' Rights.[8]

Basic Principles of the Banjul Charter

The Banjul Charter came into force on 21 October 1986, thereby creating binding legal obligations on all the parties thereto to give effect to the rights enumerated therein.[9] At the time of writing fifty-one States have ratified it.[10] The Banjul Charter in many respects reflects internationally recognized fundamental rights, in many instances contained in the UDHR and the International Covenants on Human Rights, which are binding *erga omnes*. However, it is still too early to assert that some of the rights specified in the Banjul Charter and peculiar to it have generated rules of customary international law.

The Banjul Charter is composed of four sections, a preamble and three main parts. The preamble lists its aims and objectives and the duty to promote and protect human rights in Africa. The first substantive part lists human and peoples' rights and duties, namely, first and second generation rights (Articles 2–18), which include the right to life, prohibition of torture and ill-treatment, prohibition of arbitrary arrest or detention, the right to a fair trial, and freedom of conscience, expression, association and assembly; peoples' or group or third generation rights (Articles 19–24), which include the rights of self-determination and development; the duties of individuals (Articles 27–29), which include duties towards the family, society and the State, and the international community; and State duties (Articles 25, 26), which include the duty to promote and ensure awareness of and respect for rights guaranteed in the Charter through teaching, education and publication, and the duty to guarantee the independence of the courts.[11]

The second substantive part contains the measures of safeguard (Articles 30–62), specifically the establishment and organization of the African Commission on Human and Peoples' Rights (hereafter African Commission), while the third and final section (Articles 64–68) deals with general administrative issues. It is apparent that no provision was made for a judicial organ.

The preamble acknowledges that the OAU Charter strives for 'freedom, equality, justice and dignity', that it seeks to eradicate colonialism and endeavours to improve the lives of the peoples of Africa, principles which the Banjul Charter reaffirms through a commitment to eliminate colonialism in its various guises and all forms of discrimination, including apartheid, and to dismantle aggressive foreign military bases. The latter commitment is interesting and it would appear to reflect not only a policy of non-alignment, to which many African States are committed, but more importantly an attempt to maintain international peace and security.[12] The preamble stresses that civil and political rights cannot be dissociated from economic, social and cultural rights and that to guarantee the former the latter must be satisfied, and that the enjoyment of rights and freedoms carries with it obligations and the performance of duties.[13] To these ends it recognizes that fundamental human rights, intrinsic to human beings and here inspired and characterized by the historical traditions and values of African civilization, require international protection and it reaffirms adherence to the human rights instruments adopted by the OAU, the UN and Non-Aligned Movement.[14]

The preamble makes it clear that the Banjul Charter is influenced throughout by the African conception of law and human rights.[15] This fact is important because it helps to explain the resistance to a judicial organ, the protection and promotion of family and community values, and the emphasis on economic and social rights. The Banjul Charter is also distinctive in that it accentuates the notion that the individual owes obligations to the community and the State, an idea that is gaining some credibility in the West where the traditional, perhaps excessive, stress on individualism is under attack as a factor in the decline of civil society. It is also important to note that the Banjul Charter provides for a right to development and other third generation rights, so as to redress the iniquities of the established international economic order.

Distinctive Features of the Banjul Charter

The Banjul Charter contains a number of distinctive features which, as has been mentioned, reflects the African philosophy of law and conception of human rights. This explains in part why the Banjul Charter deals with second and third generation rights as well as civil and political rights and why it imposes obligations upon the individual towards the State and the community. However, these features are also explicable on the basis of Marxist philosophy which was then followed by some States. However, the ideological distinction between the different categories of rights now seems less important in light of the Vienna Declaration on Human Rights 1993 which stresses that all human rights are universal, indivisible and interdependent.[16]

The want of a court was similarly justified on the basis that the African conception of law is averse to the solution of disputes by adverserial means. Disputes are traditionally settled through reconciliation aimed at reaching a consensus. In addition, it has been said that a judicial body would have proved counterproductive in that few African States would have been prepared to ratify the Banjul Charter if that had required submission to the jurisdiction of a court. The lack of a judicial remedy nevertheless attracted considerable criticism as undermining the effective enforcement of rights in Africa.[17] The OAU has since accepted that the attainment of human and peoples' rights requires the establishment of a court and this project is now on the verge of realization, a subject considered in greater detail below.

No provision is made in the Banjul Charter for derogation from human rights in times of emergency.[18] However, this is not as positive a feature as may appear at first sight since, as will become apparent, the Banjul Charter makes extensive use of 'clawback' clauses which make the enforcement of the right dependent on national law or at the discretion of the national authorities. Article 10(1) is one such example stating that, 'Every individual shall have the right to free association *provided that* he abides by the law'(emphasis added). The attainment of these rights is thereby considerably weakened because they are subject to whatever national law dictates.[19] Nevertheless, this does not mean that the State is able to act in an arbitrary manner.[20]

The Banjul Charter makes no provision for reservations, denunciation and withdrawal as a matter of deliberate policy. However, unless a treaty expressly forbids the making of reservations, which is not the case with the Banjul Charter, States may formulate a reservation when signing or ratifying a treaty so long as the reservation is compatible with the object and purpose of the treaty.[21] The denunciation of, or withdrawal from, the Banjul Charter is similarly not prohibited since it was the clear intention of the parties during the drafting stage that this contingency should be available.[22]

The Application of the Banjul Charter

As an international human rights treaty, and notwithstanding any lack of reference on this point, it is clearly established that the Banjul Charter must be interpreted in a dynamic and creative manner so as best to achieve its aims and objectives.[23]

Article 1 imposes a binding legal obligation on the signatories to recognize the rights, duties and freedoms enshrined in the Banjul Charter which must be given effect to through the adoption of legislative or other measures.[24] An analysis of the relevant constitutional law of each OAU Member State[25] is beyond the scope of this work but it suffices to say that this provision imposes a clear requirement on States parties to enshrine the Banjul Charter in domestic law and would appear to be aimed in particular at those States that adhere to the dualist doctrine of incorporation.[26] There are a number of ways in which the Banjul Charter can be given effect to in national law, by constitutional amendment or incorporation, by the enactment of a legislative act or through the adoption of an administrative measure. Whichever system prevails the end result must be the same, i.e., the rights, duties and freedoms must be enforceable in domestic law. It is important to note that the attempts of the Nigerian regime to limit or revoke the domestic effect of the Banjul Charter were condemned by the African Commission.[27] Article 65 specifies that the Banjul Charter will take effect three months after ratification by a State party but no time limit is set by which it must be given effect to within the domestic legal system. This requirement of the Banjul Charter can be favourably compared with the ECHR which does not oblige the High Contracting Parties to incorporate the ECHR into domestic law, although effective remedies before national authorities must exist.[28]

Unlike other human rights instruments the Banjul Charter makes no explicit reference to the fact that once aliens are allowed into the territory of a State party they are generally entitled to the rights and freedoms set out therein.[29] However, the wording of the Banjul Charter leads to the conclusion that the enjoyment of these rights and freedoms is secured to all individuals under the jurisdiction of a State party unless compelling reasons of public policy dictate otherwise, e.g., running for high public office.

Article 2 of the Banjul Charter guarantees every individual the rights and freedoms enumerated therein without discrimination.[30] This provision is phrased in categorical terms and since the individual is 'entitled' to the enjoyment of these rights, positive obligations appear to have been undertaken by the State.[31] Its importance is axiomatic and its place in the Banjul Charter is designed to permeate the subsequent provisions and secure the enjoyment of these rights without discrimination. It does not constitute a sweeping prohibition on discrimination *per se*, reflecting the international legal principles on non-discrimination. Following the principles extracted from other jurisdictions it is likely that not *all* discrimination is prohibited as long as some rational and objective basis, which must also be proportionate to the legitimate aim pursued, exists.[32]

The use of the words 'such as' suggests that the list of prohibited categories of discrimination is not meant to be exhaustive. It might therefore be interpreted to extend to sexual orientation,[33] the aged,[34] children[35] and the disabled.[36] Whereas other international instruments contain similar provisions none includes the category of 'ethnic groups'. This reference is a very significant addition given that many African States are multicultural and ethnic conflict sometimes seems endemic, often brought about by the lack of equal opportunities. Events in the Great Lakes region of Central Africa in 1994 demonstrate that some semblance of impartial authority must exist if ethnic groups are to be protected.[37] There is no express protection of 'minorities' but given that a definition of this term has proved elusive it may be that the adjectives race, ethnic, colour, religion and language suffice. While the individual, as opposed to a group, is the subject of this article in legal terms there may be a collective aspect to the exercise of these rights. It has thus been suggested that this provision not only seeks to protect the individual but would also appear to allow a citizen to complain that the national authorities are discriminating against a particular tribe or ethnic group.[38]

Civil and Political Rights

Article 3 also mirrors the principle of non-discrimination by guaranteeing the individual's right to equality before the law and his right to equal protection before the law. It prohibits discrimination in law and in fact in any field regulated and protected by public authorities. All are given equal access to the courts and general laws bind all in equal measure.[39] It applies both to the substantive content of the law and the manner in which laws are administered. Consequently, it applies to a law containing a discriminatory provision, on grounds of sex or race for instance, as well as to the arbitrary application of an otherwise unobjectionable law. An absolute obligation is imposed upon the State and reflects the principles of due process and the rule of law,[40] as well as the international law principle of non-discrimination, which in this context should be understood to imply any distinction, exclusion, restriction or preference based on any ground such as race,[41] sex,[42] language,[43] religion,[44] birth[45] or other status[46] which has the purpose or effect of nullifying or impairing the recognition, enjoyment or exercise of all rights and freedoms on an equal footing.

Article 4 guarantees the right to life but the provision is broadly worded and the guarantee is not absolute.[47] Thus only the 'arbitrary' deprivation of life is prohibited, which it is universally accepted requires States parties to provide security and stability and to take effective measures not only to prevent and punish the loss of life by criminal acts[48] but also to prevent arbitrary killing by their own security forces.[49] The shooting by police of peacefully striking workers in Malawi was condemned by the African Commission as a violation of the right to life.[50] Extrajudicial killings have also been condemned by the African Commission.[51] In this context, States are also under an obligation to prevent the disappearances of individuals.[52]

The language used in this provision impliedly accepts the imposition of the death penalty in accordance with the law.[53] That the Banjul Charter is not intended to prohibit capital punishment can also be deduced from the fact that the overwhelming majority of African States retain the death penalty.[54] However, it should be observed that Article 5(3) of the African Charter on the Rights and Welfare of the Child prohibits the sentence of death being pronounced on a child.[55] Because human beings are held to be inviolable it is accepted that any form of abuse, expressly considered in article 5, is unacceptable. In this context, it means that in capital cases all safeguards and guarantees for due process, both at pre-trial stages and during the trial itself, must be respected, including an adequate defence, a right of appeal and a right to seek pardon or commutation of sentence.[56]

The trial in Nigeria which pronounced the sentence of death on Ken

Saro-Wiwa and other human rights activists in November 1995 amply demonstrates the importance of such safeguards. The human rights of the Ogoni people who were protesting about the pollution of their land and water by transnational oil companies were progressively nullified by the military. Ken Saro-Wiwa was at the forefront of the campaign of protest. Since 1994 the military has occupied the area and has persecuted the Ogonis.[57] Following unrest and the deaths of four pro-government Ogoni leaders, Ken Saro-Wiwa and others were charged with their murders. A special military tribunal, the Civil Disturbances Tribunal, was established pursuant to the Special Tribunal Edict 1994 to try them. However, the trial has been widely criticized as falling well below international standards and failing to meet the most elementary requirements of a right to a fair trial. The independence and impartiality of the judges was highly questionable, facilities for the defence were lacking, the evidence was tainted, and there was no right of appeal to a higher judicial body.[58] Clearly, the accused did not receive a fair hearing in what was a trial with a predetermined outcome. It is unlikely that the accused would ever have benefited from all the safeguards and guarantees of due process in such a politically motivated case.

The definition of 'human being' in Article 4 raises the question of abortion but in the absence of any such reference it may be that the Banjul Charter does not intend to protect the unborn child.[59] In addition, the question arises how the right to life stands in relation to the issue of assisted death. Furthermore, scientific and technological developments raise the issue of bioethics.[60] Ultimately, in common with the other international instruments, the Banjul Charter appears to be more concerned with protecting the quality of life, by reducing infant mortality and increasing life expectancy, rather than life itself.[61]

Article 5 is also concerned with the dignity and integrity of the individual, regarded as one of the essentials of justice in a democratic society, and categorically prohibits '[a]ll forms of exploitation and degradation of man, particularly slavery ... torture, cruel, inhuman or degrading punishment and treatment', and is applicable to any one deprived of liberty by the State. It must be emphasized that this provision contains an absolute guarantee.[62] This provision reflects aspects of general international law. Thus it has been argued that the prohibition against slavery is a norm of *jus cogens*.[63] This can be evidenced from, *inter alia*, a number of international conventions expressly dealing with the slave trade, namely, Convention to Suppress Slave Trade and Slavery 1926 as amended, and Supplementary Convention on the Abolition of Slavery, the Slave Trade, and Institutions and Practices Similar to Slavery 1956.[64] However, it seems that the practice of slavery still survives in Africa.[65] It appears that the civil war in Mozambique led to the smuggling of people into South Africa which itself led to trafficking in women and children for immoral purposes.[66] Concern remains whether slavery has been effectively abolished in practice in Mauritania.[67]

While traditional forms of slavery have been almost universally eradicated contemporary forms of slavery are matters of increasing concern which have been condemned by the Vienna Declaration and Programme of Action. Examples of contemporary forms of slavery include the sale of children,[68] child labour,[69] bonded labour, prostitution,[70] child pornography[71] and prostitution,[72] sex tourism,[73] organ transplantation,[74] and child soldiers. According to the UN the use of child soldiers has been a feature of many conflicts in Africa, including Ethiopia, Liberia, Mozambique, Rwanda, Sudan and Uganda, amongst many others. The problem is compounded by the fact that in many of these cases children, some as young as six, have been kidnapped and coerced into soldiering.[75] Articles 2 and 22(2) of the African Charter on the Rights and Welfare of the Child in combination seem to set eighteen as the threshold age for recruitment to the armed forces or participation in hostilities.[76]

Torture is also prohibited by international law though the emergence of this rule is of more recent origin. In *Filartiga* v. *Peña-Irala* the US Court of Appeals for the Second Circuit stated that 'official torture is now prohibited by the law of nations' and that 'deliberate torture . . . violates universally accepted terms of the international law of human rights'.[77] That the prohibition on torture is part of customary international law, and has acquired the status of *jus cogens*, can be further evidenced by the reaction of the international community, including the adoption of UN General Assembly Resolution 3452 (XXX) 1975 Declaration on the Protection of all Persons from Torture and other Cruel, Inhuman, or Degrading Treatment or Punishment, the Vienna Declaration and Programme of Action, the UN Convention Against Torture and Other Cruel, Inhuman or Degrading Treatment or Punishment 1984,[78] the Inter-American Convention to Prevent and Punish Torture 1985 and the European Convention for the Prevention of Torture and Inhuman or Degrading Treatment or Punishment 1987 which establishes mechanisms for investigating allegations of torture.

Torture may be distinguished from cruel, inhuman or degrading treatment or punishment by the degree of pain or cruelty inflicted. Thus, in *Ireland* v. *United Kingdom* the European Court of Human Rights stated that torture amounted to suffering of a particularly intense and cruel nature.[79] Specific examples of physical assault amounting to torture and cruel, inhuman and degrading treatment and punishment exist in the practice of the HRC relating to communications concerning African States.[80] Thus, in *Mukong* v. *Cameroon* an opponent of the one-party system in Cameroon was arrested for advocating political change. The applicant contended successfully that the conditions of his detention, including overcrowding, and deprivation of food and clothing, amounted to cruel, inhuman and degrading treatment. With regard to conditions of detention in general, the HRC observed that certain minimum standards, as set by the UN Standard Minimum Rules for the Treatment of Prisoners, must be met regardless of a State's level of development. This required minimum floor space and sufficient air, adequate sanitary facilities, a separate bed, clothing which is not degrading or humiliating, and nutritional food. Apart from the general conditions of detention, the applicant had been singled out for exceptionally harsh and degrading treatment. He was kept detained incommunicado, was threatened with torture and death, deprived of food, and kept locked in a cell for days on end without the possibility of recreation.[81]

In *Isidore Kanana* v. *Zaire* a political opponent of the regime was subjected to electrical shocks and heavy beatings with metal bars wrapped in barbed wire. He was then left for dead by the roadside. The HRC concluded that he had been subjected to torture, cruel and inhuman treatment and that the inherent dignity of the person had been violated.[82]

In addition, the decision of the African Commission in the case of *Amnesty International on behalf of Orton and Vera Chirwa* v. *Malawi* is of interest. The Commission found that excessive solitary confinement, over-crowding, shackling within a cell, poor quality food, denial of access to medical care, acts of beating and torture violated Article 5.[83]

It is clear that the prohibition against cruel, inhuman, or degrading treatment or punishment in international human rights law extends to corporal punishment.[84] However, it is equally clear that this injunction is problematic for many African States which continue to retain its use as punishment for many crimes.[85]

While it has already been observed above that capital punishment is not *per se* prohibited under general international law, it is manifest that the sentence of death must be performed in such a way as to cause the least possible physical and mental suffering.[86] Barbaric modes of execution that entail a lingering death or the affliction of acute pain and suffering, such as burning at the stake, crucifixion or disembowelment, or which may offend our sense of decency, such as public beheadings, would evidently constitute cruel, inhuman and degrading punishment.[87] For some though, the death penalty is by its very nature cruel and inhuman.[88]

Account should additionally be taken of the fact that unjustifiably prolonged delays in the execution of a death sentence amount to cruel and inhuman punishment.[89]

Article 5 of the Banjul Charter can be favourably compared with other international documents in that it prohibits *all* forms of exploitation and degradation so that the list of offences cited, while clearly the worst envis-aged, is not meant to be exhaustive. This provision can be favourably compared with the analogous provision in the ECHR, Article 3, which is not as extensive. Accordingly, a prohibition on forced or compulsory labour, though not mentioned in the Banjul Charter, may be implied.[90]

Another problematic issue are harmful traditional practices affecting the health of women and children, especially female circumcision and infibulation which is practised in many African countries, notably Ethiopia, Somalia, and Egypt.[91] The practice is painful and has lasting physiological and psychologi-cal effects, in addition to the dangers of infection. It is self-evident that such practices are degrading and dehumanizing and have been condemned by the Beijing Platform for Action.[92] However, it could be argued that tradition and custom, whatever their nature, are protected by Article 17(3) of the Banjul Charter. The question therefore arises as to how mutually incompatible rights are reconciled. Priority must be given to the more fundamental right, either by reference to its non-derogable status – the Banjul Charter is unhelpful in this regard – or by reference to its status as a norm of *jus cogens*.[93] In this particular context, therefore, considerations of humanity must prevail over traditional values. Nevertheless, if these cultural practices enjoy active support an immediate prohibition may give rise to the accusation of 'cultural imperialism' and, as Sudan has admitted, the practice can persist despite the fact it is illegal.[94] Education may be the most appropriate answer.

Article 6 protects the right to liberty and security of person,[95] which should be applicable to all deprivations of liberty, not just criminal cases,[96] and prohibits arbitrary arrest or detention, i.e., they must be based on grounds and procedures established by law.[97] Again this provision is phrased in broad terms and may be unfavourably compared to Article 9 ICCPR,[98] Article 5 ECHR,[99] and Article 7 ACHR which specify these guarantees in greater detail. Thus the Banjul Charter is silent on, *inter alia*, the right to be informed at the time of the arrest for the reasons of the arrest;[100] the right to be brought promptly before a judicial officer[101] and to a trial within a reasonable time;[102] the right to challenge the lawfulness of the detention before a court and to be released if the lawfulness is not established;[103] the right to compensation for unlawful arrest or detention;[104] and the prohibition on imprisonment for civil suits.[105] It appears from the jurisprudence of the African Commission that these guarantees are implied[106] but the omission is nevertheless regrettable and, because deprivation of freedom by the authorities ranks as one of the most serious infringements of a person's fundamental rights, surely the grounds upon which a person can be detained by the authorities should have been set out in detail.

Article 7 enshrines the right to a fair trial[107] and the use of the word 'cause' suggests a wider application to take into account not only civil actions and criminal cases[108] but also customary law and non-judicial disputes with the authorities and traditional dispute settlement by village or tribal elders.[109] This is apparent from sub-paragraph (a) which provides for a right to appeal to a competent national organ concerning the violation of rights recognized by, *inter alia*, customs. International practice makes clear that this principle extends to all courts and tribunals, including emergency and military courts.[110] However, the UN has expressed concern about the use of military courts to try ordinary offences.[111]

According to Article 7(1) the right to a fair trial comprises four elements. First, the right to appeal to a competent national organ against acts violating fundamental rights, which therefore does not restrict this right solely to judicial bodies, but could apply to ombudsmen or government ministers.[112] The African Commission has held that the impossibility of 'any avenue of appeal to competent national organs in criminal cases' is a clear violation of this provision.[113] Ouster clauses have been similarly condemned.[114] Secondly, the presumption of innocence,[115] which might extend to the right against self-incrimination.[116] Thirdly, the right to a defence, which must also refer to the right to prepare adequately one's defence, including the right to be defended by counsel of one's choice.[117] The African Commission found a violation of this provision in *Constitutional Rights Project* v. *Nigeria (in respect of Zamani Lakwot)* where the defence counsel was harrassed into resigning from a trial.[118] This also raises practical questions concerning the availability of advocates, legal costs and legal aid, questions that are not specifically addressed by the Banjul Charter.[119] However, there is some cause for optimism in that Article 26 obliges States parties to allow the establishment and improvement of appropriate national institutions entrusted with the promotion and protection of the rights and freedoms enshrined in the Charter.[120] And fourthly, the right to a trial within a reasonable time.[121] The provision requires the court or tribunal to be competent and impartial and their independence is further guaranteed by Article 26.[122] The African Commission has held in the *Chirwa case* that a tribunal composed of members of the armed forces, police and judiciary violates this obligation.[123] As has been seen, the trial of Ken Saro-Wiwa fails abjectly to pass this test.

Article 7(2) includes the principle of non-retroactivity of the criminal law and criminal penalties.[124] In addition, punishment is personal and may only be imposed on the offender.[125]

Article 7 of the Banjul Charter does not appear to require that cases be heard in public[126] but neither does it make provision for cases to be heard *in camera* in the interests of national security or public order, or in the interest of the parties or justice.[127] However, the power of the courts in this respect must be presumed.[128] In a negative sense there are other internationally accepted elements of a fair trial that Article 7 omits,[129] including the right to examine witnesses;[130] the right to be present at one's trial;[131] the right not to be re-tried according to the principles of *ne bis in idem* or *autrefois acquit, autrefois convict*;[132] and the right to the free assistance of an interpreter in court, which would appear to be a regrettable oversight given the multiplicity of languages and dialects.[133] Moreover, the Banjul Charter does not address the question of the administration of juvenile justice.[134]

Article 8 broadly guarantees freedom of conscience, or personal conviction,[135] the profession[136] and the free practice of religion.[137] Under international human rights law restrictions cannot be placed on the freedom of conscience or religious belief, so that the freedom to change one's beliefs must be guaranteed.[138] At the same time, the freedom not to believe is also guaranteed.[139] Consequently, one cannot be compelled to adhere to, for instance, a State religion and neither should one suffer discrimination for failing to adhere to the State religion or other official ideology.[140]

It is unclear whether the phrase 'the free practice of religion' is analogous to the freedom to manifest one's religion 'individually or in community with others and in public or private'.[141] The freedom guaranteed by the Banjul Charter may not be as wide-ranging as other international instruments for it omits any mention of a freedom to disseminate one's religion or belief or manifest it in public. While this need not mean that worship must be in secret, it may entail limitations so that religious groups may not have a right to express their beliefs on the public highway by way of processions.[142] Moreover, it may negate the freedom to proselytize.[143] Nevertheless, the guarantee is inherently weak in that the general exception that these freedoms are 'subject to law and order' is too far-reaching and could easily be invoked to undermine these freedoms.[144]

One of the questions that arises is whether the freedom of conscience encompasses conscientious objection to compulsory military service.[145]

Article 9 guarantees what should be one of the essential pillars of a democratic society, the freedom to receive information and to express and disseminate opinion.[146] The concept of 'opinion' appears to refer to political or secular thought, as opposed to 'conscience' which seems to have a religious or more fundamental connotation,[147] but both share much in common, including the fact that they admit of no interference.[148] This includes coercion of any sort to reveal one's opinion.[149] However, it is regrettable that there is no explicit reference to a freedom of speech or other forms of expression since the concepts of 'opinion' and 'expression' do not appear to be interchangeable.[150] Thus, the scope of this freedom is unclear.[151] However, the freedom of political expression, speech and the freedom of the press in society is fundamental.[152] The pre-eminent role of the press has been emphasized by international human rights law because the press provides the public with an optimum mean of discovering and forming an opinion on political leaders and it also gives politicians an opportunity to comment.[153] Moreover, politicians acting in a public capacity must accept a wide degree of criticism. The press has a role as a public watchdog in politics and to restrict the press from passing legitimate comment or making value judgments would amount to censorship.[154] In addition, imposing restrictions on the press by requiring journalists to register with a licensing authority is also incompatible with the freedom of expression.[155]

The Banjul Charter appears to draw a distinction between the two freedoms. Thus, while the right to receive information seems to be absolute[156] the freedom to express an opinion must be exercised ' within the law'. It is generally accepted that the freedom of expression entails duties and responsibilities[157] and therefore that some interference may be necessary[158] but this limitation appears to be more sweeping than that contained in comparable international documents where the limitation constitutes the exception to the general rule[159] and Amnesty International has therefore expressed concern that the limitation in the Banjul Charter should not be interpreted in such a way that governments would be allowed to enact arbitrary or punitive measures which would unnecessarily curb these freedoms.[160]

Given the damaging legacy of racism in Africa it is unlikely that the Banjul Charter will tolerate the expression of racist ideas since the rights of others are directly affected and human rights themselves are undermined.

Moreover, further to Article 28 thereof individuals are under an obligation to respect other individuals without discrimination and to maintain relations aimed at enhancing mutual respect and tolerance. International human rights law regards restrictions to combat racism as legitimate.[161]

Article 10 broadly guarantees the right of free association. This implies that individuals must be free to create and join trades unions and professional bodies.[162] Thus, in *Civil Liberties Organization in respect of Nigerian Bar Association* v. *Nigeria* the African Commission held that 'there must always be a general capacity for citizens to join, without State interference, in association in order to attain various ends'.[163] However, this does not seem to mean that such bodies are owed any preferential treatment by the State[164] nor does it imply an automatic right to strike, which can be subject to limitations under national law.[165] Again this provision is subject to limitations which compare unfavourably with other international documents. As in Article 9, Article 10 contains a general exception in that the right is conditional on the individual abiding by the law. This limitation could render the freedom guaranteed worthless since priority is given to national law. Thus, if the formation of trade unions is prohibited under domestic law Article 10 provides no redress. By comparison, the limitations contained in other international documents are specific thereby lessening the possibility of abuse.[166]

Article 10(2) contains a correlative right in that 'no one may be compelled to join an association.'[167] However, this guarantee may again be rendered worthless because it is made subject to the obligation of solidarity contained in Article 29 which imposes upon the individual duties towards the family, the community and the State. While the sentiment of these obligations may be laudable in that they reflect traditional African values and attempt to imbue the individual with good citizenship, the potential for abuse exists. For example, individuals may be compelled to join a political party not of their choice under the guise that it preserves and strenthens social and national solidarity.[168]

Article 11 guarantees the right of assembly, which includes demonstrations, subject to certain restrictions and limitations.[169] The right of assembly cannot be absolute because it impacts on the rights of others and because of the threat of disorder and these reasonable restrictions can be found in democratic societies.[170]

Article 12 guarantees various aspects of the right of free movement. First, individuals, whether national or alien it seems, can move freely within the State.[171] Secondly, they can elect where they wish to reside, both important considerations in view of apartheid's restrictions on these rights.[172] The individual's right to freedom of movement or residence within a State is guaranteed provided 'he abides by the law'.[173] This not only suggests that the individual must be lawfully within the territory, having complied with immigration requirements, but that his continued presence is contingent on observing domestic law, a requirement that seems to be wholly legitimate.

Squatting or trespass would not therefore be protected under this provision. This right is often compromised in Africa because of the many situations giving rise to massive dislocations of people.

Article 12(2) grants the individual the right to leave a State subject to restrictions imposed by the law for the protection of national security, law and order, public health or morality.[174] Consequently, inability to leave as a result of having to serve a lawful prison sentence would not violate this right. In addition, the right of an individual to enter his own State is also guaranteed but the Banjul Charter, in common with other international instruments, restricts the right of entry to nationals only. Aliens do not have the right to enter another State's territory since in principle it is for the State to determine who it will admit.[175] However, it should be observed that the Banjul Charter is unique in apparently making the national's right of entry to his own country subject to restrictions. This provision would appear to be incompatible with international law.[176] A positive feature is Article 12(3) which grants a right, when persecuted,[177] to seek and obtain asylum. The question of asylum is to be considered in accordance with national and international law and it is clear that this provision is inspired by, and is a complement to, the OAU Convention on Refugees 1969.[178] The right of asylum enshrined in the Banjul Charter is extensive since potentially it could be granted to anyone who is persecuted whereas Article 22(7) ACHR, for example, restricts it to situations where the individual is 'being pursued for political offences or related common crimes'.

The right of asylum is qualified, however, by Article 23(2)(a) which obliges States parties to ensure that individuals enjoying the right of asylum under Article 12 do not engage in subversive activities against their country of origin or any other State party. This provision emphasizes an analogous requirement in the OAU Charter. Regrettably, the Banjul Charter does not expressly guarantee the right of *non-refoulement* although this would appear to be implied in the wording of Article 12(3).

Article 12(4) protects a non-national who is legally within another State from summary expulsion as expulsion can only be legitimate by virtue of a decision taken in accordance with the law.[179] Unlike Article 13 ICCPR and Article 1 of the Seventh Protocol ECHR, the Banjul Charter does not confer upon the non-national a right to have the case reviewed, to appeal to the competent authority or to give reasons against his expulsion.[180] It would appear that the Banjul Charter is too broadly worded[181] and that this right would have been better safeguarded if the provision had been drafted along the lines of the aforementioned instruments to list procedural guarantees.

Finally, Article 12(5) prohibits the mass expulsion of non-nationals aimed at national, racial, ethnic or religious groups. The expulsion by Idi Amin of thousands of Asian residents in Uganda in the 1970s would clearly have come within the scope of this proscription. Article 4 of the Fourth Protocol ECHR and Article 22(9) ACHR prohibit in absolute terms the collective expulsion of aliens and it is submitted that their wording is preferable to that of the Banjul Charter. As has been stated previously, the list enumerated in this clause might not be exhaustive as the expulsion of non-nationals *en masse* for, say, economic reasons would not appear to fall within the terms of the prohibition. It has already been observed that the mass expulsion of migrant workers occurs frequently in Africa.[182] However, protection against the mass expulsion of nationals, a practice not unknown in Africa, is omitted from the terms of this Article.[183]

Article 13(1) broadly guarantees the right to participate freely in government but it does not expressly grant a right to participate in elections on the basis of universal adult suffrage nor a right to elected representative government.[184] This right is confined to citizens and contains a further limitation in that participation in government, either directly or through freely chosen representatives, must be in accordance with the law. Hence a right to form a political party cannot be guaranteed as neither can a right to multipartism. This provision reflected the fact that the overwhelming majority of African States have been one-party States and that liberal democracy has been considered largely alien to Africa and allegedy unsuitable to tackle its needs. Nonetheless, the African Commission has affirmed that the best government is one elected by and accountable to the people and has thus called upon military governments to hand over political power to democratically elected governments.[185] In addition, it has condemned the military takeover in The Gambia in 1994 as a clear violation of the fundamental principle of democracy that governments should be based on the consent of the people and a 'flagrant violation of the right of the Gambian people to freely choose their government',[186] and further, it has called upon the Nigerian military government to respect the right of free participation in government. Moreover, it needs to be recalled that under the terms of the Harare Declaration 1991 members of the Commonwealth committed themselves to an agenda of democracy and human rights.

Article 13(2) gives the citizen the right of equal access to the public service of his country but nowhere is the concept of public service defined.[187] However, it is interesting to note that the ECJ has interpreted the concept of public service in Article 39(4) (ex Art 48(4)) EC Treaty as referring to activities which involve participation in the exercise of powers conferred by public law or safeguard the general interests of the State, such as the armed forces, the police, or the judiciary.[188] However, sectarianism has sometimes led to the exclusion of some ethnic groups from participating in the public affairs of a country.

Article 13(3) grants every individual, thereby including non-nationals, the right of equal access to public property and services before the law.[189]

Article 14 guarantees the right to property.[190] Although the concept of 'property' is undefined it is submitted that it must be given a wide interpretation.[191] The question arises as to the compatibility of this provision with the customary laws of many African societies where women, often as a result of inheritance laws, lose their property.[192]

Enjoyment of this right may be limited 'in the interest of public need or in the general interest of the community' in accordance with the law, which means that property may not be interfered with or confiscated arbitrarily.[193] The rights guaranteed in the Banjul Charter may be less extensive than those in comparable international documents in that it makes no express reference as to the appropriate level of compensation for the expropriation of property.[194] Hence Article 1 of the First Protocol ECHR further subjects the prerogative of the State to deprive an individual of his property[195] to the general principles of international law[196] while Article 21(2) ACHR provides for the payment of just compensation, which is left to the individual State to determine.[197]

It is interesting to note that the right to property does not extend to condoning tax evasion or avoidance since Article 29(6) imposes an obligation upon the individual to pay taxes according to the law in the interest of society.[198] It is unclear whether punitive levels of taxation which may force an owner to give up property are compatible with the Banjul Charter.[199]

It is significant that nowhere does the Banjul Charter make provision for a right to privacy. The right to privacy found in comparable international documents extends to respect for private life, home and correspondence, subject to the usual derogations in the interests of the law and democratic society, and is an important guarantee against the arbitrary interference by the State in the affairs of the individual.[200] Its omission is therefore regrettable.

Economic, Social and Cultural Rights

Articles 15–18 guarantee rights which have a plural nature, transcending both first and second generation rights, which, in the context of the Banjul Charter, may be better classified as economic, social and cultural.[201] However, many doubt the legal capacity of such 'rights' considering them social and political desiderata incapable of enforcement. In addition, it is argued that the State is under no legal duty to provide these societal goals. The extent to which a State provides social assistance or basic amenities to its citizens is viewed as a political and not a legal matter.[202] How can a right exist in the absence of a corresponding duty? It is true that the ICES, for instance, provides for progressive realization and acknowledges constraints due to the limits of available resources. Yet these views do not take account of the growing awareness of the importance of these 'rights' and of the work of international bodies to achieve their full realization. In the UN an Expert Committee on Economic, Social and Cultural Rights was established by ECOSOC in 1985, which became operational in 1987, to supervise the implementation of the ICES by State parties. The Committee has expressed the view that State parties have assumed clear obligations in respect of the full realization of the rights in question which require them to move expeditiously and effectively towards that goal.[203] In addition, as a result of an international conference held in 1986 under the auspices of the International Commission of Jurists to consider the obligations of the State parties to the International Covenants, the Limburg Principles describe economic, social and cultural rights as an integral part of international human rights law.[204] Notice must also be taken of the Revised European Social Charter, the Protocol of San Salvador and to a lesser extent EC law which, however, does impose binding legal obligations on Member States. But most significantly, the Vienna Declaration in 1993 stressed the universality, indivisibility and interdependence of all human rights.[205] There is therefore cause for believing that certain economic, social and cultural rights are, in addition to an expression of ideals, legally enforceable rights under international law while other principles are merely *de lege ferenda*. However, under the Banjul Charter these rights are guaranteed not only for the individual but are also considered indispensable if the economies of the African States are to become less dependent. This becomes apparent when considering third generation rights below.

Article 15 guarantees distinct rights, the right to work under equitable and satisfactory conditions, and the right to equal pay for equal work. The way in which the provision is phrased appears to impose an absolute obligation which, it is believed, may impose too onerous a burden upon the signatory States for full and immediate realization. It is unclear whether the right to work is guaranteed.[206] The language used strongly suggests that it is not the right to work as an independent right that is guaranteed but rather facilitation of the right to work or the right to work in a safe environment. It is interesting to note that according to Article 29(6) the individual is under a duty to work to the best of his abilities and competence.

As has been stated Article 15 provides for an equitable and satisfactory working environment but nowhere is it specified how this is to be achieved.[207] However, it would appear to be a reference to healthy and safe standards and just working conditions.[208] The Banjul Charter is silent on rest and leisure[209] and the right to reasonable remuneration[210] but it may be that these rights come within the definition of 'equitable and satisfactory conditions'.

Finally, Article 15 enshrines the right to equal pay[211] for equal work.[212] This right seems to extend to all workers and does not appear to be solely designed to eliminate discrimination in pay between the sexes. A reference to the EC Treaty demonstrates the complexities surrounding this issue.[213]

Article 16 guarantees in general terms the right to health, which includes both physical and mental health,[214] and obliges States parties to adopt the measures necessary to protect the health of their people and to ensure medical attention when they are sick.[215] The right to health is not absolute but is the 'best attainable'.[216] It implies access to medical and social facilities and rehabilitation services. Curative treatment is expensive and current thinking emphasizes preventive care, all of which necessitates substantial investment by the State. But Africa seems to be losing the war against disease as chronic, degenerative diseases, such as tuberculosis, malaria and AIDS, appear to be on the rampage.[217] Resources, already scarce, are stretched beyond their limits. Nonetheless, the Committee on Economic, Social and Cultural Rights has stated that States must continue to endeavour to secure the widest possible enjoyment of these rights.[218] However, it has been pointed out that some cultural practices, such as female genital mutilation and traditional delivery of children, undermine the enjoyment of this right.[219]

Paragraph 1 extends the right to health to every individual, not only citizens, which is particularly significant in the light of the refugee problem. By contrast the State obligation contained in paragraph 2 would appear to extend to citizens only and may be designed to conserve scarce resources or limit the liability of the State for a failure to provide adequate medical facilities to tourists or other foreigners.

Article 16 is supplemented by Article 18(1) and (4) which have a social and moral objective, reflecting in part African traditional values. Thus, paragraph 1 provides, *inter alia*, that the State is to take care of the physical health of the family while paragraph 4 seeks to protect the rights of the aged[220] and disabled.[221]

Article 17(1) protects the right to education but unlike other international documents it does not state how this is to be achieved.[222] Thus, it does not provide for compulsory education or free education at any level,[223] nor does it provide for different kinds of education,[224] nor does it provide for equality of opportunity.[225] It is therefore not clear to what extent education is made dependent upon means but given the collectivist ideals that inspire much of the Banjul Charter it would not be surprising if education at certain levels, particularly primary education, was meant to be at public expense as far as financially feasible.

It would seem that 'education' must be seen to have a wide definition to include not only all levels of academic education but also technical and vocational training. However, in light of paragraph 2 which guarantees the individual the right freely to participate in the cultural life of his community, 'education' must be deemed to include art, music, dance, and other cultural pursuits.

Whereas the lack of resources means that the effective enjoyment of this right is denied to many children throughout Africa it is again the case that girls are particularly disadvantaged as a result of the inferior status of women in traditional societies.[226]

According to paragraph 3 the State is under a duty to promote and protect morals and traditional values recognized by the community. Thus, the obligation does not seem to be confined to children or students but applies to any individual. The promotion and protection of traditional values may be justified as an attempt to preserve indigenous culture and way of life.[227] By comparison other documents give parents or legal guardians the right to have their children educated in accordance with their religious, philosophical and moral convictions.[228] As has been seen, however, some cultural traditions can have an awkward relationship with human rights guarantees and if incompatibility exists priority must be given to the more fundamental right.

Article 18 declares the family the natural unit and basis of society and the custodian of morals and traditional values, and its physical and moral health is to be protected by the State.[229] Furthermore, paragraph 2 provides that the State is to assist the family and although this assistance is not specified it may include social, financial and other support.[230] The Banjul Charter is virtually unique in declaring that the aged and disabled are entitled to protection.[231]

The Banjul Charter is silent on the right to marry[232] and the right to found a family[233] but these rights must be implied in the general tenor of the provision. The question of divorce is not addressed.[234] With its emphasis on morals and traditional values and the lack of a right to privacy it would seem that the Banjul Charter is not intended to respect homosexual relationships.[235]

Paragraph 3 seeks to eliminate discrimination against women and to protect the rights of women in the context of the family by reference to international instruments.[236] It needs to be recalled that sex-based discrimination is further prohibited by Articles 2 and 3 of the Banjul Charter. Again, the Banjul Charter is not specific about which rights are guaranteed but its reference to international instruments rather than national law is to be welcomed. In practice this provision should have the effect of guaranteeing these international rights in national law even if the State has not ratified those instruments. The HRC has expressed the view that sex-based discrimination relating to, *inter alia*, acquisition or loss of the family name, acquisition or loss of nationality, divorce, child custody and maintenance, is prohibited, and that spouses have equal rights and responsibilities within the family.[237] This should ensure that the wife and her property are not considered chattels of the husband.[238]

The rights of children are similarly protected[239] which would appear to encompass the status and rights of children born out of wedlock.[240] According to the HRC children have the right to, *inter alia*, a name from birth, the right to acquire a nationality, the right to an education and the right to know and be cared for by their parents where possible.[241] In addition, and mentioned elsewhere in association with other rights, the State must take measures to reduce infant mortality and reduce malnutrition, to protect abandoned or orphaned children, and to protect children from acts of violence and inhuman and degrading treatment, such as forced labour or prostitution.[242]

The right to family life is complemented by Articles 27(1) and Article 29(1) which impose duties upon the individual towards his family.[243] Again these duties are inspired by their special nature in traditional African society.

Peoples' Rights

The importance of the rights of 'peoples', or third generation or group rights, as an element of the African concept of human rights is illustrated by its inclusion in the Banjul Charter, specifically in Articles 19–24.[244] The significance of the community in African traditional life cannot be overstated as it is within the community that the individual could express his identity to the utmost; the community and the individual are thus inextricably linked. By protecting the community the individual is thereby also protected. However, the problem with such rights is that they are difficult to reconcile with any classical theory of human rights, which emphasizes an individualistic approach. Even when rights are ascribed to groups of persons, women and children for instance, the rights themselves have still been regarded as belonging to the individual members of the group rather than the group as an abstract entity itself.[245] Peoples' rights are afforded to human beings communally, i.e., in conjunction with others as a group, and require that they be exercised collectively. A feature of the dichotomy between the different categories of rights is that the two may often conflict. In resolving such conflicts opposing rights have to be balanced and weighed against each other. In practice, there can be widespread recognition of peoples' rights. Most States have now legislated to protect the environment and such laws may accord priority to the rights of the many over the individual right to property. Peoples' rights are thus sometimes accepted as permissible, even if not required by international human rights law. However, it is still uncommon in legal and political theory to view peoples' rights as human rights. As with second generation rights, it is argued that States have not assumed immediate legal obligations, at most they are socially or politically desirable ideals to be achieved, and that such 'rights' are unenforceable and cannot be vindicated because no one is correspondingly obligated.[246] Nevertheless, some arguments in favour of a conception of peoples' rights, claiming that they have the same nature and justification as individual rights, have compelling force. Peoples' rights are rights the bearers of which are collectivities which are justified by the essential value that human beings have in the quality of their own lives. As such they are not derivative from individual rights but exist as an independent, though sometimes intertwined, category of human rights. Yet the conclusion must be arrived at that at the present stage of development of international law the majority of States are unwilling to accept the concept of peoples rights. However, before examining the substantive measures it is necessary to discuss what is meant by the concept of 'peoples', which is nowhere defined in the Banjul Charter.

The definition of 'peoples' is a difficult task given that no universally accepted version has yet been drafted. Furthermore, because of its abstract nature it suffers from inherent weaknesses and it may therefore be as difficult to identify the peoples or groups entitled to these rights as it may be to identify the entities that owe them these rights.[247] Whilst no definition was ultimately forthcoming, discussions on the draft Charter provide an insight into the African notion of a 'people' for these purposes.[248]

It emerges that the African and Western conceptions of a 'people' differ in that the African notion refers to the national community as a whole as distinct from ethnic, linguistic or tribal communities, whereas the Western notion includes such groups and is closely identified with minority or group rights. The African interpretation would therefore appear to refer to the population of a State as a whole, or the State itself, and not to sections of it, a conclusion that becomes apparent by reference to Article 21(4)-(5) which begin with the phrase, 'States parties to the present Charter'. The rights of peoples in the sense of national communities and the rights of minorities was distinguished which suggests that minorities are not specifically protected by the Banjul Charter but only insofar as an individual cannot be discriminated against on the grounds of race, ethnic group or national origin under Article 2 and insofar as the Banjul Charter reflects general principles of international law. In this respect the Banjul Charter is little different from other international instruments in that members of minorities do not enjoy rights because they are bestowed on a community but simply because that person is an individual who has rights and the fact that he or she may be a member of a minority is purely incidental. The guarantee in Article 19 that nothing justifies the domination of one people by another appears thereby to be considerably weakened. The International Commission of Jurists has suggested the following criteria as relevant in determining the notion of a 'people' and it is submitted that they have considerable merit. These are: (1) a common history; (2) racial and ethnic ties; (3) cultural and linguistic ties; (4) religious and ideological ties; (5) a common geographic location; (6) a common economic base; and (7) a reasonably sized population.

Article 19 seems to serve as an introduction to the rights that are elaborated further in subsequent provisions. It extends the principle of non-discrimination to the community as a whole by proclaiming the equality of all peoples. Considering the African notion of 'peoples' as a national community this provision would appear to refer to the principles of equal rights and sovereign equality contained in Articles 1(2) and 2(1) of the UN Charter. Moreover, the total prohibition on the domination of one people over another would appear to be a reference to the principles of political independence and political and economic self-determination. In addition, it can also be interpreted as an attempt to address the problems of racial oppression and intolerance, not only as characterized by *apartheid* and white-minority rule in Rhodesia, but also the descent into genocide in the Great Lakes region of central Africa seemingly as a result of ethnic inequalities.[249]

Article 20 enshrines a principle of international law cherished by the OAU, the inalienable right to political and economic self-determination. African States have established a link between the right to self-determination and the principles of sovereignty and non-interference whereby self-determination reinforces those fundamental principles of international law.[250] The Banjul Charter is one of the few international conventions that proclaims self-determination as a fundamental human right[251] since even its existence as a norm of international law has been challenged. A reason for this doubt concerns the content and scope of self-determination, i.e., is it a principle of general application or does it apply solely in the context of decolonization? What people are entitled to exercise this right, colonial subjects, discontented minorities? Does it legitimize secession? Many of these questions are still unresolved because general agreement has proved well-nigh impossible but the Banjul Charter addresses some of these questions and it is significant that it considers this issue in three paragraphs.

The reference in paragraph 1 to *all* peoples having the right to existence and the right to self-determination appears not only to include national communities but also colonized and oppressed peoples. This is apparent from paragraph 2, and the practice and *opinio juris* of African States, but the distinction between the two must be made given that the content of the right varies between categories. Therefore, with regard to external self-determination, it is now clearly established that the inhabitants of non-self-governing territories have a legal right freely to determine their future political, economic and cultural status.[252] States entrusted with the responsibility of administering non-self-governing territories are under a corresponding duty to decolonize them.[253] In this context self-determination is synonymous with decolonization. Independence must be an available choice. However, if self-determination is a right of all peoples does this mean that self-determination operates internally and that secession is legitimized? The ministerial conference reviewing the draft charter was adamant in its view that this was certainly not the case. This position is not surprising given the emphasis placed on the principles of territorial integrity and *uti possidetis* by the African States.[254] The current position is clearly reflected by the African Commission's opinion in *Katangese Peoples' Congress* v. *Zaire* where it stated that the 'Commission is obliged to uphold the sovereignty and territorial integrity of Zaire'.[255] Generally, the international community appears reluctant to recognize a right of self-determination when the exercise of that right involves a threat of secession, a view apparently reinforced by paragraph 6 of General Assembly Resolution 1514 (XV) Declaration on the Granting of Independence to Colonial Countries and Peoples 1960.[256] In this sense, self-determination operates 'externally' and once independence is attained no further recourse to the right is permissible. Accordingly, in Africa the right of self-determination is presently being denied to the Sahrawis of Western Sahara.[257] Nevertheless, it should be observed that there exists considerable support for the view that internal self-determination requires good and democratic governance and that the oppression of racial, linguistic and religious minorities justifies secession.[258] A link with Article 13 may thereby be established.

Also relevant in this context are paragraphs 2 and 3 which give colonized and oppressed peoples the right to free themselves by resorting to any means recognized by the international community and the right to the assistance of African States in their liberation struggle against foreign domination. These provisions give rise to numerous controversial questions that have not yet been adequately resolved but which, with the virtual elimination of colonialism from Africa, appear to have less contemporary relevance.

The reference to 'oppressed peoples' in paragraph 2 was designed to include those in Rhodesia, South Africa and Namibia who were not labouring under classical colonial situations. However, it seems unlikely that the definition of 'oppressed peoples' was meant to extend to those whose rights were being violated by a tyrannical ruler, e.g., Idi Amin. Given the OAU's traditional stand on subversion and on the principle of domestic jurisdiction, it must be doubted whether the Banjul Charter had been intended to recognize a right to revolution. Nevertheless, taking into account more recent developments, such as the concept of internal self-determination, the commitment to human rights and good governance under the Harare Declaration, the widespread belief that gross violations of human rights undermine international peace and security, good grounds exist for seeking to interpret this provision in such a way as to include any form of domestic oppression.[259]

The next question that arises concerns the right of oppressed peoples to resort to any means recognized by the international community to free themselves from domination, a proposition that has been advanced by General Assembly resolutions.[260] There seems to be a consensus that political and non-violent opposition is permissible but does a right to use force exist? Completely divergent views exist on this point. Many Western States claim that the use of force is permissible only in limited circumstances, for instance, in response to prior force used by the occupying power.[261] Developing States argue that the use of force is valid *ab initio* and is justified on the grounds of 'just war' and self-defence. The war, usually known as a war of national liberation,[262] is just because it is being waged in furtherance of a norm of international law, the principle of self-determination, and because the forcible deprivation of a people's right to self-determination constitutes a breach of international law. They have a right to self-defence because prior force has been used against them, although considerable doubt exists as to whether a non-State entity can claim a right to self-defence.[263]

Paragraph 3 enshrines a further controversial point, namely, the right of liberation movements to assistance. The question that arises is, what form of assistance? Three possibilities exist: military intervention by third States; military aid; and political and moral support. The position generally adopted by Western States has been that aid to liberation movements excludes material aid and has usually been confined to humanitarian and economic aid.[264] This assertion is based not only on the view that wars of national liberation are a species of internal conflict but also on the belief that the supply of material aid violates the norm on non-intervention. Furthermore, with the exception of the customary right to self-defence, it is argued that the Security Council has a monopoly on the use of force. Moral assistance appears to be legitimate given the fact that a general consensus exists to that effect in the international community. Such moral and diplomatic support can be expressed in two ways: (a) by recognizing the legitimacy of the struggle; and (b) by recognizing the national liberation movement as the legitimate representative of the people and/or the independence of the State proclaimed by the movement. One example of a general nature is Resolution 3103 (XXVIII), paragraph 1 of which states:

> The struggle of peoples under colonial and alien domination and racist regimes for the implementation of their right to self-determination and independence is legitimate and in full accordance with the principles of international law.

However, many developing States have actively contributed to the material support of liberation movements. It is argued that the calls in numerous General Assembly resolutions for oppressed peoples to struggle for their freedom and to seek and receive support does not necessarily, in the absence of a definition, exclude military or material aid.[265] Direct military aid is thus justified on the grounds of collective self-defence and the implementation of the right to self-determination. Ultimately, however, the conclusion appears to be that, at best, indirect military aid is legitimate.[266]

As has been stated, Article 20 includes economic self-determination and the content of this right seems to have various manifestations. Article 21 clearly refers to the concept of permanent sovereignty over natural resources and must be viewed in the context of the attempts of the developing nations over the last thirty years to create a NIEO.[267] The strong language in which this provision is couched reflects the strength of feeling among the African States that economic, and even political, independence will not be achieved until such time as they genuinely control their natural resources. Thus, paragraph 1 declares that '[a]ll peoples shall freely dispose of their wealth and natural resources', a right that must be exercised in their exclusive interest and of which they cannot be deprived.[268] Paragraph 4 extends this right to the States themselves, with the added obligation of strengthening African unity and solidarity. Moreover, in order for their peoples to benefit fully from the riches of their natural resources, paragraph 5 obliges the Member States to eliminate all forms of foreign economic exploitation, particularly that practised by international monopolies.[269] Given the excesses that have been committed, and are still being committed, by certain multinational companies this duty comes as no surprise,[270] although the negative effect on foreign investment may be unwelcome, and paragraph 2 states that in cases of spoliation the dispossessed people are to have the right to the lawful recovery of their property and adequate compensation. However, by whom will compensation be payable, by the host State, the multinational corporation or the State which administered the non-self-governing terri-tory?[271] This provision appears to be particularly significant to the people of the Western Sahara whose natural resources, in particular phosphates and the rich fishing grounds off its coast, are being plundered by Morocco, and to the people of Namibia.[272] However, the undesirable consequences that such policies could have on foreign investment are tempered somewhat by paragraph 3 which imposes an obligation to 'promote international co-operation based on mutual respect, equitable exchange and the principles of international law'. This suggests that the expropriation or nationalization of foreign property and businesses must be in accordance with current inter-national legal standards, including the payment of compensation. However, as has already been noted, the Banjul Charter is silent as to the appropriate level of compensation, paragraph 2 simply refers to 'adequate compensa-tion'. At present international law requires compensation to be prompt, adequate and effective but the developing States have maintained that the less rigid standard of adequate compensation is appropriate and it may be that this is a principle *de lege ferenda*.[273] It should also be noted that Article 14 makes the compulsory acquisition of property subject to the 'public need' or to 'the general interest of the community and in accordance with the provisions of appropriate laws.'[274]

Article 22 enshrines a controversial right, that to development, specifi-cally economic, social and cultural development which forms part of the NIEO.[275] This definition, which as will be seen is narrower than that existing under general international law, takes into account factors such as the standard of living and opportunities for advancement of the individual, and are designed to address a human dimension, such as the problems of poverty,[276] illiteracy[277] and unemployment.[278] The right to development as such was first promulgated only in 1968 in the Proclamation of Tehran which provided that the implementation of human rights was dependent upon sound and effective policies of economic and social development.[279] It then received the support of a number of commentators.[280] In resolution 37/199 the General Assembly declared that the right to development is an inalienable human right and stressed that the UN should pay particular attention to the developmental aspects of human rights.[281] However, a seminal event in the history of human rights was the proclamation of the Declaration on the Right to Development in 1986 which asserts that human rights are interdependent and indivisible, thus seeking to reconcile the separate paths taken by the International Covenants in 1966.[282] It defines the right to development as 'an inalienable human right by virtue of which every human person and all peoples are entitled to participate in, contribute to, and enjoy economic, social, cultural and political development, in which all human beings and fundamental freedoms can be fully realized'. It should be emphasized that the Declaration adopts a dynamic view of development, necessitating a continuous process of improvement. Nevertheless, a consen-sus on the right to development was only achieved subsequently, at the

World Conference on Human Rights in 1993, and strengthened by the Cairo Declaration adopted at the International Conference on Population and Development in 1994, the Copenhagen Declaration adopted at the Summit for Social Development in 1995 and the Declaration and Platform for Action adopted at the World Conference on Women at Beijing, also in 1995.[283] The right to development can now be said to encompass the concepts of sustainability and respect for the environment, democracy, good governance and respect for all human rights, social as well as economic development, and the fundamental role played by women.[284] Nevertheless, some still reject the concept of a right to development arguing either that this 'right' is merely an aspiration or that its enforcement would necessarily violate civil and political rights. However, there is no evidence to support this allegation and in any event the Declaration on the Right to Development emphasizes the need to give equal weight to civil and political rights. Furthermore, popular participation, democracy and social justice are considered essential elements of the right to development. It should also be noted that Article 22(1) of the Banjul Charter qualifies the right to development by requiring that due regard be paid to the freedom and identity of peoples.

Article 22(2) imposes a duty upon States individually or collectively to ensure the exercise of this right, which is reflected by Articles 3 and 4 of the Declaration. This reflects the widely held view that development can only take place in the context of a favourable international climate, based on a new and equitable economic order. Changes to the present international economic system will obviously be required, entailing international co-operation.[285] Measures at the national level are also necessary, focussing on equality of opportunity,[286] but taking into account the specific needs of each country.[287]

Article 22(1) additionally declares the right of peoples to the equal enjoyment of the common heritage of mankind. The common heritage of mankind is a concept which has received some limited recognition by the international community and is of particular significance with regard to the deep sea-bed and the moon and other celestial bodies.[288] It therefore supplements the right to development and seeks to bring about its realization by having fair access to natural resources beyond national jurisdiction. An alternative interpretation is that the concept of common heritage of mankind refers to the protection for posterity of the cultural heritage of a nation or the wonders of nature, a species of international conservation law.[289]

Article 23 enshrines a principle fundamental to the international community, that of peace and security.[290] Violations of human rights are a constant threat to international peace and security, and vice versa. In addition, it must be stressed that the maintenance of peace and security is a prerequisite for the realization of the right to development.[291] Wars and civil conflicts obstruct development through their consumption of economic and human resources whereas the reduction of military expenditure would help to further development. It is interesting that the Banjul Charter refers not only to international peace and security but also to national peace and security. While the Banjul Charter does not expressly define 'peace and security' it does refer to the principles of solidarity and friendly relations affirmed by the UN and the OAU and it would seem that the principles contained in the UN Declaration on the Principles of International Law Concerning Friendly Relations and Co-operation Among States in Accordance with the UN Charter are directly relevant. It is obvious that human rights cannot be adequately protected in times. of conflict and it follows that to secure their fulfilment a state of peace should prevail. Unfortunately there are currently many African States that cannot be said to be enjoying this right.

Article 24 asserts another recent 'right' interconnected with development,[292] that to environment, and the Banjul Charter is unique in that it is the first human rights document to do so.[293] The right to environment is not defined, and as with Article 22(1) it could be interpreted as seeking to protect natural wonders, but it is submitted that it refers to the international protection of the environment from, *inter alia*, pollution and in particular the principle that States must ensure that activities within their jurisdiction or control do not cause damage to the environment of other States or of areas beyond the limits of national jurisdiction.[294] The dangers of acid rain and the Chernobyl nuclear disaster illustrate the importance of this principle. It is important to note that the OAU has addressed the vexed issue of toxic waste by adopting the Bamako Convention banning the import of waste into Africa. The right to environment could additionally extend to include measures designed to protect the land from ecological disasters such as overgrazing.[295]

It should be observed that the collective rights of minorities are not expressly protected by the Banjul Charter. In light of the recent history of communal violence in parts of Africa, exemplified by the genocidal atrocities in Rwanda in particular, it seems regrettable that the Banjul Charter has not addressed this omission.[296]

Duties

A salient feature of the Banjul Charter, by virtue of Article 27(1), is the emphasis on the individual's obligations towards 'his family and society, the State and other legally recognized communities and the international community'.[297] The scope and extent of these obligations goes considerably further than those imposed by most other international documents. It is clear that the Banjul Charter has been influenced here by traditional African values.

The list of duties contained in Articles 27–29 gives rise to the questions whether they impose legally binding obligations upon the individual and to what extent these duties are enforceable. By definition many of these duties are of a general nature but answers to these questions are particularly important, e.g., can an individual be prosecuted because he has not placed his physical and intellectual abilities at the service of his community as required by Article 29(2)? What is the relationship between such an obligation and the guarantee against forced labour or the right to (intellectual) property? But given that the individual cannot be arraigned before the Commission, how can the Commission seek to enforce these duties? During the drafting conference it was made clear that only States could be held responsible for any violations of the Charter. Furthermore, it was stated that not all the duties were to be carried out to the letter but reference was made to principles which the community accepts but whose immediate application is not envisaged.[298] Nevertheless, some duties are enforceable and the individual who failed in his duty would be answerable under municipal law.

Enforceable duties would appear to include the duty under Article 28 to respect other individuals without discrimination; the duty under Article 29(1) to maintain one's parents in case of need; the duty under paragraph 3 thereof not to compromise the security of the State; the duty under paragraph 5 thereof to contribute to the defence of one's country, which would appear to include military service; and the duty under paragraph 6 thereof to pay taxes. Other duties, such as that involving the harmonious development of the family under Article 29(1) or the preservation and strengthening of positive African values under paragraph 7 thereof, or the promotion and achievement of African unity under paragraph 8 thereof, place a moral rather than a legal obligation upon the individual. It may be that the concept of duties as a whole serves as a code of good citizenship for the people of Africa.[299]

The African Commission on Human and Peoples' Rights

The implementation of the rights enshrined in the Banjul Charter is entrusted to the African Commission on Human and Peoples' Rights (hereafter referred to as the Commission) which by virtue of Article 30 is mandated with promoting human and peoples' rights and ensuring their protection.[300] Its organization does not furnish very many original features by comparison with its counterparts, the European Commission on Human Rights (now abolished by virtue of Protocol 11 ECHR) and the Inter-American Commission on Human Rights, and it should be noted at the outset that its powers of implementation and investigation are comparatively weaker.

Article 31 establishes that the Commission is composed of eleven members, chosen to serve in their personal capacities from amongst African personalities of the highest reputation, integrity and impartiality, with competence in the field of human rights, particular consideration being given to those with legal experience, although legal training is not a prerequisite since the Commission will not be performing a strict legal role.[301] The independence of the Commission must be beyond doubt if it is to perform its functions satisfactorily and if it is secure the trust and co-operation of the State parties, and this is reinforced by Article 38 which requires the members of the Commission upon their election to make a solemn declaration that they will discharge their duties impartially and faithfully.[302] The odd number of commissioners will facilitate the taking of decisions in that a tie in voting may thus be avoided but in the event of a tie Article 64 provides that the Chairman has the casting vote. It has been suggested that the size of the Commission is small by comparison with the membership of the OAU[303] but the Commission would become unwieldly if each Member State could nominate a commissioner.

Article 34 stipulates that the members of the Commission must be the nationals of one of the State parties to the Banjul Charter. Each State party may nominate a maximum of two candidates who must not be of the same nationality. In addition, according to Article 32, the Commission may not include more than one national of the same State. The size of the Commission is supposed to correspond to an equitable geographic distribution reflecting the OAU.[304]

Article 33 requires the members of the Commission to be elected by secret ballot by the OAU Assembly from a list of persons nominated by the States parties to the Banjul Charter. It seems unsatisfactory that States that are not parties to the Banjul Charter should influence the composition of the Commission. According to Article 36 the members of the Commission are elected to serve a renewable six-year term.

The Commission's Chairman and Vice-Chairman are elected under Article 42(1) by its members for a renewable two-year term.[305] It should be noted, however, that the Chairman has few executive powers.[306] In the performance of their duties Article 43 provides that the members of the Commission are to enjoy diplomatic privileges and immunities.

In the event of the death or resignation of a member Article 39 provides that the seat will be declared vacant by the OAU Secretary-General. The OAU Secretary-General can additionally declare the seat vacant if, in the unanimous opinion of his colleagues, a member ceases to fulfil his functions or is incapable of continuing to fulfil them, unless such failure is of a temporary nature.[307] In either case the OAU Assembly must fill that seat unless the remaining period of office was less than six months in which event the seat will be filled in due course. A member of the Commission elected to replace another member must complete their predecessor's mandate.

Article 64(2) provides that the Chairman may convene the Commission whenever necessary but at least once a year.[308] In addition, extraordinary sessions may be convened.[309] To be quorate at least seven members must be present[310] and decisions are taken by a majority of the voting members, with the Chairman having the casting vote in the event of a tie.[311] The OAU's

Secretary-General may attend the Commission's meetings and although he may be invited to speak he does not vote nor participate in the discussions.[312]

The Commission held its constituent meeting in November 1987 under the chairmanship of Izak Nguema of Gabon, who declared that the role of the Commission would not be one of 'embarrassing' African governments. The then OAU Secretary-General, Ide Oumarou, warned the Commission to tread carefully in its 'delicate task' and advised it that its investigative methods should take account of 'our environment, our people and our governments'.[313]

The Commission's mandate is defined by a number of guidelines set out in Article 45. It should be noted at the outset that while the Commission was created to promote and protect human and peoples' rights in Africa its competence in the field of protection is not exclusive but is shared with the OAU Assembly, which has a supervisory role, and the Court on Human and Peoples' Rights. However, the Commission does perform a quasi-judicial function and it possesses jurisdiction to interpret the Banjul Charter and to carry out tasks conferred upon it by the OAU Assembly. It is therefore necessary to consider separately the various functions of the Commission, which may be divided into three categories: promotion; protection; and other areas of competence.

The first, and fundamental, function of the Commission, as provided for by Article 45(1), is to promote human and peoples' rights in Africa, which it is doing with the assistance of NGOs. There appear to be three elements to this function: a studies and information function; a quasi-legislative function; and co-operative functions.[314] In addition, under the Protocol establishing the Court on Human and Peoples' Rights the Commission has access to the Court.

Subparagraph (a) requires the Commission to perform its study and information function in several ways. Thus the Commission acts as a documentation centre. It therefore gathers, classifies and keeps information on human rights in Africa. In addition, it is responsible for disseminating information, either systematically or in response to inquiries, and one method of achieving this is by organizing conferences. Furthermore, the Commission can undertake studies and conduct research. The Commission is also entrusted with encouraging national and local institutions concerned with human and peoples' rights. Finally, the Commission can advise governments.

Subparagraph (b) endows the Commission with a quasi-legislative function by giving it responsibility for developing principles and rules aimed at solving legal problems relating to human rights generally upon which governments may base their legislation. This rather vague requirement is important because of the influence that the Commission can exert upon States parties and it is clear that the drafting of model laws is envisaged.

Finally, subparagraph (c) requires the Commission to co-operate with other African and international institutions concerned with human rights.[315]

The Commission has thus co-operated with non-governmental agencies, such as the UNHCR, and NGOs such as Amnesty International and the International Commission of Jurists.

Article 45(2) requires the Commission to ensure the protection of the specified rights and the importance of this aspect of the Commission's functions cannot be overemphasized. The various procedural devices which the Commission employs are considered in greater detail below and it suffices here to say that the attention of the Commission can be drawn by a State party, individual or organization to any alleged violation of the Banjul Charter by another State party. The Commission will then investigate the complaint and submit its report to the OAU Assembly. Alternatively, it can refer the matter to the Court.

The Commission has two other areas of competence. According to Article 45(3) it can interpret the provisions of the Banjul Charter at the request of a State party, the OAU, or an African organization recognized by the OAU.[316] In the absence of a court at this time it was reasonable to expect the Commission to perform this quasi-judicial function which is similar to the advisory jurisdiction of international judicial bodies. Such a function was necessary given certain ambiguities and innovations contained in the Banjul Charter. In addition, in the course of investigating complaints the Commission must necessarily interpret the Banjul Charter. The Commission's powers in this context are therefore important given that it is performing a quasi-judicial function in defining and declaring the extent of fundamental freedoms and duties.

Finally, Article 45(4) assigns to the Commission the duty of performing any task entrusted to it by the OAU Assembly which would seem to obviate the need of creating *ad hoc* committees on human rights.[317] The tasks envisaged could include special studies or on-site investigations such as allegations of violations by a State party that may have been declared inadmissible on procedural grounds.

Clearly the Commission has an extremely important role to play in the protection of human and peoples' rights and its jurisdiction and powers are set out in Articles 46–58, as supplemented by the Rules of Procedure, and in the Protocol. The Commission is empowered to examine inter-State complaints and 'other communications'. It should be noted that under Article 46 the Commission has broad investigative powers in that it may resort to any appropriate method of investigation in accordance with international law, including the creation of committees and working groups in accordance with Rules 28 and 29, and the Banjul Charter and it may hear from the OAU Secretary-General or any other person capable of enlightening it, including, as has been observed, NGOs and national liberation movements. It appears that the Commission has invoked Article 46 creatively by recommending interim measures of protection and requesting permission for on-site investigations.[318] One of its primary functions is to discover the facts and attempt to reach an amicable settlement based on respect for human rights.[319]

Articles 47–54 govern inter-state complaints.[320] The Banjul Charter provides States with various types of actions if they have good reason to believe that human and peoples' rights are being violated by other State parties. The types of actions provided for envisage a negotiation procedure and a complaint procedure. Under Article 47 and Rule 87 the complainant State can draw the attention of the State that may be at fault to possible violations of the Banjul Charter through a written communication. At the same time this communication is also submitted to the OAU Secretary-General and the Chairman of the Commission, providing a detailed account of the facts denounced and the Charter provisions allegedly breached. The State receiving the communication then has three months in which to issue a written reply which should include information regarding the relevant laws and administrative measures applied or applicable and any redress given or the course of action available.[321] If the complainant State is not satisfied with this statement or if no reply is forthcoming and the question is not settled through bilateral negotiation or 'any other peaceful procedure' Article 48 and Rules 90–92 empower either State to submit the matter to the Commission.[322] The phrase 'any other peaceful procedure' would appear to refer to mediation, good offices or any other method of settling disputes peacefully in accordance with international law. These provisions underline the African emphasis on conciliation rather than adversarial adjudication.

Alternatively, however, a State can submit a complaint directly to the Commission under Article 49.[323] It is interesting to note that the jurisdiction of the Commission is not dependent upon a State party's prior acceptance of its competence, i.e., a State automatically accepts the compulsory jurisdiction of the Commission upon ratification or accession to the Banjul Charter.[324]

It is now necessary to consider procedural issues regarding the Commission's jurisdiction with regard to inter-state complaints. Its jurisdiction *ratione materiae* is broad since Article 47 clearly indicates that its attention may be drawn to any violation, whether by omission or commission, of the Banjul Charter. Its jurisdiction *ratione personae* extends to acts committed by, or imputable to, a State party. Thus acts committed by individuals in a private capacity or private companies lie outside the competence of the Commission. However, caution must be exercised that a State does not renounce its responsibilities by attributing fault to a State servant in an individual capacity. Its jurisdiction *ratione loci* poses some difficulty. It is clear from the wording of the Banjul Charter that many of the rights guaranteed are available not only to the nationals of State parties but also to *any* individual under their jurisdiction. But does the Commission's jurisdiction extend extraterritorially? It would seem that a State party can be responsible for a violation in relation to a national or protected person who is outside the national territory.[325]

Article 50 requires the exhaustion of all existing local remedies. However, States cannot profit by deliberately delaying redress since the Commission can ignore this stricture if it is apparent that exhausting those remedies would entail an inordinate length of time.[326] The Commission's investigative powers are contained in Articles 51 and 52. Once an issue has been referred to it the Commission can request the States concerned to provide it with all relevant information.[327] However, it is not clear whether the States are obliged to supply this information although any lack of co-operation will doubtless feature in the Commission's report. During this stage the States concerned may be represented before the Commission and may submit written or oral observations.[328] In addition, the Commission can approach 'other sources' for any information it deems necessary and this would appear to include other States, individuals, NGOs, the OAU and other international organizations. Nonetheless, during this time the Commission must attempt by all possible means to reach an amicable settlement which must be based on respect for human and peoples' rights.[329]

If no settlement is forthcoming the Commission is required to draft a report stating the facts and its findings which it must subsequently submit to the States concerned and the OAU Assembly.[330] Article 53 allows the Commission to make to the OAU Assembly such recommendations as it considers necessary when submitting the report, so that it could recommend that the matter be closed and no further action be taken, that a resolution be adopted, or that the report be published.[331] The ultimate responsibility however, lies with the OAU Assembly.

As has been observed, the Banjul Charter envisages complaints, or 'communications', 'other than those of State parties' under Article 55. This includes complaints from individuals and NGOs.[332] It is interesting to note that the *locus standi* requirements before the Commission are comparatively broad since individuals and organizations other than the victim can submit a complaint.[333] A number of procedural hurdles have to be overcome before the Commission will entertain a communication, which it will do by a simple majority of its members. Article 56 enumerates seven admissibility requirements and although similar criteria are to be found in comparable international instruments the Banjul Charter goes further in introducing unique and more restrictive requirements of admissibility.[334]

The first condition of admissibility is that the communication must not be anonymous, even if the authors request anonymity, so that 'adequate information with a certain degree of specificity concerning the victim' must be provided.[335] However, if there are fears of reprisals, a real fear in much of Africa, the Commission can protect the author's identity.

The second condition is that the communication must be compatible with the OAU Charter and the Banjul Charter. A claim that the people of Katanga had a right to secede from Zaïre in accordance with the right to self-determination raised the question of compatibility with the basic principles of the OAU.[336] This provision could also be interpreted as a reference to the conditions *ratione materiae, personae* and *temporis*.[337] With regard to subject matter, a communication must refer to specific violations of 'any one of the rights enunciated in the Charter'.[338] Thus vague complaints about the general political climate cannot suffice.[339] Complaints can only be submitted against States parties.[340] Finally, as regards the time of the alleged violation, communications must be submitted against African States which were parties to the Banjul Charter at the time the violations were alleged to have occurred.[341]

The third condition is that the communication must not be disparaging or insulting towards the State concerned, its institutions or the OAU.[342] The Commission hence has the authority to dismiss patently absurb complaints that amount to an abuse of the right of petition. It is important that the adjectives 'disparaging' and 'insulting' should not be interpreted narrowly.

The fourth condition is that the communication must not be based exclusively on information obtained from the mass media. The rationale for this requirement seems to be that communications should not be based on secondary and unsubstantiated allegations[343] although it appears that the Commission has itself taken notice of events disseminated by the media.[344]

The fifth condition requires the exhaustion of existing domestic remedies.[345] This provision reflects a general principle of international law which affords the State the initial opportunity to right any wrongdoing[346] and exists in all major human rights instruments.[347] The Commission has held that domestic remedies refer to 'those normally available in the domestic court system and excluding those available only as a pure discretionary matter from the executive'.[348] It seems that the burden of proof is initially on the applicant.[349]

Domestic remedies must exist, however, and their exhaustion is not required where it is apparent that such procedures would be 'unduly prolonged'. Although the wording of the Banjul Charter may appear prima facie restrictive[350] the practice of the Commission suggests a more liberal approach. Thus remedies do not need to be exhausted if they are 'unavailable, ineffective or unreasonably prolonged',[351] or 'impractical or undesirable'.[352]

The sixth condition is that the communication must be submitted within a reasonable period from the time local remedies were exhausted or from the date the Commission was seized of the matter. No indication is given as to what constitutes 'reasonable' but the Commission seems to have been given considerable flexibility.[353] This should ensure that any imputed State does not profit from delaying tactics.

The final condition is that the communication must not be concerned with cases that have previously been settled under the UN Charter, the OAU Charter or the Banjul Charter.[354] The Commission can therefore reject communications which have been considered by the HRC or which have already been considered by the Commission, unless, for example, new facts emerge.[355] It appears, however, that the Commission itself is divided as to whether it has competence to receive communications identical to those submitted to another international body or whether it is simply precluded from receiving communications which, in the language of the provision, have 'previously been settled'.[356] In order to avoid the duplication of effort the former interpretation seems preferable.[357]

No other formal conditions of admissibility are required and it appears that these criteria are meant to be exhaustive. However, prior to the substantive examination of any communication Article 57 requires that the State concerned be notified by the Commission.[358] That State then has three months in which to respond to the allegations,[359] and the complainant has a right of reply.[360] The Commission must take a decision on admissibility 'as early as possible'.[361]

It should be observed that provision is made under Article 58 for exceptional cases where communications reveal 'the existence of a series of serious or massive violations of human and peoples' rights'.[362] This phrase is not defined but it would seem that specific, isolated violations, however serious, lie beyond the scope of this provision. On the other hand, the violations do not have to be serious *and* massive since these adjectives are divisible.[363] It seems beyond doubt that the gross violations of human rights in Nigeria and Rwanda would meet this description.[364]

Under Article 58(2) the OAU Assembly may request the Commission to undertake in-depth studies of such cases and present factual reports with findings and recommendations. In addition, under paragraph 3 thereof, a case of emergency duly noticed by the Commission must be submitted to the OAU Chairman who may request an in-depth study.[365] This latter provision is designed to overcome the difficulty presented by the fact that the OAU usually meets only once a year and that prolonged delays might otherwise ensue. The Banjul Charter does not define what is meant by 'in-depth study'[366] and it is still too early to state what these procedures may consist of.[367]

In comparison with other human rights bodies the formal powers of the Commission seem weak. This can best be illustrated by reference to Article 58(1) which empowers the Commission to draw the OAU's attention to cases of serious or massive violations. Under Rule 111 the Commission may recommend, but not require, States parties to take interim measures to avoid 'irreparable prejudice' being caused to an alleged victim.[368] The salutary effect that international publicity can have on errant States is not available to the Commission to the same degree. Article 59 provides that all measures adopted by the Commission remain confidential until such time as the OAU decides otherwise. Nevertheless, there is room for optimism. Article 54 requires the Commission to submit an annual report on its activities to the OAU Assembly and these and other measures are now published in, *inter alia*, specialist law journals.[369] In addition, the Commission has assumed a supervisory role monitoring the compliance of States parties with their human rights obligations. Under Article 62 States parties must submit every two years a report on legislative or other measures taken to give effect to the rights and freedoms guaranteed by the Banjul Charter.[370] And as will now be seen, the Commission has an enhanced role under the Protocol. Thus, although the Commission is not strictly speaking a judicial body, it shares more similarities with the UN Human Rights Committee than the European Court of Human Rights, the nature of its work will inevitably involve it in evaluating legal concepts, rules and situations. In Articles 60 and 61 the Banjul Charter gives the Commission various principles from which it can draw inspiration. The primary measures relate to the international law of human rights, and in particular various African and UN documents, such as the UDHR and the International Covenants to which many African States are parties. The secondary sources include other international conventions, presumably such instruments as the ECHR and the ACHR, insofar as they reflect rules expressly recognized by OAU Member States, African practices consistent with international standards, customary law, general principles of law recognized by African States, and legal precedents and doctrine. The African States thereby declare their adherence to, *inter alia*, general international law.

The Nouakchott Protocol on the Establishment of an African Court on Human and Peoples' Rights

The observation has already been made that the Banjul Charter makes no provision for a court to enforce the rights guaranteed thereunder. This omission was justified on the basis that the African conception of law is averse to third party adjudication, which is considered as confrontational, but alternatively is traditionally based on reconciliation reached through consensus. In addition, many African States would have been reluctant to ratify the Charter had provision been made for compulsory judicial settlement. However, this difficulty could easily have been overcome. The jurisdiction of the court need not have been automatic but could have been made contingent on acceptance by States through separate declarations,[371] including the possibility of appending reservations.[372]

The lack of a judicial remedy has attracted considerable criticism as undermining the effective application of human and peoples' rights in Africa.[373] Events, such as in Nigeria, appear to have proved the critics correct. The Commission is mandated under the Banjul Charter with promoting human and peoples' rights and ensuring their protection. However, as has been seen, its powers of implementation and investigation are relatively weak. It has no powers of enforcement. Its decisions either have declaratory effect or are merely recommendatory. Ultimate power resides with the OAU, a political body the resolutions of which have no binding force.

The Africa-wide system of human rights has therefore been resting on shaky foundations. The Commission has generally proved unable to act as a strong guardian of human and peoples' rights.[374] Consequently, continued opposition to a court could no longer be credibly maintained as compatible with respect for human and peoples' rights.

In June 1994 the OAU, meeting in its thirtieth ordinary session in Tunis, requested its Secretary-General to 'convene a Government experts' meeting to ponder, in conjunction with the African Commission, over the means to enhance the efficiency of the African Commission in considering particularly the establishment of an African Court of Human and Peoples' Rights.'[375]

The resultant Draft Protocol to the African Charter on Human and Peoples' Rights on the Establishment of an African Court of Human and Peoples' Rights was adopted by a group of government experts meeting in Cape Town in September 1995.[376] Comments were invited from the OAU Member States and a second meeting was held in Mauritania in April 1997.[377] The draft protocol underwent some revision but was adopted by consensus and named the Nouakchott Protocol.[378] A third government experts meeting was convened in December 1997 in Addis Ababa to review any further proposals for amending the Nouakchott Protocol following the failure of the OAU Assembly to adopt the Protocol at its summit in Harare in June 1997. The Addis Ababa draft, which amended the Nouakchott draft in some significant, and even retrograde, ways, was adopted by the OAU Assembly at its thirty-fourth ordinary session in Ouagadougou, Burkina Faso, in June 1998.[379]

The Establishment of the Court

The Preamble seeks initially to place the Nouakchott Protocol in the wider context of a natural progression in the achievement of the legitimate aspirations of the African peoples and draws a causal link between the objectives of the OAU, including freedom, equality and justice, and the establishment of the Court. More immediately, it recalls that the Banjul Charter reaffirms adherence to human and peoples' rights and, acknowledging that its objectives are to promote and protect such rights, it is firmly convinced that their attainment requires the establishment of an African Court of Human and Peoples' Rights, an aim achieved under Article 1 of the Nouakchott Protocol. The Court is an integral part of the OAU.

The seat of the Court, according to Article 25(1), is to be determined by the OAU Assembly although this place need not be permanent since, under paragraph 2 thereof, it may be changed by the Assembly after due consultation with the Court. It should be noted that if the Court deems it desirable it may convene in the territory of any OAU Member State with its prior permission.

The Court and the Commission

There had been some early speculation that the Commission, criticized as ineffectual, should be abolished and replaced entirely by a court but the prevailing consensus was that the court should reinforce the work of the Commission.[380] Thus, according to the Preamble and Article 2 of the Nouakchott Protocol the Court is to complement the protective mandate of the Commission in accordance with the terms of the Banjul Charter. As will become apparent, the Commission will play a prominent role as a filter mechanism. The Nouakchott Protocol consequently envisages a two-tier system comparable to that currently operating under the ACHR.

Jurisdiction and Seizin

It is self-evident that the effective guarantee of human and peoples' rights will be largely dependent on the jurisdiction conferred upon, and assumed by, the Court. The Nouakchott Protocol provides for various heads of jurisdiction. It should be noted that the jurisdiction of the Court with regard to cases brought by the Commission or State parties under Article 5(1) is automatic upon ratification of the Protocol and is not dependent on further declarations by State parties.[381] However, jurisdiction is optional with regard to the standing of NGOs and individuals and States must make a separate declaration under Article 34(6) accepting the competence of the Court to receive petitions from such complainants under Article 5(3).[382] The Court cannot entertain an individual petition against a State party that has not made such a declaration.

Under Article 3(1) the jurisdiction of the Court extends to all cases and disputes submitted to it concerning the interpretation and application of the Banjul Charter, the Nouakchott Protocol and any other applicable African human rights instrument. This final clause is of particular interest because of its innovative character. It is broader in scope than Article 32 ECHR and Article 62(3) ACHR which restrict the respective Courts to those treaty systems. It would appear to extend the jurisdiction of the Court over, e.g., the OAU Convention on Refugees, and the African Charter on the Rights and Welfare of the Child, and even UN treaties such as the International Covenants on Human Rights. This particular power of the Court to pronounce on other African human rights treaties seems a welcome development but it does not appear to be without its problems. Perhaps controversially it could include regional African instruments such as the revised ECOWAS Treaty or the AEC Treaty.[383] What would the relationship be between the African Court of Human and Peoples' Rights and the AEC Court?[384] It is unclear whether the Nouakchott Protocol enshrines the principle of exclusivity of competence.[385] Nevertheless, the African Court of

Human and Peoples' Rights seems to be the only competent judicial authority to pronounce on the Banjul Charter and Protocol. Potential problems of concurrent jurisdiction or conflicting judgments do not appear to have been properly addressed.

An additional source of potential conflict arises in relation to the Commission's quasi-judicial function under Article 45(3) of the Banjul Charter to interpret the provisions of the Banjul Charter at the request of a State party, the OAU, or an African organization recognized by the OAU.[386] The Commission retains this power notwithstanding the creation of the Court. It is unclear what effect the establishment of the Court will have in practice in this context since the potential for duplication exists. One can only speculate that it may be that this specific role of the Commission will fall into desuetude or it may be that the Court will be asked to review the Commission's interpretations and provide definitive rulings.

Given the traditional reluctance among African States to submit to third-party adjudication, the power of the Court to *apply* the law is a welcome and necessary development if human rights are to have any meaningful protection in Africa.[387] The concern that the jurisdiction of the Court might have been restricted to issuing declaratory judgments only, similar to that of the Commission under Article 45(3) of the Banjul Charter described above, has been allayed. However, the composition of the Court assumes added significance if the judges elected are prepared to interpret the law in a dynamic and teleological fashion so as to make it truly effective.[388] Nevertheless, this provision has the potential of giving the Court ample opportunities to develop a significant and distinctive human rights jurisprudence.

If the jurisdiction of the Court is disputed Article 3(2) declares that the matter must be settled by the decision of the Court. This is identical to Article 32(2) ECHR and corresponds to a fundamental principle of international law, namely, 'the inherent power of a tribunal to interpret the text establishing its jurisdiction'.[389] However, as has been observed above, issues of disputed jurisdiction might arise.

The Nouakchott Protocol does not make express provision for parties to file preliminary objections, although Article 3(2) would appear to make allusion to this procedure by envisaging challenges to the Court's jurisdiction. It is likely that this question will be addressed by the Court's Rules of Procedure.[390]

Contentious Jurisdiction

According to Article 5(1) the following are entitled to submit contentious cases to the Court: (a) the Commission; (b) a State party which has lodged a complaint to the Commission; (c) a State party against which a complaint has been lodged at the Commission; (d) a State party whose citizen is a victim of human rights violations. These, in contrast to applicants under

Article 5(3), could be described as privileged applicants in that their standing is not dependent on an additional declaration accepting the competence of the Court.[391] The wording of this provision suggests that States do not have a general right of access to the Court, but that a prior communication to the Commission seems a condition precedent for the initiation of proceedings before the Court by States, with the exception of subparagraph (d). Only the Commission appears to have unlimited access to the Court in the sense that it can refer new cases to the Court. This may be important in relation to Article 58 of the Banjul Charter. The wording of subparagraphs (b) and (c) further suggests that the States in question need not await the outcome of the Commission's deliberations before approaching the Court.

Article 5(2) enshrines what appears to be a welcome development in human rights instruments in that it permits a State party which has an interest in a case to request the Court to be permitted to join.[392] There is no guidance as to what the phrase 'a legal interest' might mean but the Court may choose to be guided by either the jurisprudence of the ICJ, which has adopted a strict approach to requests for intervention,[393] or that of the European Court of Human Rights.[394] It is instructive to note that the requirement in previous drafts that States show a *legal* interest has been omitted. The procedure has now been simplified. However, a danger exists that States may be too ready to intervene. It is not clear whether the time limit of three months within which *judgments* should be delivered in accordance with Article 27(1) applies to this procedure.

The Nouakchott Protocol also recognizes the *locus standi* of other applicants and provides for *actio popularis*, albeit to a limited extent. Thus, according to Article 5(3), the Court may allow individuals and NGOs with observer status before the Commission to bring cases before the Court.[395] However, the Court is not compelled to entertain such an application since Article 6(3) gives the Court the option of referring it to the Commission. The Court might prefer to take this route in circumstances where other forms of peaceful settlement would seem more appropriate, either because of sensitive political issues or because a State accepts responsibility. Hurdles of admissibility must still be satisfied by these applicants.

While the Court deliberates on admissibility it may request the Commission's opinion on the matter. While the Commission is obliged to respond promptly, the wisdom of what will necessarily be a dilatory procedure appears questionable. However, this may be a means of addressing the concern of some States on the vexed issue of domestic jurisdiction which undermined the Cape Town draft.[396] The end result has been a compromise which makes the Court accessible to individuals and NGOs subject to the prior acceptance of such jurisdiction by States. The danger does exist that the Court might not become fully functional when the Protocol enters into force. It is likely that some of the worst perpetrators of serious abuses of human rights, Nigeria, Sudan, may not be brought to account since it is improbable that they will accept the Court's exceptional jurisdiction. However, it needs to be recalled that the Commission could invoke Article 5(1)(a) and refer the matter to the Court, as could a State under Article 5(1)(b). Nevertheless, it is encouraging that individuals and NGOs have been given a role in protecting human rights.

The Protocol does not address the possibility of a non-appearing State party. Provision for such a contingency should be made.[397]

Advisory Jurisdiction

The Protocol bestows advisory jurisdiction upon the Court. Article 4 thus confers upon the Court competence to give advisory opinions on any legal matter relating to the Banjul Charter or other African human rights instrument at the request of a member State of the OAU, any OAU organ, or any African organization recognised by the OAU.[398] This power is considerably broader in scope than the advisory jurisdiction of the European Court of Human Rights under Article 47 ECHR but is similar to that of the IACHR under Article 64(1) ACHR[399] although the Nouakchott Protocol goes further by granting *locus standi* to other African organizations. However, unlike Article 64(2) ACHR, no express provision is made for allowing the Court to render opinions regarding the compatibility of a State's domestic laws with human rights instruments, although it could be implied in the language of the provision.[400] Given the adherence to the principle of non-interference in the internal affairs of States by African States it should come as no surprise if the assumption of such jurisdiction were resisted.

It is interesting to note that all member States of the OAU appear able to request an opinion, whether or not they are parties to the Nouakchott Protocol. This would include parties to the Banjul Charter which have not ratified the Protocol. The recognition of a broad range of applicants, including African organizations, could give rise to problems similar to those discussed above in relation to the contentious recognition under Article 3(1). On the other hand, such a wide jurisdiction, if patterned on the Inter-American model, has the potential of strengthening the commitment to human rights and giving rise to a rich jurisprudence.

It is important to note that the power of the Court to render advisory opinions is purely discretionary, as evidenced by the inclusion of the word 'may' in Article 4(1). It remains to be seen in what circumstances the Court may choose to decline to exercise its advisory jurisdiction but the Court could make creative use of this jurisdiction were it to follow the precedent set by the IACHR.[401]

Article 4(2) requires the Court to give reasons for its advisory opinions and enables the judges to deliver separate or dissenting opinions. This appears to be standard international judicial practice.[402]

It is a trite observation that advisory opinions are not legally binding as such but it would be surprising if the Court's opinions were not to acquire the authoritative or persuasive status accorded to the opinions of the ICJ and the IACHR.

Conditions for Considering Communications

Individuals and NGOs invoking the jurisdiction of the Court must overcome the hurdles of admissibility listed in Article 56 of the Banjul Charter.[403] Thus Article 6(2) of the Protocol requires that the Court rule on the admissibility of cases taking account of Article 56 of the Banjul Charter. The Court appears to have been given flexibility since the provision does not state that the hurdles of admissibility *must* be satisfied, only that the Court must take account of them. If the Court approached this matter in a dynamic manner the cause of justice could be advanced considerably. There seems to be no reason why communications previously declared inadmissible by the Commission could not be reopened by the Court.[404] All other conditions for the consideration of communications are to be addressed by the Rules of Procedure.

It is interesting to note that under Article 9 the Court is given the power to attempt amicable settlements. It is submitted that this function seems more appropriate for the Commission.[405] Nonetheless, a settlement should be reached only when the public interest is not compromised.

Hearings and Presentations

Under Article 10(1) the Court is required to conduct its proceedings in public. However, proceedings may be held in camera in circumstances to be addressed by the Rules of Procedure.[406]

Under Article 10(2) any party to the case is entitled to be represented by a legal representative of the party's choice.[407] Free legal representation may be provided in the interests of justice.[408] Given the abject poverty in many parts of Africa this circumstance appears significant but it will only prove effective if proper funding is forthcoming. The work of the Commission has suffered as a result of inadequate funding[409] but the international community must ensure that the Court avoids this fate.

Article 10(3) guarantees protection to any person, witness or representative of parties who appears before the Court necessary for the proper discharging of their functions and duties before the Court. Individuals and others should therefore be able to appear before the Court without fear of retribution. This is a welcome development since arbitrary detention and even death is all too common in parts of Africa. It is interesting to observe that in the Inter-American system the IACHR has utilised its power to indicate provisional measures under Article 63(2) ACHR to protect witnesses due to testify before it when their safety was believed to be at risk.[410] Furthermore, Article 40(2) of the IACHR's Rules of Procedure obliges States to refrain from instituting proceedings or taking reprisals against any person on account of their testimony before the Court. It is unclear how, if at all, individuals are to be effectively protected within the jurisdiction of a State party to the Nouakchott Protocol but it is submitted that this guarantee could be strengthened were the Court to use creatively its competence to indicate provisional measures under Article 27(2).[411]

Sources of Law

According to Article 7 the Court must apply the provisions of the Banjul Charter and other human rights instruments. The Court, which in time will no doubt give rise to a distinctive jurisprudence, can thus draw inspiration from the wealth of general and particular international law, including the UDHR, the ICCPR, the ECHR and the ACHR. No express mention is made of the norms of *jus cogens*, which incorporate human rights law,[412] but as part of general international law they should undoubtedly influence the Court. It will be interesting to see if the Court builds a distinctive jurisprudence emphasizing the second and third generation rights advanced by the developing world but which are still a matter of controversy within conservative western circles.

Composition of the Court

According to Article 11(1) the Court will consist of eleven judges, who must be nationals of OAU Member States. This is only a fraction of the actual membership of the OAU and should ensure that the bench does not become unwieldly.[413] The possibility exists that a national of an OAU Member State that has not ratified the Banjul Charter nor the Nouakchott Protocol may be elected to serve on the bench.[414] However, only States parties to the Protocol may nominate candidates.[415] No two judges can be nationals of the same State.[416]

The judges are elected in an individual capacity, i.e., they must not follow instructions from any State or other agency. This requirement should be read in conjunction with Article 17(1) which guarantees the independence of the judges. A general obligation exists to ensure that judges consider all cases impartially, free from inducements, pressure, influence, threats or other interference.[417] Additionally, the judges enjoy all immunities extended to diplomatic agents under international law during their term of office.[418] Article 17(2) seeks to avoid conflict of interest by requiring a judge who has previously been involved in a case to recuse himself. All judges, except for the President,[419] are to be part-time[420] but they must not perform any activity which is incompatible with their independence or impartiality or the demands of their office.[421] As is standard practice in international tribunals, judges may be drawn from varied backgrounds.[422] A novel provision is the requirement to give due consideration to adequate gender representation in the nomination process.[423]

Judges are elected by secret ballot by the OAU Assembly.[424] Again, adequate gender representation must be observed[425] which implies that the candidatures of certain women must survive the nomination process. Article 14(2) requires that Africa's main regions and its principal legal traditions (civil, common, Roman-Dutch and Islamic law, but is customary law included?) are represented on the Court.[426] It is curious that no similar direction is required at the nomination stage.

The judges' term of office is six years with the possibility of a further renewable period.[427] However, a judge may be suspended or removed from office when the other members of the Court are unanimously of the view that he or she no longer fulfils the requirements of the office.[428] The Court's decision can be overturned by the OAU Assembly.[429]

Procedural Issues

Article 23 provides that the Court will meet with a quorum consisting of at least seven judges. No provision is made for chambers.[430] Neither does the Nouakchott Protocol envisage the appointment of *ad hoc* judges. This is curious in light of the requirement under Article 22 that judges holding the nationality of a State party to a case before the Court are disqualified from hearing the case.[431]

Article 26 obliges the Court to hear submissions by all parties and to this end it may receive written and oral evidence and other representations including expert testimony. The Court has a wide discretion as to the evidence and witnesses it will admit but the effective protection of human rights would be greatly enhanced if the Court were to allow representations from a broad category of *amici curiae*.[432] If it considers it necessary, the Court can hold an enquiry.

If the Court concludes that human rights have been violated, Article 27(1) requires that it 'shall make appropriate orders to remedy the violation, including the payment of fair compensation or reparation.' The Court is thus obliged to make an award.[433] It is unclear whether the Nouakchott Protocol envisages restitution in kind as a remedy although it could be covered by the concept of 'reparation' and the general wording of the provision.[434]

Under Article 27(2) the Court must adopt such provisional measures as it deems necessary in cases of 'extreme gravity and urgency', and 'to avoid irreparable harm to persons'.[435] Stringent requirements must therefore be met. It is nevertheless not entirely clear when the Court is authorized to adopt such measures, that is, can it act *proprio motu*, is it at the request of a party to the case, is it only in relation to a case already pending before the Court, or at the request of the Commission with respect to a case not yet submitted to the Court,[436] or will the Court want to satisfy itself that it has jurisdiction, *prima facie* or otherwise, before adopting provisional measures? These issues must be addressed by the Rules of Procedure.

Article 28 governs the Court's judgments in contentious cases. Thus, judgments must be taken by majority, and must be final and not subject to appeal.[437] Moreover, judgments must be reasoned, as are advisory opinions under Article 4(2), read in open court and separate and dissenting opinions may be attached.[438] It is interesting to note that Article 28(1) requires the Court to render its judgment within three months of having completed its deliberations. This does not seem an unreasonable expectation in the context of the protection of human rights.

The judgments of the Court are binding; thus States parties to cases decided by the Court 'undertake to comply with the judgment ... and to guarantee its execution'.[439] International practice suggests that the Court's jurisprudence will have a persuasive effect on other States. However, the Court has no power to enforce its judgments, although it can draw the Assembly's attention to any cases in which a State has not complied with a judgment in its annual report under Article 31. Under Article 29(2) the Council of Ministers is entrusted with the task of monitoring the execution of judgments on the Assembly's behalf.[440] Without further clarification it is unlikely that the Council of Ministers will have any powers to ensure compliance. Yet a creative interpretation of Article 27(1) could allow the Court to award punitive damages in cases where the applicant establishes that a State has flouted a judgment of the Court and has failed to make reparation to a victim.[441]

Conclusion

The post-war era has been distinguished by the momentous advances in the protection of human rights. Although Africa made a late arrival it is nevertheless making a distinctive contribution. The Banjul Charter is a welcome development in the regional protection of human rights and reinforces the universal commitments to human rights made by many African States. The Banjul Charter is not, however, a duplicate of other international or regional human rights instruments but represents an African notion of human and peoples' rights. To that end it incorporates a number of distinctive features expressly reflecting traditional African values and was innovative in imposing obligations on the individual towards the State and the community. In addition, the Banjul Charter includes economic, social and cultural rights as well as the more controversial third generation or peoples' rights, with particular emphasis placed on the right to development. The rights of survival are given prominence. However, in other respects the achievements of the Banjul Charter are more modest. Individual rights are undermined through the extensive use of clawback clauses and the national authorities retain considerable discretion. Furthermore, its enforcement mechanisms are comparatively weak. Consequently, the Nouakchott Protocol on an African Court is an exciting prospect which should enhance the protection of human rights. Although the right of access by individual applicants is limited and justly deserves criticism, the creation of a court is a seminal development. The Banjul Charter attracted a remarkable degree of consensus and entered into force within a relatively short period of time. It is to be hoped that the Nouakchott Protocol will be adopted in the not too distant future. Ultimately, however, an effective guarantee for the enjoyment of human and peoples' rights is a culture of pluralism and tolerance, and respect for the rule of law. In this respect, much remains to be done in parts of Africa.

Notes

1. I. Brownlie, (ed.) *Basic Documents on International Law* (4th edn 1995) p. 255; *United States Diplomatic and Consular Staff in Tehran* (*United States of America* v. *Iran*) ICJ Reports 1980, p. 3.
2. See, e.g., the statement made by the Observer for Swaziland to the Human Rights Commission in 1997, UN Doc. E/CN.4/1997/SR.4, paras. 46, 47. See also *Mika Miha* v. *Equatorial Guinea*, Communication No. 414/1990, UN Doc. CCPR/C/51/D/414/1990, where Equatorial Guinea had sought to argue, unsuccessfully, that the communication constituted an interference in its internal affairs even though it had ratified the Optional Protocol to the ICCPR accepting the HRC's competence to consider complaints from individuals subject to the State party's jurisdiction.
3. It has been argued that the one-party State is not necessarily less democratic or more likely to abuse human rights than a pluralist democracy, see Y. Khushalani, 'Human Rights in Asia and Africa', 4 *HRLJ*(1983) 403 at pp. 418–21, who also puts forward a number of principles which, if observed, would preserve the rule of law and human rights in a one-party State. But see *contra*, B.P. Wanda, 'The One-Party State and the Protection of Human Rights in Africa with Particular Reference to Political Rights', 3 *RADIC* (1991) 756. In Western circles a pluralistic democracy protecting human rights within the framework of the rule of law is advanced as the optimum means of government. The question arises whether this system of government is suitable for the very different conditions of Africa. Africa has not had a history of constitutionalism and, barring a few exceptions, liberal democracy has not taken root. National unity, order and development have usually taken precedence over democracy. Multipartism is often equated with tribalism and division. Certainly, democracy must be more than mere majority rule. However, the fear of tribalism can be no more than an excuse to perpetuate a dictatorship. The seeming success of Museveni's Uganda provides an interesting possibility out of this dilemma whereby politics is partyless and elections are non-partisan, see further, J. Oloka-Onyango, 'Constitutional Transition in Museveni's Uganda: New Horizons or Another False Start?' 39 *JAL* (1995) 156. Nevertheless, in recent years there has been a reaction against the abuses of authoritarian one-party rule and

political pluralism, good governance and constitutionalism have been widely introduced with a view to restoring legitimacy, e.g., in Burkina Faso, UN Doc. HRI/CORE/1/Add.30, p. 5, Chad, UN Doc. HRI/CORE/1/Add.88, p. 12, Gabon, UN Doc. HRI/CORE/1/Add.65/Rev.1, pp. 5, 6, Guinea, UN Doc. HRI/CORE/1/Add.80, p. 4, South Africa, UN Doc. HRI/CORE/1/Add.92, Tanzania, UN Doc. ICCPR/C/79/Add.97, para. 4, and Tunisia, UN Doc. E/CN.4/1998/SR.31, paras. 46, 47. See further, the ECA's African Economic Report – 1998, Part II.A. The momentum of these changes is so overwhelming that the adoption of multipartism is inevitable even when the people seem to support a single party system, as in Tanzania, UN Doc. CCPR/C/83/Add.2, paras. 2–6. The transition to democracy is not without its problems, however, as ethnic and social tensions can sometimes be exacerbated, as in Burundi, UN Doc. E/CN.4/1998/72, or Togo, UN Doc. HRI/CORE/1/Add.38/Rev.1, p. 10. Cf. Article 25 ICCPR, and General comment 25, UN Doc. HRI/GEN/1/Rev.3, pp. 49–54, Article 3 of the First Protocol ECHR, and Article 23 ACHR. It has therefore been suggested that there is a right to democratic governance, see T.M. Franck. 'The Emerging Right to Democratic Governance', 86 *AJIL* (1992) 46; UN Commission on Human Rights, Working paper on the promotion and protection of human rights by the exercise of democracy and the establishment of a democratic society, submitted by Osman El-Hajje, UN Doc. E/CN.4/Sub.2/1997/30. For an African view, see D.M. Ayine, 'Ballots as Bullets?: Compliance with Rules and Norms Providing for the Right to Democratic Governance: An African Perspective', 10 *RADIC* (1998) 709. See further *supra*, p. 126.

4. I. Brownlie, *Basic Documents on Human Rights* (2nd edn 1981) p. 426. See further, U.O. Umozurike, *The African Charter on Human and Peoples' Rights* (1997) p. 24.

5. See further Chapter 3 of this book.

6. Article 10(2). Cf. Article 20(2) UDHR which states that no one may be compelled to belong to an association. See further note 167 *infra*.

7. On the substantive amendments, see P. Kunig, 'The Protection of Human Rights by International Law in Africa', 25 *German Yearbook of International Law* (1982) 138.

8. Text in *Naldi*, p. 109.

9. See Article 63. On the Banjul Charter generally, see Umozurike, note 4 *supra*; C.E. Welch, Jr. 'The OAU and Human Rights: Regional Promotion of Human Rights', in Y. El-Ayouty (ed.), *The Organization of African Unity after Thirty Years* (1994) Chapter 5; R. D'Sa, 'Human and Peoples' Rights: Distinctive Features of the African Charter', 29 *JAL* (1985) 72; R. Gittleman, 'The African Charter on Human and Peoples' Rights: A Legal Analysis', 22 *Virginia Journal of International Law* (1982) 667; O. Ojo and A. Sesay, 'The OAU and Human Rights: Prospects for the 1980s and Beyond', 8 *Human Rights Quarterly* (1986) 89. It is interesting to note by way of comparison that the Inter-American Court of Human Rights has held that the ACHR comes into force for those States that ratify or accede to it on the date of deposit of the instrument of ratification or accession, 'The Effects of Reservations on the Entry into Force of the American Convention on Human Rights', 22 *ILM* 37 (1983).

10. Only Eritrea and Ethiopia have still to sign or ratify.

11. Welch, note 9 *supra*, pp. 55, 56.

12. In this context, see the African Nuclear-Weapon-Free Zone Treaty (Treaty of Pelindaba) 1996, 8 *RADIC* (1996) p. 456.

13. See the Vienna Declaration and Programme of Action adopted by the UN World Conference on Human Rights at Vienna in 1993 which emphasized that all human rights are universal, indivisible and interdependent, 32 *ILM* 1661 (1993), Part I, para. 5.

14. In order better to understand the strengths and weaknesses of the Banjul Charter comparisons will be drawn with international human rights law where relevant. The following OAU Member States are parties to the International Covenants: Algeria (including Optional Protocol); Angola (including Optional Protocol); Benin (including Optional Protocol); Burundi; Cameroon (including Optional Protocol); Cape Verde; Central African Republic (including Optional Protocol); Chad (including Optional Protocol); Congo (including Optional Protocol); Côte d'Ivoire (including Optional Protocol); Democratic Republic of the Congo (including Optional Protocol); Egypt; Equatorial Guinea (including Optional Protocol); Ethiopia; Gabon; Gambia (including Optional Protocol); Guinea (including Optional Protocol); Guinea-Bissau (ICES only); Kenya; Lesotho; Libya (including Optional Protocol); Madagascar (including Optional Protocol); Malawi (including Optional Protocol); Mali; Mauritius (including Optional Protocol); Mozambique; Namibia (including Optional Protocol); Niger (including Optional Protocol); Nigeria; Rwanda; Senegal (including Optional Protocol); Seychelles (including Optional Protocol); Sierra Leone (including Optional Protocol); Somalia (including Optional Protocol); Sudan; Tanzania; Togo (including Optional Protocol); Tunisia; Uganda (including Optional Protocol); Zambia (including Optional Protocol); Zimbabwe. Liberia, São Tomé e Príncipe and South Africa have signed the International Covenants. Morocco is also a party to the International Covenants. For scholarly articles providing a comparative analysis of the Banjul Charter with other international human rights documents, see Gittleman, note 9 *supra*; B. Obinna Okere, 'The Protection of Human Rights in Africa and the African Charter on Human and Peoples' Rights: A Comparative Analysis with the European and American Systems', 6 *Human Rights Quarterly* (1984) 141, who, at p. 158, describes the Banjul Charter as 'modest in its objectives and flexible in its means'.

15. Umozurike, note 4 *supra*, Chapter 8; J. Cobbah, 'African Values and the Human Rights Debate: An African Perspective', 9 *Human Rights Quarterly* (1987) 322.

16. See note 13 *supra*. African States have traditionally emphasized the link between development and human rights, and development and democracy, that the promotion and protection of civil and political rights are dependent on social justice, UN Doc. E/CN.4/1993/SR.47, paras. 5, 6, 24. See further, Vienna Declaration and Programme of Action, Part II, C.

17. See Gittleman and D'Sa, note 9 *supra*..

18. But see Article 27(2). Cf. Articles 15 ECHR, 4 ICCPR and 27 ACHR; and see General comment 5, UN Doc. HRI/GEN/1/Rev.3; *Lawless* v. *Ireland* Series A, Vol. 3 (1961); *Ireland* v. *United Kingdom* Series A, Vol. 25 (1978); *Brogan* v. *United Kingdom* Series A, Vol. 145-B (1988); *Brannigan and McBride* v. *United Kingdom* Series A, Vol. 258-B (1993). See further, J. Oraa, *Human Rights in States of Emergency in International Law* (1992); D.J. Harris, M. O'Boyle and C. Warbrick, *Law of the European Convention on Human Rights* (1995) Chapter 16.

19. See E.A. Ankumah, *The African Commission on Human and Peoples' Rights* (1996) Chapter 5.5.4. Gittleman, note 9 *supra*, p. 159, writes that the Banjul Charter is 'incapable of supplying even a scintilla of external restraint upon a government's power to create laws contrary to the spirit of the rights granted'. Umozurike, who is less critical, divides the Banjul Charter's civil and political rights into unrestricted and restricted rights, note 4 *supra*, Chapter 3.

20. See *Commission Nationale des Droits de l'Homme et des Libertés* v. *Chad* (Communication No. 74/92) 18 *HRLJ* (1997) 34 at para. 21, where the African Commission stated that the impossibility of derogating during emergencies meant that 'even a civil war in Chad cannot be used as an excuse by the State violating or permitting violations of rights in the African Charter.' The jurisprudence of the European Court of Human Rights is of interest. For example, the

Court has consistently held that limitations, which must have a legitimate aim and be prescribed by law, must be interpreted narrowly, for example, by being 'necessary in a democratic society', *Handyside* v. *United Kingdom* Series A, Vol. 24 (1976), para. 48; *Olsson* v. *Sweden* Series A, Vol. 130 (1988), para. 67; and proportionate, *Campbell* v. *United Kingdom* series A, Vol. 233 (1993); see Harris, O'Boyle and Warbrick, note 18 *supra*, pp. 289–301. The phrase 'in accordance with the law' has been interpreted to mean that there has to be a measure of legal protection in domestic law against arbitrary interference by public authorities, Harris, O'Boyle and Warbrick, note 18, *supra*, pp. 285–9. However, in all these circumstances it is acknowledged that the State has a 'margin of appreciation', see, e.g., *Lithgow* v. *United Kingdom* Series A, Vol. 102 (1986) where the European Court of Human Rights stated that 'it will respect the legislature's judgment ... unless that judgment was manifestly without reasonable foundation' (para. 122). For further examples, see *Dudgeon* v. *United Kingdom* Series A, Vol. 45 (1981); *Rees* v. *United Kingdom* Series A, Vol. 106 (1986); *Mueller* v. *Switzerland* Series A, Vol. 133 (1988). See also, H.C. Yourow, *The Margin of Appreciation Doctrine in the Dynamics of European Human Rights Jurisprudence* (1996). The ECJ also recognizes this concept, see e.g., Case 34/79 *R* v. *Henn and Darby* [1978] ECR 3795.

21. *Reservations to the Genocide Convention Case* ICJ Reports 1951, p. 15; Article 19 Vienna Convention on the Law of Treaties 1969. It seems that two States, Egypt and Zambia, entered reservations, Umozurike, note 4 *supra*, p. 27.

22. International Commission of Jurists, *Human and Peoples' Rights in Africa and the African Charter* (1986) p. 34. See Article 56 of the Vienna Convention on the Law of Treaties. Denunciation of a human rights treaty seems inconceivable in the present political climate, but cf. Article 58 ECHR. It should also be observed that in common with other human rights treaties the Banjul Charter makes no provision for the expulsion of States parties, see Article 60(5) of the Vienna Convention on the Law of Treaties.

23. In *Wemhoff* v. *Germany* Series A, Vol. 7 (1968) p. 23, the European Court of Human Rights stated that as a law-making treaty, the ECHR must be interpreted in the manner 'most appropriate in order to realise the aim and achieve the object of the treaty, and not that which would restrict to the greatest possible degree the obligations undertaken by the parties'. Furthermore, in *Tyrer* v. *United Kingdom* Series A, Vol. 26 (1978) para. 31, the Court said that the ECHR is 'a living instrument which ... must be interpreted in the light of present day conditions'. See also *Compulsory Membership of Journalists Association Case* 25 ILM 123 (1986). A similar approach has been taken by the judiciary in Africa in relation to constitutional interpretation, see, e.g., *Attorney-General and Another* v. *Kasonde and Others* [1994] 3 LRC 144; *Dow* v. *Attorney-General* [1992] LRC (Const) 623 at p. 636; *Minister of Defence, Namibia* v. *Mwandinghi* 1992 (2) SA 355 (NmS) at pp. 360, 364; *Government of the Republic of Namibia* v. *Cultura 2000* 1994 (1) SA 407 (NmS) at p. 418; *Ex parte Attorney-General, Namibia: In re Corporal Punishment by Organs of State* 1991 (3) SA 76 (NmS) at p. 86; *S* v. *Ncube* 1988 (2) SA 702 (ZS) at p. 717; *Catholic Commission for Justice and Peace, Zimbabwe* v. *Attorney-General, Zimbabwe* 1993 (4) SA 239 (ZS) at p. 252. In *Attorney-General of the Gambia* v. *Mamodun Jobe* [1984] AC 689 at p. 700, and *Société United Docks and Others* v. *The Government of Mauritius* [1985] 1 AC 585 at p. 603, the Judicial Committee of the Privy Council called for a 'generous and purposive construction'. See also section 39 of the Constitution of South Africa, and further, *S* v. *Zuma and Others* 1995 (2) SA 642 (CC) at pp. 650–1; *S* v. *Makwanyane* 1995 (3) SA 391 (CC) at p. 403.

24. See C. Anyangwe, 'Obligations of States Parties to the African Charter on Human and Peoples' Rights', 10 *RADIC* (1998) 625 at pp. 627–35. In *Commission*

Nationale des Droits de l'Homme et des Libertés v. *Chad* (Communication No. 74/ 92) 18 *HRLJ* (1997) 34 at para. 20, the African Commission expressed the view that 'if a state neglects to ensure the rights in the African Charter, this can constitute a violation, even if the State or its agents are not the immediate cause of the violation.' The HRC has stated that implementation does not depend solely on constitutional or legislative enactments which are often not *per se* sufficient. State parties must ensure the enjoyment of human rights to all individuals under their jurisdiction which requires the adoption of 'all appropriate means' to that end, General comment 3 adopted by the HRC, UN Doc. HRI/GEN/1/Rev.2 (1996) pp. 4, 55–9. See also *Mika Miha* v. *Equatorial Guinea*, Communication No. 414/1990 . In the case of *Velasquez Rodriguez* v. *Honduras* 9 *HRLJ* (1988) 212, paras. 166, 174, the Inter-American Court on Human Rights stated that as a consequence of Article 1 ACHR, 'States must prevent, investigate and punish any violation of the rights recognized by the Convention and, moreover, if possible attempt to restore the rights violated and provide compensation as warranted for damages arising from the violations'. Additionally, the Court ruled that the 'State has a legal duty to use the means at its disposal to carry out a serious investigation of violations committed within its jurisdiction, to identify those responsible, to impose the appropriate punishment and to ensure the victim compensation'. It should be observed that many African States have set up statutory commissions with jurisdiction over human rights issues, e.g., Algeria, UN Doc. CCPR/C/101/Add.1, paras. 23–7, Benin, UN Doc. HRI/CORE/1/Add.85, para. 59, Cameroon, UN Doc. CCPR/C/102/ Add.2, paras. 5–7, Ghana, UN Doc. CERD/C/338/Add.5, para. 13, Lesotho, UN Doc. HRI/CORE/1/Add.98, para. 77, Senegal, UN Doc. CCPR/C/102/ Add.2, paras. 28–31, Togo, UN Doc. HRI/CORE/1/Add.38/Rev.1, pp. 8–10, Tunisia, UN Doc. HRI/CORE/1/Add.46, pp. 19–21, Uganda, UN Doc. HRI/ CORE/1/Add.69, paras. 29, 30.

25. However, references to domestic judgments or legislation to illustrate points will be made from time to time. The majority of African States have constitutional provisions guaranteeing fundamental rights and a number, e.g., Burkina Faso, Chad, Congo, Gabon, Mali and Togo, make specific reference to the Banjul Charter, see generally, C. Heyns, (ed.) *Human Rights in Africa 1996* (1996).

26. Generally States that follow the English common law approach, e.g., Lesotho, UN Doc. HRI/CORE/1/Add.98, para. 62, Tanzania, UN Doc. CCPR/C/ SR.1689, para. 13, Uganda, UN Doc. HRI/CORE/1/Add.69, paras. 40, 41, and Zambia, UN Doc. HRI/CORE/1/Add.22/Rev.1, para. 69. It is thus interesting to note that in *Nemi and Others* v. *The State* [1994] 1 LRC 376, the Supreme Court of Nigeria found that the Banjul Charter had been made part of domestic law by the legislation ratifying it. States that adhere to the monist tradition generally give priority to international law over municipal law. See, e.g., Article 40 of the Constitution of Cameroon; Article 79 of the Constitution of Guinea, UN Doc. HRI/CORE/1/Add.80, para. 36; Article 79 of the Constitution of Senegal, UN Doc. HRI/CORE/1/Add. 51, para. 26; Article 32 of the Tunisian Constitution, UN Doc. HRI/CORE/1/Add.46, paras. 68. See also Ankumah, note 19 *supra*, Chapter 5.5.1. Once a treaty is ratified by Senegal it becomes an operative part of municipal law and can be directly cited before domestic courts, UN Docs. HRI/CORE/1/Add. 51, para. 26, CAT/C/17/Add.14, para. 7. To the same effect, see Article 123 of the Algerian Constitution, UN Doc. CERD/C/280/ Add.3, para. 4; Article 222 of the Constitution of Chad, UN Doc. HRI/CORE/ 1/Add.88, para. 48; Article 79 of the Constitution of Guinea, UN Doc. HRI/ CORE/1/Add.80, para. 36. This also appears to be the position in Benin, UN Doc. HRI/CORE/1/Add.85, para. 53; Burkina Faso, UN Doc. HRI/CORE/1/ Add.30, para. 27, Madagascar, UN Doc. HRI/CORE/1/Add.31, para. 46, and

Tunisia, UN Doc. HRI/CORE/1/Add.46, paras. 69–70. The HRC has expressed concern about the lack of clarity in the implementation of international instruments in Libya, UN Doc. CCPR/C/79/Add.101, paras. 2, 6. See generally, F. Viljoen, 'Application of the African Charter on Human and Peoples' Rights by domestic courts in Africa', 43 *JAL* (1999) 1.

27. *Civil Liberties Organization* v. *Nigeria* (Communication No. 129/94) 18 *HRLJ* (1997) 35.

28. Article 13 ECHR. See *Klass* v. *Germany* Series A, Vol. 28 (1979) para. 64; *Soering* v. *United Kingdom* Series A, Vol. 161 (1989) para. 120; *Boyle and Rice* v. *United Kingdom* Series A, Vol. 131 (1988). Cf. Article 46(1)(a) ACHR. See further, Harris, O'Boyle and Warbrick, note 18 *supra*, Chapter 14.

29. Cf. Article 2 ICCPR, and General comment 3, UN Doc. HRI/GEN/1/Rev.2, para. 1, Article 1 ECHR and Article 1 ACHR.

30. Cf. Article 2(1) ICCPR and Article 14 ECHR; and see Harris, O'Boyle and Warbrick, note 18 *supra*, Chapter 15. See *Aumeeruddy-Cziffra* v. *Mauritius* 4 *HRLJ* (1983) 139.

31. General comment 4, UN Doc. HRI/GEN/Rev.2 (1996) pp. 4, 5. See also the Guidelines for National Periodic Reports adopted by the African Commission, *Naldi*, p. 155 at pp. 175, 76, requiring details on the measures undertaken by States parties against racial discrimination by public authorities and individuals, including the criminalization and prohibition of organizations that promote and incite racial hatred.

32. *Belgian Linguistic Case* Series A, Vol. 6. (1968); *Rasmussen* v. *Denmark* Series A, Vol. 87 (1984); Case 170/84 *Bilka-Kaufhaus* v. *Weber von Hartz* [1986] ECR 1607; Case 171/88 *Rinner-Kuhn* v. *FWW Spezial Gebaudereinigung GmbH* [1989] *ECR* 2743. See further Article 2(2), (3) of Directive 76/207, OJ [1976] L 39, on Equal Treatment, and Case 165/82 *Commission* v. *United Kingdom (Re Equal Treatment for Men and Women)* [1983] ECR 3431. See also General comment 18, UN Doc. HRI/GEN/1/Rev.2 (1996) p. 28.

33. See *Toonen* v. *Australia*, Communication No. 488/1992, UN Doc. A/49/40, Annex IX, EE, para. 8.7, where the HRC expressed the view that the reference to 'sex' in Article 2(1) ICCPR included sexual orientation. However, it must be acknowledged that homosexuality is repugnant to most African societies, e.g., Tanzania, UN Doc. CCPR/C/SR.1690, para. 49. Cf. Article 9(3) of the Constitution of South Africa and see *National Coalition for Gay and Lesbian Equality and Others* v. *Minister of Justice and Others* 1998 (12) BCLR 1517 (CC). *Cf.* Case C-249/96 *Grant* v. *South West Trains Ltd* [1998] All ER (EC) 193 where the ECJ held, contrary to the opinion of the Advocate-General, that the denial of job perks to same-sex partners did not breach EC law on equal pay. But now see Article 13 EC Treaty.

34. Article 13 EC Treaty.

35. See Article 3 of the African Charter on the Rights and Welfare of the Child 1990, text in *Naldi*, pp. 183–99 (not yet in force).

36. See Article 18(4) of the Banjul Charter; Vienna Declaration and Programme of Action, Part II, paras 63–5.

37. See, e.g., UN Doc. E/CN.4/1996/69.

38. Gittleman, note 9 *supra*, p. 683. Cf. Article 27 ICCPR and see *Lovelace* v. *Canada* 2 *HRLJ* (1981) 158; and *Bernard Ominayak, Chief of the Lubicon Lake Band* v. *Canada*, Communication No. 167/1984.

39. See, e.g., Article 40 of the Egyptian Constitution (and see further, UN Doc. E/1990/5/Add.38, pp. 15–17), section 20(1) of the Constitution of Malawi, Article 10(1) of the Namibian Constitution, section 9 of the South African Constitution, Articles 13 and 29(2) of the Tanzanian Constitution, Article 6 of the Tunisian Constitution, Article 11 of the Constitution of Togo, section 23(1)(b) of the

Constitution of Zimbabwe, and Articles 5 and 30 of Libya's Constitutional Declaration, UN Doc. CERD/C/299/Add.13, para. 35. See also *S* v. *Ntuli* 1996 (1) BCLR 141 (CC), *Harksen* v. *Lane NO and Others* 1997 (11) BCLR 1489 (CC), *City Council of Pretoria* v. *Walker* 1998 (3) BCLR 257 (CC). As has been observed elsewhere, complete equality in all circumstances is not possible and 'rational differentiation' is permissible, see section 9(5) of the South African Constitution, and *Prinsloo* v. *Van der Linde and Another* 1997 (3) SA 1012 (CC), *President of the Republic of South Africa and Another* v. *Hugo* 1997 (6) BCLR 708 (CC). This issue raises particular difficulties for many African countries where different legal systems may co-exist, customary, Islamic and Western, and can cause unequal treatment between races, e.g., Lesotho, UN Doc. CERD/C/337/Add.1, para. 50, and see, the observations of the Committee on the Elimination of Racial Discrimination on Zimbabwe which expressed serious concern about a dual legal system regulating marriage and inheritance, UN Doc. CERD/C/304/Add.3. Similar concerns have been expressed about Tanzania, UN Doc. E/CN.4/Sub.2/1997/SR.14, para. 5, and Zambia, UN Doc. CCPR/C/79/Add.62, para. 9. Since the introduction of the Constitution in Uganda in 1995 reforms have been underway to ensure the supremacy of the Constitution over Islamic and customary law, UN Doc. CRC/C/SR.409, paras. 32, 33.

40.   P. Sieghart, *The International Law of Human Rights* (1983) pp. 263–8. Because of their basic and general character, the principles of equality before the law and equal protection of the law as well as that of non-discrimination are sometimes expressly referred to in other provisions concerning particular categories of rights. It is encouraging to observe that over the last decade a process of democratization has swept through Africa. New constitutions guaranteeing fundamental rights have been adopted, legal reforms have been introduced, human rights commissions have been established, and there have been moves towards multi-party systems. However, a culture of respect for the rule of law has not always kept pace with the transition to democracy. The armed forces and the police often act with seeming impunity and above the law, the arbitrary use of force and detention is sometimes widespread, human rights violations are not always properly investigated. A culture of accountability and transparency is not always apparent. Nevertheless, there are reasons to be less than pessimistic.

41.   Article 1(1) of the International Convention on the Elimination of All Forms of Racial Discrimination 1966, ratified by forty-five African States, provides that the term 'racial discrimination' is to mean any distinction, exclusion, restriction or preference based on race, colour, descent, or national or ethnic origin which has the purpose or effect of nullifying or impairing the recognition, enjoyment or exercise, on an equal footing, of human rights and fundamental freedoms in the political, economic, social cultural or any other field of public life. The prohibition on racial discrimination is reinforced by the International Convention on the Suppression and Punishment of the Crime of Apartheid 1973. See also the Vienna Declaration and Programme of Action, Part II, paras. 19–24. The principle of non-discrimination on the ground of race is a norm of customary international law, see Judge Tanaka's Dissenting Opinion in the *South West Africa Cases* (Second Phase) ICJ Reports 1966, p. 6 at p. 300; *Barcelona Traction Case* (Second Phase) ICJ Reports 1970, p. 3 at p. 32; *Namibia Case* ICJ Reports 1971, p. 16, which may have acquired the status of a norm of *jus cogens*, see I. Brownlie, *Principles of Public International Law* (4th edn 1990) pp. 513, 600–1. See also *Koowarta* v. *Bjelke-Petersen* (1982) 39 ALR 417; *Gerhardy* v. *Brown* (1985) 57 ALR 472. Important ECHR cases are *East African Asian Cases* 3 EHRR 76 and *Abdulaziz, Cabales and Balkandali* v. *United Kingdom* Series A, Vol. 94 (1985). The Supreme Court of Namibia has made clear its revulsion at apartheid.

In *S* v. *Van Wyk* 1992 (1) SACR 147 (NmS) Ackermann AJA, at p. 169, emphasized 'how deep and irrevocable the constitutional commitment is to ... equality before the law and non-discrimination and to the proscription and eradication of the practice of racial discrimination and apartheid and its consequences. These objectives may rightly be said to be fundamental aspects of public policy.' Whereas Mohamed AJA, at p. 172, stated that throughout the Constitution there is 'one golden and unbroken thread – an abiding "revulsion" of racism and apartheid ... no other Constitution in the world ... seeks to identify a legal ethos against apartheid with greater vigour and intensity'. In relation to South Africa the Constitutional Court has declared that fundamental to the spirit and tenor of the Constitution is the 'promise of the equal protection of the laws to all the people of this country and a ringing and decisive break with a past which perpetuated inequality and irrational discrimination', *S* v. *Mhlungu and Others* 1995 (7) BCLR 793 (CC) at p. 799; see also *Shabalala and Others* v. *Attorney-General of the Transvaal and Another* 1995 (12) BCLR 1593 (CC) at p. 1605. See also section 23 of the Constitution of Zimbabwe, UN Doc. CCPR/ C/74/Add.3, pp. 4, 42, Articles 10(2) and 23(1) of the Namibian Constitution, section 9(3) of the South African Constitution and *Democratic Party* v. *Minister of Home Affairs* (1999, unreported) (CC). See further, W. McKean, *Equality and Discrimination under International Law* (1983) Chapter 15; T. Meron, *Human Rights Law-Making in the United Nations* (1986) Chapter 1. It should be noted further that discrimination based on race constitutes inhuman or degrading treatment, *East African Asians* v. *United Kingdom* (1981) 3 EHRR 76. It is not clear whether affirmative action, or positive discrimination, allowable under Article 1(4) of the International Convention on the Elimination of All Forms of Racial Discrimination, would be permissible under the Banjul Charter, but see Umozurike, note 4 *supra*, p. 30. It is interesting to note that the Committee on the Elimination of Racial Discrimination has welcomed Namibia's policy of affirmative action, see Article 23(2), (3) of the Constitution, and *Kauesa* v. *Minister of Home Affairs* 1994 (3) BCLR 1 (NmH), although discrimination persists in many areas, UN Doc. A/51/18, paras. 494, 496. Note section 20(2) of the Constitution of Malawi, and section 9(2) of the South African Constitution.

42. Discrimination on the basis of sex is condemned by a number of multilateral instruments, including the ICCPR, the ACHR, the Inter-American Convention on the Granting of Political Rights to Women 1948, the EC Treaty and the Revised European Social Charter. See also the Vienna Declaration and Programme of Action, Part II, paras. 36–44. Article 1 of the UN Convention on the Elimination of All Forms of Discrimination Against Women 1979 provides that discrimination against women shall mean any distinction, exclusion or restriction made on the basis of sex which has the effect or purpose of impairing or nullifying the recognition, enjoyment or exercise by women, irrespective of their marital status, on a basis of equality with men and women, of human rights and fundamental freedoms in the political, economic, social, cultural, civil or any other field. And see *Aumeeruddy-Cziffra* v. *Mauritius* 4 HRLJ (1983) 139; *Abdulaziz, Cabales and Balkandali* v. *United Kingdom* Series A, Vol. 94 (1985); *Proposed Amendments to the Naturalization Provisions of the Constitution of Costa Rica* 5 HRLJ (1984) 161; Case 149/77 *Defrenne* v. *SABENA* (*No. 3*) [1978] ECR 1365; Case 152/84 *Marshall* v. *Southampton and South West Area Health Authority* (*Teaching*) (*No. 1*) [1986] ECR 723. See further Meron, *Human Rights Law-Making in the UN*, note 41 *supra*, Chapter 2. The ECJ has held that the scope of EC law on non-discrimination extends to transsexuals, Case C-13/94 *P* v. *S and Cornwall County Council* [1996] ECR I-2143. The existence of different legal systems, secular, customary and religious (Islamic), in many African countries, gives rise to difficulties and may result in discrimination against women, often designated

as 'junior males', in areas such as succession, marriage and divorce, UN Doc. A/51/18, para. 497 (Namibia, notwithstanding Article 10(2) of the Constitution); UN Doc. CCPR/C/79/Add.62, para.9 (Zambia); UN Doc. CRC/C/15/Add.55 (Zimbabwe, notwithstanding the fact that it has adopted various pieces of legislation prohibiting discrimination on the basis of sex, UN Doc. CCPR/C/74/Add.3, pp. 4, 9–11); UN Doc. E/C.12/1993/SR.37, para. 66 (Senegal). Women are routinely in an inferior position and suffer discrimination, e,g., in Equatorial Guinea, UN Doc. E/CN.4/1996/67, para. 51. But see *Dow* v. *Attorney-General* [1992] LRC (Const) 623; *Ephrahim* v. *Pastory* [1990] LRC (Const) 757; sections 13(a), 20(1) and 24 of the Constitution of Malawi; and section 9(3) of the South African Constitution. By virtue of the Mauritius (Amendment) Act 1995 gender has been added to the grounds on which discrimination by law is prohibited under section 16 of the Constitution. It is not clear that affirmative action, or positive discrimination, would be permissible under the Banjul Charter, but see Umozurike, note 4 *supra*, p. 30; and see Case C-450/93 *Kalanke* v. *Freie Hansestadt Bremen* [1996] All ER (EC) 66; Case C-409/95 *Marschall* v. *Land Nordrhein-Westfalen* [1998] I CMLR 547.

43. See section 20(1) of the Constitution of Malawi, section 9(3) of the South African Constitution and section 23 of the Constitution of Zimbabwe. However, the Committee on the Elimination of Racial Discrimination has expressed concern that not all minority languages are used in education in Zimbabwe, UN Doc. A/51/18, para. 92. See further, Article 2(1) of the Declaration on the Rights of Persons Belonging to National or Ethnic, Religious and Linguistic Minorities, General Assembly Resolution 43/135 (1992), which, *inter alia*, proclaims the right of linguistic minorities to use their own language; and the European Charter for Regional or Minority Languages 1992. See also the Council of Europe's Framework Convention for the Protection of National Minorities 1994, which is criticized as rather vague, H. Klebes, 'The Council of Europe's Framework Convention for the Protection of National Minorities', 16 *HRLJ* (1995) 92; and further, the Vienna Declaration and Programme of Action, Part II, paras. 25–7. And see the *Belgian Linguistic Case* Series A, Vol. 6 (1968).

44. See section 20(1) of the Constitution of Malawi, Article 10(2) of the Constitution of Namibia, section 9(3) of the South African Constitution, and section 23 of the Constitution of Zimbabwe. Discrimination on the ground of religion is condemned by General Assembly Resolution 36/55 (1981) Declaration on the Elimination of All Forms of Intolerance and of Discrimination Based on Religion or Belief, and Article 2(1) of the Declaration on the Rights of Persons Belonging to National, Ethnic, Religious or Linguistic Minorities which, *inter alia*, proclaims the rights of persons belonging to religious minorities to profess and practise their own religion. See also General comment 22, UN Doc. HRI/GEN/1/Rev.2, pp. 37, 38; Vienna Declaration and Programme of Action, Part II, paras. 25–7; and Article 13 EC Treaty. An important case is *Hoffmann* v. *Austria* Series A, Vol. 255-C (1993) where the European Court of Human Rights upheld the applicant's complaint that the decision of the Austrian courts to award custody of the child to the husband was based on her religious beliefs as a Jehovah's Witness. The Special Rapporteur on extrajudicial, summary or arbitrary executions has expressed deep concern at the situation in Algeria where considerable loss of life has occurred as a result of religious intolerance and discrimination, UN Doc. E/CN.4/1994/35, para. 107.

45. Discrimination on the ground of birth is condemned by the African Charter on the Rights and Welfare of the Child, Articles 3, 6. See also the European Convention on the Legal Status of Children Born Out of Wedlock; and see *Marckx* v. *Belgium* Series A, Vol. 31 (1979); *Johnston* v. *Ireland* Series A, Vol. 112 (1986); *Inze* v. *Austria* Series A, Vol. 126 (1987). See further section 20(1) of the

Constitution of Malawi, and section 9(3) of the South African Constitution. See also *Fraser* v. *Children's Court, Pretoria North* 1997 (2) BCLR 153 (CC) where dispensing with the father's consent for the adoption of an illegitimate child was held to violate section 8(2) of the Interim Constitution of South Africa.

46. As has been noted above, included in this category could be discrimination against the aged, persons with disabilities and persons of different sexual orientation, see section 9(3) of the South African Constitution. See also Article 13(5) of the Tanzanian Constitution. While neither the International Covenants nor the UDHR explicitly prohibit discrimination on the basis of age the omission is best explained by the fact that when adopted the problem of demographic ageing was not as evident nor as pressing as at present. The Committee on Economic, Social and Cultural Rights, while accepting that 'other status' could be interpreted as applying to age, has recognized that it may not yet be possible to conclude that discrimination on the grounds of age is comprehensively prohibited by the ICES. However, the Committee has emphasized that the unacceptability of discrimination against the aged is underlined in many international policy documents and national legislation of many States and that there is a clear trend towards the elimination of existing barriers. The Committee has therefore urged States to expedite this trend to the greatest extent possible, UN Doc. HRI/GEN/1/Rev.2 (1996) p. 79. With regard to persons with disabilities the Committee on Economic, Social and Cultural Rights has stated that the absence of any mention of disability in the ICES was due to a lack of awareness at the time but that its provisions apply equally to them and that the Banjul Charter (Article 18(4)), the Additional Protocol to the American Convention on Human Rights in the Area of Economic, Social and Cultural Rights (Article 18), and the UN Convention on the Rights of the Child (Article 23) expressly address this issue. Consequently, the Committee was of the view that it is now widely accepted that the rights of such persons must be protected and promoted through general and specific laws and policies and it has called upon States to adopt comprehensive anti-discrimination legislation, General comment 5, UN Doc. HRI/GEN/1/Rev.2 (1996) pp. 66–70. Note Zimbabwe's Disabled Persons Act which protects disabled persons from discrimination on the basis of their disability, UN Doc. CCPR/C/74/Add.3, para. 6(c). See further sections 13(g) and 20(1) of the Constitution of Malawi, and section 9(3) of the South African Constitution. Discrimination on the grounds of, *inter alia*, disability or age is implicitly condemned by Article 13 EC Treaty. With regard to sexual orientation, without a specific reference thereto in the treaty, it seems that the courts are reluctant to read such protection. In Case 249/96 *Grant* v. *South West Trains Ltd* [1998] All ER (EC) 193 the Advocate-General expressed the opinion that there was nothing in EC law to indicate that the rights and duties flowing from the law, including the right not to be discriminated against, should not apply to homosexuals and to the disabled although it needs to be recalled that the ECJ rejected this argument. In *R* v. *Ministry of Defence, ex parte Smith* [1996] QB 517, Lord Bingham MR said, 'I find nothing whatever in the EEC Treaty or in the Equal Treatment Directive which suggests that the draftsmen of these instruments were addressing their minds in any way whatever to the problem of discrimination on grounds of sexual orientation.' These decisions may now have been reversed by Article 13 EC Treaty. However, note *Toonen* v. *Australia*, Communication No. 488/1992, para. 8.7, where the HRC expressed the view that the reference to 'sex' in Article 26 ICCPR included sexual orientation. See also section 9(3) of the South African Constitution. On sexual orientation see further, *William H. Webster, Director of Central Intelligence, Petitioner* v. *John Doe* (1988) 108 S. Ct. 2047; R. Wintemute, *Sexual Orientation and Human Rights* (1995). It should be observed that section 9(3) of the South African Constitution is

wide-ranging in scope, including pregnancy in the prohibited categories. See *Fraser* v. *Children's Court, Pretoria North* 1997 (2) BCLR 153 (CC) where the Constitutional Court of South Africa considered discrimination on the basis of gender and marital status contrary to section 8(2) of the Interim Constitution. It is also important that people should not suffer discrimination because of their beliefs or political opinions, see, e.g., section 20(1) of the Constitution of Malawi, section 9(3) of the South African Constitution. See further, *Oló Bahamonde* v. *Equatorial Guinea*, Communication No. 468/1991, UN Doc. A/49/40, Annex IX, BB.

47. The HRC proclaims it 'the supreme right' from which no derogation is permissible and which must not be interpreted narrowly since Article 6(1) ICCPR describes the right to life as 'inherent', General comment 6, UN Doc. HRI/GEN/1/Rev.2 (1996) p. 6. Cf. Article 5(1), (2) of the African Charter on the Rights and Welfare of the Child which states, *inter alia*, that every child, i.e., every person under the age of eighteen (Article 2), has an inherent right to life. Note *S* v. *Tcoeib* 1996 (7) BCLR 996 (NmS) where the Supreme Court of Namibia found that a sentence of life imprisonment did not violate the right to life guaranteed by Article 6 of the Constitution.

48. See *Commission Nationale des Droits de l'Homme et des Libertés* v. *Chad* (Communication 74/92) 18 *HRLJ* (1997) 34 at para. 22, where the African Commission stated that, 'Even where it cannot be proved that violations were committed by government agents, the government had a responsibility to secure the safety and the liberty of its citizens, and to conduct investigations into murders'. The increasing trend in enacting amnesty laws as a means of achieving national reconciliation gives rise to fears about impunity and disregard for the rights of victims, including the right to compensation, see, e.g., the Vienna Declaration and Programme of Action, Part II, paras. 60, 62, and 91. The HRC has stated that amnesty for the perpetrators of serious human rights violations is incompatible with the right of every individual to a fair hearing before an impartial and independent court, General Comment 20, UN Doc. HRI/GEN/1/Rev. 3 (1997) para. 15. States are obliged to investigate human rights violations, to carry out justice by prosecuting and punishing the perpetrators and providing just compensation. See the concern expressed by the UN Special Rapporteur on the amnesty law adopted in Togo in 1995, Report by the Special Rapporteur, Bacre Waly Ndiaye, UN Doc. E/CN.4/1996/4, p. 111, and the amnesty laws in Mauritania and South Africa, UN Doc. E/CN.4/1994/7, para. 691. However, it is interesting to note that the Constitutional Court of South Africa has held that there are compelling reasons of public policy, namely, national reconciliation, why the amnesty law (Promotion of National Unity and Reconciliation Act 1995, noted in 39 *JAL* (1995) 231) should not be deemed unconstitutional, *Azanian Peoples Organization (AZAPO) and Others* v. *President of the Republic of South Africa and Others* 1996 (8) BCLR 1015 (CC).

49. See General comment 6, UN Doc. HRI/GEN/1/Rev.2 (1996) p. 6, where the HRC states that the protection against arbitrary deprivation of life is of 'paramount importance'. The HRC adds that the 'deprivation of life by the authorities of the State is a matter of the utmost gravity. Therefore, the law must strictly control and limit the circumstances in which a person may be deprived of life by such authorities.' See further, *Miango* v. *Zaire* UN Doc. A/43/40, p. 218; *McCann, Farrell and Savage* v. *United Kingdom* Series A, Vol. 324 (1995). Cf. section 16(1) of the Constitution of Malawi. Allegations of such violations have been made against Algeria, Burundi, Democratic Republic of the Congo, Egypt, Nigeria, Rwanda, Senegal, Sierra Leone and Sudan, UN Doc. E/CN.4. 1999/39/Add. 1. See further, Ankumah, note 19 *supra*, Chapter 5.2.1. It is interesting to note that section 4(2) of the Constitution of Botswana and

Article 12(3)(a)-(d) of the Zambian Constitution provide for circumstances where the taking of life is regarded as reasonably justifiable. See also section 12(2) of the Constitution of Zimbabwe and section 42(2) of the Criminal Procedure and Evidence Act, UN Doc. CCPR/C/74/Add.3, paras. 51–5. The UN has expressed concern about incidents of communal violence in Burundi, Nigeria, Rwanda and Zaïre where it was reported that allegedly not only did the authorities not intervene to stop the violence but actively supported one side or even began it, UN Doc. E/CN.4/1994/35, para. 709.

50. *Krischna Achutan (on behalf of Aleke Banda) v. Malawi* (Communication No. 64/92); *Amnesty International on behalf of Orton and Vera Chirwa v. Malawi* (Communication Nos. 68/92, 78/92) 3 *IHRR* (1996) 134. Cf. *Camargo v. Colombia*, Communication No. 46/1979 UN Doc. CCPR/C/OP/1, p. 112; *McCann, Farrell and Savage v. United Kingdom* Series A, Vol. 324 (1995).

51. *Free Legal Assistance Group and Others v. Zaire* (Communication No. 25/89) 18 *HRLJ* (1997) 32. In addition, the UN Special Rapporteur on Extrajudicial, Summary or Arbitrary Executions has expressed concern about instances of extrajudicial, summary or arbitrary executions in Equatorial Guinea, UN Doc. E/CN.4/1994/56, pp. 15–18, Algeria, Angola, Burundi, Chad, Liberia, Mali, Sierra Leone, UN Doc. E/CN.4/1996/4, Senegal, South Africa, UN Doc. CAT/C/SR.247, Ethiopia, UN Docs. E/CN.4/1996/4, pp. 47, 48, E/CN.4/1996/38, pp. 38, 39, Sudan, UN Doc. E/CN.4/1996/38, pp. 76, 77, Somalia, see, e.g., UN Doc. E/CN.4/1994/35, p. 4, Togo, UN Doc. E/CN.4/1994/59, pp. 7, 8, 13, Egypt, UN Doc. E/CN.4/1996/4, pp. 44, 45, and even massacres amounting to genocide in Rwanda, Report by B.N. Ndiaye, Special Rapporteur, on his mission to Rwanda from 8 to 17 April 1993, UN Doc. E/CN.4/1994/7/Add.1, amongst others. See also UN Doc. E/CN.4/1999/39/Add. 1.

52. *Velasquez Rodriguez v. Honduras* 9 *HRLJ* (1988) 212; *Tshishimbi v. Zaire*, Communication No. 542/1993. In 1992 the General Assembly, by resolution 47/133, proclaimed the Declaration on the Protection of All Persons from Enforced Disappearance, according to which the systematic practice of disappearance violates, *inter alia*, the right to life. See also the Draft International Convention on the Protection of All Persons From Forced Disappearance, UN Doc. E/CN.4/Sub.2/1998/19, pp. 21–38. The World Conference on Human Rights welcomed the adoption of the Vienna Declaration and called upon States 'to take effective legislative, administrative, judicial or other measures to prevent, terminate and punish acts of enforced disappearances', Part II, para. 62. See further the Inter-American Convention on Forced Disappearances of Persons 1994. In the recent past Rwanda and Zaïre have seen many cases of involuntary disappearances of persons, see UN Docs. E/CN.4/1995/70, p. 11; E/CN.4/1994/49, para. 30, respectively. See further UN Doc. E/CN.4/1996/38, where Algeria, Burundi, Ethiopia, Rwanda, and Sudan were highlighted for particular concern, as have been Nigeria, UN Doc. CCPR/C/79/Add.65, para. 18, and Togo, UN Doc. CCPR/C/79/Add.36, para. 6.

53. See, e.g., section 16 of the Constitution of Malawi. See also *Constitutional Rights Project (in respect of Wahab Akamu, G. Adega and others) v. Nigeria* (Communication No. 60/91) 3 *IHRR* (1996) 132; and *Constitutional Rights Project (in respect of Zamani Lakwot and others) v. Nigeria* (Communication No. 87/93) 3 *IHRR* (1996) 137. See also *Mbushuu and Another v. Republic* [1995] 1 LRC 216. It is interesting to note that the Constitutional Court of South Africa has ruled capital punishment unconstitutional as violating, *inter alia*, the right to life in *S v. Makwanyane and Mchunu* 1995 (3) SA 391 (CC). Capital punishment is not yet prohibited in itself under customary international law, although see W.A. Schabas, *The Abolition of the Death Penalty in International Law* (2nd edn 1997), but universal and regional instruments do provide for its abolition, see, e.g., the

Second Optional Protocol to the ICCPR aiming at the abolition of the death penalty 1989, which has been ratified by Mozambique, Namibia and Seychelles, and the note by the present author, 'United Nations Seeks to Abolish the Death Penalty' 40 *ICLQ* (1991) 948. Nearly a hundred States still maintain the death penalty, UN Doc. E/CN.4/1999/52, and apply it to vulnerable groups such as pregnant women, mothers of young children, the mentally disabled, and the elderly, UN Doc. E/CN.4/Sub.2/1998/WG.1/CRP.3. Although States parties to the ICCPR and the ACHR are not obliged to abolish the death penalty both treaties are abolitionist in outlook and must restrict its application to the 'most serious crimes', e.g., offences with lethal consequences, so that the death penalty is an exceptional measure, General comment 6, UN Doc. HRI/GEN/1/Rev.2, p. 7; *Restrictions to the Death Penalty Case* 4 *HRLJ* (1983). Consequently, in *Lubuto* v. *Zambia*, Communication No. 390/90, 339 the HRC held that the sentence of death was an excessive punishment for aggravated robbery. The HRC has been critical of, *inter alia*, Libya, UN Doc. CCPR/C/79/Add.101, para. 8, Nigeria, UN Doc. CCPR/C/79/Add.65, para. 16, and Togo, UN Doc. CCPR/C/79/Add.36, para. 10. Death sentences have been pronounced on some of those found guilty of genocide in Rwanda, *Keesing's* Vol. 43, 1997, p. 41622, although it is interesting to note that the International Criminal Tribunal for Rwanda itself, established pursuant to Security Council Resolution 955 (1994) cannot impose the death sentence, imprisonment being the sole penalty. For the statute of the Tribunal, see 33 *ILM* 1602 (1994). The UN has expressed concern about the extension of the application of the death penalty in Côte d'Ivoire, which, however, has not been applied since 1960, UN Doc. E/CN.4/1996/4, pp. 40, 41, and Egypt, UN Doc. E/CN.4/1994/35, p. 5; and the large number of offences punishable by death in Libya, UN Docs. CCPR/C/79/Add.45, para. 8, CCPR/C/79/Add.101, para. 8. Cf. Article 4(2) ACHR. It should be observed further that Article 4(3) ACHR prohibits the re-establishment of the death sentence in States that have abolished it, see further *International Responsibility for the Promulgation and Enforcement of Laws in Violation of the Convention (Articles 1 and 2 of the American Convention on Human Rights)* 16 *HRLJ* (1995) 9. The Gambia has been criticized for reinstating the death penalty, which had been abolished in 1993, in 1995, UN Doc. E/CN.4/1996/4, p. 49.

54. Angola, Cape Verde, Guinea-Bissau, Mauritius, Mozambique, Namibia, São Tomé e Príncipe, Seychelles and South Africa have abolished the death penalty while a number of others are abolitionist *de facto*, e.g., Gabon, UN Doc. CCPR/C/31/Add.4, para.28, Madagascar and Tunisia, UN Doc. E/CN.4/1998/SR.31, p. 5. The HRC thus recommended that Zambia abolish the death penalty, UN Doc. CCPR/C/79/Add.62, para. 23. See further, R. Hood, *The Death Penalty* (2nd edn 1996) Appendix 1, Tables 1–3; UN Doc. E/CN.4/1999/52.

55. See also Article 37(a) of the UN Convention on the Rights of the Child, Article 6(5) ICCPR and Article 4(5) ACPR. The death penalty does not apply to minors in Chad nor Sudan, UN Docs. CRC/C/3/Add.50, para. 90, CCPR/C/75/Add.2, para. 71. See further, Article 80 of the Criminal Code of Cameroon, UN Doc. CCPR/C/63/Add.1, para. 52. It has been pointed out that the death penalty is still applied to minors in many countries, UN Doc. E/CN.4/Sub.2/1998/WG.1/CRP.3. Concern has been expressed about legislation allowing for the imposition of capital punishment on minors in Algeria, UN Doc. E/CN.4/1995/47, para. 380, although Articles 49 and 50 of the Penal Code state that the death penalty cannot be imposed on anyone aged under eighteen, UN Doc. CRC/C/28/Add.4, para. 56. Somalia is the only African State not to have ratified the UN Convention on the Rights of the Child.

56. General comment 6, UN Doc. E/CN.4/1994/35, pp. 6, 7; Safeguards Guaranteeing Protection of the Rights of Those Facing the Death Penalty 1984, General

Assembly Resolution 39/118; *Mbenge* v. *Zaire* UN Doc. A/38/40, p. 134; *Constitutional Rights Project (in respect of Wahab Akamu, G. Adega and others)* v. *Nigeria* (Communication No. 60/91) 3 *IHRR* (1996) 132; *Constitutional Rights Project (in respect of Zamani Lakwot and others)* v. *Nigeria* (Communication No. 87/93) 3 *IHRR* (1996) 137. Such safeguards appear to exist in, e.g., Cameroon, UN Doc. CCPR/C/63/Add.1, paras. 50, 51, Gabon, UN Doc. CCPR/C/31/Add.4, paras. 27–9, Sudan, UN Doc. CCPR/C/75/Add.2, paras. 69, 70, and Zimbabwe, UN Doc. CCPR/C/74/Add.3, paras. 20, 68–70. Thus the UN has called upon Algeria, Central African Republic, Chad, Côte d'Ivoire, Egypt, Libya, Malawi, Nigeria, Rwanda and Sierra Leone to revise the administration of justice where the death sentence is at stake, UN Docs. E/CN.4/1995/47, para. 376, E/CN.4/1994/35, p. 7, E/CN.4/1996/4, pp. 41, 130. Egypt and Nigeria have been singled out for particular criticism because of the establishment of special courts with jurisdiction over capital offences with the aim of speeding proceedings. The Special Rapporteur noted that standards of due process and respect for the right to life before such courts were lower than normal, UN Doc. E/CN.4/1996/4, para. 550. It should be noted further that in *Nemi and Others* v. *The State* [1994] 1 LRC 376 at p. 398, the Nigerian Supreme Court stated *obiter* that the lack of legal representation at a capital trial did not violate fundamental rights.

57. Condemned by General Assembly Resolution 50/199.
58. UN Doc. E/CN.4/1996/4, pp. 80–4. The HRC has criticized special tribunals for their failure to safeguard procedural and substantive rights, UN Doc. CCPR/C/79/Add.65.
59. Only the ACHR seems to make reference to this issue, article 2(1) thereof stating, *inter alia*, that the right to life must be protected 'in general, from the moment of conception', which has, however, been interpreted restrictively, *Baby Boy Case* 2 *HRLJ* (1981) 110. The European Commission on Human Rights has held that the right to life of a foetus may be limited in certain circumstances, *Paton* v. *United Kingdom* (1981) 3 EHRR 408, see further, Harris, O'Boyle and Warbrick, note 18 *supra*, pp. 42, 43. It should be observed that by virtue of the Choice on Termination of Pregnancy Act 1996, noted in 41 *JAL* (1997) 248, South Africa liberalized its abortion law. A constitutional challenge to this Act failed, see *Christian Lawyers Association of SA and Others* v. *Minister of Health and Others* 1998 (11) BCLR 1434 (T). In Cameroon abortion is limited to cases of serious threats to the health of the mother or pregnancy resulting from rape, UN Doc. CCPR/C/63/Add.1, paras. 44, 46. In Zimbabwe abortion is also allowed only in exceptional circumstances, UN Doc. CCPR/C/74/Add.3, para. 59, whereas in Chad only for medical purposes, UN Doc. CRC/C/3/Add.50, para. 67. In Zambia the unborn child is given considerable protection, see Article 12(2) of the Constitution and sections 151–3 of the Penal Code, while the Malian and Tunisian Penal Codes protect life from the moment of conception, UN Docs. CRC/C/3/Add.53, para. 36, and CCPR/C/84/Add.1, para. 77, respectively. In Algeria abortion is prohibited under the Penal Code, UN DOC. CRC/C/28/Add.4, para. 24, whereas in Niger it is prohibited under the Criminal Code, UN Doc. CRC/C/3/Add.29, para. 18.
60. UN Doc. E/CN.4/1995/74. See *S* v. *Mcgown* 1995 (1) ZLR 4, where a doctor was charged with culpable homicide, including a charge relating to the administration of drugs using a new technique and thus experimenting without the patient's consent. Note section 19(5) of the Constitution of Malawi, and section 12(2) of the South African Constitution. In Tunisia non-therapeutic scientific experimentation with the aim of protecting the life and health of the subject can take place with the written consent of the subject, UN Doc. CCPR/C/84/Add.1, para. 102. The position seems to be similar in Sudan, UN Doc. CCPR/C/75/Add.2, para. 85. It is instructive to note that Cameroon has established an ethics

committee on research involving human subjects, UN Doc. CCPR/C/63/Add.1, para. 57, whereas in Zimbabwe a Medical Research Council has been established to ensure that no medical research or experimentation is performed without the free consent of the patients. Note the European Convention on Human Rights and Biomedicine 1997.

61. General comment 6, UN Doc. HRI/GEN/1/Rev.2, p. 7; Sieghart, note 40 *supra*, pp. 128–35. See also Article 5(2) of the African Charter on the Rights and Welfare of the Child. For details on the policies adopted by African countries in this area, see, e.g., UN Docs. CRC/C/28/Add.4, pp. 21–4, (Algeria), UN Doc. E/1990/5/Add.38, para. 183 (Egypt), CRC/C/3/Add.53, pp. 23–9 (Mali), CRC/C/3/Add.29, pp. 3, 6–8 (Niger), CCPR/C/74/Add.3, paras. 60–61 (Zimbabwe). Libya in particular has been praised for the range of services for children in the field of health, UN Doc. CRC/C/15/Add.84, para. 4.

62. This is the case with Articles 7 and 10 ICCPR, General comments 20, UN Docs. HRI/GEN/1/Rev.2, para. 3, and 21, HRI/GEN/1/Rev.2, para. 4; Article 3 ECHR, Harris, O'Boyle and Warbrick, note 18 *supra*, pp. 55–56; and Article 5(1), (2) ACHR. See also, Vienna Declaration and Programme of Action, Part II, paras. 55–6. And see *S* v. *Williams and Others* 1995 (7) BCLR 861 (CC) pp. 869–70. Even the need to combat terrorism cannot justify violations of physical integrity, *Tomasi* v. *France* Series A, Vol. 241-A (1992).

63. *Barcelona Traction Case* (Second Phase) ICJ Reports 1970, p. 3 at p. 32.

64. For example, the Libyan Penal Code prohibits dealing or trafficking of persons in a state of slavery or semi-slavery and designates the slave trade as a punishable offence, UN Doc. E/CN.4/Sub.2/AC.2/1994/4, p. 6. See also Article 6 of the Constitution of Botswana, the Criminal Code of Cameroon, UN Doc. CCPR/C/63/Add.1, para. 59; the Labour Code of Gabon, UN Doc. CCPR/C/31/Add.4, para. 32; section 27(1), (2) of the Constitution of Malawi; Article 189 of the Penal Code of Mali, UN Doc. E/CN.4/Sub.2/AC.2/1991/4, para. 4; Article 9 of the Namibian Constitution; section 13 of the South African Constitution; Article 14 of the Constitution of Zambia and sections 261–3 of the Penal Code; and section 14 of the Constitution of Zimbabwe. Ethiopia has reported that almost all the provisions of the Slavery Conventions have been given domestic effect, UN Doc. E/CN.4/Sub.2/AC.2/1994/4, p. 3. It should be noted that the following are not parties to any treaty prohibiting slavery: Angola (although it has expressed its intention to ratify the conventions on slavery, UN Doc. E/CN.4/Sub.2/AC.2/1996/1, p. 3), Botswana, Burkina Faso, Chad, Equatorial Guinea, Eritrea, Gabon, Gambia, Guinea-Bissau, Kenya, Mozambique, Namibia, Rwanda, São Tomé e Príncipe, Somalia and Swaziland.

65. Ankumah, note 19 *supra*, pp. 94, 119, 20, who refers to the cultural practice of Trokosi in Ghana and Togo, whereby young girls are sold to priests to expiate alleged crimes committed by members of their family, and which has been condemned by the Committee on the Rights of the Child, UN Doc. CRC/C/15/Add.73, para. 21. It is claimed that in Sudan children from the African south of the country are regularly kidnapped and taken to northern Sudan to work as servants without pay. They are also forcibly converted to Islam, UN Doc. E/CN.4/Sub.2/1996/24, pp. 19–20, and further, UN Doc. E/CN.4/Sub.2/1998/NGO/6. These allegations are denied by the Sudanese government, UN Doc. CCPR/C/75/Add.2, paras. 95–8.

66. UN Doc. E/CN.4/Sub.2/1993/30, para. 45.

67. Officially abolished under Ordinance 81–234 (1981), UN Docs. E/CN.4/Sub.2/AC.2/1991/5/Add.2, para. 10; E/CN.4/Sub.2/1993/30, paras. 43, 44; E/CN.4/Sub.2/1996/24, p. 20.

68. Article 29 of the African Charter on the Rights and Welfare of the Child and Article 35 of the UN Convention on the Rights of the Child prohibit the

abduction, sale, and traffic in children. Although Vitit Muntarbhorn, Special Rapporteur on the Sale of Children, has reported that the sale of children for adoption is not a major problem in Africa, sporadic reports of children in Burkina Faso and the children of Mozambican refugees being sold to foreigners have surfaced, UN Doc. E/CN.4/1993/67, para. 64. The abduction, sale and traffic of children in Sudan seems widespread, UN Doc. E/CN.4/1997/95, para. 47. Traffic in children from Togo to other African countries has also been reported, UN Doc. E/CN.4/Sub.2/1997/13, para. 74. The sale of children is prohibited in Mauritius by section 15 of the Child Protection Act 1994. See also Zimbabwe's Criminal Procedure and Evidence Act, UN Doc. CCPR/C/74/ Add.3, para. 87(b). It should be noted that the Commission on Human Rights is working on a draft optional protocol to the Convention on the Rights of the Child on the sale of children, child prostitution and child pornography, UN Doc. E/CN.4/1998/103.

69. There appears to have been an increase in the exploitation of child labour across Africa as a result of the harsh economic climate, including being used in crime and drugs-related activities, UN Docs. E/CN.4/Sub.2/1993/30, para. 39; E/ CN.4/1993/67, paras. 97, 98. Like many poor countries, Zimbabwe is faced with a child labour problem but has been taking steps to address the issue, UN Doc. CCPR/C/74/Add.3, p. 43. The HRC has expressed concern about the employment of children in Tanzania although progress has been made in that field, UN Doc. CCPR/C/79/Add.97, paras. 7, 25. Article 15 of the African Charter on the Rights and Welfare of the Child and Article 32 of the UN Convention on the Rights of the Child seek to protect children from child labour. See further, Article 24 ICCPR and General comment 17, UN Doc. HRI/ GEN/1/Rev.3, para. 3. See also section 23(4) of the Constitution of Malawi, Articles 15(2) and 95(b) of the Namibian Constitution, section 28(1)(e), (f) of the South African Constitution, and Article 24 of the Zambian Constitution. Egypt places age restrictions on the employment of young persons, UN Doc. E/1990/ 5/Add.38, para. 143.

70. Prostitution and brothels are prohibited under Zimbabwe's Criminal Law Amendment Act, UN Doc. CCPR/C/74/Add.3, para. 87(a). Incitement to engage in prostitution is a criminal offence in Egypt, UN Doc. E/1990/5/ Add.38, pp. 43, 44.

71. Article 27(c) of the African Charter on the Rights and Welfare of the Child and Article 34(c) of the UN Convention on the Rights of the Child prohibit the use of children in pornographic activities. Child pornography materials through videos appears to be on the increase in Africa, UN Doc. E/CN.4/1993/67, para. 211; but see section 16(3) of the Child Protection Act 1994 of Mauritius. Child pornography is absolutely prohibited in Angola, UN Doc. E/CN.4/Sub.2/ AC.2/1991/1, p. 3. Section 30(1)(d) of the South African Constitution proclaims that children have a right not to be subjected to abuse, which would appear to protect children from sexual exploitation. Zimbabwe claims that child pornography is not a major problem, UN Doc. CCPR/C/74/Add.3, para. 87(b). Note the draft optional protocol to the Convention on the Rights of the Child on the sale of children, child prostitution and child pornography, UN Doc. E/CN.4/ 1998/103, paras. 48–52.

72. Article 27(b) of the African Charter on the Rights and Welfare of the Child and Article 34(b) of the UN Convention on the Rights of the Child prohibit the use of children in prostitution. Poverty and migration to urban areas is giving rise to increasing child prostitution problems in countries such as Burkina Faso, Côte d'Ivoire, and Ethiopia, UN Doc. E/CN.4/1993/67, p. 32. Child prostitution is said to be widespread in Kenya, UN Doc. E/C.12/1993/SR.4, para. 15, Nigeria and Zambia, UN Doc. E/CN.4/1997/95, p. 12. Zimbabwe claims that

child prostitution is not a major problem and that children are protected from sexual exploitation by the prohibition of marriage by minors, UN Doc. CCPR/C/74/Add.3, paras. 87(b), 223. Section 14 of the Child Protection Act 1994 of Mauritius makes it a criminal offence for a person to cause a child to engage in prostitution. See also Article 183 of the Penal Code of Mali, UN Doc. E/CN.4/Sub.2/AC.2/1991/4, para. 5. Note the draft optional protocol to the Convention on the Rights of the Child on the sale of children, child prostitution and child pornography, UN Doc. E/CN.4/1998/103, paras. 41–7.

73.   Article 27(a) of the African Charter on the Rights and Welfare of the Child and Article 34(a) of the UN Convention on the Rights of the Child prohibit sexual exploitation. Although not yet a major area of concern as in Asia the advent of tourism in Africa and curbs in Asia mean that many African countries will probably be faced with an increasing problem. It is reported that Mauritania has been targeted by foreign paedophiles, UN Doc. E/CN.4/1993/67, para. 181. Note the draft optional protocol to the Convention on the Rights of the Child on the sale of children, child prostitution and child pornography, UN Doc. E/CN.4/1998/103, paras. 53, 54.

74.   Ethiopia has legislation in force to counteract the removal of organs from children, while Libya has legislation regarding the transplantation and removal of organs, UN Doc. E/CN.4/Sub.2/AC.2/1994/8, pp. 3, 4.

75.   UN Docs. E/CN.4/1993/67, pp. 23–6; E/CN.4/1999/71, p. 16.

76.   See also Article 38 of the UN Convention on the Rights of the Child which sets fifteen as the threshold age, an age which has been criticized as too low but which should be raised to eighteen, UN Doc. E/CN.4/1993/67, para. 138. The UN is working on a draft optional protocol to the Convention on the Rights of the Child on involvement of children in armed conflict that would raise the minimum age at which children can serve in armed conflict, UN Doc. E/CN.4/1998/102. See also UN Doc. E/CN.4/1998/119.

77.   (1980) 630 F.2d 876. See also *Prosecutor* v. *Furundzija* 38 *ILM* 317 (1999).

78.   Ratified by Algeria, Benin, Burundi, Cameroon, Cape Verde, Chad, Côte d'Ivoire, Democratic Republic of the Congo, Egypt, Ethiopia, Guinea, Libya, Malawi, Mauritius, Namibia, Senegal, Seychelles, Somalia, Togo, Tunisia and Uganda. Signed by Gabon, Gambia, Nigeria, Sierra Leone, South Africa and Sudan.

79.   Series A, Vol. 25 (1978). See further, Harris, O'Boyle and Warbrick, note 18 *supra*, Chapter 3. Article 1(1) of the UN Convention Against Torture defines torture as, 'any act by which severe pain or suffering, whether physical or mental, is intentionally inflicted on a person for such purposes as obtaining from him or a third person information or a confession, punishing him for an act he or a third person has committed or is suspected of having committed, or intimidating or coercing him or a third person, or for any reason based on discrimination of any kind, when such pain or suffering is inflicted by or at the instigation of or with the consent or acquiescence of a public official or other person acting in an official capacity. It does not include pain or suffering arising only from, inherent in or incidental to lawful sanctions.' Furthermore, Article 1(2) states that, 'Torture constitutes an aggravated and deliberate form of cruel, inhuman or degrading treatment or punishment.' See further, *Prosecutor* v. *Furundzija* 38 *ILM* 317 (1999) para. 162; *Aksoy* v. *Turkey* Reports 1996-VI; and *Aydin* v. *Turkey* Reports 1997-VI. The HRC has expressed the view that it is unnecessary to draw sharp distinctions between the different kinds of treatment or punishment; the distinctions depend on the nature, purpose and severity of the treatment applied, General comment 20, UN Doc. HRI/GEN/1/Rev.2, para. 4. However, the Constitutional Court of South Africa discussed the meaning of the words 'cruel, inhuman or degrading' at some length in *S* v. *Williams and Others* 1995 (7) BCLR 861 (CC) at pp. 869–73.

80. Ankumah writes that torture is practised with 'impunity' in Africa, note 19 *supra*, p. 116, notwithstanding the fact that the practice is outlawed. Torture and ill-treatment of persons arrested by the security forces was commonplace in Zaire which operated with complete impunity. Electric shocks, sexual violence, mock executions and whippings were used to punish and humiliate Mobutu's political opponents, UN Doc. E/CN.4/1994/49, para. 29. Allegations of ill-treatment are also common in Zambia, UN Doc. CCPR/C/79/Add.62, paras. 12, 24. In many African countries torture in police custody to coerce detainees to incriminate others is reported to be routine, e.g., Djibouti, UN Doc. E/CN.4/1993/26, para. 158–60, Nigeria, UN Doc. CCPR/C/79/Add.65, para. 18, Sudan, UN Docs. E/CN.4/1993/26, paras. 412–22, E/CN.4/1994/48, paras. 41–51 (although prohibited by law, UN Doc. CCPR/C/75/Add.2, pp. 24, 25), and Togo, UN Doc. CCPR/C/79/Add.36, para. 6 (although prohibited by the Constitution, UN Doc. CCPR/C/63/Add.2, paras. 22–4). Torture and inhuman and degrading treatment or punishment is prohibited under the constitutions of many African States, e.g., Algeria, UN Doc. CRC/C/28/Add.4, para. 55, Botswana (section 7(1)), Chad (Article 18), Gabon (Article 1(1)), Lesotho (Article 8(1)), section 19(2) of the Constitution of Malawi, Mali (Article 3), Namibia (Article 8(2)(b)), South Africa (section 12(1)(d), (e)), Tanzania (Article 13(6)(e)), Zambia (Article 15), and Zimbabwe (section 15(1)). Egypt has reported to the Committee Against Torture that torture is a crime under Egyptian law, defined as an act of inflicting suffering. It was left to the courts to determine in each instance whether an act of torture had occurred. Psychological, mental and physical torture were covered, as was the threat of torture. Moreover, the Convention Against Torture could be invoked before Egyptian courts, UN Doc. CAT/C/SR.163/Add.1, para. 6. However, torture by the police and security forces seems routine, UN Docs. E/CN.4/1993/26, paras. 167–200, E/CN.4/1994/31, para. 226. Senegal reported that its Constitution implicitly condemns the practice of torture and is expressly covered by the Penal Code and the Code of Criminal Procedure, although cases of torture by the police have been reported, UN Doc. CAT/C/17/Add.14. Allegations of the systematic resort to torture by the security forces, with full impunity, combating the separatist movement in Casamance have also been made, UN Doc. CAT/C/SR.247, para. 25. The Committee against Torture recommended, *inter alia*, a blanket prohibition on torture, UN Doc. CAT/C/SR.249, p. 11. Mauritius reported that torture was covered by its constitutional provisions but there were lacunae so that mental torture was not covered, UN Doc. CAT/C/SR.213, para. 3. Libya made a similar confession, UN Doc. CAT/C/SR.135, p. 6, and the HRC expressed concern about allegations of torture, UN Doc. CCPR/C/79/Add.45. The HRC has emphasized that the prohibition or criminalization of torture or similar practices is insufficient but that effective machineries of control must exist, General comment 7, UN Doc. HRI/GEN/1/Rev.2, para. 1. Thus, concern was expressed that allegations of abuses in Zambia are not investigated by an independent body, UN Doc. CCPR/C/79/Add.62, paras. 12, 24. Lesotho was criticized for the inaction of its authorities, UN Doc. E/CN.4/1993/26, para. 307. The UN Special Rapporteur on Extrajudicial, Summary or Arbitrary Executions has received reports of deaths in custody as a result of torture in Cameroon, Egypt, and Morocco, UN Doc. E/CN.4/1995/47, para. 388.

81. Communication No. 458/1991, UN Doc. CCPR/C/51/D/458/1991. Cameroon has reported to the Commission on Human Rights that its Penal Code was amended in 1996 to make torture an offence, UN Doc. E/CN.4/1998/SR.31, para. 58. See also *Bozize* v. *Central African Republic* which concerned a former military officer who had gone into exile after a coup d'etat he had instigated

failed. He was repatriated by force and imprisoned. The HRC was of the view that Bozize had been subjected to maltreatment, held incommunicado and detained in conditions which did not respect the inherent dignity of the human person, Communication No. 428/1990, UN Doc. HR/94/24. In *Mika Miha* v. *Equatorial Guinea* a political opponent of the regime claimed that he had been tortured and kept in detention without medical assistance. The HRC concluded that he had been subjected to torture, and that the deprivation of food and water and the denial of medical attention after ill-treatment amounted to cruel and inhuman treatment, Communication No. 414/1990, UN Doc. CCPR/C/51/ D/414/1990. See further, *Marais* v. *Madagascar*, Communication No. 49/1979, *Birhashwirwa and Mulumba* v. *Zaire*, Communication Nos. 241 and 242/1987, UN Doc. A/45/40, Annex IX, I, and *El-Megreisi* v. *Libya*, concerning a Libyan citizen who was arrested by the Libyan security police on suspicion of active involvement in politics. The HRC found that El-Megreisi had been subjected to arbitrary arrest and detention, Communication No. 440/1990, UN Doc. HR/ 94/24. The HRC has expressed concern about the lack of information about people held in incommunicado detention in Libya, UN Doc. CCPR/C/79/ Add.45, para.9. It should be observed that the UN Convention Against Torture is part of Libyan domestic law and that torture is prohibited under the Penal Code, UN Doc. CAT/C/25/Add.3. In its general comment on Article 7 ICCPR, the HRC has stated that prolonged solitary confinement may violate the ICCPR, UN Doc. HRI/GEN/1/Rev.2, para. 6. See also, *Velasquez Rodriguez* v. *Honduras* 9 *HRLJ* (1988) 212, para. 187. Cf. *S* v. *Masitere* 1991 (1) SA 821 (ZS) where the Supreme Court of Zimbabwe held solitary confinement and a spare diet to be unconstitutional; and *Conjwayo* v. *Minister of Justice, Legal and Parliamentary Affairs* 1992 (2) SA 56 (ZS) where the same court held that prisoners are entitled to a minimum daily exercise period in the open air. And see section 42(1)(b) of the Constitution of Malawi, and section 35(2)(e) of the South African Constitution. The UN has received numerous reports of deaths in custody as a result of torture or other cruel, inhuman and degrading treatment in Sierra Leone, or inhuman prison conditions or medical neglect in Togo, UN Doc. E/CN.4/1994/ 35, para. 702. Cameroon has acknowledged that whereas the rights of prisoners are protected under law economic constraints mean that prison conditions are 'unpleasant', UN Doc. E/CN.4/1998/SR.31, paras. 58, 59.

82. Communication No. 366/1989, UN Doc. A/49/40, Annex IX, J.

83. Note 50 *supra*. See further, *Free Legal Assistance Group and Others* v. *Zaire* (Communication No. 25/89) 18 *HRLJ* (1997) 32, and *Commission Nationale des Droits de l'Homme et des Libertés* v. *Chad* (Communication No. 74/92) 18 *HRLJ* (1997) 34.

84. *Tyrer* v. *United Kingdom* Series A, Vol. 26 (1978); General comment 20, UN Doc. HRI/GEN/1/Rev.2, para. 5.

85. Thus, the HRC has called for the abolition of corporal punishment in Zambia, UN Doc. CCPR/C/79/Add.62, para. 27, and has deplored the introduction in Libya of cruel punishments such as flogging and amputation, UN Doc. CCPR/ C/79/Add.45, para. 9. In Lesotho male juveniles are exposed to corporal punishment, UN Doc. CRC/C/11/Add.20, p. 30. But see section 19(4) of the Constitution of Malawi. The imposition of judicial corporal punishment on adults was declared unconstitutional as inhuman or degrading punishment by the Court of Appeal of Botswana, *S* v. *Petrus* [1985] LRC (Const) 699, Supreme Court of Zimbabwe, *S* v. *Ncube* 1988 (2) SA 702 (ZS), and the Supreme Court of Namibia, *Ex Parte Attorney-General, Namibia: In re Corporal Punishment by Organs of State* 1991 (3) SA 76 (NmS). Furthermore, the imposition of corporal punishment on juveniles has similarly been adjudged unconstitutional by the Supreme Court of Namibia, *Ex Parte Attorney-General, Namibia, idem*, the Supreme Court

of Zimbabwe, *S* v. *Juvenile* 1990 (4) SA 151 (ZS), although reversed by the Constitution of Zimbabwe Amendment (No. 11) Act 1990, and the Constitutional Court of South Africa, *S* v. *Williams and Others* 1995 (7) BCLR 861 (CC).

86. General comment 20, UN Doc. HRI/GEN/1/Rev.2, para. 6.

87. *Soering* v. *United Kingdom* Series A, Vol. 161 (1989) para. 104; *Gregg* v. *Georgia* (1976) S. Ct. 2909.

88. *S* v. *Makwanyane and Mchunu* 1995 (3) SA 391. Cf. *State* v. *Ntesang* [1995] 2 LRC 338, where the Court of Appeal of Botswana held that execution by hanging was a lawful punishment since the Constitution expressly preserved the death penalty as a competent punishment even though torture, inhuman or degrading punishment was prohibited. In *Mbushuu* v. *Republic* [1995] 1 LRC 216 the Court of Appeal of Tanzania found that the death penalty and the mode of execution, hanging, offended the constitutional protection against cruel, inhuman and degrading punishment but that the death sentence was saved by other constitutional provisions and that it was also favoured by society. See also *Amasimbi* v. *State* (1992) MR 227. Under the Constitution of Zimbabwe Amendment (No. 11) Act 1990, section 15 of the Constitution was amended so as to render constitutional hanging as the method of carrying out the death sentence. This was a legislative response to developments in the Supreme Court after the Court, in considering an appeal against the death sentence imposed on a convicted murderer, had called for argument on whether hanging offended the constitutional prohibition on inhuman or degrading punishment, *S* v. *Ketose* No. 64/90.

89. *Catholic Commission for Justice and Peace in Zimbabwe* v. *Attorney-General, Zimbabwe* 1993 (4) SA 239 (ZS); *Nkomo* v. *Attorney-General, Zimbabwe* 1994 (1) SACR 302 (ZS). However, with the passage of the Constitution of Zimbabwe Amendment (No. 13) Act 1993 any delay in the execution of sentence of death would no longer be unconstitutional as inhuman or degrading punishment. See also *Pratt and Morgan* v. *Jamaica*, Communication Nos. 210/1986 and 225/1987, UN Docs. CCPR/C/35/D/210/1986.

90. Cf. Article 4 ECHR; see further, Harris, O'Boyle and Warbrick, note 18 *supra*, Chapter 4. In *Van der Mussele* v. *Belgium* Series A, Vol. 70 (1983) the European Court of Human Rights stated that 'labour' is forced if it involves physical or mental constraint. However, prison work imposed in the ordinary course of detention does not amount to forced or compulsory labour, *Van Droogenbroeck* v. *Belgium* Series A, Vol. 50 (1982). See also ILO Convention Concerning Forced or Compulsory Labour 1930 and ILO Convention Concerning the Abolition of Forced Labour 1957. For constitutional prohibitions, see, e.g., Botswana (section 6), Malawi (section 27(3), (4)), Namibia (Article 9), South Africa (section 13), Zambia (Article 14), and Zimbabwe (section 14). Sexual violence could also be caught by Articles 4 and 5 of the Banjul Charter, see further note 236 *infra*.

91. It has been reported that female circumcision exists in at least twenty-five countries in Africa, UN Doc. E/CN.4/Sub.2/1991/6, p. 3. Egypt's highest civil court has recommended the legalization of female circumcision whilst acknowledging that the practice was not mandatory under Islam, UN Doc. E/CN.4/Sub.2/1997/10, para. 104. By contrast, Egypt's supreme administrative court has upheld a ban on government health workers performing female circumcision, *The Guardian* (London), 29 December 1997, p. 11. It appears that among States directly concerned with female genital mutilation only Burkina Faso, Sudan, UN Doc. E/CN.4/Sub.2/1996/6, para. 159, and Senegal, UN Doc. E/CN.4/Sub.2/1998/SR.16, para. 57, have legislated to condemn and punish such practices. Guinea, Niger and Sudan were singled out for their determination to put an end to these practices, ibid., pp. 6–11. A WHO Regional Plan of Action

to Accelerate the Elimination of Female Genital Mutilation was launched in many African countries in March 1997, UN Doc. E/CN.4/Sub.2/1997/SR.14, para. 15.

92. UN Fourth World Conference on Women, 35 *ILM* 401 (1996), paras. 113, 118, 124 and 224; Vienna Declaration and Programme of Action, Part II, paras 38, 49. See also Article 21(1) of the African Charter on the Rights and Welfare of the Child.

93. See *Dow* v. *Attorney-General* [1992] LRC (Const) 623, where the Botswana Court of Appeal held that custom and tradition must always yield to the Constitution and to express legislation. Furthermore, para. 224 of the Beijing Plan of Action states that 'any harmful aspect of certain traditional, customary or modern practices that violates the rights of women should be prohibited and eliminated'.

94. For example, in Tanzania, UN Doc. CCPR/C/SR.1690, para. 19. It must be stressed, however, that consent to the infliction of grievous bodily harm does not make it any the less a crime and the State can have well-founded reasons of public policy to prosecute, see *Laskey* v. *United Kingdom* Reports 1997 I.

95. Including the security of non-detained persons, *Bwalya* v. *Zambia*, Communication No. 314/1988, UN Doc. A/48/40, Annex XII.I; *Oló Bahamonde*, Communication No. 468/1991; *Tshishimbi* v. *Zaire*, Communication No. 542/1993.

96. General comment 8, UN Doc. HRI/GEN/1/Rev.2, para. 1; Harris, O'Boyle and Warbrick, note 18 *supra*, p. 97. See also *Bernstein and Others* v. *Bester NO and Others* 1996 (4) BCLR 449 (CC).

97. *Bouamar* v. *Belgium* Series A, Vol. 129 (1988). In *Sheriff* v. *District Magistrate of Port Louis* (1989) MR 260 the Supreme Court of Mauritius observed that deprivation of liberty was an exceptional measure. For constitutional guarantees see, e.g., section 5 of the Constitution of Botswana, section 18 of the Constitution of Malawi, Article 11 of the Namibian Constitution, sections 12(1) and 35(1), (2) of the South African Constitution, Article 15 of the Constitution of Togo, Article 13 of the Zambian Constitution, and section 13 of the Constitution of Zimbabwe. See also the Bail Act 1989 of Mauritius, and Cameroon's Code of Criminal Procedure and Criminal Code, UN Doc. CCPR/C/63/Add.1, paras. 61, 62. In Senegal police custody and pre-trial detention are regulated by the Code of Criminal Procedure, UN Doc. CAT/C/17/Add.14, pp. 13–5. In *Koné* v. *Senegal*, Communication No. 386/1989, the HRC was of the view that the applicant's arrest and detention were not arbitrary in light of the procedural guarantees. However, in *Kanana* v. *Zaire*, Communication No. 366/1989, the fact that the applicant had been brought to the police station under false pretences meant that his arrest and detention were arbitrary. In *Free Legal Assistance Group and Others* v. *Zaire* Communication 25/89 the African Commission found that indefinite detention violated Article 6. It appears that in Nigeria detention without charge is commonplace, UN Doc. CCPR/C/79/Add.65, para. 20.

98. See General comment 8, UN Doc. HRI/GEN/1/Rev.2, pp. 8, 9.

99. See Harris, O'Boyle and Warbrick, note 18 *supra*,. Chapter 5.

100. Described by the European Court of Human Rights as an 'elementary safeguard', *Fox, Campbell and Hartley* v. *United Kingdom* Series A, Vol. 182 (1990), para. 41. See, e.g., section 5(2) of the Constitution of Botswana, section 42(1)(a) of the Constitution of Malawi, section 35(1)(e), (2)(a) of the South African Constitution, Article 13(2) of the Zambian Constitution, and section 13(3) of the Constitution of Zimbabwe. See further, *Birhashwirwa and Mulumba* v. *Zaire*, Communication Nos. 241 and 242/1987; *Mika Miha* v. *Equatorial Guinea*, Communication No. 414/90. In *El-Megreisi* v. *Libya*, Communication No. 440/1990, the applicant had still not been charged five years after his arrest.

101. On the meaning of judicial officer, see *Schiesser* v. *Switzerland* Series A, Vol. 34

(1979); *Huber* v. *Switzerland* Series A, Vol. 188 (1990). The HRC has stated that delays must not exceed a few days, General comment 8, UN Doc. HRI/GEN/ 1/Rev.2, para. 2; see also, section 5(3) of the Constitution of Botswana; section 42(2)(b) of the Constitution of Malawi; Article 11(3) of the Namibian Constitution; section 35(1)(d) of the South African Constitution; the Tunisian Code of Penal Procedure, UN Doc. CCPR/C/84/Add.1, para. 155(a); Article 13(3) of the Zambian Constitution; section 32 of the Criminal Procedure and Evidence Act of Zimbabwe, UN Doc. CCPR/C/74/Add.3, para. 95; *Brogan* v. *United Kingdom* Series A, Vol. 145-B (1988); *DPP* v. *101B & Shanto* (1989) MR 110; *Mika Miha* v. *Equatorial Guinea*, Communication No. 414/90; *Birhashwirwa and Mulumba* v. *Zaire*, Communication Nos. 241 and 242/1987; *Bozize* v. *Central African Republic*, Communication No. 428/1990; *Oló Bahamonde* v. *Equatorial Guinea*, Communication No. 468/1991.

102. *Wemhoff* v. *Germany* Series A, Vol. 7 (1968); *Herczegfalvy* v. *Austria* Series A, Vol. 244 (1992). In *Koné* v. *Senegal*, Communication No. 386/1989, a violation of Article 9(3) was established. The applicant had been subjected to a delay of four years and four months, during which time he was kept in custody, and no special circumstances were present justifying such delay. See also, section 12(1) of the Constitution of Lesotho, section 25(3)(a) of the South African Interim Constitution; the Tunisian Code of Penal Procedure, UN Doc. CCPR/C/84/ Add.1, paras. 109–16, 155(c), section 18 of the Constitution of Zimbabwe; *Director of Public Prosecutions and Another* v. *Lebona* 1998 (5) BCLR 618 (Les CA); *Hossen* v. *District Magistrate of Port Louis* (1993) MR 9; *In re Mlambo* 1991 (2) ZLR 339; *Mlauzi* v. *Attorney-General* 1993 (1) SA 207 (ZS); *Sanderson* v. *Attorney-General, Eastern Cape* 1997 (12) BCLR 1675 (CC); *Smyth* v. *Ushewokunze and Another* 1998 (2) BCLR 170 (ZS); *Wild and Another* v. *Hoffert NO and Others* 1998 (6) BCLR 656 (CC). Article 12(1)(b) of the Namibian Constitution requires that the accused be released if a trial fails to take place within a reasonable time, see *S* v. *Strowitski and Another* 1995 (1) BCLR 12 (Nm), *S* v. *Heidenreich* [1996] 2 LRC 115. However, a 'speedy trial' is not required, *S* v. *Strowitski and Another* 1995 (1) BCLR 12 (Nm). See further, section 5(3) of the Constitution of Botswana, and Article 13(3) of the Zambian Constitution.

103. This right is comparable to the writ of *habeas corpus*, which the Inter-American Court of Human Rights has held to be of a fundamental nature, *Habeas Corpus in Emergency Situations* 27 *ILM* 512 (1988). The HRC has stated that pre-trial detention should be an exception and as short as possible, UN Doc. HRI/GEN/ 1/Rev.2, para. 3; and see futher, *De Jong, Baljet and Van den Brink* v. *The Netherlands* Seies A, Vol. 77 (1984), and *Brogan* v. *United Kingdom* Series A, Vol. 145-B (1988). See section 35(2)(d) of the South African Constitution. See also *Mika Miha* v. *Equatorial Guinea*, Communication No. 414/90; *Bozize* v. *Central African Republic*, Communication No. 428/1990; *El-Megreisi* v. *Libya*, Communication No. 440/1990. It has been observed in note 102 *supra* that the Constitutions of Botswana, Namibia and Zambia require the release of the accused if he or she is not tried within a reasonable time. See also section 42(1)(e)(f) of the Constitution of Malawi.

It appears that the term 'habeas corpus' is unknown to the francophone African legal system, although the principle is applied, UN Doc. E/CN.4/ Sub.2/1998/19, para. 79. Under Tunisia's Code of Criminal Procedure the length of custody and of pre-trial detention is usually four days but cannot exceed ten days, UN Doc. CCPR/C/84/Add.1, para. 109. However, the HRC has expressed concern that the law is not adhered to strictly, UN Doc. CCPR/ C/79/Add.43, para. 8. The HRC has also expressed concern about the absence of habeas corpus in Senegal, UN Doc. CCPR/C/SR.1180.

104. See *Brogan* v. *United Kingdom* Series A, Vol. 145-B (1988); Harris, O'Boyle and

Warbrick, note 18 *supra*, pp. 158–60. Compensation is available in Tunisia, UN Doc. CCPR/C/84/Add.1, para. 117, Botswana under section 5(4) of the Constitution, Zambia under Article 13(4) of the Constitution, and Zimbabwe under section 13(5) of the Constitution, UN Doc. CCPR/C/74/Add.3, para. 101.

105.   Cf. Article 11 ICCPR, Article 1 of the Fourth Protocol ECHR, and Article 7(7) ACHR; Sieghart, note 40 *supra*, pp. 135–59. In Cameroon and Sudan imprisonment on the ground of inability to fulfil a contractual obligation is prohibited, UN Docs. CCPR/C/63/Add.1, para. 69, CCPR/C/75/Add.2, para. 107. See also, section 19(6)(c) of the Constitution of Malawi; *Pelladoah* v. *Development Bank of Mauritius* (1992) MR 5. Although in Zimbabwe a person cannot be imprisoned for the inability to fulfil a contractual obligation, UN Doc. CCPR/C/74/Add.3, para. 110, section 13(2)(c) of the Constitution does allow for imprisonment for judgment debtors who wilfully refuse to do so, *Chinamora* v. *Angwa Furnishers (Pvt) Limited (Attorney-General intervening)* 1997 (2) BCLR 189 (ZS). Imprisonment for non-payment in civil claims is possible in Gabon, UN Doc. CCPR/C/31/Add.4, para. 36. The HRC has recommended that Zambia abolish imprisonment for civil debt, UN Doc. CCPR/C/79/Add.62, para. 26.

106.   Amnesty International, *The Organization of African Unity and Human Rights* (1987) p. 11. Ankumah is critical of the wording of this provision and again points out that this right is violated with impunity in Africa, note 19 *supra*, Chapter 5.2.3. The African Commission found violations of Article 6 in the *Chirwa case*. Arrests *en masse* of the regime's political opponents were categorized as 'arbitrary', as was the detention without charge or trial of another opponent. See also *Commission Nationale des Droits de l'Homme et des Libertés* v. *Chad* (Communication No. 74/92). In *Free Legal Assistance Group and Others* v. *Zaire* (Communication No. 25/89), at para. 42, indefinite detention of individuals was held to be in violation of Article 6.

107.   See *Lawyers' Committee for Human Rights* v. *Zaire* (Communication 47/90), *Commission Nationale des Droits de l'Homme et des Libertés* v. *Chad* (Communication 74/92). Cf. section 12(1) of the Constitution of Lesotho, section 42(2)(f) of the Constitution of Malawi, Article 12 of the Namibian Constitution, section 35(3) of the South African Constitution, and section 18 of the Zimbabwean Constitution. The primary objective of this guarantee is 'the protection of the individual interest in fundamental justice', see *In re Mlambo* 1992 (4) SA 144 (ZS).

108.   Cf. Article 14(1) ICCPR, Article 6(1) ECHR and Article 8(1) ACHR. See further, Article 12(1)(a) of the Namibian Constitution and section 18(9) of the Zimbabwean Constitution, and see *Holland and Others* v. *Minister of the Public Service, Labour and Social Welfare* 1997 (6) BCLR 809 (ZS).

109.   For example, the legal system of Lesotho includes customary law with its own court structure, UN Doc. CERD/C/337/Add.1, paras. 4, 5.

110.   General comment 13, HRI/GEN/1/Rev.2, p. 14; Harris, O'Boyle and Warbrick, note 18 *supra*, pp. 166–96. The European Court of Human Rights has therefore held that military courts martial must meet the requirements of the right to a fair trial, *Findlay* v. *United Kingdom* Reports 1997–I. For the position in Tunisia, see UN Doc. CCPR/C/84/Add.1, paras. 161–3. It should be observed that disciplinary proccedings conducted by a parliamentary legislature appear to fall outside the scope of this provision, *Smith* v. *Mutasa NO and Another* 1990 (3) SA 756 (ZS); *Mutasa* v. *Makombe NO* 1997 (6) BCLR 841 (ZS).

111.   Since the use of military courts involves serious risks of arbitrariness, because of the applicable procedure and the fact that double standards seem to be applied depending on whether the accused is a civilian or a soldier, the UN has called on such trials to be 'exceptional', UN Doc. E/CN.4/1994/35, p. 33. In resolution 1993/69, the Commission on Human Rights called upon Equatorial

Guinea to terminate the use of military courts to try civilians, UN Doc. E/CN4/1996/67, para. 14. Nigeria has been criticized by the HRC for its use of military courts, UN Doc. CCPR/C/79/Add.65, para. 12.

112.   Cf. Article 14 ICCPR; General comment 13, UN Doc. HRI/GEN/1/Rev.2, para. 15. On the right of access to a court under Article 6(1) ECHR, see *Golder* v. *United Kingdom* Series A, Vol. 18 (1975); Harris, O'Boyle and Warbrick, note 18 *supra*, pp. 196–202. According to Ankumah, the right to appeal under the Banjul Charter does not encompass a right to resort to a superior court but refers simply to the right to seek a judicial remedy, note 19 *supra*, p. 124. Access to the courts is guaranteed in Gabon, UN Doc. CCPR/C/31/Add.4, para. 41, section 41 of the Constitution of Malawi, Articles 12 and 24(3) of the Namibian Constitution, section 34 of the South African Constitution, Togo, UN Doc. CCPR/C/63/Add.2, para. 45. However, see *Oló Bahamonde* v. *Equatorial Guinea*, Communication No. 468/1991. On the right of appeal, cf. Article 14(5) ICCPR and see General comment 13, UN Doc. HRI/GEN/1/Rev.2, para. 17. Under the ECHR it is expressly provided for by Article 2 of the Seventh Protocol, see Harris, O'Boyle and Warbrick, note 18 *supra*, pp. 566, 567. The right of appeal is provided for in the legal systems of various African States, e.g., Gabon, UN Doc. CCPR/C/31/Add.4, para. 50, section 42(2)(viii) of the Constitution of Malawi, section 35(3)(o) of the South African Constitution, Tunisia, UN Doc. CCPR/C/84/Add.1, paras. 157, 158, and Zimbabwe, UN Doc. CCPR/C/74/Add.3, para. 139.

113.   *Constitutional Rights Project* v. *Nigeria (in respect of Wahab Akamu, G. Adega and Others)*(Communication No. 60/91) 3 *IHRR* (1996) 132; and *Constitutional Rights Project* v. *Nigeria (in respect of Zamani Lakwot and Others)*(Communication No. 87/93) 3 *IHRR* (1996) 137.

114.   *Civil Liberties Organization* v. *Nigeria* (Communication No. 129/94) 18 *HRLJ* (1997) 35. See also *Akonaay* v. *Attorney-General* [1994] 2 LRC 399.

115.   Cf. Article 14(2) ICCPR; Article 6(2) ECHR. The HRC has stated that the presumption of innocence is fundamental to the protection of human rights and that no guilt can be presumed until the charge has been proved beyond a reasonable doubt. The burden of proof is on the prosecution and the accused has the benefit of the doubt. All public authorities must refrain from prejudging the outcome of a trial, General comment 13, UN Doc. HRI/GEN/1/Rev.2, para. 7. See further, *Barbera, Messegue and Jabardo* v. *Spain* Series A, Vol. 146 (1989) para. 77; Harris, O'Boyle and Warbrick, note 18 *supra*, pp. 241–8. See also, Articles 22–5 of the Constitution of Chad, Article 1(4) of the Constitution of Gabon, section 42(2)(f)(iii) of the Constitution of Malawi, Article 12(1)(d) of the Namibian Constitution, section 35(3)(h) of the South African Constitution, Article 18 of the Constitution of Togo, Article 12 of the Tunisian Constitution, UN Doc. CCPR/C/84/Add.1, para. 154, Article 18(2)(a) of the Zambian Constitution, section 18(3)(b) of the Constitution of Zimbabwe. The issue of 'reverse onus' has been challenged before the courts as incompatible with the presumption of innocence, see *S* v. *Zuma* 1995 (2) SA 642 (CC), *S* v. *Bhulwana* 1996 (1) SA 388 (CC), *S* v. *Coetzee and Others* 1997 (4) BCLR 437 (CC), *S* v. *Chogugudza* 1996 (3) BCLR 427 (ZS).

116.   Article 14(3)(g) ICCPR; General comment 13, HRI/GEN/1/Rev.2, para. 14; *Funke* v. *France* Series A, Vol. 256-A (1993); Harris, O'Boyle and Warbrick, note 18 *supra*, pp. 213, 214. Cf. section 42(2)(f)(iii) of the Constitution of Malawi, Article 12(1)(f) of the Namibian Constitution and section 35(3)(j) of the South African Constitution, and see *Ferreira* v. *Levin and Others* 1996 (1) BCLR 1 (CC), *Nel* v. *Le Roux NO and Others* 1996 (4) BCLR 592 (CC), *Parbhoo and Others* v. *Getz NO and Another* 1997 (10) BCLR 1337 (CC), *S* v. *Shikunga* 1997 (9) BCLR 1321 (Nm S).

117. See section 42(2)(f)(v) of the Constitution of Malawi, section 35(3)(b)(f) of the South African Constitution, Article 18(2)(c) of the Zambian Constitution and section 18 of the Constitution of Zimbabwe. See further, *Paweni* v. *Minister of State Security* 1984 (1) ZLR 236. Cf. Article 14(3)(b), (d) ICCPR; *Marais* v. *Madagascar*, Communication No. 49/1979; Article 6(3)(c) ECHR; *Poitrimol* v. *France*, Series A, Vol. 277-A (1993), para. 34; Harris, O'Boyle and Warbrick, note 18 *supra*, pp. 256–66; General comment 13, UN Doc. HRI/GEN/1/Rev.2, paras. 9, 11.

118. Note 113 *supra*.

119. See section 42(2)(f)(v) of the Constitution of Malawi, section 35(3)(g) of the South African Constitution, and Article 18(2)(d) of the Zambian Constitution. See further, *Granger* v. *United Kingdom* Series A, Vol. 174 (1990); *Quaranta* v. *Switzerland* Series A, Vol. 205 (1991). Moreover, in *Airey* v. *Ireland* Series A, Vol. 32 (1979), the European Court of Human Rights found that the right of access to the courts was effectively foreclosed due to prohibitive legal costs and that the availability of legal aid was one of the means of securing such access.

120. The work of NGOs in this sphere and in providing legal services in rural areas must not be overlooked.

121. See section 42(2)(f)(i) of the Constitution of Malawi, Article 12(1)(b) of the Namibian Constitution, section 35(3)(d) of the South African Constitution, Article 18(1) of the Zambian Constitution, and section 18 of the Constitution of Zimbabwe. See further, *Corbett* v. *The State* [1990] LRC (Crim) 30. The European Court of Human Rights has interpreted the term 'reasonable time' to have a relative meaning in that there is no one period of time which can be described as reasonable but is dependent on all the circumstances of the case, *Wemhoff* v. *Germany* Series A, Vol. 7 (1968), *Stogmuller* v. *Austria* Series A, Vol. 9 (1969), which, however, does not excuse unjustified delays on the part of the authorities, see Harris, O'Boyle and Warbrick, note 18 *supra*, pp. 225–9. According to the HRC, the requirement of a trial 'without undue delay' applies at all stages, including on appeal, General comment 13, UN Doc. HRI/GEN/1/Rev.2, para. 10. This latter point was reaffirmed by the HRC in *Lubuto* v. *Zambia*, Communication No. 390/1990, where a delay of eight years between arrest and final judgment was blamed on the lack of administrative support for the judiciary. Resource constraints in many African countries make compliance difficult, e.g., Cameroon, UN Doc. CCPR/C/63/Add.1, para. 68.

122. The European Court of Human Rights has defined 'court' as an organ with a judicial character, independent of the executive and the parties to the case and offering procedural guarantees, *Belilos* v. *Switzerland* Series A, Vol. 132 (1988) para. 64; Harris, O'Boyle and Warbrick, note 18 *supra*, pp. 230–9. The HRC requires courts to be 'independent, impartial and competent', General comment 13, UN Doc. HRI/GEN/1/Rev.2, para. 3. As Ankumah points out, pressure on the judiciary from the executive is common in much of Africa, note 19 *supra*, pp. 125, 126. Thus, the independence of the judiciary has been questioned in Equatorial Guinea, UN Doc. E/CN.4/1996/67, paras. 13, 17; *Oló Bahamonde* v. *Equatorial Guinea*, Communication No. 468/1991. In *S* v. *Heita and another* 1992 (3) SA 785 (Nm), at pp. 789, 791, the significance of judicial independence for the effective functioning of the judiciary 'without which the Constitution itself cannot survive' was emphasized. O'Linn J stated that the courts in Namibia are subject only to the Constitution and the law, which 'simply means that it is also not subject to the dictates of political parties, even if that party is the majority party. Similarly it is not subject to any other pressure group.' See further Article 78(2), (3) of the Namibian Constitution. See also, sections 42(2)(f)(i) and 103(1) of the Constitution of Malawi, Article 65 of the Tunisian Constitution, UN Doc. CCPR/C/84/Add.1, para. 142, Articles 18(1) and 91(3) of the Zambian Consti-

tution. The independence of the judiciary is also recognized in Zimbabwe, UN Doc. CCPR/C/74/Add.3, paras. 21–3, and see *Smyth* v. *Ushewokunze and Another* 1998 (2) BCLR 170 (ZS).

123. Note 106 *supra*.

124. See (Communication No. 101/93) *Civil Liberties Organization in respect of Nigerian Bar Association* v. *Nigeria*, Eighth Annual Activity Report 1994–1995. Cf. Article 15 ICCPR; Article 7 ECHR; *Kokkinakis* v. *Greece* Series A, Vol. 260-A (1993); *Welch* v. *United Kingdom* Series A, Vol. 307-A (1995); Harris, O'Boyle and Warbrick, note 18 *supra*, Chapter 7. See also, e.g., section 10(4) of the Constitution of Botswana, section 42(2)(f)(vi) of the Constitution of Malawi, Article 12(3) of the Namibian Constitution, section 35(3)(l) of the South African Constitution, Article 18(4) of the Zambian Constitution, and section 18(5) of the Constitution of Zimbabwe. And further, Articles 3 and 4 of the Criminal Code of Cameroon, UN Doc. CCPR/C/63/Add.1, para. 79, Article 13 of the Tunisian Constitution and Article 1 of the Penal Code, UN Doc. CCPR/C/84/Add.1, para. 164. See also *S* v. *Kalize* 18 *CLB* (1992) 50.

125. See Ankumah, note 19 *supra*, pp. 129–30, who refers to two complaints to the African Commission alleging violation of this guarantee.

126. Ankumah regrets the absence of this requirement since political opposition is often suppressed through secret trials, note 19 *supra*, pp. 124, 125. Apart from exceptional circumstances, hearings should be open to the public in general, General comment 13, UN Doc. HRI/GEN/1/Rev.2, para. 6. Cf. section 42(2)(f)(i) of the Constitution of Malawi, Article 12(1)(a) of the Namibian Constitution, section 35(3)(c) of the South African Constitution, and section 194 of Zimbabwe's Criminal Procedure and Evidence Act. In *Andony* v. *State* (1992) MR 249 the Supreme Court of Mauritius held that the accused cannot, in a democratic society, be deprived of the right to a public trial unless there are compelling reasons to do so, the reasons for which must be set out. Cf. Article 14(1) ICCPR; Article 6(1) ECHR. See also, *Pretto* v. *Italy* Series A, Vol. 71 (1983); *Barbera, Messegue and Jabardo* v. *Spain* Series A, Vol. 146 (1988); Harris, O'Boyle and Warbrick, note 18 *supra.*, pp. 218, 219.

127. *Campbell and Fell* v. *United Kingdom* Series A, Vol. 80 (1984). Cf. the position in Cameroon, UN Doc. CCPR/C/63/Add.1, para. 76, Tunisia, UN Doc. CCPR/C/84/Add.1, para. 152, Zambia (Article 18(11) of the Constitution) and Zimbabwe, UN Doc. CCPR/C/74/Add.3, para. 131.

128. *Duval* v. *District Magistrate of Flacq* (1990) MR 36.

129. The African Commission on Human and Peoples' Rights has called for Article 7(1) to be expanded so as to guarantee several additional rights, including notification of charges, appearance before a judicial officer, right to release pending trial, adequate preparation of the defence, speedy trial, examination of witnesses and the right to an interpreter, ACHR/COMM/FIN(XI)/Annex VII.

130. Cf. Article 14(3)(e) ICCPR; General comment 13, UN Doc. HRI/GEN/1/Rev.2, para. 12; Article 18(2)(e) of the Zambian Constitution, and section 18(3)(e) of the Constitution of Zimbabwe. See further, *Bacha, Kowlessur & Barbeau* v. *Boodhoo* (1989) MR 51; *Bonisch* v. *Austria* Series A, Vol. 92 (1985); Harris, O'Boyle and Warbrick, note 18 *supra*, pp. 266–9.

131. *Goddi* v. *Italy* Series A, Vol. 76 (1984); *Colozza and Rubinat* v. *Italy* Series A, Vol. 89 (1985). Note, however, that in Case 98/79 *Pecastaing* v. *Belgium* [1980] ECR 691 the ECJ held that an EC national does not have the right under EC law to remain in the host State during the conduct of proceedings so long as a fair hearing, including an adequate defence, was not compromised. See section 35(3)(e) of the South African Constitution, and the Tunisian Code of Penal Procedure, UN Doc. CCPR/C/84/Add.1, para. 155(d).

132. Cf. Article 14(7) ICCPR; General comment 13, UN Doc. HRI/GEN/1/Rev.2,

para. 19; Article 4(1) Seventh Protocol to the ECHR. See also, section 42(2)(f)(vii) of the Constitution of Malawi, Article 12(2) of the Namibian Constitution, section 35(3)(m) of the South African Constitution, the Tunisian Code of Penal Procedure, UN Doc. CCPR/C/84/Add.1, para. 159, Article 18(5), (6) of the Zambian Constitution, and section 18(6) of the Constitution of Zimbabwe, and see *Mlauzi* v. *Attorney-General* 1992 (1) ZLR 260.

133. General comment 13, UN Doc. HRI/GEN/1/Rev.2, para. 13; *Luedicke, Belkacem and Koç* v. *Germany* Series A, Vol. 29 (1978); Harris, O'Boyle and Warbrick, note 18 *supra*, pp. 269–72; Ankumah, note 19 *supra*, pp. 130, 131. See also section 42(2)(f)(ix) of the Constitution of Malawi, section 35(3)(k) of the South African Constitution, and Article 18(2)(f) of the Zambian Constitution. For the position in Zimbabwe, see UN Doc. CCPR/C/74/Add.3, para. 134. In Tunisia interpreters are appointed by the courts, UN Doc. CCPR/C/84/Add.1, para. 155(f).

134. But see Article 17 of the African Charter on the Rights and Welfare of the Child. Cf. Article 37(b) of the UN Convention on the Rights of the Child; Articles 10(2)(b), (3), 14(4) and 24(1) ICCPR; Article 5(5) ACHR; UN Standard Minimum Rules for the Administration of Juvenile Justice 1985 (the Beijing Rules), UN Doc. A/RES/40/33; UN Rules for the Protection of Juveniles Deprived of their Liberty 1990, UN Doc. A/RES/45/113. See also section 6(1)(f) of the Constitution of Lesotho, section 42(2)(g) of the Constitution of Malawi, Article 15(5) of the Namibian Constitution, section 28(1)(g) of the South African Constitution (see further, UN Doc. E/CN.4/1996/31, pp. 20–2). A system of juvenile courts operates in Botswana, UN Doc. E/CN.4/1997/26, p. 5, Guinea, UN Doc. E/CN.4/1998/35, pp. 9, 10; and Zimbabwe, see UN Doc. CCPR/C/74/Add.3, paras. 137, 138. For the positions in Algeria, Ethiopia and Mauritius, see UN Docs. CRC/C/28/Add.4, VII, B; E/CN.4/1996/31, pp. 3–6; E/CN.4/1998/35, para. 37. In Botswana and Lesotho children cannot be imprisoned, see UN Docs. E/CN.4/1997/26, p. 5, CRC/C/11/Add.20, para. 42, respectively. However, it appears that many African countries lack special jurisdictions for juveniles, UN Doc. E/CN.4/Sub.2/1991/50, para. 32. It is important that juvenile offenders be segregated from adults, General comment 21, UN Doc. HRI/GEN/1/Rev. 3, para. 13. Swaziland has acknowledged failings in this respect due to scarce facilities, UN Doc. E/CN.4/1998/35, para. 49. Similarly Lesotho, UN Doc. CRC/C/11/Add.20, para. 115.

135. See section 11(1) of the Constitution of Botswana, section 33 of the Constitution of Malawi, section 15(1) of the South African Constitution, Article 19(1) of the Zambian Constitution, and section 19 of the Constitution of Zimbabwe. In Sudan the right to freedom of conscience is routinely violated as minorities are subjected to a policy of cultural, linguistic and religious assimilation, UN Doc. E/CN.4/1994/48, paras. 66, 67, although the Sudanese government claims a policy of toleration, UN Doc. CCPR/C/75/Add.2, p. 31.

136. Cf. *Van Marle* v. *The Netherlands* Series A, Vol. 101 (1986). See section 22 of the South African Constitution.

137. Cf. Article 18 ICCPR, Article 9 ECHR and Article 12 ACHR. See also the UN Convention on the Elimination of All Forms of Intolerance and Discrimination Based on Religion or Belief 1981. See generally, Harris, O'Boyle and Warbrick, note 18 *supra*, Chapter 10. See also section 11(1) of the Constitution of Botswana, section 33 of the Constitution of Malawi, section 15(1) of the South African Constitution, Article 19 of the Tanzanian Constitution, Article 5 of the Tunisian Constitution, UN Doc. CCPR/C/84/Add.1, paras. 173–6, section 19(1) of the Constitution of Zimbabwe. See further, *In re Chikweche* 1995 (4) BCLR 533 (ZS); *S* v. *Lawrence; S* v. *Negal; S* v. *Solberg* 1997 (10) BCLR 1348 (CC). Although Egypt's Constitution prohibits discrimination on grounds of religion and guarantees freedom of belief (Articles 40 and 46) it is widely reported that the

Coptic Christian minority suffers discrimination in many spheres of public life, UN Doc. E/CN.4/1994/79, pp. 45–52. Sudan has been singled out for especial criticism for its policy of forced conversions, UN Doc. E/CN.4/1994/48, para. 79. The enactment of personal laws (*in casu* Islamic law) as an essential component for the enjoyment of religious freedom was rejected by the Supreme Court of Mauritius in *Bhewa* v. *Government of Mauritius* (1990) MR 79. But see the Civil Status (Amendment No.2) Act 1990 which allows for a register of marriages and divorces according to Islamic rites.

138.   General comment 22, UN Doc. HRI/GEN/1/Rev.2, paras. 3, 5; Article 9(1) ECHR; *Otto-Preminger-Institut* v. *Austria* Series A, Vol. 295 (1994). See further, Harris, O'Boyle and Warbrick, note 18 *supra*, pp. 360–3. See also section 11(1) of the Constitution of Botswana and Article 19(1) of the Zambian Constitution. The freedom to change religion is problematic for Islamic cultures since such an eventuality is likely to be considered as heresy, see the concern expressed by the HRC at restrictions on this freedom in Libya where Islamic law decrees the death penalty for apostasy, although it does not appear to have been applied to date, UN Doc. CCPR/C/79/Add.45, para. 13. Sudan claims that conversion from Islam is not an offence, only the manifestation of such conversion if it upsets public order, UN Doc. CCPR/C/75/Add.2, para. 127. The HRC has also expressed the view that the terms 'belief' and 'religion' must be construed broadly and are not limited to traditional or accepted religions.

139.   General comment 22, UN Doc. HRI/GEN/1/Rev.2, para. 2; *Kokkinakis* v. *Greece* Series A, Vol. 260-A (1993) para. 31. See *In re Chikweche* 1995 (4) BCLR 533 (ZS) where the Supreme Court of Zimbabwe found that beliefs based on secular morality were also protected by section 19(1) of the Constitution.

140.   Article 18(2) ICCPR; General comment 22, UN Doc. HRI/GEN/1/Rev.2, paras. 9, 10. See section 11(4) of the Constitution of Botswana; Article 19(4) of the Zambian Constitution; *S* v. *Lawrence; S* v. *Negal; S* v. *Solberg* 1997 (10) BCLR 1348 (CC). Persecution of non-Muslims appears to be a factor behind the civil war in Sudan, see UN Doc. E/CN.4/1994/48, paras. 71–80; Ankumah, note 19 *supra*, p. 134, although see UN Doc. CCPR/C/75/Add.2, p. 31.

141.   Cf. Article 18(1) ICCPR, Article 9(1) ECHR. According to the HRC a broad range of acts is caught by this exposition, including ceremonial acts, the building of places of worship, the observance of holidays and days of rest, the observance of dietary laws, the wearing of special clothing, and the use of customary languages, as by Coptic Christians in Egypt and Ethiopia, General comment 22, UN Doc. HRI/GEN/1/Rev.2, para. 4. In *Aumeer* v. *L'Assemblée de Dieu* (1988) MR 229 the Supreme Court of Mauritius held that the right to freedom of religion included the right to manifest and propagate one's religion or belief in worship, teaching, practice and observance. For guarantees, see section 11(1) of the Constitution of Botswana, section 31 of the South African Constitution, Article 19(2) of the Tanzanian Constitution, and Article 19(1) of the Zambian Constitution. See further, Harris, O'Boyle and Warbrick, note 18 *supra*, pp. 363–65.

142.   In *Aumeer* v. *L'Assemblée de Dieu* (1988) MR 229 the Supreme Court of Mauritius held that the right to freedom of religion should be exercised in a civilized society in such a way so as not to cause inconvenience to others.

143.   In *Kokkinakis* v. *Greece* Series A, Vol. 260-A (1993), paras. 45–50, the European Court of Human Rights drew a distinction between Christian evangelism and improper proselytism which used coercion or manipulation or offered inducements and which was therefore not protected by Article 9. Article 19(2) of the Tanzanian Constitution permits evangelization.

144.   In *Les Témoins de Jéhovah* v. *Zaire* (Communication 56/91) the African Commission found that the harassment of Jehovah's Witnesses violated Article 8 as

there was no evidence that the practice of their religion threatened law and order. Cf. Article 18(3) ICCPR and Article 9(2) ECHR. See also section 11(5) of the Constitution of Botswana and Article 19(5) of the Zambian Constitution. Limitations in the interests of, *inter alia*, public order exist in Sudan, UN Doc. CCPR/C/75/Add.2, para. 127. According to the HRC the limitations must be strictly interpreted and must be prescribed by law and must be proportionate, General comment 22, UN Doc. HRI/GEN/1/Rev.2, para. 8; see also, Harris, O'Boyle and Warbrick, note 18 *supra*, pp. 365–8. See *Gay News Ltd* v. *Lemon* (1983) 5 EHRR 123 where the European Commission on Human Rights found that restrictions imposed on blasphemous libel did not constitute an illegitimate interference with the freedom of thought and religion.

145. According to the HRC conscientious objection is to be read into Article 18 ICCPR, UN Doc. HRI/GEN/1/Rev.2, para. 11. In *Arrowsmith* v. *United Kingdom* (1981) 3 EHRR 218 the European Commission on Human Rights expressed the view that pacifism as a philosophy comes within the scope of Article 9 ECHR; see further, Harris, O'Boyle and Warbrick, note 18 *supra*, pp. 368–70. The Committee of Ministers of the Council of Europe has recommended that the Member States recognize conscientious objection to compulsory military service and make provision for alternative service in civilian service, Recommendation No. R (87) 8, 9 April 1987. Sudan claims that there is no conscientious objection to military service since such service is voluntary, UN Doc. CCPR/C/75/Add.2, para. 131. In Angola conscientious objectors are required to serve in the administrative sector in lieu, UN Doc. E/CN.4/1995/99, p. 2. The HRC has expressed concern at the lack of provision for conscientious objection in Libya, UN Doc. CCPR/C/79/Add.45, para. 13.

146. Ankumah, note 19, *supra*, Chapter 5.2.6. See, *Aduayom et al.* v. *Togo*, Communications Nos. 422–4/1990, and further, e.g., section 34 of the Constitution of Malawi, section 15(1) of the South African Constitution, Article 18 of the Tanzanian Constitution, Article 8 of the Tunisian Constitution, UN Doc. CCPR/C/84/Add.1, paras. 177, 178, section 19 of the Constitution of Zimbabwe (freedom of thought). The observations of the Special Rapporteur on the promotion and protection of the right to freedom of opinion and expression in Malawi seem applicable to much of Africa, Report of Special Rapporteur Mr Abid Hussain, UN Doc. E/CN.4/1995/32, pp. 18, 19. Particularly relevant are his observations that the right to freedom of opinion and expression could not be enjoyed fully because of structural constraints, namely, widespread poverty, high rate of illiteracy and lack of education.

147. UN Doc. E/CN.4/1995/32, para. 25.

148. UN Doc. E/CN.4/1995/32, paras. 26, 27. In *Attorney-General* v. *Guardian Newspapers Ltd. and others* [1987] 3 All ER 316, at pp. 346, 347, Lord Bridge, dissenting, said, 'Freedom of speech is always the first casualty under a totalitarian regime. Such a regime cannot afford to allow the free circulation of information and ideas among its citizens. Censorship is the indispensable tool to regulate what the public may and what they may not know'. The UN has expressed concern about the violent repression of political opposition, journalists and human rights activists in Chad, Equatorial Guinea, Kenya, Zaïre, UN Doc. E/CN.4/1994/35, paras. 712, 713, and Sudan, UN Doc. E/CN.4/1994/48, para. 81.

149. Harris, O'Boyle and Warbrick, note 18 *supra*, p. 379.

150. *Handyside* v. *United Kingdom* Series A, Vol. 24 (1976) para. 49; *Lingens* v. *Austria* Series A, Vol. 103 (1986) para. 41; Harris, O'Boyle and Warbrick, note 18 *supra*, p. 379. Cf. Article 19 ICCPR and Article 10 ECHR.

151. The freedom of expression covers art, film, television and radio, amongst others, UN Doc. E/CN.4/1995/32, para. 31; Harris, O'Boyle and Warbrick, note 18 *supra*, pp. 377–86. Thus, in *Retrofit (Pvt) Limited* v. *Minister of Information, Posts*

and Telecommunications 1996 (3) BCLR 394 (ZS) the Supreme Court of Zimbabwe held that a monopoly in telecommunications services curtailed the freedom of expression in contravention of section 20(1) of the Constitution. It extends to the military, *South African National Defence Force Union* v. *Minister of Defence* (1999, unreported) (CC).

152.   *Lingens* v. *Austria* Series A, Vol. 103 (1986) para. 42; *Oberschlick* v. *Austria* Series A, Vol. 204 (1991) para. 58; *The Observer and The Guardian* v. *United Kingdom* Series A, Vol. 216 (1991) para. 59; *Castells* v. *Spain* Series A, Vol. 236 (1992) para. 42; General comment 10, UN Doc. HRI/GEN/1, p. 10. In *Free Press of Namibia (Pty) Ltd v. Cabinet for the Interim Government of South West Africa* 1987 (1) SA 614 (SWA) at p. 623, the Court stated that, 'If freedom of speech is to have any significance in a democratic country, its concomitant, freedom of the press, must be recognised because it is only by reaching a large number of people and rallying their support that these freedoms can be utilised for the benefit of society'. The Supreme Court of Zimbabwe has emphasized the vital importance of the freedoms of speech and expression in a democratic society, *Woods and Others* v. *Minister of Justice, Legal and Parliamentary Affairs and Others* 1995 (1) BCLR 56 (ZS); *United Parties* v. *Minister of Justice, Legal and Parliamentary Affairs and Others* 1998 (2) BCLR 224 (ZS). Cf. Article 21(1)(a) of the Constitution of Namibia, Article 20(1) of the Zambian Constitution and section 16(1) of the Constitution of South Africa. Freedom of expression is restricted in, *inter alia*, Nigeria, UN Doc. CCPR/C/79/Add.65, para. 22, and Togo, UN Doc. CCPR/C/79/Add.36, para. 11. In Algeria journalists in particular have been targeted by terrorists which has led the UN to appeal to the Algerian government to protect journalists in their work, UN Doc. E/CN.4/1995/32, pp. 21–4.

153.   *Aduayom et al.* v. *Togo*, Communications Nos. 422–4/1990; *Lingens* v. *Austria* Series A, Vol. 103 (1986); *Oberschlick* v. *Austria* Series A, Vol. 204 (1991); *Compulsory Membership of Journalists Association Case* 25 ILM 123 (1986) para. 70. The HRC has stated that criticism of the government is not fully tolerated in Tunisia and that laws on defamation, insult and false information unduly limit the freedom of the press, UN Doc. CCPR/C/79/Add.43, para. 11. In Zimbabwe statements which bring the President into contempt are considered subversive under the Law and Order Maintenance Act, UN Doc. CCPR/C/74/Add.3, para. 159(a).

154.   *Lingens* v. *Austria* Series A, Vol. 103 (1986); *Oberschlick* v. *Austria* Series A, Vol. 204 (1991). It should be noted that compelling grounds must exist for prior restraint, *The Observer and The Guardian* v. *United Kingdom* Series A, Vol. 216 (1991) para. 60.

155.   *Compulsory Membership of Journalists Association Case* 25 ILM 123 (1986) paras. 70–81.

156.   International human rights law restricts the freedom to receive or seek information insofar as information is generally accessible, UN Doc. E/CN.4/1995/32, para. 34; Harris, O'Boyle and Warbrick, note 18 *supra*, p. 379. It would not appear that the freedom to receive information could be interpreted to include access to information which is guaranteed in certain States, such as under the US Freedom of Information Acts 1967 and 1974. But see section 32 of the South African Constitution. It should be observed, however, that the Banjul Charter does not guarantee the freedom to *impart* information, cf. Article 19(2) ICCPR, Article 10(1) ECHR. The UN regards the freedom to impart and receive information as distinct rights, UN Doc. E/CN.4/1995/32, para. 35.

157.   UN Doc. E/CN.4/1995/32, paras. 36, 37; *Jersild* v. *Denmark* Series A, Vol. 298 (1994) para. 31; Harris, O'Boyle and Warbrick, note 18 *supra*, pp. 388, 389.

158.   Thus, there would appear to be no right to perpetrate slander or libel or to display obscene material, see, e.g., section 12(2) of the Constitution of Botswana,

section 16(2) of the South African Constitution and Article 20(3) of the Zambian Constitution. In Zimbabwe the freedom of expression is circumscribed by, *inter alia*, the law of defamation and contempt of court, UN Doc. CCPR/C/74/ Add.3, paras. 157, 159, 160. Under Act No. 90/052 (1990) freedom of expression and of the press was liberalized in Cameroon, although public order, morality and the reputation of others is protected, UN Doc. CCPR/C/63/Add.1, paras. 85, 86. In *R* v. *Boodhoo and another* (1990) MR 191 the Supreme Court of Mauritius held that the restriction on publishing false news likely to disturb public order without taking reasonable steps to inquire as to its veracity was justified. Cf. Article 19(3) ICCPR and Article 10(2) ECHR. In *Lingens* v. *Austria* Series A, Vol. 103 (1986) the European Court of Human Rights, in finding that an Austrian law on criminal defamation violated press freedom, set different standards of acceptable criticism as between politicians and private individuals. Although the definition of 'obscenity' is not free from difficulty the European Court of Human Rights has held that artistic freedom was not absolute so that the State retained a discretion which justified its confiscating obscene paintings in order to protect public morals, *Mueller* v. *Switzerland* Series A, Vol. 133 (1988). See also the report of the UN Special Rapporteur on the right to freedom of opinion and expression, UN Doc. E/CN.4/Sub.2/1991/9. Censorship is permissible in Zimbabwe to protect societal morals, UN Doc. CCPR/C/74/ Add.3, para. 167.

159. UN Doc. E/CN.4/1995/32 paras. 38–55; Harris, O'Boyle and Warbrick, note 18 *supra*, pp. 389–414.

160. Amnesty International, note 106 *supra*, p. 11. Note that in *Handyside* v. *United Kingdom* Series A, Vol. 24 (1976) para. 49, the European Court of Human Rights observed that the freedom of expression required pluralism, tolerance and broadmindedness for ideas or information that may offend, shock or disturb the State or a sector of the population.

161. See Articles 5(1) and 20 ICCPR, Article 17 ECHR, Articles 13(5) and 29(a) ACHR and Article 4 of the International Convention on the Elimination of All Forms of Racial Discrimination; General comment 11, UN Doc. HRI/GEN/1/Rev.2, p. 12; Harris, O'Boyle and Warbrick, note 18 *supra*, pp. 409–11; UN Doc. E/ CN.4/Sub.2/1991/9, pp. 8–20. See the statement by the Attorney-General of Kenya, UN Doc. E/CN.4/1993/SR.47, para. 23. Note *Kauesa* v. *Minister of Home Affairs* 1994 (3) BCLR 1 (NmH) where the High Court of Namibia held that 'hate speech' was not protected under the Namibian Constitution, see Article 21(2) of the Constitution. See further, *J.R.T. and the W.G. Party* v. *Canada*, Communication No. 104/1981. See also section 16(2) of the South African Constitution, section 70 of the Zambian Penal Code, section 44 of Zimbabwe's Law and Order Maintenance Act. On action taken by Tunisia in this respect, see UN Doc. E/CN.4/1995/32, pp. 33–5.

162. *Swedish Engine Drivers Union* v. *Sweden* Series A, Vol. 20 (1976); *Schmidt and Dahlstrom* v. *Sweden* Series A, Vol. 21 (1976); Harris, O'Boyle and Warbrick, note 18 *supra*, pp. 424–30; Ankumah, note 19 *supra*, p. 137. See also the ILO Convention on Freedom of Association and Protection of the Right to Organize 1948 and ILO Convention on the Right to Organize and Bargain Collectively 1949. Cf. section 13(1) of the Constitution of Botswana, Article 56 of the Egyptian Constitution, section 32(1) of the Constitution of Malawi, Article 21(1)(e) of the Namibian Constitution, section 23(2)(a)(b) of the South African Constitution, Article 20(1) of the Tanzanian Constitution, Article 21 of the Zambian Constitution, section 21 of the Constitution of Zimbabwe.

163. Note 124 *supra*. The right to form trade unions, even if provided by law, is often illusory in Africa, e.g., in Kenya, UN Doc. E/C.12/1993/SR.4, para. 13.

164. *Schmidt and Dahlstrom* v. *Sweden* Series A, Vol. 21 (1976); *National Union of Belgian Police* v. *Belgium* Series A, Vol. 19 (1975).

165. The right to strike is recognized by Article 8(1)(d) ICES, Article 6(4) of the Revised European Social Charter and Article 8(1)(b) of the Protocol of San Salvador, and in *Schmidt and Dahlstrom* v. *Sweden* Series A, Vol. 21 (1976) the European Court stated that striking could be a means of complying with Article 11 but that such a right was not unlimited. These treaties combine legally enforceable rights with the progressive realization of social policies. On the ESC see D.J. Harris, *The European Social Charter* (1984). See further, Article 21(1)(f) of the Namibian Constitution and section 23(2)(c) of the South African Constitution. It is interesting to note that section 17 of the South African Constitution enshrines a right to picket. Strikes are legal in Egypt and Zimbabwe subject to certain procedures, UN Docs. E/1990/5/Add.38, paras. 111 and 112, CCPR/C/74/Add.3, para. 186. The right to strike, even if provided by law, is often illusory in Africa, eg., Kenya, UN Doc. E/C.12/1993/SR.4, para. 13.

166. Cf. Article 22(2) ICCPR, Article 11(2) ECHR, Article 16(2), (3) ACHR and Articles 5 and 6 of the Revised European Social Charter; Harris, O'Boyle and Warbrick, note 18 *supra*, pp. 430–2. See further, *Engel* v. *The Netherlands* Series A, Vol. 22 (1976). But cf. *South African National Defence Force Union* v. *Minister of Defence* (1999, unreported) (CC). See also section 13(2) of the Constitution of Botswana, Article 21(2) of the Zambian Constitution. In Cameroon restrictions may be imposed under Act No. 90/053 (1990) on the grounds of national security, anti-Constitutionalism and against laws and morality, UN Doc. CCPR/C/63/Add.1, para. 92. In Nigeria the freedom of assembly is severely curtailed, UN Doc. CCPR/C/79/Add.65, para. 22.

167. Cf. Article 20(2) UDHR; section 32(2) of the Constitution of Malawi. In *Young, James and Webster* v. *United Kingdom* Series A, Vol. 44 (1981) the European Court of Human Rights held that compulsion to join a trade union notwithstanding an employee's objections itself interfered with the right of association.

168. Article 19(2) of the Tanzanian Constitution prohibits forced membership of a political party.

169. The State is under a obligation to secure the exercise of this right, *Plattform 'Artze für das Leben'* v. *Austria* Series A, Vol. 139 (1988); Harris, O'Boyle and Warbrick, note 18 *supra*, pp. 418, 419. It is assumed that it is the right of *peaceful* assembly that is guaranteed, cf. Article 21 ICCPR and Article 11(1) ECHR, see Harris, O'Boyle and Warbrick, *supra*, p. 418. Although the right of assembly and demonstrations may sometimes be guaranteed by law in many African countries, e.g., section 13(1) of the Constitution of Botswana, section 38 of the Constitution of Malawi, Article 21(1)(d) of the Namibian Constitution, section 17 of the South African Constitution, Article 21(1) of the Zambian Constitution, section 21 of the Constitution of Zimbabwe, it is not so in practice, e.g., Equatorial Guinea, UN Doc. E/CN.4/1996/67, para. 47. The right of peaceful assembly is severely limited and subject to arbitrary interference in Nigeria, UN Doc. CCPR/C/79/Add.65, para. 22, Sudan, UN Doc. E/CN.4/1994/48, para. 85, and Togo, UN Doc. CCPR/C/79/Add. 36, para. 12. However, see *In re Davison Mhunhumeso and Others* 1994 (1) ZLR 49; *Seeiso* v. *Minister of Home Affairs and Others* 1998 (6) BCLR 765 (Les CA).

170. See *Ezelin* v. *France* Series A, Vol. 202 (1991) where the European Court of Human Rights held that there must be a sense of proportionality between the prevention of disorder and the right to protest peacefully. In the case of *In re Davison Mhunhumeso and Others* 1994 (1) ZLR 49 the Supreme Court of Zimbabwe held that although the power to prohibit or control a public demonstration was necessary in the interest of public order or public safety, the statutory limitations were not reasonably justifiable in a democratic society. See

also *Bizlall* v. *Commissioner of Police* (1993) MR 213; *Seeiso* v. *Minister of Home Affairs and Others* 1998 (6) BCLR 765 (Les CA). Cameroon's Act No. 90/055 (1990) allows public meetings to be held freely if prior notification is given. Demonstrations in public thoroughfares may be prohibited or venues changed if serious public disturbances seem likely, UN Doc. CCPR/C/63/Add.1, para. 91.

171. Cf. Article 13 UDHR, Article 12(1) ICCPR, Article 2(1) of the Fourth Protocol ECHR and Article 22(1) ACHR. See section 14(1) of the Constitution of Botswana, section 39(1) of the Constitution of Malawi, Article 21(1)(g) of the Namibian Constitution, section 21(1) of the South African Constitution, Article 22(1)(a) of the Zambian Constitution, and section 22(1) of the Constitution of Zimbabwe. In *Rattigan and Others* v. *The Chief Immigration Officer and Others* 1994 (2) ZLR 54 the Supreme Court of Zimbabwe extended the freedom of movement to an alien married to a Zimbabwean national. It should be observed that international law does not recognize a right of aliens to enter or reside in a another State. Consent for entry may be given subject to conditions relating to movement, residence and employment, General comment 15, UN Doc. HRI/GEN/1/Rev.2, paras. 5, 6. Freedom of movement is severely restricted in Sudan, UN Doc. E/CN.4/1994/48, paras. 109–13. It appears that internal banishments contravene the freedom of movement enshrined in Article 12(1) ICCPR, see *Birhashwirwa and Mulumba* v. *Zaire*, Communication Nos. 241 and 242/1987.

172. Cf. Article 13 UDHR, Article 12(1) ICCPR, Article 2(1) of the Fourth Protocol ECHR and Article 22(1) ACHR. See section 14(1) of the Constitution of Botswana, section 39(1) of the Constitution of Malawi, Article 21(1)(h) of the Namibian Constitution, section 21(3) of the South African Constitution, Article 22(1)(b) of the Zambian Constitution, and section 22(1) of the Constitution of Zimbabwe. See further, *Patricia Ann Salem* v. *Chief Immigration Officer and Another* 1994 (2) ZLR 287.

173. By contrast, international instruments either employ the phrase 'lawfully within the territory' or contain restrictions, e.g., Article 12(3) ICCPR, see General comment 15, UN Doc. HRI/GEN/1/Rev.2, para. 8; *Ackla* v. *Togo*, Communication No. 505/1992. See also section 14(2), (3) of the Constitution of Botswana, Article 22(2), (3) of the Zambian Constitution, section 22(3) of the Constitution of Zimbabwe (see further, UN Doc. CCPR/C/74/Add.3, paras. 114, 120–2).

174. Article 12(2) ICCPR, Article 2(2) of the Fourth Protocol ECHR and Article 22(2) ACHR; *Oló Bahamonde* v. *Equatorial Guinea*, Communication No. 468/1991; Harris, O'Boyle and Warbrick, note 18 *supra*, p. 562. Cf. section 39(2) of the Constitution of Malawi, Article 21(1)(i) of the Namibian Constitution, section 21(2) and (4) of the South African Constitution, and Article 22(1)(c) of the Zambian Constitution. See also Zimbabwe's Immigration Act, UN Doc. CCPR/C/74/Add.3, para. 112. See further, *Nyirongo* v. *Attorney-General of Zambia* [1993] 3 LRC 256.

175. General comment 15, UN Doc. HRI/GEN/1/Rev.2, para. 5.

176. See Article 12(4) ICCPR, Article 3(2) of the Fourth Protocol ECHR, Article 22(5) ACHR; *East African Asians* v. *United Kingdom* 3 EHRR 76 (1981); Harris, O'Boyle and Warbrick, note 18 *supra*, pp. 562, 563. For constitutional guarantees, see section 14(1) of the Constitution of Botswana, section 39(2) of the Constitution of Malawi, Article 21(1)(i) of the Namibian Constitution, section 21(1)(c) of the South African Constitution, and Article 22(1)(c) of the Zambian Constitution. See further, *Nyirongo* v. *Attorney-General of Zambia* [1993] 3 LRC 256.

177. The concept of persecution is nowhere defined in the Banjul Charter and it would seem that reference should therefore be made to the OAU Convention on Refugees 1969, see further Chapter 3 of this book.

178. Cf. Article 14 UDHR, Article 22(7) ACHR. The right of asylum has been held to be a conventional, and not a customary, right of international law, *Asylum Case* ICJ Reports 1950, p. 266. See further Chapter 3 of this book.

179. According to the HRC Article 13 ICCPR is applicable to all procedures aimed at the expulsion of an alien who is lawfully in the territory of a State party, so that illegal entrants are not covered unless the legality of the alien's entry or stay is directly at issue, General comment 15, UN Doc. HRI/GEN/1/Rev.2, para. 9.

180. The HRC has stated that Article 13 is clearly designed to prevent arbitrary expulsions and that only 'compelling reasons of national security' can excuse less than full compliance with procedural safeguards, General comment 15, UN Doc. HRI/GEN/1/Rev.2, para. 10. Furthermore, if the procedure for expulsion entails arrest, the safeguards relating to deprivation of liberty may be applicable, ibid., para. 9. See also, Harris, O'Boyle and Warbrick, note 18 *supra*, pp. 565, 566.

181. Cf. for a similar effect Article 22(6) ACHR.

182. UN Docs. A/50/476, Annex, para. 101; E/C.12/1/Add.15, para. 16.

183. It seems that in 1989 Mauritania deported more than 100,000 of its citizens of African descent, UN Doc. E/CN.4/1997/SR.39, para. 30.

184. Cf. Article 21 UDHR, Article 25 ICCPR, Article 3 of the First Protocol ECHR, and Article 23 ACHR. See also, *Mathieu-Mohin and Clerfayt* v. *Belgium* Series A, Vol. 113 (1987); Harris, O'Boyle and Warbrick, note 18 *supra*, Chapter 20; Ankumah, note 19 *supra*, p. 141. And see section 40 of the Constitution of Malawi, Article 17 of the Namibian Constitution, section 19 of the South African Constitution, and see *New National Party of South Africa* v. *Government of the Republic of South Africa* (1999, unreported) (CC), Article 21 of the Tanzanian Constitution. For the position in Zimbabwe, see UN Doc. CCPR/C/74/Add.3, pp. 45–50. In *Margaret Dongo* v. *Vivian Mwashita and Registrar-General of Elections and Chairman, Electoral Supervisory Commission and Chairman Election Directorate* (unreported) the High Court of Zimbabwe set aside the results of a parliamentary election on the grounds of electoral irregularities.

185. Eighth Annual Activity Report, 3 *IHRR* (1996) p. 242.

186. Ibid., pp. 244, 245.

187. Cf. Article 21(2) UDHR, Article 25(c) ICCPR, *Aduayom* v. *Togo*, Communications Nos. 422–4 1990. Zambia claims that its citizens are free to participate in public affairs, UN Doc. CCPR/C/63/Add.3, paras. 100–2. Note that in *Glasenapp* v. *Germany* Series A, Vol. 104 (1986) and *Kosiek* v. *Germany* Series A, Vol. 105 (1986) the European Court of Human Rights held that the ECHR does not recognize a right to recruitment to the civil service.

188. Case 149/79 *Commission* v. *Belgium* [1980] ECR 3881; Case 225/85 *Commission* v. *Italy* [1987] ECR 2625.

189. Cf. Articles 25(c) ICCPR and Article 23(1)(c) ACHR which are not as extensive in scope. This provision may refer to equal access to public services such as education and health, see sections 27 and 29 of the South African Constitution. Zimbabwe has acknowledged that the economic situation has adversely affected the ability of low-income groups to use these services, UN Doc. CCPR/C/74/Add.3, para. 257.

190. Ankumah, note 19 *supra*, p. 142. Cf. Article 17 UDHR, Article 1 of the First Protocol ECHR, and Article 21 ACHR. The right to property has been described as 'inalienable', UN Doc. E/CN.4/1993/15, para. 83; and see General Assembly resolution 41/132. On the right to property generally, see Harris, O'Boyle and Warbrick, note 18 *supra*, Chapter 18. Although this provision is silent on the question of ownership it should be read as such; cf. Article 17(1) UDHR and Article 1 of the First Protocol ECHR. It is interesting to observe that the

European Court of Human Rights has held that Article 1 of the First Protocol is designed to protect existing property and does not guarantee the right to *acquire* property, *Marckx* v. *Belgium* Series A, Vol. 31 (1979); but cf. *contra*, UN Doc. E/ CN.4/1993/15, para. 95. The right to property is recognized by the Constitutions of, *inter alia*, Algeria, Botswana, Egypt, Kenya, Malawi, Mauritius, Namibia, Senegal, South Africa, Tanzania, Zambia and Zimbabwe. In Africa account must also be taken of traditional forms of land tenure whereby land, often considered divine, is a sacred and inalienable community possession and that individuals enjoy the usufruct, UN Doc. E/CN.4/1993/15, para. 154.

191. UN Doc. E/CN.4.1993/15, para. 94; *Van Marle* v. *The Netherlands* Series A, Vol. 101 (1986); *Tre Traktorer Aktiebolag* v. *Sweden* Series A, Vol. 159 (1989); *Hewlett* v. *Minister of Finance* 1981 ZLR 571. Customary rights in land are forms of property, *Akonaay* v. *Attorney-General* [1994] 2 LRC 399.

192. Ankumah, note 19 *supra*, p. 142; UN Doc. E/CN.4/Sub.2/1991/6, para. 33. See further, *supra*, p. 130.

193. Cf. Article 1 of the First Protocol ECHR; Article 21 ACHR; section 8(1) of the Constitution of Botswana, section 28(2) of the Constitution of Malawi; Article 16(2) of the Namibian Constitution; section 25(1), (2) of the South African Constitution; Article 16(1) of the Zambian Constitution; section 16(1) of the Constitution of Zimbabwe. In the *Case concerning certain German Interests in Polish Upper Silesia* PCIJ, Series A, No. 7 (1926) at p. 22, the PCIJ expressed the opinion that according to customary international law only 'expropriation for reasons of public utility, judicial liquidation and similar measures' was permissible. The jurisprudence of the European Court of Human Rights demonstrates that the State has wide powers to take and to control the use of property, Harris, O'Boyle and Warbrick, note 18 *supra*, pp. 527–30, 534–8. On the deprivation of property in Zimbabwe, see *Davies* v. *Minister of Land, Agriculture and Water Development* 1996 (9) BCLR 1209 (ZS). Property can be regulated by the State to comply with, for example, environmental standards, health and safety standards, building and planning regulations, and rent controls, UN Doc. E/CN.4/1993/15, pp. 75, 76. A pressing problem that is being addressed in Southern Africa is the question of land rights and land redistribution to redress the iniquitous acquisition of land by settlers during the era of white domination, see the article by the present author, 'Constitutional challenge to land reform in Zimbabwe', 31 *Comparative and International Law Journal of Southern Africa* (1998) 78. The expropriation of farms in Zimbabwe for the resettlement of communal farming families has been held to be legitimate in the public interest, *Davies* v. *Minister of Land, Agriculture and Water Development* 1995 (1) BCLR 83 (ZH). In South Africa a Land Claims Commission and a Land Claims Court have been established to consider restitution of land rights, see sections 121 and 122 of the Interim Constitution and Land Restitution and Reform Laws Amendment Act 1997. Section 25(4)-(9) of the Constitution also addresses the inequalities of the historical legacy. See also, *James* v. *United Kingdom* Series A, Vol. 98 (1986) para. 41; and UN Doc. E/ CN.4/1993/15, para. 464.

194. Although Article 21(2) thereof stipulates 'adequate compensation' in cases of spoliation, this is with reference to the wealth and natural resources of dispossessed peoples rather than individuals.

195. *James* v. *United Kingdom* Series A, Vol. 98 (1985). In relation to foreign owed property see Article 2(2)(c) of the Charter of Economic Rights and Duties of States, General Assembly Resolution 3281 (XXIX) 1974.

196. This is a reference to the general principles of international law which require the payment of prompt, adequate and effective compensation in respect of expropriation of property of foreign nationals, Harris, O'Boyle and Warbrick,

note 18 *supra*, pp. 530–2. Developing States favour the less rigid requirement of adequate, fair or just compensation, see *Texaco* v. *Libya* 17 *ILM* 1 (1978).

197.   Thus, the Civil Code of Egypt (Article 34 of the Constitution refers solely to 'compensation') and section 16(1)(c) of the Constitution of Zimbabwe stipulate the payment of fair compensation, whereas Article 16(2) of the Namibian Constitution requires the payment of just compensation. Section 25(3) of the South African Constitution refers to 'just and equitable' payment, while section 8(1)(b)(i) of the Constitution of Botswana and Article 16(1) of the Zambian Constitution require 'adequate compensation'. See also, *Akonaay* v. *Attorney-General* [1994] 2 LRC 399. The reference to 'general principles of international law' in Article 1 of the First Protocol ECHR does not apply to the taking by a State of the property of its nationals who, nevertheless are entitled to some compensation. There is no right to full compensation in all circumstances since legitimate objectives of 'public interest' might call for less than full reimbursement, *Lithgow* v. *United Kingdom* Series A, Vol. 102 (1986); Harris, O'Boyle and Warbrick, note 18 *supra*, pp. 532–4; UN Doc. E/CN.4/1993/15, para. 465.

198.   Cf. to a similar effect Article 1 of the First Protocol ECHR.

199.   Although a State party has a considerable margin of appreciation in this area an excessive burden on an individual devoid of reasonable foundation has been held to be contrary to the ECHR, see Harris, O'Boyle and Warbrick, note 18 *supra*, pp. 537, 538.

200.   Cf. Article 12 UDHR, Article 17 ICCPR, Article 8 ECHR and Article 11 ACHR. See further, General comment 16, UN Doc. HRI/GEN/1/Rev.2, pp. 21–3; Harris, O'Boyle and Warbrick, note 18 *supra*, Chapter 9. The right to privacy, home and correspondence is guaranteed by, e.g., Articles 37 and 38 of the Algerian Constitution, section 9 of the Constitution of Botswana, Articles 17 and 42 of the Constitution of Chad, section 21 of the Constitution of Malawi, Article 6 of the Constitution of Mali, Article 13 of the Namibian Constitution, section 14 of the South African Constitution, Articles 28 and 29 of the Togolese Constitution, Article 17 of the Zambian Constitution.

201.   Ankumah, note 19 *supra*, Chapter 5.3; Umozurike, note 4 *supra*, Chapter 4.

202.   Thus some African States do not guarantee such rights but consider them principles of state policy, see, e.g., section 13 of the Constitution of Malawi, Chapter 11 of the Namibian Constitution. See also section 27(2) of the South African Constitution.

203.   General comment 3, HRI/GEN/1/Rev.2, pp. 55–9. Note further the Protocol amending the European Social Charter providing for a system of collective complaints 1995.

204.   *The Review* (International Commission of Jurists), No. 37 (1986) pp. 43–55.

205.   See note 13 *supra*.

206.   Article 1 of the Revised European Social Charter and Article 6 ICES provide for a qualified and progressive right to work where States undertake to do their utmost to create the conditions necessary to achieve as high a level of employment as possible. See also Ankumah, note 19 *supra*, Chapter 5.3.1. The right to work is guaranteed in Egypt, UN Doc. E/1990/5/Add.38, paras. 82, 83, Libya, UN Doc. CERD/C/299/Add.13, paras. 65–8, and Tanzania (Articles 11(1) and 22(1) of the Constitution). Yet many African countries lack sources of employment with consequent high rates of unemployment and underemployment, e.g., Equatorial Guinea, UN Doc. E/CN.4/1996/67, para. 68. According to the ECA it is estimated that during 1996 and 1997 urban unemployment stood at approximately 20–30%, underemployment at some 25–50%, and youth unemployment at 25–40%, African Economic Report – 1998, para. 81. However, it reports that many African countries have indictated that they are creating a favourable employment environment by undertaking institutional reforms,

supporting small-scale enterprises and modernizing agriculture, ibid., para. 83. By way of contrast, it is interesting to note that under Article 25 of the Tanzanian Constitution every person is under an obligation to engage in productive labour.

207. Cf. Articles 2 and 3 of the Revised European Social Charter, and First Protocol thereto; Harris, note 165 *supra*, pp. 37–48. See further the Social Charter of the EC and Framework Directive 89/391 on Health and Safety.

208. Cf. Article 23(1) UDHR; Article 7 ICES. Only Articles 2 and 3 of the Revised European Social Charter actually require just conditions of work and safe and healthy working conditions; Harris, note 165 *supra*, pp. 43–8, but see also Article 140 (ex Art 118c) EC Treaty. Egypt and Kenya appear to have detailed regulations on health and safety, UN Docs. E/1990/5/Add.38, pp. 27, 28, E/C.12/1993/SR.4, para. 12.

209. Cf. Article 24 UDHR; Article 7(d) ICES; Article 2 of the Revised European Social Charter; and the Working Time Directive 93/104. See further, Harris, note 165 *supra*, pp. 37–43. Again Egypt seems to have detailed laws on these areas, UN Doc. E/1990/5/Add.38, pp. 28–30. See also Nigeria's Labour Act 1990, UN Doc. E/1990/5/Add.31, para. 5. The ECA reports that working conditions are deteriorating, African Economic Report – 1998, para. 81.

210. Cf. Article 23(3) UDHR, Article 7(a) ICES, Article 4 of the Revised European Social Charter and Article 7(a) of the Protocol of San Salvador. See also Egypt's Labour Act 1981, UN Doc. E/1990/5/Add.38, para. 95; Article 95(i) of the Namibian Constitution; Nigeria's Labour Act 1990, UN Doc. E/1990/5/Add.31, para. 5; and Article 23 of the Tanzanian Constitution; and further, Harris, note 165 *supra*, pp. 48–59. The ECA reports that real wages are decreasing, African Economic Report-1998, para. 81. Senegal has acknowledged the imposition of unfavourable wage trends as a result of its economic situation, UN Doc. E/C.12/1993/SR.37, para. 23.

211. The ECJ has interpreted the concept of 'pay' broadly to include, for instance, non-pay benefits, Case 12/81 *Garland* v. *British Rail Engineering Ltd* [1982] ECR 359, contributions under a contractual scheme, Case 170/84 *Bilka-Kaufhaus GmbH* v. *Weber von Hartz* [1986] ECR 1607, sick pay, Case 171/88 *Rinner-Kuhn* v. *FWW Spezial Gebaudereinigung GmbH* [1989] ECR 2743, retirement pensions and redundancy payments, Case C-262/88 *Barber* v. *Guardian Royal Exchange Assurance Group* [1990] ECR I-1889.

212. Cf. Article 23(2) UDHR; Article 7(a)(i) ICES; Articles 4(3) and 20(c) of the Revised European Social Charter; and Article 1 of the First Protocol ESC. See also ILO Convention on Equal Remuneration 1951, and Article 141 (ex Art 119) EC Treaty, and further Case 43/75 *Defrenne* v. *SABENA (No. 2)* [1976] ECR 455. Nigeria's Labour Act 1990 guarantees equality of pay without gender discrimination, UN Doc. E/1990/5/Add.31, para. 6.

213. See also Directive 75/117 and further, e.g., Case 96/80 *Jenkins* v. *Kingsgate (Clothing Productions) Ltd* [1981] ECR 911; Case C-177/88 *Dekker* v. *Stichting Vormingscentrum Voor Jong Volwassenen* [1990] ECR I-3941; Case C-127/92 *Enderby* v. *Frenchay Area Health Authority* [1993] ECR I-5535.

214. Only Article 12 ICES expressly mentions both physical and mental health. See also the Declaration on Rights of Mentally Retarded Persons, General Assembly Resolution 2856 (XXVI) 1971. Neither is health made dependent on the standard of living, although the two are inextricably linked, but is considered to be an independent right, only Article 25(1) UDHR expressly connects the two.

215. The Banjul Charter does not enumerate the steps necessary to achieve these purposes, cf. Article 25(1) UDHR, Article 12(2) ICES, Article 11 of the Revised European Social Charter, and Articles 10 and 11 of the Protocol of San Salvador. See also Article 15 of Libya's Constitutional Declaration, UN Doc. CERD/C/

229/Add.13, para. 72, section 13(c) of the Constitution of Malawi, Article 95(j) of the Namibian Constitution, Article 11(1) of the Tanzanian Constitution and section 27(1)(a) of the South African Constitution.

216. In *Union Interafricaine des Droits de l'Homme* v. *Zaire* (Communication 100/93) the African Commission found a violation of Article 16 when the State failed to provide safe drinking water, electricity and medicines. Cf. Article 12(1) ICES, and Articles 11 and 13 of the Revised European Social Charter. See Ankumah, note 19 *supra*, Chapter 5.3.2.; Harris, op. cit., pp. 105–8, 121–9. According to the Committee on Economic, Social and Cultural Rights essential primary health care is a core obligation under the ICES, General comment 3, UN Doc. HRI/ GEN/1/Rev.2, para. 10. According to the ECA, access to health care is generally poor in Africa, with the greatest number of countries with the lowest access to health services, African Economic Report – 1998, paras. 78, 80. It is estimated that 32% of the population of sub-Saharan Africa will not reach the age of forty, UN Doc. E/C.12/1997/SR.27, para. 27. Nevertheless, progress in health care has been made in some countries, including Algeria, Botswana, Cape Verde, Mauritius, African Economic Report – 1998, para. 80, Egypt, UN Doc. E/1990/ 5/Add.38, pp. 55–7, and Kenya, UN Doc. E/C.12/1993/SR.4, para. 18. By way of contrast, international aid programmes have resulted in the deterioration of Zimbabwe's once highly prized health services, UN Doc. CCPR/C/74/Add.3, para. 257.

217. African Economic Report – 1998, para. 79.

218. General comment 3, UN Doc. HRI/GEN/1/Rev.2, paras. 11 and 12.

219. Ankumah, note 19 *supra*, p. 147; UN Doc. E/CN.4/Sub.2/1991/6, pp. 8–12. The Beijing Platform for Action reaffirms that women have the right, on a basis of equality with men, to enjoy the highest attainable standard of physical and mental health throughout their lives, paras. 89 and 92.

220. See Article 9 ICES, which recognizes the right to old-age benefits, General comment 6, UN Doc. HRI/GEN/1/Rev.2, para. 10; Article 25(1) UDHR; Article 9 of the Protocol of San Salvador; and Article 23 of the Revised European Social Charter, which provides that the elderly have a right to social protection. Some African countries do provide some form of pension or social security, e.g., Kenya, UN Doc. E/C.12/1993/SR.4, para. 14, Libya, UN Doc. E/1990/5/ Add.26, pp. 15–18, Senegal, UN Doc. E/C.12/1993/SR.37, paras. 24, 61. See also Article 95(f) of the Namibian Constitution, Article 11(1) of the Tanzanian Constitution and section 27(1)(c) of the South African Constitution providing for a right to social security. See further, section 13(j) of the Constitution of Malawi. In 1982 the World Assembly on Ageing adopted the Vienna International Plan of Action on Ageing which details the measures to be taken by States to safeguard the rights of older persons within the context of the International Covenants, Report of the World Assembly on Ageing (1982). In 1991 the General Assembly adopted the UN Principles for Older Persons, resolution 46/91, which correspond closely to the rights in the ICES, including access to adequate food, water, shelter, clothing, health care, and educational, cultural, spiritual and recreational facilities, as well as the right to live in dignity and security free from exploitation and abuse. Moreover, in 1992 the General Assembly adopted the Proclamation on Ageing, resolution 47/5, encouraging the support of families providing care, and urging recognition of the contributions to society by older women. In addition, the Committee on Economic, Social and Cultural Rights has stated that older people are equally entitled to enjoy the rights recognized in the ICES and has therefore elaborated on the application of its specific provisions to the aged, General comment 6, UN Doc. HRI/GEN/1/Rev.2, pp. 77–84.

221. See Article 25(1) UDHR; Article 18 of the Protocol of San Salvador; Article 15 of

the Revised European Social Charter. Cf. section 13(g) of the Constitution of Malawi, Article 95(g) of the Namibian Constitution and Article 11(1) of the Tanzanian Constitution.

222. Cf. Article 26 UDHR, Articles 13 and 14 ICES, Articles 9 and 10 of the Revised European Social Charter, and Article 13 of the Protocol of San Salvador. See further Ankumah, note 19 *supra*, Chapter 5.3.3; Harris, note 165 *supra*, pp. 98–105. For developments in Libya, see UN Doc. E/1990/5/Add.26, pp. 39–47.

223. Cf. Article 2 of the First Protocol ECHR which is drafted in negative terms. What is guaranteed is a right to access to state institutions, the right to an effective education, and the right to official recognition of studies, see Harris, O'Boyle and Warbrick, note 18 *supra*, pp. 541–4. There also appears to be a positive obligation on the State to make education available. Thus in *Union Interafricaine des Droits de l'Homme* v. *Zaire* (Communication 100/93) the African Commission found a violation of Article 17 when universities and secondary schools were shut. Only Article 13(2)(b), (c) ICES calls for free education at secondary and higher levels. The educational system has expanded in most African countries since independence. Basic education is compulsory and free in Libya, UN Doc. E/1990/5/Add.26, para. 174(a), while in Algeria and Tunisia education is free at all levels, UN Docs. CRC/C/28/Add.4, para. 104, CCPR/C/84/Add.1, para. 226(d). See further, section 13(f) of the Constitution of Malawi, Article 20(2) of the Namibian Consitution and section 29(1)(a) of the Constitution of South Africa which confers the right to a 'basic education'. The Supreme Court of South West Africa declared the child's right to schooling a fundamental right, *S* v. *Namseb* 1991 (1) SACR 223 (SWA). Education is said to be a priority in Nigeria, UN Doc. E/1990/5/Add.31, pp. 10–14. Nevertheless, problems still exist insofar as resources, equal opportunities, enrolment, etc. are concerned, e.g., in Chad, UN Doc. CRC/C/3/Add.50, pp. 31–4; Equatorial Guinea, UN Doc. E/CN.4/1996/67, paras 66, 67, Kenya, UN Doc. E/C.12/1993/SR.4, paras. 19, 20; Lesotho, UN Doc. CRC/C/11/Add.20, pp. 50–2; Mali, UN Doc. CRC/C/3/Add.53, pp. 37–43; Niger, UN Doc. CRC/C/3/Add. 29, pp. 8–10. The Committee on Economic, Social and Cultural Rights has expressed concern about the absence of compulsory education in Gambia, UN Doc. E/C.12/1994/9, para. 17. Zaïre was found to be in violation of Articles 13 and 14 ICES by failing to secure primary education free of charge, UN Doc. E/C.12/1998/4, para. 297.

224. It is unclear whether a right to operate private schools is acknowledged, see on this issue Harris, O'Boyle and Warbrick, note 18 *supra*, pp. 543, 544. Cf. *contra* Article 20(4) of the Namibian Constitution, section 29(3) of the South African Constitution. In Lesotho most secondary schools are owned by the churches, UN Doc. CRC/C/11/Add.20, para. 201.

225. Cf. Article 11(3) of the Tanzanian Constitution. Insofar as discrimination and minority rights are concerned see *Belgian Linguistic Case* Series A, Vol. 6 (1968) and the Convention Against Discrimination in Education 1960. See further, Harris, O'Boyle and Warbrick, note 18 *supra*, pp. 547–9. Women seem to be disadvantaged educationally in Gambia, UN Doc. E/C.12/1994/9, para. 17. In South Africa independent educational establishments cannot discriminate on the basis of race, section 29(3)(a) of the Constitution. Needless to say, *de jure* discrimination characterized the educational system during the apartheid era in South Africa, UN Doc. E/CN.4/1989/8, paras. 399–413.

226. UN Doc. E/CN.4/Sub.2/1991/6, pp. 6, 7. Enrolment of girls tends to be low, see, e.g., Chad, UN Doc. CRC/C/3/Add.50, para. 161, Mali, UN Doc. CRC/C/3/Add.53, para. 142, and Niger, UN Doc. CRC/C/3/Add.29, para. 44.

227. Cf. Article 27 ICCPR, which does, of course, have a much wider scope. Note, e.g., the African Cultural Centre Trust Fund Act 1984 of Mauritius.

228. Cf. Article 13(3) ICES, Article 18(4) ICCPR, Article 12(4) ACHR, and Article 2 of the First Protocol ECHR, and see *Kjeldsen, Busk Madsen and Pedersen* v. *Denmark* Series A, Vol. 23 (1976), and *Campbell and Cosans* v. *United Kingdom* Series A, Vol. 48 (1982); section 32(c) of the South African Constitution. See further, Harris, O'Boyle and Warbrick, note 18 *supra*, pp. 544–7.

229. Ankumah, note 19 *supra*, Chapter 5.3.4. Cf. Article 16(3) UDHR, Article 23(1) ICCPR, Article 10(1) ICES, Articles 8 and 12 ECHR, Article 16 of the Revised European Social Charter and Article 17(1) ACHR. See also Article 9 of the Egyptian Constitution, sections 13(i) and 22(1) of the Constitution of Malawi, Article 14(3) of the Namibian Constitution, and the Constitution of Cameroon, UN Doc. CCPR/C/63/Add.1, para. 94. For the position in Gabon, see UN Doc. CCPR/C/31/Add.4, para. 64; in Libya, see UN Doc. E/1990/5/Add.26, pp. 18–25; Nigeria, see UN Doc. E/1990/5/Add.31, pp. 14, 15; in Sudan, see UN Doc. CCPR/C/75/Add.2, para. 143; and in Togo, see UN Doc. CCPR/C/63/Add.2, paras. 84, 85. It should be observed that according to the HRC there is no standard definition of the 'family', General comment 19, UN Doc. HRI/GEN/1/Rev.2, para. 2, but a married couple, especially when there are children, constitutes a family, *Aumeeruddy-Cziffra* v. *Mauritius* 4 *HRLJ* (1983) 139. The European Court of Human Rights has stated that 'the family' must 'include the relationship that arises from a lawful and genuine marriage', *Abdulaziz, Cabales and Balkandali* v. *United Kingdom* Series A, Vol. 94 (1985) para. 62. The concept of 'family life' under Article 8 ECHR has a broader meaning, however, which takes into consideration *de facto* relationships, such as cohabitation on a permanent footing between unmarried couples, *Abdulaziz, Cabales and Balkandali* v. *United Kingdom* Series A, Vol. 94 (1985) paras. 62–63; Harris, O'Boyle and Warbrick, note 18 *supra*, pp. 312–17.

230. General comment 19, UN Doc. HRI/GEN/1/Rev.2, para. 3; Harris, note 165 *supra*, pp. 136–8. Article 16 of the Revised European Social Charter and Article 15 of the Protocol of San Salvador list specific examples of forms of assistance and protection and include social and family benefits, family housing, special natal care and adequate nutrition for children. Cf. section 22(1) of the Constitution of Malawi. It is instructive to note that the Committee on Economic, Social and Cultural Rights has expressed concern about the high maternal mortality rate in Gambia, UN Doc. E/C.12/1994/9, para. 16.

231. See General comment 5, ICES, UN Doc. E/C.12/1994/13; and further, *supra*, p. 129.

232. Ankumah, note 19 *supra*, pp. 152 and 53, 156 and 57. Cf. Article 23(2) ICCPR; Article 12 ECHR; Article 17(2) ACHR. The right to marry is not absolute under the international instruments but is subject to national laws on, for example, marriageable age or degrees of kinship, but any limitations must not restrict or reduce the right in such a way or to such an extent as to negate its very essence; General comment 19, UN Doc. HRI/GEN/1/Rev.2, para. 4; *Cossey* v. *United Kingdom* Series A, Vol. 184 (1990); Harris, O'Boyle and Warbrick, note 18 *supra*, pp. 436–9. Cf. section 22(3) of the Constitution of Malawi, Article 14(1) of the Namibian Constitution. It should be observed that the age at which marriage may be entered into in many African societies is discriminatory, e.g., in Togo, UN Doc. CCPR/C/63/Add.2, para. 85(a), Zimbabwe, UN Doc. CRC/C/SR.294, para. 3, dependent on common or customary law, e.g., in Ghana, UN Doc. CRC/C/15/Add.73, para. 7, or religion, e.g., Egypt, UN Doc. E/1990/5/Add.38, para. 143(c). It is clear that marriage should be entered into with the free and full consent of the intending spouses, Article 23(3) ICCPR, General comment 19, ibid., Article 17(3) ACHR, Harris, O'Boyle and Warbrick, note 18

supra, p. 436, problematic for some African societies, eg., Gambia, UN Doc. E/C.12/1994/9, para. 14. Cf. section 22(4) of the Constitution of Malawi, Article 14(2) of the Namibian Constitution, Article 44 of the Togolese Constitution, and the Individual and Family Code of Burkina Faso, UN Doc. E/CN.4/Sub.2/1993/31, p. 9. In Libya women must give their consent to marry, UN Doc. E/CN.4/1998/SR.39, para. 49. For the position in Cameroon, see UN Doc. CCPR/C/63/Add.1, para. 95, and Sudan, see UN Doc. CCPR/C/75/Add.2, para. 143. The practice of early marriage is prevalent in parts of Africa, UN Doc. E/CN.4/Sub.2/1991/6, p. 7, and has been condemned by the Beijing Plan of Action, UN Doc. E/CN.4/Sub.2/1997/10/Add.1, p. 4. Polygamy, connected both with customary practices and Islam, may give rise to problems with regard to the applicability of different legal systems, e.g., in Gambia, UN Doc. E/C.12/1994/9, para. 14, Nigeria, UN Doc. CCPR/C/79/Add.65, para. 25, Senegal, UN Doc. E/C.12/1993/SR.37, para. 65, Zambia, UN Doc. CCPR/C/63/Add.3, para. 93, and Zimbabwe, UN Doc. CRC/C/SR.294, para. 3. Tunisia's Code of Personal Status prohibits polygamy and polyandry, UN Doc. CCPR/C/84/Add.1, para. 54. In *Bhewa* v. *Government of Mauritius* (1990) MR 79 the Supreme Court of Mauritius upheld the exclusive status of monogamous marriage.

233. Cf. Article 23(2) ICCPR; Article 12 ECHR; Article 17(2) ACHR. According to the HRC this implies the possibility to procreate and live together, General comment 19, UN Doc. HRI/GEN/1/Rev.2, para. 5; *Abdulaziz, Cabales and Balkandali* v. *United Kingdom* Series A, Vol. 94 (1985). See section 22(3) of the Constitution of Malawi, and Article 14(1) of the Namibian Constitution. Compulsory family planning is prohibited, General comment 19, *ibid.*, Harris, O'Boyle and Warbrick, note 18 *supra*, p. 440. It should be observed, however, that there is no positive obligation on the State to provide individuals with children, either through adoption or artificial means of reproduction, Harris, O'Boyle and Warbrick, note 18 *supra*, pp. 441 and 442.

234. Cf. Article 16 UDHR; Article 23(4) ICCPR; Article 17(4) ACHR. See Article 14(1) of the Namibian Constitution. In the absence of any reference to the dissolution of marriage in the ECHR the European Court of Human Rights has held that States parties are under no obligation to make provision for divorce, *Johnston* v. *Ireland* Series A, Vol. 112 (1987). However, if divorce is allowed, the right to marry encompasses a right to remarry without unnecessary restrictions, *F* v. *Switzerland* Series A, Vol. 128 (1987); Harris, O'Boyle and Warbrick, note 18 *supra*, pp. 439 and 440. In Togo both men and women have the right to initiate divorce proceedings, UN Doc. CCPR/C/63/Add.2, para. 85(d). In Sudan there appears to be equality of rights upon dissolution, UN Doc. CCPR/C/75/Add.2, para. 143. The HRC has noted that inequality between men and women in the area of divorce exists in Libya, UN Doc. CCPR/C/79/Add.101, para. 17.

235. The legal status of homosexuals was raised in *Courson* v. *Zimbabwe* (Communication No. 136/94) 3 *IHRR* (1996) 129, but the complaint was withdrawn. However, it appears little tolerance of homosexuality was shown, Ankumah, note 19 *supra*, p. 174. Although issues of sexuality have been interpreted as coming within the definition of 'private life' and 'privacy' under Article 8 ECHR, see *Dudgeon* v. *United Kingdom* Series A, Vol. 45 (1981), the European Court of Human Rights has held that homosexuals and transsexuals have no right to marry since that right refers to 'the traditional marriage between persons of opposite biological sex', *Rees* v. *United Kingdom* Series A, Vol. 106 (1986); *Cossey* v. *United Kingdom* Series A, Vol. 184 (1990); Harris, O'Boyle and Warbrick, note 18 *supra*, pp. 438, 439. See also Article 17 ICCPR and *Toonen* v. *Australia*, Communication No. 488/1992.

236. Ankumah, note 19 *supra*, pp. 151–9. See Article 23(4) ICCPR, Article 5 of the Seventh Protocol ECHR, Article 17(4) ACHR, and the UN Convention on the

Elimination of Discrimination Against Women. Cf. Article 11 of the Egyptian Constitution and sections 13(a) and 24 of the Constitution of Malawi. See further, *Bhewa* v. *Government of Mauritius* (1990) MR 79; *Rattigan and Others* v. *Chief Immigration Officer and Others* 1994(2) ZLR 54. Only seven Africa States are not parties to the above Convention, i.e., Djibouti, Mauritania, Niger, SADR, Somalia, Sudan and Swaziland. It is reported that women are discriminated against in Sudan, UN Doc. E/CN.4/1994/48, para. 102–8. An area of concern that is being addressed is that of violence against women, which violates a variety of rights, see, e.g., the Inter-American Convention on the Prevention, Punishment and Eradication of Violence Against Women 1994, which defines violence against women as 'any act or conduct, based on gender, which causes death or physical, sexual or psychological harm or suffering to women, whether in the public or private sphere'. Violence against women is further defined as, *inter alia*, 'Physical, sexual and psychological violence occurring in the family, including battering, sexual abuse of female children in the household, dowry-related violence, marital rape, female genital mutilation and other traditional practices harmful to women, non-spousal violence and violence related to exploitation', Beijing Platform for Action, para. 113. Female infanticide and prenatal selection are also included in the definition, para. 115. See further the report of the UN Special Rapporteur on violence against women, UN Doc. E/CN.4/1996/53. In *Aydin* v. *Turkey* Reports 1997-VI, para. 83, the European Court of Human Rights stated that 'rape leaves deep psychological scars on the victim which do not respond to the passage of time as quickly as other forms of physical and mental violence'. Note section 24(2)(a) of the Constitution of Malawi. In Egypt violence against women is a criminal offence, UN Doc. E/1990/5/Add.38, para. 69. The HRC has expressed concern that in Libya women are inadequately protected by law in respect of domestic violence and rape, UN Doc. CCPR/C/79/Add.101, para. 17. Also being addressed is the situation of systematic rape, sexual slavery and slavery-like practices during armed conflict. The conflict in Rwanda gave rise to widespread rape and abduction of women, UN Doc. E/CN.4/1995/42, para. 270. Rape as a weapon of war constitutes a violation of human rights, including the prohibitions on torture and cruel, inhuman or degrading treatment or punishment, slavery, and the right to life and security and dignity of the person, international humanitarian law, and constitutes a war crime, UN Doc. E/CN4/Sub.2/1996/26, and see further, *Cyprus* v. *Turkey* 4 EHHR 482 (1976), *Prosecutor* v. *Furundzija* 38 *ILM* 317 (1999) paras. 165–86, and the Vienna Declaration and Programme of Action, Part II, para. 38.

237.   General comment 19, UN Doc. HRI/GEN/1/Rev.2, para. 6. Note section 24 of the Constitution of Malawi. In Zimbabwe a number of customary laws have been changed over the years to improve the status of women, e.g., the Matrimonial Causes Act, UN Doc. E/CN.4/AC.45/1994/4, p. 30. Under Tunisia's Code of Personal Status the wife enjoys full legal personality on an equal footing with the husband, UN Doc. CCPR/C/84/Add.1, para. 55, although the father usually has custody of the children, ibid., paras. 56–60. Although the HRC has welcomed Libya's efforts to improve the status of women, it appears much remains to be done, UN Doc. CCPR/C/79/Add.101.

238.   As Ankumah points out, in many African countries the husband is the guardian of the wife's person and property, note 19 *supra*, pp. 153, 54; customary law may adversely affect the woman's rights to succession. It appears that in Libya inequality still persists in the area of inheritance, UN Doc. CCPR/C/79/Add.101, para. 17, although women may dispose of their assets, UN Doc. E/CN.4/1998/SR.39, para. 49. Under Article 24 of Tunisia's Code of Personal Status the husband has no power to administer the wife's personal property.

239.   Cf. Article 25(2) UDHR, Article 24(1) ICCPR, Article 10(2), (3) ICES, Article 18
ACHR and Article 16 of the Protocol of San Salvador but also to the UN
Convention on the Rights of the Child and the African Charter on the Rights
and Welfare of the Child, which stress the best interests of the child as the
primary consideration. At the time of writing only two African States are not
parties to the UN Convention, namely Somalia and the SADR. Eight States
have ratified the Charter, which requires fifteen ratifications to enter into force,
i.e., Benin, Burkina Faso, Cape Verde, Mauritius, Niger, Seychelles, Uganda,
and Zimbabwe. Cf. Article 10 of the Egyptian Constitution (and see further, UN
Doc. E/1990/5/Add.38, pp. 41–8), sections 13(h) and 23 of the Constitution of
Malawi, Article 15 of the Namibian Constitution and section 30 of the Constitution of South Africa. The UN Committee on the Rights of the Child has stated
that Algerian legislation is inadequate in terms of considering children as
subjects in their own right, and is incompatible with the principle of the best
interests of the child, UN Doc. CRC/C/15/Add.76, para. 16. Multiple violations
of the rights of children have been reported in Sudan, including non-separation
of the family, the principle of non-discrimination, and the right to an identity,
UN Doc. E/CN.4/1994/48, paras. 86–101.

240.   The European Court of Human Rights has held that illegitimate children should
be placed legally and socially in a position akin to that of a legitimate child and
that the absence of an appropriate legal regime reflecting the illegitimate child's
natural family ties amounts to a failure to respect family life in contravention
of Article 8, *Marckx* v. *Belgium* Series A, Vol. 31 (1979). In addition, illegitimate
children must have equal rights under the law in accordance with the principle
of non-discrimination enshrined in Article 14 ECHR, *Inze* v. *Austria* Series A,
Vol. 126 (1987). See also Article 24 ICCPR and General comment 17, UN Doc.
HRI/GEN/1/Rev.2, para. 5, and Article 3 of the African Charter on the Rights
and Welfare of the Child. Cf. the Civil Status (Amendment No. 2) Act 1990 of
Mauritius. The HRC has expressed concern at the persistence of discrimination
against children born out of wedlock in Libya, UN Doc. CCPR/C/79/Add.101,
para. 18. For the position in Tunisia, see UN Doc. CCPR/C/84/Add.1, paras.
220–5.

241.   It should be observed that all these rights are guaranteed under the UN
Convention on the Rights of the Child and the African Charter on the Rights
and Welfare of the Child. Cf. section 23(2), (3) of the Constitution of Malawi;
section 28(1)(a)(b) of the South African Constitution; Togo's Family Code, UN
Doc. CCPR/C/63/Add.2, p. 11. See further, the positions in Algeria, UN Doc.
CRC/C/28/Add.4, pp. 10, 11, Chad, UN Doc. CRC/C/3/Add.50, pp. 17, 18,
Egypt, UN Doc. E/1990/5/Add.38, pp. 45, 46, Lesotho, UN Doc. CRC/C/11/
Add.20, pp. 23–6, Mali, UN Doc. CRC/C/3/Add.53, pp. 13, 14, Niger, UN Doc.
CRC/C/3/Add.29, p. 5.

242.   General comment 17, UN Doc. HRI/GEN/1/Rev.2, pp. 23–5. Uganda's Constitution of 1995 contains general provisions setting out the basic rights of
children. The Children's Statute 1996 incorporates the UN Convention and
establishes mechanisms for the protection of children's rights, including the
National Council for Children, composed of government representatives and
members of the public, entrusted with the formulation of policy for the
realization of children's rights, UN Doc. CRC/C/SR.409, para. 6. Mali's Penal
Code protects the sexual integrity of children, UN Doc. CRC/C/3/Add.53,
para. 30. See similarly, Lesotho, UN Doc. CRC/C/11/Add.20, para. 38. However, by way of contrast, it has been reported that in Zimbabwe sexual relations
with children are sometimes condoned by social and cultural practices, UN
Doc. E/CN.4/1997/95, para. 44. It has already been noted that the abduction
and sale of children is widespread in Sudan, UN Docs. E/CN.4/1994/48, paras.

95, 97, 98, E/CN.4/1997/95, para. 47. The issue of traditional practices arises once again. Thus child marriages, female circumcision performed on children, and discrimination must all be addressed, see UN Doc. E/CN.4/Sub.2/1991/6. With regard to the implementation of the Beijing Platform for Action Botswana announced its intention to take 'all the appropriate measures with a view to abolishing traditional practices prejudicial to the health of children', UN Doc. E/CN./Sub.2/1997/10/Add.1, para. 20.

243. Cf. Article 32 ACHR.

244. Umozurike, note 4 *supra*, Chapter 5.

245. Sieghart, note 40 *supra*, p. 367. However, some individual rights, such as the right to religion, may be contingent on the implementation of a collective right, see Y. Dinstein, 'Collective Human Rights Rights of Peoples and Minorities', 25 *ICLQ* (1976) 102 at p. 103.

246. Although the International Commission of Jurists has expressed the view that these provisions of the Banjul Charter impose a positive obligation upon States parties to realise these rights, note 22 *supra*, p. 29.

247. Sieghart, note 40 *supra*, pp. 367, 368; A. Kiss, 'The Peoples' Right to Self-Determination', 7 *HRLJ* (1986) 165 at pp. 172–73; T. van Boven, 'The Relations between Peoples' Rights and Human Rights in the African Charter', 7 *HRLJ* (1986) 183; J.-B. Marie, 'Relations between Peoples' Rights and Human Rights: Semantic and Methodological Distinctions', 7 *HRLJ* (1986) 195; I. Brownlie, 'The Rights of Peoples in Modern International Law', in J. Crawford (ed.), *The Rights of Peoples* (1988).

248. See the report of the International Commission of Jurists, note 22 *supra*, pp. 53, 54.

249. See note 41 *supra*.

250. The fact that some African countries continue to be affected by mercenary activities undermines their right to self-determination, see further Chapter 1 of this book.

251. Cf. common Article 1 of the International Covenants. See also the Vienna Declaration and Programme of Action, Part I, para. 2. According to the HRC the realization of the right of self-determination 'is an essential condition for the effective guarantee and observance of individual human rights and for the promotion and strengthening of those rights', General comment 12, UN Doc. HRI/GEN/1/Rev.2, para. 1; and further, A. Cassese, *Self-Determination of Peoples: A Legal Reappraisal* (1995) Chapter 3. See also, Sieghart, note 40 *supra.*, pp. 368–70.

252. Evidence of the legal status of the right of self-determination can be ascertained from numerous UN General Assembly resolutions, both of a general and specific nature, but in particular Resolution 1514(XV) 1960 Declaration on the Granting of Independence to Colonial Countries and Peoples, Resolution 1541(XV) 1960, and Resolution 2625(XXV) 1970 Declaration on Friendly Relations Among States in Accordance with the Charter of the United Nations, State practice and *opinio juris*, and the jurisprudence of the ICJ, see *Namibia Case* ICJ Reports 1971, p. 16, *Western Sahara Case* ICJ Reports 1975, p. 12, *Frontier Dispute Case* ICJ Reports 1986, p. 554, and the *East Timor Case* ICJ Reports 1995, p. 90. See further, General comment 12, UN Doc. HRI/GEN/1/Rev.2, paras. 6, 7; Vienna Declaration and Programme of Action, Part I, para. 2(2); Cassese, note 251 *supra*, Chapter 4. It has been further asserted that the right of self-determination is a norm of *jus cogens* from which no derogation is permissible and this assertion is supported by the use of the adjective inalienable in all the more recent texts, see General comment 12, UN Doc. HRI/GEN/1/Rev.2, para. 2. Indeed, the Banjul Charter also describes it as 'unquestionable'. See Brownlie, *Principles of Public International Law*, note 41 *supra*, pp. 513, 515; Cassese, *supra*,

pp. 133–40. Whereas *dicta* in the *Frontier Dispute Case* ICJ Reports 1986, p. 554, suggest that this may not be the case, see further Chapter 1, the finding by the ICJ in the *East Timor Case* ICJ Reports 1995, p. 90 at para. 29, that self-determination is an obligation *erga omnes* lends support to the view that it is a peremptory norm of international law.

253. General comment 12, UN Doc. HRI/GEN/1/Rev.2, para. 6, which makes plain that the obligation to promote and realize the right to self-determination is incumbent on all States parties. This is mirrored by the *dicta* of the ICJ in the *East Timor Case* that self-determination imposes an *erga omnes* obligation, ICJ Reports 1995, p. 90 at para. 29. It should be observed further that any forcible denial of the right to self-determination is a violation of international law which may constitute an international crime, Vienna Declaration and Programme of Action, Part I, para. 2(2); Cassese, note 251 *supra*, pp. 180–5, 194–7.

254. See Chapter 1 of this book. For example, Tanzania has made clear its opposition to the view that the right to self-determination includes a right to secession, UN Doc. CCPR/C/SR.1690, para. 48. It is instructive to note that because the so-called 'homelands' of Transkei, Bophuthatswana, Venda and Ciskei were granted, nominal, independence by South Africa in violation of, *inter alia*, the right to self-determination, they went unrecognized by the international community, see, e.g., UN General Assembly resolution 36/172A (1982). The independence of the homelands was repealed by section 190(1) of the Interim Constitution of South Africa of 1994 and all four were eventually reintegrated.

255. Communication No. 75/92, 3 *IHRR* (1996) 136, para. 5. See also Ankumah, note 19 *supra*, pp. 163, 164. It is interesting to note that in *Reference re Secession of Quebec* 37 *ILM* 1340 (1998), the Supreme Court of Canada expressed the view that no right of unilateral secession existed in international law.

256. Cassese, note 251 *supra*, pp. 102–8, 122–4; Vienna Declaration and Programme of Action, Part I, para. 3. See also the report of the Special Rapporteur of the Sub-Commission on the Prevention of Discrimination and Protection of Minorities, UN Doc. E/CN.4.Sub.2/1993/34, paras. 59, 161–3.

257. See Chapter 2 of this book.

258. Cassese, note 251 *supra*, pp. 108–125. Thus the Vienna Declaration and Programme of Action requires that States conduct themselves 'in compliance with the principle of equal rights and self-determination of peoples' and possess a government 'representing the whole people . . . without distinction of any kind', Part I, para. 3. See also, UN Doc. E/CN.4/Sub.2/1993/34, para. 165, which, however, sets a high standard of proof, requiring 'beyond reasonable doubt' evidence 'that there is no prospect within the foreseeable future that the Government will become representative of the whole people', or if 'it can be shown that the majority is pursuing a policy of genocide', para. 84. See the submission of the Sudanese government that it complies with this requirement, UN Doc. CCPR/C/75/Add.2, paras. 21, 22. It should be observed that Sudan has accepted a political arrangement with the southern rebels giving them the opportunity of exercising the right to a referendum, ibid., para. 23.

259. It needs to be recalled that human rights instruments must be interpreted purposively, see note 23 *supra*.

260. For instance, resolution 2625(XXV) 1970 Declaration on Friendly Relations and resolution 3103(XXVIII) 1973 Basic Principles on the Legal Status of the Combatants Struggling Against Colonial and Alien Domination and Racist Regimes.

261. Cassese, note 251 *supra*, p. 198.

262. Such struggles have been defined as 'armed conflicts in which peoples are fighting against colonial domination and alien occupation and against racist regimes in the exercise of their right to self-determination', Article 1(4) of Protocol I Additional to the Geneva Conventions relating to the Protection of

Victims of International Armed Conflicts 1977. See generally, G. Abi-Saab, 'Wars of National Liberation and the Laws of War', 3 *Annales d'Etudes Internationales* (1972) 93; N. Ronzitti, 'Wars of National Liberation – A Legal Definition', 1 *Italian Yearbook of International Law* (1975) 192; H. Wilson, *International Law and the Use of Force by National Liberation Movements* (1988).

263. Cassese, note 251 *supra*, pp. 197, 198. See further, C.J.R. Dugard, 'The Organisation of African Unity and Colonialism: An Inquiry into the Plea of Self-Defence as a Justification for the Use of Force in the Eradication of Colonialism', 16 *ICLQ* (1967) 157.

264. In the *Nicaragua Case* ICJ Reports 1986, p. 14 at p. 351, Judge Schwebel stated that 'it is lawful for a foreign State or movement to give to a people struggling for self-determination moral, political and humanitarian assistance'.

265. See. e.g., resolution 2105(XX) 1965.

266. Cassese, note 251 *supra*, pp. 199, 200; K. Ginther, 'Liberation Movements', in R. Bernhardt, (ed.) *Encyclopedia of Public International Law* (1983) Vol. III, pp. 245–9.

267. Articles 1(2) and 47 ICCPR, General comment 12, UN Doc. HRI/GEN/1/Rev.2, para. 5; Articles 1(2) and 25 ICES; General Assembly resolutions 1803(XVII) 1962 on Permanent Sovereignty over Natural Resources and 3281(XXIX) 1974 Charter on the Economic Rights and Duties of States; Sieghart, note 40 *supra*, pp. 372–4.

268. See para. 4(e) of the Declaration on the Establishment of a New International Economic Order, General Assembly Resolution 3201 (S-VI) 1974. See further Judge Weeramantry in the *East Timor Case* ICJ Reports 1995, p. 90 at pp. 221, 222.

269. See the Charter of Economic Rights and Duties of States, note 267 *supra*.

270. On the relationship between the enjoyment of human rights and the activities of transnational corporations, see the reports of the UN Secretary-General, UN Docs. E/CN.4/Sub.2/1995/11 and E/CN.4/Sub.2/1996/12.

271. In this context, it is interesting to note the action commenced by Nauru seeking compensation from its former administering power for spoliation amongst other things, see *Certain Phosphate Lands in Nauru* ICJ Reports 1992, p. 240, which was settled out of court by the payment of compensation.

272. Thus Namibia obtained compensation from South Africa.

273. See *Texaco* v. *Libya* 17 *ILM* 1 (1978) where the arbitrator observed that developed States regarded the formulation as *contra legem*. Note that in *Lithgow* v. *United Kingdom* Series A, Vol. 102 (1986) the European Court of Human Rights declared that under Article 1 of the First Protocol ECHR the taking of property without payment of an amount reasonably related to its value would normally constitute a disproportionate interference which could not be considered justifiable. See *supra*, pp. 126–7.

274. See *supra*, pp. 126–7.

275. Sieghart, note 40 *supra*, pp. 374, 375; Ankumah, note 19 *supra*, pp. 165–7; A. Rich, 'A Right to Development: A Right of Peoples?', in Crawford, note 247 *supra*, Chapter 3.

276. The Vienna Declaration and Programme of Action states that extreme poverty inhibits the enjoyment of human rights, Part I, para. 14. For the link between poverty and human rights, see Special Rapporteur Despouy's Final Report on human rights and extreme poverty, UN Doc. E/CN.4/Sub.2/1996/13. It is estimated that 40% of the population in sub-Saharan Africa live in poverty, UN Doc. E/C.12/1997/SR.27, para. 27.

277. According to the ECA, the literacy rate in Africa seems to be 61%, African Economic Report – 1998, para. 75.

278. Unemployment in Africa is high, see note 206 *supra*. The main elements of the right to development are: the right to effective participation in all aspects of

development at all stages of the decision-making process; the right to equal opportunity in access to resources; the right to fair distribution of the benefits of development; the right to respect for civil, political, economic, social and cultural rights; the right to an international environment in which these rights can be realized; see UN Doc. E/CN.4/1996/24, p. 16.

279. International Conference on Human Rights at Tehran, 13 May 1968. See also General Assembly resolution 2542 (XXIV) 1969 Declaration on Social Progress and Development.

280. K. M'Baye, 'Le droit au développement comme un droit de l'homme', 5 *Revue des Droits de l'Homme* (1972) 503; O. Schacter, 'The Emerging International Law of Development', 15 *Columbia Journal of Transnational Law* (1976) 1; C. Weeramantry, 'The Right to Development', 25 *IJIL* (1985) 482.

281. See also resolution 37/200.

282. General Assembly resolution 41/128. See also the Vienna Declaration and Programme of Action which reaffirms the right to development as a universal and inalienable right and an integral part of fundamental human rights, Part I, para. 10.

283. The Working Group of the UN Commission on Human Rights on the Right to Development has stated that two elements are required for the right to development to be fully effective as a human right: the need to establish minimum standards and targets, and the need for a process of accountability, UN Doc. E/CN.4/1995/27, para. 63.

284. Ibid., p. 15. See further, the Vienna Declaration and Programme of Action, Part I, paras. 10 and 11.

285. Vienna Declaration and Programme of Action, Part I, para. 10; UN Doc. E/CN.4/1995/27, p. 16. A number of problems that need to be overcome have been identified, including the external debt burden of many developing countries, especially in Africa, unbalanced international trade relations, which often make developing States dependent on the export of commodities, the prices of which are unstable and often in decline, and inadequate development assistance, see UN Doc. E/CN.4/1996/24, pp. 22–5. Debt servicing entails the net transfer of financial resources from developing to developed countries. Between 1982 and 1992, debts owed to international financial institutions amounted to 23% of the total African debt, UN Doc. E/CN.4/1995/25, para. 24. Madagascar has identified the debt crisis as a particular obstacle to the implementation of the right to development, UN Doc. E/CN.4/1995/25/Add.2. Fears have been expressed that the debt burden will lead to political destabilization and social disintegration, ibid., para. 16. In 1989 the OAU called for structural adjustment programmes to be replaced with alternative people-centred programmes, the African Alternative Framework to Structural Adjustment Programmes for Socio-Economic Recovery and Transformation. Balanced and rational economic approaches must be found. Debt reduction and cancellation have been proposed as priorities, see further UN Doc. E/CN.4/1995/25, Part IV. A concerted, albeit limited, response by the international community to the debt crisis has been the HIPC Initiative developed in 1996 by the IMF and the World Bank. Although thirty-four African States come within the category of heavily indebted poor countries to date only Uganda is eligible for assistance under the strict terms of the HIPC Initiative, African Economic Report – 1998, Part I.A.6.

286. Article 8(1) of the Declaration on the Right to Development calls for 'equality of opportunity for all in their access to basic resources, education, health services, food, housing, employment and the fair distribution of income'. Obstacles which have been identified at the national level include persistent violations of human rights, armed conflicts, widespread corruption, lack of

educational and employment opportunities, capital flight, structural adjustment programmes which have had a negative impact on social policies, marked differences in income distribution, and other socially and economically exclusive policies, see UN Doc. E/CN.4/1996/24, pp. 20–2. Zimbabwe has identified the unequal distribution of land as an obstacle, UN Doc. E/CN.4/AC.45/1994/ 4, paras. 159–61, and has embarked on a controversial policy of acquisition of prime commercial farmland which is proving divisive and which could undermine the economy, *The Guardian* (London), 20 November 1997, p. 2. Policies of social and cultural favouritism can undermine development as people are driven off land to be handed over to agro-industrial enterprises or other ethnic groups.

287. The Constitutions of Mauritius and Tanzania seem to provide for a right to development. Senegal and Zimbabwe, for example, have undertaken various development programmes, including liberalization and indigenization of the economy, UN Docs. E/CN.4/AC.45/1994/4, pp. 29–31, E/CN.4/AC.45/1995/ 2, pp. 5, 6, respectively.

288. See General Assembly resolution 2749(XXV) 1970 Declaration of Principles Governing the Sea-Bed and the Ocean Floor, and the Subsoil Thereof, Beyond the Limits of National Jurisdiction; Articles 136–40 UN Convention on the Law of the Sea 1982; and the Agreement Governing the Activities of States on the Moon and other Celestial Bodies 1979. There is considerable doubt as to whether the concept of the common heritage of mankind has acquired the status of customary law, P. Malanczuk, *Akehurst's Modern Introduction to International Law* (7th edn 1997), p. 208; M. Shaw, *International Law* (4th edn 1997) p. 362.

289. See, e.g., UNESCO Convention for the Protection of the World Cultural and Natural Heritage 1972, and *Commonwealth of Australia* v. *Tasmania* (1983) 46 ALR 625. Note further the Australian Aboriginal and Torres Strait Islander Heritage Protection Act 1984. See also, UNESCO Convention on the Means of Prohibiting and Preventing the Illicit Import, Export and Transfer of Ownership of Cultural Property 1970, Article 30 (ex Art 36) EC Treaty, and the New Zealand Antiquities Act 1975.

290. The linkage between human rights and international peace is reflected in the UN Charter, see, e.g., Article 1. See further, UN Doc. E/CN.4/Sub.2/1991/32.

291. See Article 7 of the Declaration on the Right to Development.

292. See the Rio Declaration on Environment and Development 1992.

293. Sieghart, note 40 *supra*, p. 376; Ankumah, note 19 *supra*, pp. 168–70. See, e.g., section 24 of the South African Constitution. For a fuller discussion of this question, see Chapter 5 of this book.

294. See *Trail Smelter Arbitration* (1938 and 1941) 3 RIAA 1905; Articles 24 and 25 Geneva Convention on the High Seas 1958; Articles 192–4 UN Convention on the Law of the Sea 1982; the Nuclear Test Ban Treaty 1963; Geneva Convention on Long-Range Transboundary Air Pollution 1979; Vienna Convention for the Protection of the Ozone Layer 1985 and Montreal Protocol on Substances that Deplete the Ozone Layer 1987; and the Stockholm Declaration on the Human Environment 1972.

295. See UN Convention to Combat Desertification 1994, 21 *CLB* (1995) 1222.

296. Although the UN has set up the International Criminal Tribunal for Rwanda to prosecute individuals for the crime of genocide, UN Security Council resolution 955 (1994). See R.S. Lee, 'The Rwanda Tribunal', 9 *Leiden Journal of International Law* (1996) 37. It is clear that the massacres in Rwanda meet the definition of genocide, UN Doc. /CN.4/1995/71. It is interesting to note that in *Prosecutor* v. *Kanyabashi, Decision on Jurisdiction* 92 AJIL (1998) 66, at p. 70, n. 21, the International Criminal Tribunal for Rwanda stated that the law applicable to it

was influenced by African human rights instruments, including the Banjul Charter. Ethiopia is engaged in investigating and prosecuting the human rights violations of the Mengistu regime which resulted in the deaths of hundreds of thousands, UN Doc. E/CN.4/1994/103. The prohibition on genocide is a norm of *jus cogens*, see Brownlie, *Principles of Public International Law*, p. 513. See also *Barcelona Traction Case* ICJ Reports 1970, p. 3 at p. 32; *Application of the Convention on the Prevention and Punishment of the Crime of Genocide Case* ICJ Reports 1993, p. 3; and Article 19 of the ILC's Draft Articles on State Responsibility.

297. Umozurike, note 4 *supra*, pp. 64, 65. Cf. Articles 25–8 of the Tanzanian Constitution.

298. International Commission of Jurists, note 22 *supra*, pp. 54, 55. See also Ankumah, note 19 *supra*, Chapter 5.4.3.

299. D'Sa, note 9 *supra*, p. 77. It should be observed further that the African Charter on the Rights and Welfare of the Child refers both to rights and responsibilities, so that children are deemed to have obligations towards their parents, their community and their nation, a fact stressed in Uganda, UN Doc. CRC/C/SR.409, para. 53.

300. See generally, Ankumah, note 19 *supra*, Chapter 2. The Commission, which became operational in 1987, is based in Banjul, The Gambia. The Commission is assisted by a secretariat to help ensure that the Commission discharges its duties effectively, Article 41 and Rule 23 of the Commission's Rules of Procedure, hereinafter 'Rules'; see further, Ankumah, *supra*, Chapter 2.6.1.-3.

301. See also Rules 11 and 12.

302. See also Rule 16. Ankumah observes that this has not been without its problems, note 19 *supra*, Chapter 2.4.

303. Ankumah, note 19 *supra*, Chapter 2.3; D'Sa, note 9 *supra*, p. 79.

304. Although it seems that West Africa is disproportionately represented, Ankumah, note 19 *supra*, Chapter 2.3.2, who goes on to write that the important consideration is that the different legal and language traditions from across Africa are represented. No provision is made for equitable gender balance, ibid., Chapter 2.3.1.

305. See further Rule 17. Rule 17(2) requires a secret ballot.

306. See Rules 18 and 44.

307. Rule 14. See further, Ankumah, note 19 *supra*, p. 15, who has highlighted some personnel problems.

308. However, Rule 2 requires at least two ordinary sessions a year.

309. Rule 3.

310. Rule 43.

311. Rule 60.

312. Rule 22(1).

313. *The Independent* (London), 5 November 1987, p. 6.

314. International Commission of Jurists, note 22 *supra*, pp. 38, 39; Ankumah, note 19 *supra*, Chapter 2.5.1.

315. Including national liberation movements, see Rules 72, 75 and 76.

316. Ankumah, note 19 *supra*, Chapter 2.5.4. Although it was initially thought that the Commission did not have the power to act on its own volition, it has interpreted some Charter provisions on its own initiative.

317. Ankumah, note 19 *supra*, Chapter 2.5.5.

318. Ankumah, note 19 *supra*, pp. 41–3.

319. Rule 97; D'Sa, note 9 *supra*, p. 80. Note that the European Court of Human Rights and the Inter-American Commission on Human Rights are under similar expectations to reach friendly settlements, see Article 38(1) ECHR and Article 48(1)(f) ACHR.

320. Ankumah, note 19 *supra*, pp. 23, 24. To date no such complaints have been submitted.
321. See also Rule 89.
322. Cf. Article 48 ACHR; Article 4 Optional Protocol ICCPR. Rule 99 makes provision for the representation of State parties before the Commission.
323. See also Rule 92. Cf. Article 45 ACHR.
324. Cf. Article 45 ACHR which makes the jurisdiction of the Inter-American Commission dependent upon prior acceptance of its competence by States parties.
325. See *Soering* v. *United Kingdom* Series A, Vol. 161 (1989).
326. See Harris, O' Boyle and Warbrick, note 18 *supra*, pp. 613, 614.
327. See also Rule 98.
328. Rule 99.
329. See note 319 *supra*.
330. Rule 100(1) requires the Commission to adopt its report 'within a reasonable period of time' not exceeding twelve months from when the issue was referred to it.
331. See Rule 100.
332. Old Rule 114 clarified the meaning of Article 55 by specifying who was entitled to lodge a complaint. This has been replaced by amended Rule 116 which is clearly unsatisfactory since it provides that the Commission must determine questions of admissibility pursuant to Article 56, see Ankumah, note 19 *supra*, Chapter 3.2. But Article 56 lists the conditions of admissibility and is silent on who can submit a complaint. However, the practice of the Commission clearly establishes that it is competent to receive complaints from individuals and NGOs.
333. Old Rule 114. See *Baes* v. *Zaire* (Communication No. 31/89) 3 *IHRR* (1996) 123. Cf. Article 44 ACHR. By contrast the ECHR was more restrictive, requiring the complainant to be a victim, see Harris, O'Boyle and Warbrick, note 18 *supra*, pp. 635–7.
334. Ankumah, note 19 *supra*, Chapter 3.3.3. Cf. Articles 46 and 47 ACHR.
335. *Centre for Independence of Judges and Lawyers* v. *Algeria*, (Communication Nos. 104/94, 109–126/94) Eighth Annual Report 1994–1995; *Dioumessi, Kande, Kaba* v. *Guinea* (Communication No. 70/92) 4 *IHRR* (1997) 85; see also Rule 104(1)(a).
336. *Katangese Peoples' Congress* v. *Zaire* (Communication No. 75/92) 3 *IHRR* (1996) 136; Ankumah, note 19 *supra*, pp. 64, 164.
337. Cf. Article 3 Optional Protocol ICCPR. See *Njoka* v. *Kenya* (Communication No. 142/94) 3 *IHRR* (1996) 130. Because the Commission's reasoning on admissibility is not always clear, Ankumah draws a distinction between admissibility and receivability. The former are assessed against the criteria of Article 56, whereas the latter are *prima facie* inconsistent and are summarily dismissed, note 19 *supra*, Chapter 3.3.1.-3.3.2.
338. Rule 104(1)(d), (e). Cf. the ECHR which allowed the European Commission to reject an application if it was 'manifestly ill-founded', see Harris, O'Boyle and Warbrick, note 18 *supra*, pp. 627, 628; or 'manifestly groundless' under Article 47(c) ACHR.
339. See note 335 *supra*. See also *Njoka* v. *Kenya* (Communication No. 142/94).
340. See Rule 102(2); and Ankumah, note 19 *supra*, p. 56, who writes that a communication was submitted against the USA!
341. *Co-ordinating Secretary of the Free Citizens Convention* v. *Ghana* (Communication No. 4/88); *Njoka* v. *Kenya* (Communication No. 142/94). It will be interesting to observe if the Commission takes note of the European case, *Loizidou* v. *Turkey*, Report 1996–V, where it was adjudged that the European Court of Human Rights had jurisdiction because even though the violation had taken place

before the State had become a party to the ECHR its effects continued after that time. See also, *Aduayom* v. *Togo*, Communications Nos. 422–4 (1990).

342. Cf. Article 47(c) ACHR; and Article 3 Optional Protocol ICCPR. See further, Harris, O'Boyle and Warbrick, note 18 *supra*, pp. 628, 629.

343. International Commission of Jurists, note 22, *supra*, p. 46. Cf. Article 47(b) ACHR.

344. Ankumah, note 19 *supra*, p. 64.

345. *Kenya Human Rights Commission* v. *Kenya* (Communication No. 135/94) 4 *IHRR* (1997) 86; *Buyingo* v. *Uganda* (Communication No. 8/88) 3 *IHRR* (1996) 121.

346. *Interhandel Case* ICJ Reports 1959, p. 6 at pp. 26, 27; C.F. Amerasinghe, *Local Remedies in International Law* (1990). With reference to the practice of the African Commission see, e.g., *El Had Boubacare Diawara* v. *Benin* (Communication No. 18/88 joined with Nos. 16/88 and 17/88) 3 *IHRR* (1996) 122 (case pending before domestic courts); *Paul S. Haye* v. *The Gambia* (Communication No. 90/93) 3 *IHRR* (1996) 126 (failure to appeal to a higher court); *International PEN (in respect of Kemal al-Jazouli)* v. *Sudan* (Communication No. 92/93) 3 *IHRR* (1996) 127 (denial in general terms by the government of human rights violations did not mean the matter had been tried in the Sudanese courts); *Free Legal Assistance Group* v. *Zaire* (Communication No. 25/89) 18 *HRLJ* (1997) 32.

347. Cf. Article 2 Optional Protocol ICCPR; and Article 46(1) ACHR.

348. *Account of the Internal Legislation of Nigeria and the Disposition of the African Charter on Human and Peoples' Rights* (Communication No. 129/94).

349. *Buyingo* v. *Uganda* (Communication No. 8/88) 3 *IHRR* (1996) 121; *Sana Dumbuya* v. *The Gambia* (Communication No. 127/94) 3 *IHRR* (1996) 129. By contrast, the practice of the ECHR demonstrates that the burden of proof is swiftly assumed by the defendant State, Harris, O'Boyle and Warbrick, note 18 *supra*, pp. 615, 616.

350. Ankumah, note 19 *supra*, pp. 67–9.

351. *Alberto Capitao* v. *Tanzania* (Communication No. 53/91) 3 *IHRR* (1996) 123, para. 3. Cf. Rule 97 on inter-State complaints. Furthermore, Rule 104(1)(f) allows the complainant to explain why local remedies will be 'futile'. The practice of the ECHR requires adequate and effective remedies, Harris, O'Boyle and Warbrick, note 18 *supra*, pp. 616–20. See also Article 5(2)(b) Optional Protocol ICCPR and Article 46(2) ACHR.

352. *Free Legal Assistance Group, Lawyers Committee for Human Rights, Union Interafricaine des Droits de l'Homme, and Les Témoins Jéhovahs* v. *Zaire* (Communication Nos. 25/89, 47/90, 59/91, 100/93), relating to large numbers of victims and abuses in cases of serious or massive violations. In *Free Legal Assistance Group* v. *Zaire* (Communication No. 25/89) 18 *HRLJ* (1997) 32, para. 37, the Commission stated that it, 'has never held the requirement of local remedies to apply literally in cases where it is impractical or undesirable for the complainant to seize the domestic courts in the case of each violation.' Ankumah suggests that an exception should be made to the rule where individuals cannot resort to domestic remedies as a result of lack of funds, note 19 *supra*, pp. 69, 70; and see Harris, O'Boyle and Warbrick, note 18 *supra*, p. 610.

353. See Ankumah, note 19 *supra*, pp. 65, 66, who writes that the Commission should take account of factors 'such as the general nature of the case, the continuity or lack thereof of the alleged violation, the seriousness of the alleged violation and the domestic remedies procedure in the country concerned'. Cf. Article 5(2)(b) Optional Protocol ICCPR; Article 46(1)(b) ACHR. See further, Harris, O'Boyle and Warbrick, note 18 *supra*, pp. 621–4. Note also *International PEN* v. *Sudan* (Communication No. 92/93).

354. Cf. Article 5(2)(a) Optional Protocol ICCPR; and Article 47(d) ACHR. See further, Harris, O'Boyle and Warbrick, note 18 *supra*, pp. 626, 627.
355. Rule 118(2) allows the Commission to reconsider a communication declared inadmissible if it receives a request for reconsideration.
356. See also Rule 104(1)(g). See *Amnesty International* v. *Tunisia* (Communication No. 69/92).
357. Cf. *contra*, Ankumah, note 19 *supra*, pp. 66, 67.
358. See also Rules 112 and 119(1).
359. Rule 119(2). Note further Rule 117(4) which obliges the Commission to decide on admissibility where the State fails to respond within the time limit.
360. Rule 119(3). See, e.g., *Badjogoume* v. *Benin* (Communication No. 17/88) 3 *IHRR* (1996) 122.
361. Rules 113 and 118(1).
362. See *Commission Nationale des Droits de l'Homme et des Libertés* v. *Chad* (Communication No. 74/92) 18 *HRLJ* (1997) 34, para. 15; *Free Legal Assistance Group* v. *Zaire* (Communication No. 25/89) 18 *HRLJ* (1997) 32, paras. 15, 35.
363. International Commission of Jurists, note 22, *supra*, pp. 46, 47.
364. In *Jean Yaovi Degli (au nom du Caporal N. Bikagni), Union Interafricaine des Droits de l'Homme, Commission Internationale de Juristes* v. *Togo* (Communication Nos. 83/92, 88/93, 91/93 (joined)) 3 *IHRR* (1996) 125, though held inadmissible, torture and ill-treatment, extortion and killings, electoral irregularities, and a general breakdown in law and order, amounted to grave and massive violations.
365. See the criticisms by Ankumah, note 29 *supra*, pp. 40–41.
366. See Amnesty International, note 106 *supra*, p. 15.
367. Ankumah, note 19 *supra*, pp. 42, 73. But cf. on-site investigations under Article 46, of the Banjul Charter, folio 252, *supra*.
368. Ankumah, note 19 *supra*, Chapter 3.4.1.
369. It seems that the Rules of Procedure have enabled the Commission to publicize many of its activities Article 59 notwithstanding, Ankumah, note 19 *supra*, Chapters 2.8.2., 3.4.4.
370. Although Article 62 did not make it clear that the Commission had been expressly assigned this role, it was given this responsibility by the OAU, Ankumah, note 19 *supra*, Chapter 4.1. The Commission has issued guidelines to assist States parties in drafting their reports, reproduced in *Naldi*, pp. 155–82, analysed by Ankumah, note 19 *supra*, Chapter 4.3.2.-4.3.3.
371. Cf. Article 62(1) ACHR; and see Harris, O'Boyle, and Warbrick, note 18 *supra*, pp. 652–4; S. Davidson, *The Inter-American Court of Human Rights*, (1992) p. 62.
372. See Article 64 ECHR, and P. van Dijk and G.J.H. van Hoof, *Theory and Practice of the European Convention on Human Rights* (2nd edn 1990) pp. 606–13; Article 62(2) ACHR, and the decision of the IACHR in *The effect of reservations on the entry into force of the American Convention* 3 *HRLJ* (1982) 153.
373. Gittleman, note 9 *supra*; D'Sa, note 9 *supra*.
374. Ankumah, note 19 *supra*, Chapter 6; J. Oloka-Onyango, 'Beyond the Rhetoric: Reinvigorating the Struggle for Economic and Social Rights in Africa', 26 *California Western International Law Journal* (1996) 1. For a more optimistic assessment, see Umozurike, note 4 *supra*, Chapter 7.
375. Resolution AHG/230 (XXX).
376. OAU/LEG/EXP/AFC/HPR (I), reproduced in 8 *RADIC* (1996) 493. Adama Dieng, Secretary-General of the International Commission of Jurists, stated that the proposed Court was an urgent necessity to curb human rights abuses, *African Topics*, Issue 10, November–December 1995, p 11. In addition, the meeting approved various measures to strengthen the Commission's mandate. These included the need for the implementation of the Commission's and

relevant OAU resolutions; the need to improve the Commission's rules of procedure relating to the examination of complaints; the need to strengthen the rights of women, either by a protocol to the Banjul Charter or by a separate instrument; the participation by the Commission in all OAU activities affecting human and peoples' rights; the creation of national institutions within OAU member States for the effective implementation of the Banjul Charter; and the need for adequate staffing and funding; ibid., For an analysis of the Cape Town Draft, see G.J. Naldi, and K. Magliveras, 'The Proposed African Court of Human and Peoples' Rights: Evaluation and Comparison', 8 *RADIC* (1996) 944.

377. 9 *RADIC* (1997) 423.
378. 9 *RADIC* (1997) 432.
379. 9 *RADIC* (1997) 953. At the time of writing the Protocol has not been ratified by any State, although it has been signed by thirty. The Nouakchott Protocol will come into force one month after the fifteenth instrument of ratification has been deposited with the OAU Secretary-General, Article 34(3).
380. Ankumah, note 19 *supra*, Ch 6.4.1.; *African Topics*, note 376 *supra*.
381. Article 34 of the Nouakchott Protocol, and see further *supra*, pp. 150–2. Tunisia proposed to the second government legal experts meeting that the jurisdiction of the Court be subjected to a requirement of a declaration from each State party accepting such jurisdiction, 9 *RADIC* (1997) pp. 426, 427. Cf. Article 33 ECHR. Article 62(1) ACHR makes the jurisdiction of the IACHR contingent on a declaration by a State.
382. Cf. Article 34 ECHR which gives applicants direct access to the Court.
383. The text of the Revised Treaty of the Economic Community of West African States (ECOWAS) 1993 can be found at 8 *RADIC* (1996) 187. Although the AEC Treaty and the revised ECOWAS Treaty are principally concerned with issues of economic development, both make reference in identical terms to protecting human rights in accordance with the Banjul Charter in Articles 3(g) and 4(g) respectively. The experience of the EC proves that economic law can have a human rights dimension, see, e.g., Case 11/70 *Internationale Handelsgesellschaft GmbH* [1970] ECR 1125, and further, Article 6 of the Treaty on European Union.
384. On the jurisdiction of the AEC Court of Justice, see Articles 18–20, 87 AEC Treaty, and *infra*, pp. 245–7, and on that of the ECOWAS Court, see Articles 9 and 10 of the Protocol on the ECOWAS Court of Justice, 8 *RADIC* (1996) 228.
385. Note that Article 87(2) AEC Treaty, which appears to enshrine the principle of exclusivity of competence, states that the 'decisions of the Court of Justice shall be final and shall not be subject to appeal'. It should also be observed that Article 22(1) of the Protocol on the ECOWAS Community Court of Justice states that, 'No dispute regarding interpretation or application of the provisions of the Treaty may be referred to any other form of settlement except that which is provided for by the Treaty or this Protocol', an apparent reference to the Arbitration Tribunal established under Article 16 of the Revised ECOWAS Treaty. Article 2 of said Protocol describes the Court as 'the principal legal organ of the Community'.
386. The Banjul Charter does not elucidate whether the Commission's interpretations under this provision are to be considered binding. It is submitted that the interpretations are not binding but may be considered persuasive, performing a function similar to advisory opinions.
387. Note Article 28 of the Nouakchott Protocol and see *supra*, p. 156.
388. *Wemhoff* v. *Germany* Series A, Vol. 7 (1968) p. 23; Harris, O'Boyle and Warbrick, note 18 *supra*, pp. 6–9; Article 29 ACHR; *Compulsory Membership in an Association Prescribed by Law for the Practice of Journalism* 7 *HRLJ* (1986) 153; *'Other Treaties' Subject to the Consultative Jurisdiction of the Court* 3 *HRLJ* (1982) 140; Davidson,

note 371 *supra*, pp. 129–42. On the election of the judges, see folios 271, 272 *supra*.

389. See Judge Lauterpacht's Separate Opinion in the *Norwegian Loans Case* ICJ Reports 1957, p. 9 at p. 34.

390. It should be observed that the issue of preliminary objections in the American and European systems is regulated by the respective Rules of the Courts. Article 31 of the Rules of Procedure of the IACHR; and Rule of Court 55 of the European Court of Human Rights, 38 *ILM* 208 (1999); Harris, O'Boyle and Warbrick, note 18 *supra*, pp. 674–78.

391. Cf. Article 61(1) ACHR, as reinforced by the Court's judgment in *Government of Costa Rica (In the Matter of Viviana Gallardo)* 2 *HRLJ* (1981) 328; Davidson, note 371 *supra*, pp. 64–9.

392. Cf. Article 62 Statute of the ICJ and Article 36 ECHR.

393. In the *Wimbledon Case* PCIJ, Ser. A, No. 1 (1923), p. 12, the Permanent Court of International Justice required that 'the existence of this interest must be sufficiently demonstrated'. The burden of proof appears to be high, see S. Rosenne, *Intervention in the International Court of Justice* (1993) Chapter 7; C. Chinkin, *Third States in International Law* (1993) pp. 147–217.

394. See Harris, O'Boyle and Warbrick, note 18 *supra*, pp. 668–71. Note that Rule 61(3) of the European Court of Human Rights and Article 36(2) ECHR require the intervention to be in the interest of the proper administration of justice.

395. It is interesting to observe that, according to the previous draft, applicants needed to demonstate 'exceptional grounds'. Cf. Article 34 ECHR.

396. 9 *RADIC* (1997) 427.

397. The Court might choose to report such an occurrence to the OAU under Article 31 of the Nouakchott Protocol, see further, pp. 156 *supra*. Such a question could be addressed in the Rules of Procedure. Cf. Rule 64 of the European Court of Human Rights; Article 25(1) of the Rules of Procedure of the IACHR (Annual Report of the Inter-American Court of Human Rights 1991, OAS/Ser.L/V/III.25,Doc. 7, Appendix II) whereby the Court must, *proprio motu*, take whatever measures are necessary to complete consideration of the case; see also Davidson, note 371 *supra*, p. 55.

398. The potential for duplication again arises since, as has been observed, the Commission has the power of interpretation under Article 45(3) which has been described by an eminent author as amounting to authorisation 'to issue what are in effect advisory opinions', A.H. Robertson and J.G. Merrills, *Human Rights in the World* (3rd edn 1992) p. 221.

399. See Davidson, note 371 *supra*, Chapter 5; T. Buergenthal, 'The advisory practice of the Inter-American Human Rights Court', 79 *AJIL* (1985) 1. The IACHR has established that it has a wide advisory jurisdiction 'with regard to any provision dealing with the protection of human rights set forth in any international treaty applicable in the American States, regardless of whether it be bilateral or multilateral, whatever be the principal purpose of such a treaty, and whether or not non-Member States of the inter-American systems are or have a right to become parties thereto', *Interpretation of the Meaning of 'Other Treaties' in Article 64 of the American Convention* 3 *HRLJ* (1982) 140, paras. 34–8; Davidson, *supra*, pp 112–18.

400. Cf. Article 64(2) ACHR, and see *Proposed amendments to the naturalization provisions of the Constitution of Costa Rica* 5 *HRLJ* (1984) 161.

401. *Restrictions to the Death Penalty Case* 4 *HRLJ* (1983) 339; *International Responsibility for the Promulgation and Enforcement of Laws in Violation of the Convention* 16 *HRLJ* (1995) 9; Davidson, note 371 *supra*, pp. 106–12.

402. Cf. Article 66 ACHR and Article 49(2) ECHR. See also Article 28(7) of the Nouakchott Protocol in relation to the Court's judgments, p. 156 *supra*.

403. See *supra* pp. 144–6
404. Note Rule 118(2) which enables the Commission to reconsider a communication adjudged inadmissible. See also the settled practice of the IACHR, and *Godinez Cruz* v. *Honduras* (Preliminary Objections) Series C, No. 3.
405. 9 *RADIC* (1997) pp. 429, 430. Cf. Article 48(1)(f) ACHR. However, by virtue of Article 38(1)(b) of the Eleventh Protocol ECHR, the European Court must place itself at the disposal of the parties with a view to a friendly settlment. See also Rule 62.
406. Article 40(1) ECHR and Rule 33(2) state that hearings must be in public except 'in exceptional circumstances'. The protection of children's interests led the Court to place restrictions on public hearings in the cases of *O, H, W, B and R* v. *United Kingdom* (1987) Series A, Nos. 120 and 121. Some guidance at to when the Court's discretion may be exercised could be derived from the situations described in Article 6(1) ECHR, see Harris, O'Boyle and Warbrick, note 18 *supra*, pp. 218–21.
407. Cf. Articles 21 and 22 of the Rules of Procedure of the IACHR and Rule of Procedure 36(4) of the European Court of Human Rights which imposes certain conditions on the choice of legal representative; see Harris, O'Boyle and Warbrick, note 18 *supra*, p. 664.
408. Note Article 27(1) of the Nouakchott Protocol, discussed further at p. 155 *supra*, which allows the Court to order the payment of compensation, which may include the reimbursement of legal costs. Cf. Article 41 ECHR, and see Harris, O'Boyle and Warbrick, note 18 *supra*, pp. 687, 688. Legal aid before the Strasbourg organs is also available, Rules 91–6 of the European Court of Human Rights; Harris, O'Boyle and Warbrick, *supra*, pp. 664, 665.
409. Ankumah, note 19 *supra*, pp. 32, 33.
410. Supplemented by Article 24 of the Rules of Procedure of the IACHR, and see, e.g., *Colotenango* v. *Guatemala* (Provisional Measures), Resolution of the Court of 22 June 1994, Annual Report of the Inter-American Court of Human Rights 1994, OAS/Ser.L/III.31, Doc. 9, Appendix V; Davidson, note 371 *supra*, pp. 49–51.
411. See further, pp. 155–6 *supra*. Cf. Article 23 of the Rules of Procedure of the IACHR which requires States parties to a case to co-operate in order to ensure that all measures addressed to persons subject to their jurisdiction are executed, and Article 24 on Interim Measures. A commitment on the part of African governments to the fundamental principles of representative democracy, legality and the rule of law, sadly absent in many instances, would no doubt help. It is interesting to note that the IACHR has emphasized the importance of these fundamental principles, *Compulsory Membership in an Association Prescribed by Law for the Practice of Journalism* 7 *HRLJ* (1986) 153; *Restrictions of the Rights and Freedoms of the American Convention – The Word 'Laws' in Article 30* 7 *HRLJ* (1986) 231; *Habeas Corpus in Emergency Situations* 9 *HRLJ* (1988) 204; Davidson, note 371 *supra*, pp. 173–6.
412. *Barcelona Traction Case* (Second Phase) ICJ Reports 1970, 3 at p. 32; Brownlie, *Principles of Public International Law*, p. 513.
413. Cf. Article 52(1) ACHR. By contrast, the European Court of Human Rights consists of a number of judges equal to that of States parties, Article 20 ECHR, currently 40.
414. Cf. Article 34 of the Banjul Charter which stipulates that members of the Commission 'must have the nationality of one of the States Parties to the present Charter'.
415. Article 12(1), which stipulates that each State may propose up to three candidates, at least two of whom must be nationals of that State.
416. Article 11(2). Cf. Article 52(2) ACHR.

417. See also Article 16 on the oath of office.
418. Vienna Convention on Diplomatic Relations 1961; General Convention on the Privileges and Immunities of the OAU 1965. Cf. Article 59 ECHR and Article 70(1) ACHR.
419. Article 21(2). The President serves a term of office of two years and may be re-elected once, Article 21(1).
420. Article 15(4).
421. Article 18. Cf. Article 21(3) ECHR and Article 16 Statute of the ICJ which is much stricter.
422. Cf. Article 21(1) ECHR, Article 52(1) ACHR, Article 2 of the Statute of the ICJ, Article 223(1) (ex Art 167(1)) EC Treaty.
423. Article 12(2).
424. Article 14(1). It seems a two-thirds majority is required, see Article 10(2) OAU Charter and Rule 25 of the Assembly. An express requirement to this effect in Article 13(1) of the Cape Town draft was deleted from the final text.
425. Article 14(3).
426. Cf. Article 9 Statute of the ICJ.
427. Article 15(1). At the end of two years following the first election, the terms of office must expire after two years and the terms of four more judges must expire at the end of four years. Cf. Article 54(1) ACHR.
428. Article 19(1). Cf. Article 24 ECHR.
429. Article 19(2). Cf. Article 20(2) Statute of the IACHR.
430. Cf. Article 27 ECHR; Article 26 Statute of the ICJ.
431. This seems to be contrary to accepted international practice, see Article 31(1) Statute of the ICJ, Article 55(1) ACHR, Rules 28, 29 of the European Court of Human Rights.
432. The IACHR has adopted this approach, see, e.g., *International Responsibility for the Promulgation and Enforcement of Laws in Violation of the Convention* 16 *HRLJ* (1995) 9.
433. Cf. Article 63(1) ACHR. The European Court of Human Rights enjoys a large measure of discretion under Article 41 ECHR.
434. Article 24(2) of the draft Protocol adopted at Cape Town clearly envisaged this possibility since it read that fair compensation or reparation was 'to be paid or *made* to the injured party'. It is interesting to note that despite the wording of Article 63(1) ACHR, in the case of *Aloeboetoe* v. *Suriname* (*Reparations*) 14 *HRLJ* (1993) 425, the IACHR awarded non-pecuniary damages and ordered the re-opening of a school and medical dispensary in a village.
435. Cf. Article 63(2) ACHR and Rule 39 of the European Court of Human Rights.
436. Ibid., and see *Colotenango* v. *Guatemala* 2 *IHRR* (1995) 414.
437. Article 28(2). Cf. Article 44 ECHR, and Articles 66(1) and 67 ACHR.
438. Article 28(6), (7). Cf. Article 45 ECHR and Article 67(2) ACHR.
439. Article 30. Cf. Article 46(1) ECHR and Article 68(1) ACHR.
440. Cf. Article 46(2) ECHR and Article 65 ACHR. See further, Harris, O'Boyle and Warbrick, note 18 *supra*, pp. 700–5.
441. Cf. Article 41 ECHR and see Harris, O'Boyle and Warbrick, note 18 *supra*, pp. 682–6.

5

Protection of the Environment

Protection of the environment and management of environmental problems are increasingly coming under the auspices of international law.[1] This is not surprising given that major environmental crises of recent times, be it the nuclear disaster at Chernobyl, oil spillages at sea, or human activities contributing to the concentration of greenhouse gases in the atmosphere, with ensuing consequences on global warming, climate change and rising sea levels, have emphasized the transnational nature of their effect. Collective efforts to deal with such problems are therefore necessary.

International environmental law is a relatively recent phenomenon which had its inception in 1972 when the international community expressed its concern to protect the environment in the so-called Stockholm Declaration.[2] In 1992 the UN Conference on Environment and Development, the so-called Rio or Earth Summit, met to develop international environmental law into the next millennium.[3] These initiatives brought forth a number of multilateral treaties protecting the environment.[4] However, the developing world poses its own set of problems and Africa has been particularly susceptible to environmental degradation in recent years, accentuating a malaise of mismanagement. The causes are various: drought,[5] deteriorating water resources,[6] the spoliation of natural resources,[7] deforestation,[8] overgrazing and overcropping,[9] and desertification.[10] In addition, in recent years Africa, along with other developing countries, has had to contend with the growing practice by Western companies in particular of the dumping, often illicit, of toxic and dangerous substances, with all the risks that that implies for the health, life and well-being of local populations, as well as the detrimental effect on the ecosystem. The focus of this chapter is on the African response to this latter problem.

The Trade in Toxic Wastes

During the 1970s public opinion in industrialized countries demanded greater regulation of toxic wastes. Difficulties relating to the disposal of hazardous and toxic wastes in these countries became acute during the 1980s as municipal legislation regulating their treatment became stricter and as costs thereby increased. The search for less exacting domestic legal standards and cheaper costs led to increased transportation of wastes across frontiers, to be stored or dumped in developing countries.[11] By 1989, approximately 20% of the hazardous waste generated in and exported from industrialized countries was being shipped to developing countries, some 50 million tons to Africa,[12] because 'high levels of foreign debt coupled with the worldwide collapse in commodity prices made the import of hazardous waste an attractive proposal for many cash starved countries of the Third World'.[13] Environmental deterioration is consequently intrinsically linked with poverty.[14] It would seem that the volume of transboundary movements of waste from industrialized countries to developing countries continues to increase, however. The concept of trading global environmental pollution rights has been accepted as policy by the industrialized countries; waste should be dumped in the Third World.[15] And because Third World countries often lack the necessary means to treat waste even legal waste constitutes a significant threat to the environment.[16]

The international traffic and illicit dumping of toxic and hazardous wastes in developing countries represent an increasing environmental problem with a human rights dimension. Toxic waste endangers the lives, health and environmental quality of life of people. Its poor disposal results in the destruction of wildlife, leading to imbalance in the ecosystem, and the deterioration of food and water supplies and the health of the communities in which the waste is improperly disposed. Environmental degradation can lead to population displacement and migration.[17]

Dangerous and illegal disposal of wastes have come to light in several developing countries in recent years.[18] The former include recycling or recovery operations, such as the installation of incineration and lead recycling plants or the export of pollutant industries and technologies. Illicit traffic gives rise to problems of detection, since it can assume various forms beyond the capacity of the authorities to determine the exact nature of these products and it is reported that traffickers often resort to corrupt practices using front companies and even development projects as cover for what are, often, criminal activities.[19]

Africa has been one of the principal victims of the illicit movement and dumping of toxic and hazardous substances. A couple of notorious incidents in the late 1980s concerning contracts between transnational corporations and African States, whereby some countries received payment in return for the use of land for the dumping and burial of toxic waste, finally prompted reaction.[20] The Council of Ministers of the OAU thus declared that the dumping of nuclear and industrial wastes was 'a crime against Africa and the African people'.[21] The UN General Assembly also condemned the dumping of such wastes in Africa in resolution 43/75 (1988). Increased generation of hazardous waste and growing public awareness of its effects accordingly resulted in international action regulating the treatment of waste.

Basel Convention

The Basel Convention on the Control of Transboundary Movements of Hazardous Wastes and their Disposal was adopted in March 1989 under the auspices of UNEP.[22] It is the only global legal instrument dealing exclusively with the management of waste. According to the UN Special Rapporteur, the main objectives of the Convention are to 'reduce transboundary movements of hazardous and other wastes to the minimum consistent with their environmentally sound management; to treat and dispose of hazardous and other wastes as close as possible to the source of generation in an environmentally sound manner; and to minimize the generation of hazardous and other wastes in terms of both quantity and potential hazard'. The essential features of the regulatory system of the Convention are prior informed consent, the prohibition on export to a non-contracting party, the obligation to re-import, and the responsibility of States involved in transboundary movements.[23] The Convention therefore represents progress in the assumption of responsibility for this problematic issue by the international community.[24] The Convention as finally adopted was, however, a compromise between advocates of a complete ban on transboundary movements of wastes, mainly developing countries, which, often lacking the means to manage and dispose properly of such wastes, argued that regulation was no guarantee against environmental degradation, and those that wanted to define the legal framework and conditions for the international transfer of wastes, leading to their proper disposal.[25] As such the end result was a disappointment for the former which considered the Convention inadequate as institutionalizing dangerous practices and hence prompted, as will be seen below, further action.[26]

The Convention recognizes in preambular paragraph 6, and in Article 4(1), that every 'State has the sovereign right to ban the entry or disposal of foreign hazardous wastes and other wastes in its territory'. Consequently, no State party may permit hazardous wastes to be exported to a party that has prohibited their import.[27] Significantly, at the insistence of the OAU, parties must prevent the export of hazardous or other wastes to a State party or group of States parties, especially developing countries, belonging to an economic and/or political integration organization, the legislation of which prohibits such imports.[28] Nevertheless, Basel ultimately opted for a partial ban on the transboundary movement of wastes.

Article 9(1) of the Convention deems to be 'illegal traffic' any transboundary movement of hazardous or other wastes

(a)   without notification pursuant to the provisions of this Convention to all States concerned; or

(b)   without the consent pursuant to the provisions of this Convention of a State concerned; or

(c)   with consent obtained from States concerned through falsification, misrepresentation or fraud; or

(d)   that does not conform in a material way with the documents; or

(e)   that results in deliberate disposal (e.g. dumping) of hazardous wastes or other wastes in contravention of this Convention and of general principles of international law.[29]

'[I]llegal traffic in hazardous wastes or other wastes is criminal' according to Article 4(3)[30] and, under Article 9(5), each party is required to 'introduce appropriate national/domestic legislation to prevent and punish illegal traffic'.[31] Furthermore, Article 9(2) provides that when the illegal traffic is 'the result of conduct on the part of the exporter or generator', the State of export 'shall ensure that the wastes in question are: (a) taken back by the exporter or generator or, if necessary, by itself into the State of export, or, if impracticable, (b) are otherwise disposed of in accordance with the provisions of this Convention, within 30 days from the time the State of export has been informed about the illegal traffic or such other period of time as States concerned may agree'.[32]

The Convention required that Parties prevent the import of hazardous and other wastes where they had reason to believe that such wastes would not be managed in an environmentally sound manner.[33] However, the States parties recognized that the transboundary movement of hazardous wastes to developing countries might not constitute an environmentally sound management of those wastes. Exports of wastes deemed harmful by developing countries were still legal in some circumstances. The technological know-how and infrastructure to manage, store and dispose of such wastes was, and still is, generally lacking.[34] Furthermore, according to the UN Special Rapporteur, traffickers in waste, through fraudulent documentation, reclassification of wastes and corruption, are able to export dangerous wastes in the form of material intended for recycling, in violation of the laws of the exporting and importing countries.[35] As a result, the decision was taken to amend the Convention, as from 1997, in order to prohibit the export of hazardous wastes, even for recycling purposes, from OECD member countries to non-member countries,[36] thereby specifically addressing the criticisms of developing countries. The ban on the export of hazardous products to African and other developing countries should in theory eliminate, or at least decrease, the traffic and dumping of toxic wastes in those countries. Whether the OAU would have enacted a regional regime had this stricter regime been originally in place is a matter for speculation.

Bamako Convention

The Bamako Convention on the Ban of the Import of Hazardous Wastes into Africa and on the Control of their Transboundary Movements within Africa was adopted by the OAU at Bamako, Mali, in January 1991 and entered into force on 22 April 1998.[37] Such a step was considered necessary because of the perceived inadequacies of the Basel Convention in relation to developing countries, in particular the absence at that time of a total ban on the export of hazardous and other wastes to African and other developing countries.[38] The Bamako Convention complements the Basel Convention which permits the establishment of regional agreements equal to or more stringent than itself.[39]

The Bamako Convention has adopted a broader definition of waste than the Basel Convention.[40] Wastes are considered hazardous according to Article 2(1) when they are: (a) listed in the Convention's annexes; (b) defined as hazardous by the domestic legislation of a State of export, import or transit; and (c) banned, cancelled or refused registration by a State, or voluntarily withdrawn from registration in the country of manufacture for human health or environmental reasons. Whereas the Basel Convention excludes radioactive wastes,[41] 'wastes which, as a result of being radioactive, are subject to any international control systems, including international instruments, applying specifically to radioactive materials', are included, by virtue of Article 2(2), in the scope of the Bamako Convention. It additionally provides that the 'issue of the transfer to Africa of polluting technologies shall be kept under systematic review by the Secretariat of the Conference and periodic reports made to the Conference of the Parties.'[42]

The Convention distinguishes between waste generated outside of Africa and waste generated within Africa. With regard to the former, Parties to the Convention, 'aware of the risk of damage to human health and the environment caused by transboundary movements of hazardous wastes' and 'further recognizing the sovereignty of States to ban the importation into, and the transit through, their territory, of hazardous wastes and substances for human health and environmental reasons', hence agree to introduce: (a) a hazardous waste import ban; consequently, in accordance with Article 4(1), 'All Parties shall take appropriate legal, administrative and other measures within the area under their jurisdiction to prohibit the import of all hazardous wastes, for any reason, into Africa from non-Contracting Parties. Such import shall be deemed illegal and a criminal act'; and (b) a ban on dumping of hazardous wastes at sea, internal waters and waterways;[43] accordingly, under Article 4(2)(a), States parties are to 'adopt legal, administrative and other appropriate measures to control all carriers from non-Parties, and prohibit the dumping at sea of hazardous wastes'.[44] It should be observed that the ban on hazardous wastes is reinforced by the Fourth Lomé Convention 1989,[45] according to which the EC agrees to prohibit exports of such wastes to African States parties, and Article 59 of the AEC Treaty.

With regard to the production of wastes in Africa, the Convention places emphasis on the environmentally sound and efficient management of hazardous wastes, including the prohibition on exports to States where this cannot be guaranteed.[46] It provides that each Party is to, *inter alia*, 'impose strict, unlimited liability as well as joint and several liability on hazardous wastes generators',[47] seemingly as a means of encouraging the appropriate disposal of hazardous wastes.[48] The onus is on the generator because he or she is assumed to exercise effective responsibility over, and to insure, shipments.[49] In the present state of international environmental law it is probably safe to assert that the Bamako Convention imposes more stringent obligations,[50] but the advantages for the States parties appear obvious. Strict liability can displace the burden of proof onto the defendant and does not require fault. Furthermore, it 'relieves the African courts of the obligation to set standards of reasonable care, and relieves plaintiffs of the difficult task of proving the breach of these standards ... [and] has the advantages of simplifying the plaintiff's choice of defendant and establishing a clear line of responsibility'.[51] Unlimited liability sets no ceiling on the imposition of damages while joint and several liability gives the plaintiff a choice of whom to sue.[52]

The Convention additionally requires each Party to 'strive to adopt and implement the preventive, precautionary approach to pollution problems'.[53] This approach demonstrates the seriousness with which the OAU views the issue and its reluctance to become a hostage to scientific proof.[54] It should be noted further that the parties are required to apply clean production methods,[55] i.e., production or industrial systems which avoid or eliminate the generation of hazardous wastes.[56]

The Convention establishes under Article 6 a system of prior informed consent and notification procedures for proposed transboundary movement of hazardous wastes.[57] The State of export may not allow the transboundary movement until it has received written consent by the State of import and written confirmation of the existence of a contract between the exporter and the disposer specifying environmentally sound management of the wastes in question.

Article 8 imposes a duty to re-import. Where a legitimate transboundary movement of hazardous wastes cannot be completed in accordance with the terms of the contract, the State of export must ensure the re-import of the wastes by the exporter, if alternative arrangements cannot be made for their disposal in an environmentally sound manner within ninety days from the time the exporting State and the Secretariat have been informed by the importing State. The State of export and any State of transit must not oppose, hinder or prevent the return of the wastes to the State of export.[58]

The issue of illegal waste is treated by Article 9. Thus, any transboundary movement of hazardous wastes:

(a)   if carried out without notification, pursuant to the provisions of this Convention, to all States concerned; or

(b)   if carried out without the consent, pursuant to the provisions of this Convention, of a State concerned; or

(c)   if consent is obtained from States concerned through falsification, misrepresentation or fraud; or

(d)   if it does not conform in a material way with the documents; or

(e)   if it results in deliberate disposal of hazardous wastes in contravention of this Convention and of general principles of international law

is deemed to be illegal.

In addition to the imposition of liability under Article 4(3)(b), Article 9(2) requires States parties to legislate in order to allow criminal penalties, which must be sufficiently severe to punish and deter, to be imposed on illegal traffickers.[59]

If a movement is held to be illegal traffic as a result of conduct on the part of the exporter or generator, the State of export must ensure that the waste is taken back by the exporter or generator or State of export within thirty days. The return of the wastes to the State of export must not be opposed, hindered or otherwise prevented.[60] Furthermore, if a movement is deemed to be illegal traffic as a result of conduct by the importer or disposer, the State of import must ensure that the wastes are returned to the exporter by the importer.[61] It is not clear how such States are to be compelled to act in such manner but recourse could be had to the settlement of disputes procedure under the Convention.[62]

Although the Bamako Convention mirrors the Basel Convention in many respects it is significantly stricter in others. Of note are the wider scope of the Bamako Convention, the total ban on the importation of waste from outside Africa, and the adoption of the precautionary principle and the requirement to use clean production methods. Given Africa's background as a dumping ground for hazardous wastes and the lack of knowhow on the part of African States, it is understandable why the OAU should have adopted a more restrictive approach.[63] However, notable omissions include the 'polluter pays' principle and means of reinstatement of the environment.[64] The question also arises whether stringency may prove counterproductive. The inclusion of radioactive waste may prove problematic with commitments undertaken in other treaties.[65] The total ban on imported waste may hamper the development of African industry.[66] Nevertheless, it has been observed that the international community is falling in with this absolute standard. And the adoption of clean production methods may simply be beyond the capabilities of most African States at present.[67] Despite the acute nature of the problem and the profound feelings of the OAU on the subject, the Bamako Convention could prove too complex and too expensive for the majority of African States.

The Environment and Human Rights

In recent years an important question that is increasingly asked is whether international law has evolved to the extent that it is possible to assert a *right to* the environment. Does a legal obligation exist as a basis on which to affirm the right to a healthy environment as a fundamental human right? This issue deserves some attention here because of the African contribution to this debate.

One of the initial difficulties to be overcome is that of legal classification.[68] Is it possible to claim a 'right to a healthy environment' in isolation, or is it a right derived from other rights whose realization would be affected by an environment unfavourable to their implementation? How can such rights, if they exist, be enforced? Are they to be realized over a period of time or are they merely statements of desirable intent? The illicit traffic in toxic and hazardous wastes undeniably has adverse effects on the enjoyment of human rights. One has only to consider the effect of pollutants on health. It should be observed that in the Vienna Declaration and Programme of Action 1993 the international community recognized 'that the illicit dumping of toxic and dangerous substances and wastes potentially constitutes a serious threat to the human rights to life and health of everyone'. Accordingly, it called upon all States to adopt and implement rigourously existing treaties relating to the dumping of toxic and hazardous wastes and to co-operate in the prevention of illicit dumping.[69]

The right to the environment is expressly reflected in a couple of international, albeit regional, instruments, though it must be accepted that the definition of this right is uncertain.[70] Article 24 of the Banjul Charter states, 'All peoples shall have the right to a general satisfactory environment favourable to their development'.[71] The special significance of this provision is the fact that this was the first time that a satisfactory environment was asserted as a right in a legally binding instrument.[72] The 1988 Additional Protocol on Economic, Social and Cultural Rights to the ACHR (Protocol of San Salvador) contains a clause to a similar effect.[73] Article 11 thereof provides, *inter alia*, that everyone is to have the right to live in a healthy environment, and States parties are obliged to promote the protection, preservation and improvement of the environment. Article 174 (ex Art. 130r) of the EC Treaty commits the EC to a high level of protection and provides, *inter alia*, that Community policy on the environment is to contribute to pursuit of the following objectives: preserving, protecting and improving the quality of the environment; protecting human health; prudent use and rational utilization of natural resources; and promoting measures at international level to deal with regional or global environmental problems.[74] And most recently, Article 1 of the Convention on Access to Information, Public Participation in Decision-Making and Access to Justice in Environmental Matters 1998 enshrines the 'right of every person of present and future generations to live in an environment adequate to his or her health and well-being'.[75]

The effect of recommendations should not be overlooked. In this context, the Stockholm Declaration, the Rio Declaration on Environment and Development and Agenda 21 are significant developments. These documents are aspirational and have set down principles for present and future action rather than legal obligations, although they have engendered an expectation of compliance. While not binding *qua* treaties they could be classified as soft law[76] and may also reflect or have generated rules of customary international law.[77]

It is also instructive to refer to national constitutions which devote provisions to the environment, as well as other laws protecting the environment, since municipal law can be a constitutive element in the formation of customary international law.[78] Perhaps one third of the international community has adopted constitutional or other laws relating to the environment.[79] However, caution is necessary since the content and scope of such laws differ from State to State. Some expressly provide for the State's duty to protect and preserve the environment, e.g., Bahrain, Greece, The Netherlands, Sri Lanka. Some additionally assign that responsibility to citizens, e.g., Bolivia, India, Turkey. Some make provision for an enforceable right and a remedy, Burkina Faso, Chile, Congo, South Africa, whereas others simply make the protection of the environment an objective of State policy, Namibia. And others make pollution of the environment subject to the criminal law, Costa Rica, Croatia, Egypt, Spain, United Kingdom. In relation to Africa, the Constitutions of Benin (Articles 27–9), Burkina Faso (Articles 29, 30), Cape Verde (Articles 7(j), 70), Congo (Articles 46–8), Ethiopia (Article 44), Ghana (Article 36(9)), Guinea (Article 19), Lesotho (Articles 27(1)(b), 36), Madagascar (Articles 37, 39), Malawi (Article 13(d)), Mali (Article 15), Mozambique (Article 37), Namibia (Article 95(l)), Niger (Article 28), São Tomé e Príncipe (Article 10(c), 48), the Seychelles (Articles 38, 40(e)), the Republic of South Africa (Section 24), Tanzania (Section 27(1)), Togo (Article 41), and Uganda (Article 39) all make reference to the protection of the environment to a greater or lesser extent.[80] It should be noted that many allow for enforcement of rights. Reference will be made below to African national legislation relating to the environment.

Municipal jurisprudence is also of relevance. Thus attention can be drawn to various jurisdictions where the right to a healthy environment has been held to be a fundamental human right.[81]

It may also be possible to approach this issue from a different perspective and draw attention to the fact that wilful and severe damage to the environment constitutes an international crime.[82]

In light of the above it does not seem an exaggeration to assert that the right to a healthy environment has become part of international law, or at least *de lege ferenda*.[83] However, if this conclusion appears too bold it is nevertheless possible to establish a firm link between the environment and rights enshrined in international human rights instruments, including the Banjul Charter.[84] These rights, which have a multidimensional aspect, imply duties and responsibilities on the part of individuals, groups, States, international organizations and transnational corporations to protect and preserve the environment and to uphold environmental rights for present and future generations.[85] The brief survey that follows is not, however, meant to be exhaustive.

Fundamental rights affected by environmental degradation, many of which are collective or economic and social rights, but which extend to civil and political rights, include the right to life and the right to health, which encompass the right to be free of environmental conditions that endanger life and the duty of a State to protect potential victims from life-threatening environmental disasters that could occur under its jurisdiction.[86] The right to health includes the right to live and work in an environment that does not pose a threat to human health.[87] A decent environment is a prerequisite for a healthy life.

The rights of peoples to self-determination and to permanent sovereignty over their natural wealth and resources cannot be fully realized when a country's resources are spoliated and exploited, often as a result of political or economic subjection or dependence.[88] Such a state of affairs, often accompanied by intensive exploitation of raw materials that upsets the ecological balance, wastage of non-renewable energy sources, establishment of polluting and high-risk industries, has adverse consequences for the environment and produces few economic benefits. Denial of the rights of peoples to self-determination and to their natural wealth and resources has been and remains one of the root causes of underdevelopment and of serious damage inflicted on the environment in former colonies and countries still under occupation. The right to development, which encompasses the right of peoples to self-determination and to full sovereignty over all their natural wealth and resources, is thus also compromised.[89]

Others include the right to housing, which incorporates the right to housing in environmentally sound conditions;[90] the right to food, which includes the right to ecologically clean foodstuffs and consumer goods;[91] the right to information, which includes the right to environmental information;[92] the right to participate which includes the right to participate in decisions that affect the environment;[93] the freedom of expression, opinion, assembly and association which includes the right to hold and express opinions and information regarding the environment, and the right to mobilize action against ecological risks; and the right to effective remedies, including remedies for environmental harm.[94]

It can be seen from the above survey, albeit brief, that there is undeniably a close connection between assaults on the environment and the enjoyment of human rights. Damage to the environment has adverse consequences on the recognition, enjoyment and realization of fundamental rights.

Implementation and Enforcement

International and national regulation of transboundary movements of hazardous wastes would be ineffective in the absence of efficient control and implementation mechanisms. Both the Basel and Bamako Conventions make provision for monitoring mechanisms, including systems for the transmission of information by States parties.[95] In addition, the Bamako Convention creates a 'Dumpwatch',[96] the role of which is undefined but it might be an early-warning system or roving inspectorate. As has been seen, both Conventions make provision for dispute settlement through third-party adjudication. Furthermore, provision is made for the imposition of sanctions under the criminal law.

Nevertheless, the creation of appropriate legal frameworks at the national, regional and international levels for the effective implementation of a right to the environment, in this context sometimes referred to as ecological rights, remains haphazard.[97] At the present stage of development, the primary responsibility for the enforcement of international environmental law still lies with national governments. Indeed, this is reflected in the Rio Declaration on Environment and Development.[98] Strict legislation to control transboundary movements of transboundary waste must be encouraged, especially in developing countries. UNEP is seeking to provide specialist legal assistance with a view to drafting national legislation and training law officers and the judiciary. The UN Special Rapporteur has warned that while disparities in municipal legal standards continue to exist between developed and developing States there will be an incentive for traffickers to seek outlets with weaker environmental standards. And as has been seen above, the right to the environment has a procedural component so that Principle 10 of the Rio Declaration on Environment and Development proclaims, *inter alia*, that, 'Effective access to judicial and administrative proceedings, including redress and remedy, shall be provided'. In addition, it has been observed that the Basel and Bamako Conventions make the illicit traffic in toxic substances a criminal offence. States should therefore continue to develop their criminal legislation, and introduce civil and penal sanctions in order to prosecute and punish illicit traffic. Greater provision should be made for the civil and criminal liability of bodies corporate.

It has already been stated above that many African States make provision for the enforcement of fundamental rights and additionally allow for a right to indemnity. Burkina Faso (Article 30) and the Congo (Article 48) have specific constitutional provisions authorizing litigation against environmental harm and a right to compensation resulting from pollution. Furthermore, Benin (Article 28), the Congo (Article 47) and Niger (Article 28) have constitutional provisions seeking to regulate toxic wastes and the latter two States even make the illicit traffic in toxic wastes a crime (Articles 48 and 28 respectively). A number of African States have enacted legislation to similar ends, e.g., the Gambia,[99] Nigeria,[100] the Seychelles,[101] Sudan,[102] Zambia[103] and Tunisia.[104] In Cameroon, the drastic step has been taken of making the traffic in dangerous wastes punishable by death.[105] In South Africa law reform to close existing loopholes and to promote more effective policing of environmental measures have been identified as priorities.[106] Ethiopia is also giving this matter attention.[107]

Conclusion

The response of the international community to the problems posed by environmental degradation has encouraged the adoption at the national, regional and global level of measures, albeit gradual and fragmentary, which have made it possible to develop a set of standards and principles, and rights derived therefrom, with the aim of protecting the environment. The Basel and Bamako Conventions constitute progress in the struggle against the adverse effects of the illicit movement and dumping of toxic and hazardous wastes and products.

A clear link between the preservation of the environment and the promotion of human rights appears to have been established. It seems possible to assert that ecological rights have been conferred on holders of rights. A right to the environment is still evolving, and many issues regarding rights, duties and responsibilities remain to be clarified, but its essence, the right to a satisfactory environment, is recognized and can be effectively implemented under existing international and human rights law. The right to the environment includes a right of prevention of ecological risks, and in this context the Basel and Bamako Conventions have relevance. However, as has been seen, these Conventions are essentially limited to the sound management of wastes and do not expressly address violations of human rights associated with the illicit transport and dumping of toxic wastes. They are not in themselves enough to guarantee a healthy environment therefore. And it must be borne in mind that both Conventions are inoperative unless the wastes cross international frontiers.

Nevertheless, much still remains to be done and international co-operation, including the provision of financial and technical aid to Africa, seems vital. The movement of hazardous wastes from developed countries to the developing world shows little sign of abating. Traffickers seem to be able to adapt to the changing international situation and evade controls through fraud and corruption. The effect that the entry into force of the Bamako Convention will have remains to be seen. However, the ban on hazardous wastes will not prove effective unless accompanied by practical measures for the detection of illicit practices.[108] The technical capacities of developing countries to detect, monitor and prevent such traffic must therefore be strengthened, which will necessitate the transfer of technology. Accurate information is necessary if African countries are adequately to confront the illegal traffic in waste. Furthermore, strict national legislation to control transboundary movements of waste, in addition to legislation providing for stiff penal sanctions, must be enacted and enforced, including within the jurisdiction of the transgressor's country of origin. The criminal responsibility of legal persons, in addition to civil liability, should be recognized. The standing of NGOs to seek judicial relief should be extended.[109] Reduction in waste generation must continue to be encouraged. But in addition to such developments, African States should be assisted with the means of cleaning and remedying existing contamination and measures must be put in place to deal with pollution. Application of the 'polluter pays' principle should generate resources to facilitate in the implementation of such measures. Ultimately, however, the enforcement of existing, and any future, obligations seems dependent on political will.[110]

Notes

1. See the International Law Commission's Commentary on the Draft Articles on the International Responsibility of States, *Yearbook of the International Law Commission*, 1980, Vol. II, Part 2, p. 39, para. 14. In *Legality of the Threat or Use of Nuclear Weapons* ICJ Reports 1996, p. 226 at pp. 241, 242, para. 29, the ICJ stated that, 'The existence of the general obligation of States to ensure that activities within their jurisdiction and control respect the environment of other States or of areas beyond national control is now part of the corpus of international law relating to the environment'. See further Judge Weeramantry (Dissenting Opinion) p. 17. See also *Request for an Examination of the Situation in Accordance with Paragraph 63 of the Nuclear Test Case 1974* ICJ Reports 1995, p. 288 at p. 306. See further *Gabčíkovo-Nagymaros Project Case* (Hungary/Slovakia) ICJ Reports 1997, p. 7, paras. 53, 111–14, where the ICJ drew attention to newly developed norms of international environmental law. And see, P.W. Birnie and A.E. Boyle, *International Law and the Environment* (1992) p. 549.

2. Report of the United Nations Conference on the Human Environment, 5–16 June 1972 (A/CONF.48/14/Rev.1), 11 *ILM* 1416 (1972). See further L. Sohn, 'The Stockholm Declaration on the Human Environment', 14 *Harvard International Law Journal* (1973) 451.

3. 31 *ILM* 814 (1992). See, P. Sands, 'International Environmental Law after Rio', 4 *European Journal of International Law* (1993) 377.

4. These include the UN Framework Convention on Climate Change, 31 *ILM* 849 (1992), the Kyoto Protocol, 37 *ILM* (1998) 22, and the Convention on Biological Diversity, 31 *ILM* 818 (1992). The Buenos Aires Plan of Action adopted in November 1998 aims to reduce the risk of global climate change by addressing some of the issues left outstanding under the Kyoto Protocol, UN Press Release ENV/DEV/491. Also significant are the Rio Declaration on Environment and Development, 31 *ILM* 874 (1992), which, while not legally binding

qua treaty, nevertheless constitutes soft law, and the Statement of Principles for a Global Consensus of the Management, Conservation and Sustainable Development of All Types of Forests, 31 *ILM* 881 (1992). See further UN General Assembly Resolution A/RES/S-19/2 (1997) on Progress Achieved Towards Meeting Objectives of the Earth Summit, 36 *ILM* 1639 (1997). See C.A. Petsonk, 'The Role of the United Nations Environment Programme (UNEP) in the Development of International Environmental Law', 5 *American University Journal of International Law and Policy* (1990) 351; T. Gehring, 'International Environmental Regimes: Dynamic Sectoral Legal Systems', 1 *Yearbook of International Environmental Law* (1990) 35; P. Sands, 'UNCED and the Development of International Environmental Law', 3 *Yearbook of International Environmental Law* (1993) 17.

5. I.Ll. Griffiths, *The Atlas of African Affairs* (2nd, 1994) Chapter 7. It is reported that many countries in southern Africa are experiencing climate change, becoming warmer and drier, General Assembly Resolution A/RES/S-19/2, paras. 64, 65. See also UN Commission on Human Rights, Human Rights and the Environment, Preliminary Report of the Special Rapporteur, UN Doc. E/CN.4/Sub.2/1991/8, para. 52.

6. Africa is reported to have nineteen of the twenty-five countries with the highest percentage of people without safe drinking water, General Assembly Resolution A/RES/S-19/2, paras. 34, 35.

7. General Assembly Resolution A/RES/S-19/2, para. 66. But see the OAU Convention on the Conservation of Nature and Natural Resources 1968, text in *Naldi* pp. 65–75, whereby parties undertake to conserve, utilize and develop soil, water, flora and fauna resources.

8. Africa's forests are probably the world's most depleted, ever threatened by the spread of subsistence farming under pressure from population growth, with a 10.5% loss in area in the years between 1980–95, *State of the World's Forests* (FAO, 1997). See also, Griffiths, note 5 *supra*, Chapter 6. According to the NGO, Human Rights Advocates, this problem is particularly acute in the Horn of Africa, affecting Sudan, Ethiopia, Eritrea and Somalia, UN Doc. E/CN.4/Sub.2/1992/NGO/10, para. 17. See further General Assembly Resolution A/RES/S-19/2, paras. 37–41; UN Commission on Human Rights, Human Rights and the Environment, Preliminary Report of the Special Rapporteur, UN Doc. E/CN.4/Sub.2/1991/8, para. 53. In addition, the unrestrained exploitation of African forests by transnational corporations, with little or no reforestation, simply compounds the problem, UN Sub-Commission on Prevention of Discrimination and Protection of Minorities, The Question of Transnational Corporations, Working Document of the Special Rapporteur, UN Doc. E/CN.4/Sub.2/1998/6, para. 22.

9. Griffiths, note 5 *supra*, Chapter 5. It is reported that land covering 1.23 billion acres in Africa has moderate to severe soil erosion, ibid. See further, UN Doc. E/CN.4/Sub.2/1992/NGO/10, para. 17, and General Assembly Resolution A/RES/S-19/2, paras. 62. 63.

10. In response to these problems the UN Convention to Combat Desertification was adopted in 1994, 21 *CLB* (1995) 1222, and entered into force in 1996. The Convention establishes a framework of programmes, including a regional programme for Africa, to combat the degradation of land and calls for the transfer of anti-desertification technologies to developing States. See also General Assembly Resolution A/RES/S-19/2, paras. 64, 65.

11. UN Commission on Human Rights, Adverse effects of the illicit movement and dumping of toxic and dangerous products and wastes on the enjoyment of human rights, Progress Report of the Special Rapporteur, UN Doc. E/CN.4/1998/10, paras. 68–70.

12. Ibid., p. 14.
13. C. Hitz and M. Radka, 'Environmental negotiation and policy: the Basel Convention on transboundary movement of hazardous wastes and their disposal', 1 *International Journal of Environment and Pollution* (1991) 55 at p. 56; A. Kiss, 'The International Control of Transboundary Movement of Hazardous Waste', 26 *Texas International Law Journal* (1991) 521 at pp. 528, 529; C.R.H. Shearer, 'Comparative Analysis of the Basel and Bamako Conventions on Hazardous Waste', 23 *Environmental Law* (1993) 141 at pp. 144–50, who states at n. 14 that Guinea-Bissau had consented to the import of 15 million tons of waste for $600 million, twice its foreign debt. See further, C.M. Peter, 'The Proposed African Court of Justice – Jurisprudential, Procedural, Enforcement Problems and Beyond', 1 *East African Journal of Peace & Human Rights* (1993) 117 at pp. 128, 129.
14. Secretary-General of the UN Conference on Environment and Development, Progress Report on Poverty and Environmental Degradation, UN Doc. A/CONF.151/PC/15.
15. Under Article 16 bis of the Kyoto Protocol the concept of an international 'emissions trading' regime was accepted. The Buenos Aires Plan of Action further addressed this issue.
16. UN Commission on Human Rights, Adverse effects of the illicit movement and dumping of toxic and dangerous products and wastes on the enjoyment of human rights, Progress Report of the Special Rapporteur, UN Doc. E/CN.4/1998/10, pp. 15–17; C-2/90 *Commission v. Belgium* [1993] 1 CMLR 365, para. 30.
17. Vienna Declaration and Programme of Action, 32 *ILM* 1678 (1993) Part I, paragraph 11; General Assembly resolution A/RES/S-19/2, para. 57; UN Doc. E/CN.4/1988/10, p. 18; M.L. Schwartz, 'International legal protection for victims of environmental abuse', 18 *Yale Journal of International Law* (1993). See also the statement by Human Rights Advocates, UN Doc. E/CN.4/1998/NGO/44, para. 3. The ICJ has observed that 'the environment is not an abstraction but represents the living space, the quality of life and the very health of human beings, including generations unborn', *Legality of the Threat or Use of Nuclear Weapons* ICJ Reports 1996, para. 29. It seems that hydropower development in Ghana's Volta River Basin has forced thousands of people to relocate and caused thousands of cases of river blindness, UN Doc. E/CN.4/Sub.2/1992/NGO/10, para. 7.
18. *Keesing's*, Vol. 35, 1989, pp. 36788–9. Nigeria has acknowledged that it has suffered and still suffers from the illegal dumping of toxic wastes due to limited human resources in dealing with such wastes, most of which is labelled raw materials for industry, UN Commission on Human Rights, Adverse effects of the illicit movement and dumping of toxic and dangerous products and wastes on the enjoyment of human rights, Progress Report of the Special Rapporteur, UN Doc. E/CN.4/1997/19, para. 29. See also UN Doc. E/CN.4/Sub.2/1997/27, para. 12. Angola has expressed concern about its maritime and riverine coasts which risk becoming dumping sites for toxic waste, ibid., para. 26.
19. UN Commission on Human Rights, Adverse effects of the illicit movement and dumping of toxic and dangerous products and wastes on the enjoyment of human rights, Progress Report of the Special Rapporteur, UN Doc. E/CN.4/1998/10, paras. 71, 72; UN Sub-Commission on Prevention of Discrimination and Protection of Minorities, The Question of Transnational Corporations, Working Document of the Special Rapporteur, UN Doc. E/CN.4/Sub.2/1998/6, paras. 11–16. It should be noted that in resolution 3514 (XXX) 1975, the UN General Assembly condemned all corrupt practices, including bribery, by transnational and other corporations. The OAU has stated that the main

problem facing African countries was lack of information, UN Commission on Human Rights, Adverse effects of the illicit movement and dumping of toxic and dangerous products and wastes on the enjoyment of human rights, Report of the Special Rapporteur, UN Doc. E/CN.4/1998/10/Add.2, para. 45.

20. UN Commission on Human Rights, Adverse effects of the illicit movement and dumping of toxic and dangerous products and wastes on the enjoyment of human rights, Progress Report of the Special Rapporteur, UN Doc. E/CN.4/1998/10, paras. 71, 72.

21. Article 1 of resolution 1153 (XLVIII) of 25 May 1988, text in *Naldi*, pp. 76, 77. According to Article 19(3)(d) of the ILC's Draft Convention on State Responsibility 'a serious breach of an international obligation of essential importance for the safeguarding and preservation of the human environment' has been defined as an international crime, which in itself would constitute a breach of an obligation *erga omnes*, UN Commission on Human Rights, Definition of gross and large-scale violations of human rights as an international crime, UN Doc. E/CN.4/Sub.2/1993/10, para. 23.

22. 28 *ILM* 657 (1989), entered into force in May 1992. It has been ratified by one hundred and eighteen States and the EC. The twenty-one African States that have ratified the Convention are as follows: Benin, Burundi, Comoros, Côte d'Ivoire, Democratic Republic of the Congo, Egypt, Gambia, Guinea, Malawi, Mauritius, Morocco, Mozambique, Namibia, Nigeria, Senegal, Seychelles, South Africa, Tunisia, Tanzania, Zambia. See further Kiss, note 13 *supra*, p. 535.

23. UN Commission on Human Rights, Adverse effects of the illicit movement and dumping of toxic and dangerous products and wastes on the enjoyment of human rights, Progress Report of the Special Rapporteur, UN Doc. E/CN.4/1996/17, paras. 31, 32. For analysis of the Convention, see Birnie and Boyle, note 1 *supra*, pp. 332–43; M. Bothé, 'International Regulation of Transboundary Movement of Hazardous Waste', 33 *German Yearbook of International Law* (1990) 422; K. Kummer, 'The International Regulation of Transboundary Traffic in Hazardous Wastes: The 1989 Basel Convention', 41 *ICLQ* (1992) 530; V.O. Okaru, 'The Basel Convention: Controlling the Movement of Hazardous Wastes to Developing Countries', 4 *Fordham Environmental Law Reporter* (1993) 137. It should be noted that Agenda 21 (Chapters 19, 20 and 22), a comprehensive programme of action adopted by UNCED in Rio de Janeiro in June 1992, UN Doc. A/CONF.151/4 also calls for the environmentally sound management of toxic chemicals and hazardous and radioactive wastes, including the prevention of illegal international traffic in such wastes.

24. Birnie and Boyle, note 1 *supra*, pp. 334, 335.

25. Ibid., pp. 332, 333. For arguments in favour of regulation rather than prohibition, see B. Kwiatkowska, and A.H.A. Soons, 'Transboundary Movements of Hazardous Wastes and their Disposal: Emerging Global and Regional Regulation', 5 *Hague Yearbook of International Law* (1992) 68 at pp. 75–80.

26. Ibid., pp. 115, 116; Shearer, note 13 *supra*, pp. 141, 142, 151, 152; J. Ntambirweki, 'The Developing Countries in the Evolution of an International Environmental Law', 14 *Hastings International and Comparative Law Review* (1991) 905. It should be observed that the UN General Assembly regards the Basel Convention as flawed and has thus called for the development of initiatives aimed at the sound management of hazardous wastes, General Assembly resolution A/RES/S-19/2, para. 58, although it has been described as 'remarkable for its time', UN Commission on Human Rights, Adverse effects of the illicit movement and dumping of toxic and dangerous products and wastes on the enjoyment of human rights, Report of the Special Rapporteur, UN Doc. E/CN.4/1998/10/Add.2, para. 41. Human Rights Advocates has identified the following limitations: violations of human rights are inadequately addressed, if

at all; weak enforcement mechanisms; weak liability regimes; the fact that toxic substances must cross frontiers for the Convention to apply; and the fact that the USA, one of the largest generators of waste, has not ratified the Convention, UN Doc. E/CN.4/1998/NGO/44, para. 4.

27. Article 4(1)(b). See also, Principle 14, Rio Declaration on Environment and Development.

28. Kummer, note 23 *supra*, p. 542, n. 52; E.C. Eguh, 'Regulations of Transboundary Movement of Hazardous Wastes: Lessons from Koko', 9 *RADIC* (1997) 130 at pp. 140, 141.

29. Kummer, note 23 *supra*, pp. 551–3.

30. Cf. the Convention on the Protection of the Environment Through Criminal Law adopted by the Council of Europe in 1998, 38 *ILM* 259 (1999). Article 2(1)(c) and (e) thereof requires parties to adopt appropriate measures to establish as offences under its domestic law when committed intentionally, *inter alia*, 'the unlawful disposal, treatment, storage, transport, export or import of hazardous waste which causes or is likely to cause death or serious injury to any person or substantial damage to the quality of air, soil, water, animals or plants', and 'the unlawful manufacture, treatment, storage, use, transport, export or import of nuclear materials or other radioactive substances which is likely to cause death or serious injury to any person or substantial damage to the quality of the air, the soil, the water, animals or plants'. Article 3 requires parties to adopt appropriate measures to establish as criminal offences under domestic law, when committed with gross negligence, the offences enumerated in Article 2. Furthermore, under Article 6 parties must adopt measures making these offences 'punishable by criminal sanctions which take into account the serious nature of these offences. Such sanctions shall include imprisonment and may include pecuniary sanctions and reinstatement of the environment'. The Convention is innovative in that it extends liability to corporations. Thus, Article 9 obliges parties to adopt appropriate measures to enable the imposition of criminal or administrative sanctions on legal persons on whose behalf an offence as defined in Articles 2 or 3 has been committed. It should be observed further that 'a serious breach of an international obligation of essential import- ance for the safeguarding and preservation of the human environment' has been classified as an international crime, Article 19(3)(d) of the International Law Commission's Draft Articles on State Responsibility, see note 21 *supra*.

31. See, e.g., replies received from governments by the Special Rapporteur with regard to their legal obligations under the Basel Convention, UN Commission on Human Rights, Adverse effects of the illicit movement and dumping of toxic and dangerous products and wastes on the enjoyment of human rights, Pro- gress Report of the Special Rapporteur, UN Doc. E/CN.4/1998/10, pp. 6–9.

32. Kummer, note 23 *supra*, pp. 553, 554. However, it would appear that this obligation remains largely unobserved, UN Commission on Human Rights, Adverse effects of the illicit movement and dumping of toxic and dangerous products and wastes on the enjoyment of human rights, Progress Report of the Special Rapporteur, UN Doc. E/CN.4/1998/10, para. 93. In 1992, 950 tons of waste exported illegally from Germany to Egypt were denied entry to Egypt and returned to Germany, ibid., Add.1, pp. 3, 4.

33. Article 4(2)(g). See further, Birnie and Boyle, note 1 *supra*, pp. 338, 339; Kummer, note 23 *supra*, pp. 540, 541.

34. In 1997 South Africa declared its intention to open a regional training centre to promote the safe handling of hazardous and toxic wastes, UN Commission on Human Rights, Adverse effects of the illicit movement and dumping of toxic and dangerous products and wastes on the enjoyment of human rights, Pro- gress Report of the Special Rapporteur, UN Doc. E/CN.4/1997/SR.14, para. 43.

35. UN Commission on Human Rights, Adverse effects of the illicit movement and dumping of toxic and dangerous products and wastes on the enjoyment of human rights, Progress Report of the Special Rapporteur, UN Doc. E/CN.4/1997/19, para. 78.

36. Third Meeting of the Conference of the Parties to the Basel Convention, Decision 111/1, 18–22 September 1995, UN Doc. UNEP/CHW.3/35; UN Commission on Human Rights, Adverse effects of the illicit movement and dumping of toxic and dangerous products and wastes on the enjoyment of human rights, Progress Report of the Special Rapporteur, UN Doc. E/CN.4/1998/10, para. 58. The amendment has been ratified by eight State parties, including the United Kingdom, and the EC. See further, Council Regulation (EC) 120/97 on the prohibition of exports of hazardous wastes to non-OECD countries for recycling or recovery as from 1 January 1998, as decided by the parties to the Basel Convention, amending Regulation (EEC) 259/93 on the supervision and control of shipments of waste within, into and out of the EC.

37. Text in *Naldi*, pp. 78–97. The Convention has been ratified by Benin, Cameroon, Congo, Democratic Republic of the Congo, Côte d'Ivoire, Libya, Mali, Mauritius, Niger, Senegal, Sudan, Tanzania, Togo, Tunisia, and Zimbabwe, and signed by Burkina Faso, Central African Republic, Chad, Djibouti, Egypt, Guinea, Guinea-Bissau, Lesotho, Rwanda, Somalia and Swaziland. It is open only to Member States of the OAU, see Articles 21–3 thereof. For analysis, see Shearer, note 13 *supra*; I. Cheyne, 'Africa and the International Trade in Hazardous Wastes', 6 *RADIC* (1994) 493; H.S. Kaminsky, 'Assessment of the Bamako Convention on the Ban of Import into Africa and the Control of Transboundary Movement and Management of Hazardous Wastes within Africa', 5 *The Georgetown International Environmental Law Review* (1992) 77.

38. See note 26 *supra*.

39. Article 11(1) of the Basel Convention thus provides, *inter alia*, that 'Parties may enter into bilateral, multilateral, or regional agreements or arrangements regarding transboundary movement or hazardous wastes ... provided that such agreements or arrangements do not derogate from the environmentally sound management of hazardous wastes and other wastes as required by this Convention. These agreements or arrangements shall stipulate provisions which are not less environmentally sound than those provided for by this Convention, in particular taking into account the interests of developing countries'. See UN Commission on Human Rights, Adverse effects of the illicit movement and dumping of toxic and dangerous products and wastes on the enjoyment of human rights, Progress Report of the Special Rapporteur, UN Doc. E/CN.4/1996/17, para. 42; Cheyne, note 37 *supra*, pp. 493, 494. The OAU has expressed the view that the two treaties are complementary, UN Commission on Human Rights, Adverse effects of the illicit movement and dumping of toxic and dangerous products and wastes on the enjoyment of human rights, Report of the Special Rapporteur, UN Doc. E/CN.4/1998/10/Add.2, para. 44. Birnie and Boyle are of the view that such a regional measure is a more pragmatic way of protecting the interests of developing countries than a total international ban, note 1 *supra*, pp. 341 342. Other regional developments include the Waigani Convention to Ban the Importation into Forum Island Countries of Hazardous and Radioactive Wastes and to Control the Transboundary Movement and Management of Hazardous Wastes within the South Pacific Region 1995, and the Protocol to the Barcelona Convention 1976 on the Prevention of Pollution of the Mediterranean Sea by Transboundary Movements of Hazardous Wastes and their Disposal 1996, UN Commission on Human Rights, Adverse effects of the illicit movement and dumping of toxic and dangerous products and wastes on the enjoyment of human rights, Report of the Special Rapporteur, UN Doc.

E/CN.4/1998/10/Add.2, para. 41. It appears that Central American States have also agreed to ban imports of all hazardous wastes, UN Commission on Human Rights, Adverse effects of the illicit movement and dumping of toxic and dangerous products and wastes on the enjoyment of human rights, Progress Report of the Special Rapporteur, UN Doc. E/CN.4/1996/17, para. 144. See also EC Directive on Waste 75/442, OJ [1975] L 194, as amended by Directive on the Control of Wastes, 91/156, OJ [1991] L 78.

40.　Cheyne, note 37 *supra*, pp. 497–9; Shearer, note 13 *supra*, pp. 153–6. See further Article 3 of the Bamako Convention relating to national definitions of hazardous wastes. The UN General . Assembly has called for the completion of the definition according to which hazardous wastes are controlled, General Assembly resolution A/RES/S-19/2, para. 58.

41.　According to Birnie and Boyle, note 1 *supra*, p. 335, the Basel Convention is essentially limited to household and hazardous wastes and that the reason for this omission is because radioactive wastes are already subject to control by the International Atomic Energy Agency in other instruments. See further, Kummer, note 23 *supra*, pp. 543, 544. Shearer views the inclusion of radioactive wastes in the Bamako Convention as problematic, note 13 *supra*, p. 175. UN General Assembly resolution A/RES/S-19/2, at paras. 59–61, calls for the safe and responsible management of radioactive wastes.

42.　Article 4(3)(h).

43.　See Birnie and Boyle, note 1 *supra*, Chapter 6.

44.　Shearer, note 13 *supra*, pp. 156, 157. It should be observed that by virtue of Article 4(4)(c) general rights of navigation under international law through maritime zones subject to national jurisdiction remain unimpaired, see further, Birnie and Boyle, note 1 *supra*, pp. 336–337. Cf. the London Convention on the Prevention of Marine Pollution by Dumping of Wastes and Other Matters 1972, which prohibits the dumping of wastes except as provided for in the Convention, and the Oslo Convention for the Prevention of Marine Pollution by Dumping from Ships and Aircraft 1972, which bans the dumping of certain substances and regulates the dumping of others. See generally, Birnie and Boyle, note 1 *supra*, Chapter 8; Kiss, note 13 *supra*, pp. 522–8. Note the Protocol to the Barcelona Convention for the Protection of the Mediterranean Sea against Pollution which, *inter alia*, requires parties to take all appropriate measures 'to prevent and eliminate pollution of the Mediterranean Sea area which can be caused by transboundary movements and disposal of hazardous wastes'.

45.　29 *ILM* 783 (1990); see Eguh, note 28 *supra*, pp. 141, 142.

46.　Article 4(3)(i), (j), (k), (n), (o), (t).

47.　Article 4(3)(b). See further Article 12 thereof which calls for a protocol to establish the appropriate rules and procedures in the field of liabilities and compensation, Shearer, note 13 *supra*, pp. 158, 159. Again, the Bamako Convention adopts a stricter regime than that of the Basel Convention since the latter, under Article 12, merely requires parties to co-operate 'with a view to adopting, as soon as practicable, a protocol setting out appropriate rules and procedures in the field of liability and compensation', see Birnie and Boyle, note 1 *supra*, pp. 340, 341; Kummer, note 23 *supra*, pp. 554, 555. The UN General Assembly has called for the adoption and implementation of such a protocol, General Assembly resolution A/RES/S-19/2, para. 58. Note that the Council of Europe adopted in 1993 a Convention on Civil Liability for Damage Resulting from Activities Dangerous to the Environment, 32 *ILM* 1228 (1993), not yet in force, which seeks to ensure adequate compensation for damage resulting from activities dangerous to the environment and also provides for means of prevention. The system of the Convention is based on strict liability and provides for joint and several liability, Article 6. See also, the IMO International Convention on Liability and Compensation for Damage in Connection with the Carriage of Hazardous and Noxious Substances by Sea 35 *ILM* 1406 (1996); Principle 13, Rio Declaration on Environment and Development. See generally, Kwiatkowska and Soons, note 25 *supra*, pp. 130–5; S.D. Murphy, 'Prospective Liability Regimes for the Transboundary Movement of Hazardous Wastes', 88 *AJIL* (1994) 24.

48. Shearer, note 13 *supra*, pp. 157, 158.
49. Kaminsky, note 37 *supra*, p. 87. This also appears to be the case under the European Convention on Civil Liability for Damage Resulting from Activities Dangerous to the Environment, Article 8.
50. UN Commission on Human Rights, Adverse effects of the illicit movement and dumping of toxic and dangerous products and wastes on the enjoyment of human rights, Report of the Special Rapporteur, UN Doc. E/CN.4/1998/10/ Add.2, para. 41; Birnie and Boyle, note 1 *supra*, Chapter 4.2. It is instructive to note that the Bamako Convention makes no express reference to the 'polluter pays' principle, cf. Principle 16, Rio Declaration on Environment and Development, Article 174(2) (ex Art. 130r) EC Treaty, and the preamble to the European Convention on Civil Liability for Damage Resulting From Activities Dangerous to the Environment. See further, Birnie and Boyle, note 1 *supra*, pp. 109–11.
51. Kaminsky, note 37 *supra*, pp. 86, 87.
52. Shearer, note 13 *supra*, p. 158.
53. Article 4(3)(f). The UN Special Rapporteur has emphasized the salient role that prevention has in protecting life and health, UN Commission on Human Rights, Adverse effects of the illicit movement and dumping of toxic and dangerous products and wastes on the enjoyment of human rights, Progress Report of the Special Rapporteur, UN Doc. E/CN.4/1998/10, para. 93. The Bamako Convention appears to have pioneered the inclusion of the precautionary principle in the operative section of the treaty, Kaminsky, note 37 *supra*, p. 84. See further, Article 174(2) (ex Art. 130r) EC Treaty; Principle 15, Rio Declaration on Environment and Development. The ICJ seems to consider the precautionary principle to have persuasive authority as an emergent norm of international law, *Gabčíkovo-Nagymaros Project Case* ICJ Reports 1997 p. 7, paras. 112–13. See also the Dissenting Opinions of Judge Weeramantry and Judge Koroma in *Request for an Examination of the Situation in Accordance with Paragraph 63 of the Court's Judgment in the 1974 Nuclear Tests Case* ICJ Reports 1995, p. 288 at pp. 342–4, and 368 respectively, who believe the precautionary principle to be a norm of international law. However, Birnie and Boyle consider it premature to view the precautionary principle as part of international law, note 1 *supra*, pp. 95–8. See also, I. Brownlie, *Principles of Public International Law* (5th edn 1998) pp. 285, 286; M. Shaw, *International Law* (4th edn 1997) pp. 604, 605.
54. Kaminsky, note 37 *supra*, p. 85; Shearer, note 13 *supra*, pp. 160, 161. Although Shearer acknowledges that the adoption of these methods is in the best interests of African States he questions whether they possess the wherewithal to implement them, ibid., pp. 175, 176.
55. Article 4(3)(f), (g). See also Article 10. The EC has adopted similar policies, see Council Directive 91/156, note 39 *supra* amending Directive 75/442. Shearer points out that the technological and financial resources necessary to implement these policies may be beyond many African States and that the absence of enforcement mechanism undermines the effectiveness of the Convention, note 13 *supra* pp. 162, 163. Furthermore, these methods may increase costs and thereby prove a disincentive to business. He concludes that such overambitious goals may simply prove unattainable, ibid., pp. 176, 177. It should be observed that the UN General Assembly has stressed the need for developing countries

to acquire environmentally sound technologies, General Assembly Resolution A/RES/S-19/2, paras. 88–97.

56. Article 1(5).

57. Kaminsky, note 37 *supra*, pp. 79–81; Shearer, note 13 *supra*, pp. 167–9. See also Article 4(3)(u). This is the case with the Basel Convention, see Birnie and Boyle, note 1 *supra*, pp. 336–8; Kummer, note 23 *supra*, pp. 547–51; Article 13(1) providing that the parties 'shall ensure that in the case of an accident occurring during the transboundary movement of hazardous wastes or their disposal which is likely to present risks to human health and the environment in other States those States are immediately informed'. By virtue of Article 7, Article 6(2)-(4) applies *mutatis mutandis* to the movement of waste from a party through a State which is not a party. And see the Convention on Prior Informed Consent Procedure for Certain Hazardous Chemicals and Pesticides in International Trade, 38 *ILM* 1 (1999). It now seems that international law requires comprehensive environmental impact assessments to be undertaken with a view to identifying potential threats to the environment, *Gabčíkovo-Nagymaros Project Case* ICJ Reports 1997, p. 7, para. 112; and Judge Weeramantry's Dissenting Opinion in *Request for an Examination of the Situation in Accordance with Paragraph 63 of the Court's Judgment in the 1974 Nuclear Test Case* ICJ Reports 1995, p. 288 at p. 345. See also the Convention on Environmental Impact Assessment in a Transboundary Context 1991, 30 *ILM* 800 (1991), and EC Directive on the Assessment of the Effects of Certain Projects on the Environment, 85/337, OJ [1985] L 175, as amended by Directive 97/11.

58. This provision is virtually identical to Article 8 of the Basel Convention, see Kummer, note 23 *supra*, pp. 553, 554, who asserts that illegal traffic is excluded from the scope of the provision. Moreover, she draws attention to the fact that no definition of non-completion of the contract is given. Again, it would seem that this obligation is not being implemented thoroughly, UN Commission on Human Rights, Adverse effects of the illicit movement and dumping of toxic and dangerous products and wastes on the enjoyment of human rights, Progress Report of the Special Rapporteur, UN Doc. E/CN.4/1998/10, para. 93.

59. See also Article 4(4)(a), (b). See further, *supra*, pp. 223–4.

60. Article 9(3). Shearer is critical of these requirements for failure to explore cheaper or more environmentally sound options, note 13 *supra*, p. 177.

61. Article 9(4).

62. Article 20.

63. Cheyne, note 37 *supra*, pp. 499–503.

64. Cf. Article 1 of the European Convention on Civil Liability for Damage Resulting from Activities Dangerous to the Environment, and Article 8 of the European Convention on the Protection of the Environment Through Criminal Law.

65. Shearer, note 13 *supra*, p. 175.

66. Ibid.

67. Ibid., p. 176.

68. For a human rights based approach, see D. Shelton, 'Human Rights, Environmental Rights, and the Right to the Environment', 28 *Stanford Journal of International Law* (1991) 103; J. Downs, 'A Healthy and Ecologically Balanced Environment: An Argument for a Third Generation Right', 3 *Duke Journal of Comparative and International Law* (1993) 351. For a more cautious approach, see J.G. Merrills, 'Environmental Protection and Human Rights: Conceptual Aspects', in A.E. Boyle and M.R. Anderson (eds), *Human Rights Approaches to Environmental Protection* (1996) Chapter 2.

69. Part I, para. 11, 32 *ILM* 1661 (1993).

70. W.P. Gormley, 'The Legal Obligation of the International Community to Guar-

antee a Pure and Decent Environment: The Expansion of Human Rights Norms', 3 *Georgetown International Environmental Law Review* (1990) 85.

71. See further Chapter 4 *supra*, p. 138. It is interesting to note that in its 'Guidelines for National Periodic Reports', reproduced in *Naldi*, p. 155 at p. 170, the African Commission on Human and Peoples' Rights stated that the main purpose of the provision is to 'protect the environment and keep it favourable for development. Establish a system to monitor effective disposal of waste in order to prevent pollution. As a nation and in co-operation with other African States to prohibit and penalise disposal of waste on the African soil by any company'.

72. However, see R.R. Churchill, 'Environmental Rights in Existing Human Rights Treaties', in Boyle and Anderson, note 68 *supra*, p. 89 at pp. 104–7, who criticizes this provision as vague as to the actual right protected and the holder of the right.

73. 28 *ILM* 156 (1989). Churchill points out that this right is to be progressively realized as resources allow, note 72 *supra*, pp. 99, 100. The OECD has expressed the view that the promotion of a 'decent' environment should be recognized as a fundamental human right, 'Responsibility and liability of States in relation to transfrontier pollution', 13 *Environmental Policy and Law* (1984) 122.

74. Article 3(l) (ex Art 3(k)) of the EC Treaty makes environmental policy one of the policies of the EC. See also Case 302/86 *Commission* v. *Denmark* [1988] ECR 4607, para. 8. The EC has adopted a series of legislative measures on the environment, see, e.g., Directive 75/324, OJ [1975] L 147, on aquatic and air pollution, Directive 89/530 on chemical pollution, Directive 76/160, OJ [1976] L 31, on bathing water, and Directive 96/61, OJ [1996] L 257, on Integrated Prevention of Environmental Pollution; see further A. Kiss and D. Shelton, *Manual of European Environmental Law* (2nd edn 1997) pp. 74–6. The EC would also appear to provide for participatory rights, see S. Douglas-Scott, 'Environmental Rights in the European Union-Participatory Democracy or Democratic Deficit?', in Boyle and Anderson, note 68 *supra*, p. 109.

75. Done at Aarhus, Denmark, 25 June 1998.

76. M.W. Janis, *An Introduction to International Law* (2nd edn 1993) p. 220. On soft law generally, see I. Detter, *The International Legal Order* (1994) Chapter 4.

77. Janis, note 76 *supra*, pp. 220–3. One of the basic duties of States is not to act so as to injure the rights of other States, the *sic utere* principle, see *Trial Smelter Arbitration* 9 ILR 315; *Legality of the Threat or Use of Nuclear Weapons* ICJ Reports 1996, pp. 241, 242; Stockholm Conference (Principle 21); Rio Declaration on Environment and Development (Principle 2).

78. D.W. Greig, *International Law* (2nd edn 1976) pp. 24, 25. By way of contrast it is interesting to note that in *Cambridge Water* v. *Eastern Counties Leather* [1994] 2 WLR 53 at p. 80 the House of Lords expressed the view that there was no need for the common law to reflect the evolution of international environmental law.

79. UN Commission on Human Rights, Adverse effects of the illicit movement and dumping of toxic and dangerous products and wastes on the enjoyment of human rights, Progress Reports of the Special Rapporteur, UN Docs. E/CN.4/Sub.2/1992/7, E/CN.4/Sub.2/1993/7, E/CN.4/Sub.2/1994/9.

80. See C. Heyns, *Human Rights Law in Africa 1996* (1996).

81. *Minors Oposa* v. *Factoran* 33 *ILM* 173 (1994) (Supreme Court of the Philippines); *Fundepublico* v. *Mayor of Bugalagrande and Others* (Constitutional Court of Colombia), cited in UN Commission on Human Rights, Adverse effects of the illicit movement and dumping of toxic and dangerous products and wastes on the enjoyment of human rights, Progress Report of the Special Rapporteur, UN Doc. E/CN.4/Sub.2/1993/7, pp. 16, 17; *M.C. Mehta* v. *Union of India* AIR 1988 1037; *Rural Litigation and Entitlement Kendra and Others* v. *State of Uttar Pradesh and Others* AIR 1987 359 (Supreme Court of India); *Indian Council of Enviro-Legal*

Action v. *Union of India* [1996] 2 LRC 226 (Supreme Court of India). See further, F. Du Bois, 'Social Justice and the Judicial Enforcement of Environmental Rights and Duties', in Boyle and Anderson, note 68 *supra*, Chapter 8.

82. Article 19(3)(d) of the International Law Commission's Draft Articles on State Responsibility; Article 26 of the International Law Commission's Draft Code of Crimes against the Peace and Security of Mankind, see UN Commission on Human Rights, Adverse effects of the illicit movement and dumping of toxic and dangerous products wastes on the enjoyment of human rights, Progress Report of the Special Rapporteur, UN Doc. E/CN.4/Sub.2/1993/7, paras. 113–15. Article 8(2)(b)(iv) of the Rome Statute of the International Criminal Court, adopted July 1998, 37 *ILM* 999 (1998), describes such an act in the context of the *ius in bello* as a war crime. See also, *Legality of the Threat or Use of Nuclear Weapons* ICJ Reports 1996, para. 31; UN General Assembly Resolution 47/37 (1992) on the Protection of the Environment in Times of Armed Conflict; and further A. Leibler, 'Deliberate Wartime Environmental Damage: New Challenge for International Law', 23 *California Western International Law Journal* (1992–3) 67; W.D. Verwey, 'The Protection of the Environment in Times of Armed Conflict', 8 *Leiden Journal of International Law* (1995) 7.

83. On the relationship between human rights and the environment, see UN Commission on Human Rights, Adverse effects of the illicit movement and dumping of toxic and dangerous products and wastes on the enjoyment of human rights, Progress Report of the Special Rapporteur, UN Docs. E/CN.4/Sub.2/1991/8, E/CN.4/Sub.2/1992/7, pp. 22–31, E/CN.4/Sub.2/1993/7, E/CN.4/1996/17, pp. 33–5. It is interesting to observe that the UN Special Rapporteur on Human Rights and the Environment has produced a document on Draft Principles on Human Rights and the Environment which specifically recognizes a right to a healthy environment, UN Commission on Human Rights, Adverse effects of the illicit movement and dumping of toxic and dangerous products and wastes on the enjoyment of human rights, Progress Report of the Special Rapporteur, UN Doc. E/CN.4/Sub.2/1994/9. Cf. *contra*, Birnie and Boyle, note 1 *supra*, p. 192; Merrills, note 68 *supra*; and A.E. Boyle, 'The Role of International Human Rights Law in the Protection of the Environment', in Boyle and Anderson, note 68 *supra*, Chapter 3, with the possible exception of procedural rights. In 1992 the UN Special Rapporteur remarked that, 'At present we are dealing with a general social value rather than a legal principle', UN Commission on Human Rights, Adverse effects of the illicit movement and dumping of toxic and dangerous products and wastes on the enjoyment of human rights, Progress Report of the Special Rapporteur, UN Doc. E/CN.4/Sub.2/1992/7, para. 59. Arguments against the existence of such a right are based on: (a) the absence of a precise definition either of the concept of the 'right to the environment' or of the content that right should have; (b) the 'justiciability' of this right, i.e., its effective enforcement and implementation by or on behalf of beneficiaries. These arguments appear to be undermined by simple reference to successful litigation on environmental issues before domestic courts, see note 81 *supra*, and further, Kiss and Shelton, note 74 *supra*, pp. 142–51, the ECJ, see, e.g., Case 302/86 *Commission* v. *Denmark (Disposable Beer Cans Case)* [1988] ECR 4607, C-2/90 *Commission* v. *Belgium: Re Imports of Waste (Walloon Waste Case)* [1993] 1 CMLR 365, *Commission* v. *Spain* [1993] ECR I-4221, although it must be acknowledged that the prospects for individual enforcement of environmental rights seem limited at the present time, see C-236/92 *Comitato di Coordinamento per la Difesa della Cava* v. *Regione Lombardia* [1994] ECR I-483, C-321/95 P *Stichting Greenpeace Council* v. *Commission* [1998] All ER (EC) 620, the ECHR, see *López Ostra* v. *Spain* Series A, Vol. 303-C (1994), *Guerra* v. *Italy* Reports 1998-I, and the ICJ, see, e.g., *Gabčíkovo-Nagymaros Project*

Case ICJ Reports 1997, p. 7. Furthermore, interested associations have been granted *locus standi* under the European Convention on Civil Liability for Damage Resulting from Activities Dangerous to the Environment (Articles 18 and 19), and the European Convention on the Protection of the Environment Through Criminal Law (Article 11). And see also the Convention on Access to Information, Public Participation and Access to Justice in Environmental Matters. Nevertheless, individuals can be beneficiaries of rights designed to protect them but which the individual cannot enforce, that obligation binding the State at the international level. Justiciability need not be the sole prerequisite for the recognition of a right, UN Commission on Human Rights, Adverse effects of the illicit movement and dumping of toxic and dangerous products and wastes on the enjoyment of human rights, Progress Report of the Special Rapporteur, UN Doc. E/CN.4/Sub.2/1992/7, para. 59. Moreover, little account seems to have been taken of the dynamic and evolving nature of human rights. Of necessity, human rights tend to be set out in international instruments, and national constitutions, in rather abstract language as framework provisions, to be interpreted, defined and refined by the courts as circumstances require, a good example being the prohibition on torture and inhuman and degrading treatment and punishment. The lack of a definition or of precise rules need not in themselves be an obstacle to the practical application of principles which time and practice interpret.

84.   Birnie and Boyle, note 1 *supra*, pp. 192, 193; Boyle, note 83 *supra*; Churchill, note 72 *supra*. In this context it is important to note that environmental issues come within the scope of the ECHR, notwithstanding the fact that there is no right to a healthy environment *per se* in the ECHR, see, e.g., *Pine Valley Developments Ltd* v. *Ireland* Series A, Vol. 222 (1991), *López Ostra* v. *Spain* Series A, Vol. 303-C (1994), *Guerra* v. *Italy* Reports 1998-I. See further, B. van Dyke, 'A Proposal to Introduce the Right to a Healthy Environment into the European Convention Regime', 13 *Virginia Environmental Law Journal* (1993) 323.

85.   The travesty of justice that was the farcical trial of the renowned author Ken Saro-Wiwa aptly demonstrates the link between environmental issues and human rights. Complaints by the Ogoni people in southern Nigeria about environmental degradation and their calls for compensation led to numerous human rights violations by the Nigerian government. Communities in the Niger Delta of south-eastern Nigeria, which produces most of Nigeria's oil, have been protesting for a number of years that the activities of multinational oil companies, in concert with the authorities, have resulted in the pollution of their land and rivers. Following the deaths of four prominent local leaders in May 1994 the authorities crushed dissent. Ken Saro-Wiwa, who led a pressure group, and other activists, were arraigned for murder before a specially constituted tribunal, sentenced to death and executed. There is no doubt whatsoever that the charges were politically motivated and that the accused were not guilty of the charges against them. The tribunal was neither independent nor impartial and the trial was marred by procedural irregularities, including the lack of appeal to a higher judicial body. By way of contrast, the Nigerian government has stated that all oil companies must comply with local environmental regulations and has drawn attention to the material benefits brought to Ogoniland, UN Commission on Human Rights, Adverse effects of the illicit movement and dumping of toxic and dangerous products and wastes on the enjoyment of human rights, Progress Report of the Special Rapporteur, UN Doc. E/CN.4/1998/10/Add.1, p. 8.

86.   *EHP* v. *Canada* (Communication No. 67/1980), where the petitioner, a resident of Port Hope, Ontario, alleged large-scale dumping of nuclear waste within her community. The communication claimed that the wastes posed a threat to the

rights to life and health. Although the application was declared inadmissible on procedural grounds, the HRC declared that the petitioner had a *prima facie* case concerning her environmental claims. The Inter-American Commission on Human Rights has found a violation of the right to life within the context of environmental protection, cited in UN Commission on Human Rights, Adverse effects of the illicit movement and dumping of toxic and dangerous products and wastes on the enjoyment of human rights, Progress Report of the Special Rapporteur, UN Doc. E/CN.4/Sub.2/1993/7, para. 69. See also *Indian Council of Enviro-Legal Action* v. *Union of India* [1996] 2 LRC 226. It should be observed further that the Vienna Conference on Human Rights recognized that 'the illicit dumping of toxic and dangerous substances potentially constitutes a serious threat to the human rights to life and health of everyone' (Part I, para. 11). Note that the Rio Declaration on Environment and Development declared that human beings 'are entitled to a healthy and productive life in harmony with nature' (Principle 1).

87.   Article 7 ICES; Article 16 Banjul Charter; Article 3 of the Revised European Social Charter 1996. The threat to human health is acknowledged by UN General Assembly A/RES/S-19/2, para. 57. It should be noted further that protective standards governing the prohibition and regulation of the use and handling of harmful substances have also been set by the ILO, e.g., Conventions No. 13 (white lead), 115 (ionizing radiation), 139 (carcinogenic substances and agents), in addition to those prescribing general standards of protection and prevention, e.g., Convention No. 155 concerning occupational safety and health. See also Articles 137 (ex Art. 118) and 140 (ex Art. 118c) EC Treaty and Directive 89/391, OJ [1989] L 183. The ECJ has enforced measures for the protection of human health and safety, see, e.g., *Commission* v. *Germany* [1991] ECR 2567; *Commission* v. *Germany* [1991] ECR I-4983.

88.   Common Article 1 of the International Covenants; Articles 20 and 21 of the Banjul Charter; Rio Declaration on Environment and Development (Principles 2 and 23). See also the dissenting opinion of Judge Weeramantry in the *East Timor Case (Portugal* v. *Australia)* ICJ Reports, 1995, p. 90 at pp. 197–200, 203, 204, 221, 222. Of interest is the *Case concerning Certain Phosphate Lands in Nauru (Nauru* v. *Australia)* ICJ Reports 1992, p. 240, where the ICJ had to consider the issue of state responsibility for environmental damage caused by severe land degradation which occurred when Australia governed Nauru. In its Application, Nauru demanded that Australia pay compensation for the rehabilitation of certain Nauruan lands which were severely degraded through phosphate mining in the years before Nauru's independence in 1968. Nauru claimed that the compensation was owed for the ruined land and for artificially low royalties to Nauru imposed by the mining consortium, and asked the ICJ to impose an additional award for 'aggravated or moral damage'. Nauru asserted an obligation to respect the principle of self-determination and the right to permanent sovereignty over natural resources. Underlying the case was the concept of the right of future generations. The ICJ accepted jurisdiction but while the case was pending on the merits Nauru and Australia reached an out of court settlement and the case was withdrawn from the ICJ's docket. The globalized economy is presenting its own set of problems with environmental controls being perceived as undermining foreign investment. It has been alleged that private companies have influenced Kenya to delay the implementation of environmental policies, UN Commission on Human Rights, Adverse effects of the illicit movement and dumping of toxic and dangerous products and wastes on the enjoyment of human rights, Report of the Special Rapporteur, UN Doc. E/CN.4/1998/10/Add.2, paras. 49, 52.

89.   Article 1(1) of the Declaration on the Right to Development, General Assembly

Resolution 41/128 of 4 December 1986; Articles 21 and 22 of the Banjul Charter. Many still deny that a right to development exists, see, e.g., I.A. Shearer, *Starke's International Law* (11th edn, 1994) p. 358. However, it is worth noting that the Vienna Conference on Human Rights reaffirmed the right to development 'as a universal and inalienable right and an integral part of fundamental human rights' (Part I, para. 10). However, development must be compatible with the protection of the environment, with the result that the concept of sustainable development has emerged, placing human concerns at the core of the development process and hence requiring the protection of the environment and the life of present and future generations, see Vienna Conference on Human Rights (Part I, para. 11), Rio Declaration on Environment and Development (Principles 3, 4, 27), OAU Charter for Popular Participation in Development and Transformation (para. 9) (E/ECA/CM.16/11), which Judge Weeramantry found to be a recognized principle of contemporary international law in the *Gabčíkovo-Nagymaros Project Case* ICJ Reports 1997, p. 7. Furthermore, at its meeting in Rio de Janeiro in 1992, UNCED adopted Agenda 21, a comprehensive programme of action relating to sustainable development, UN Doc. E/CN.4/Sub.2/1992/7/ Add.1, pp. 4–7. In addition, Article 174 EC Treaty seems to make reference to the concept of sustainable development without actually employing the term. However, many jurists are reluctant to go this far in view of uncertainty as to its scope and content, see Brownlie, note 53 *supra*, p. 287; Shaw, note 53 *supra*, p. 606; although Birnie and Boyle seem more optimistic, note 1 *supra*, pp. 122–4.

90.   Article 7 ICES; Article 31 of the Revised European Social Charter.
91.   Article 11 ICES.
92.   Article 19(2) ICCPR; Rio Declaration on Environment and Development (Principle 10); Convention on Access to Information, Public Participation and Access to Justice in Environmental Matters. See further, section 37 of the Constitution of Malawi and section 32 of the South African Constitution. See also Directive 90/313 EEC, OJ [1990] L 158, on public access to environmental information; and T-105/95 *WWF UK (World Wide Fund for Nature) (Sweden intervening)* v. *Commission (France and United Kingdom intervening)* [1997] 2 CMLR 55. See further, *M.C. Mehta* v. *Union of India* AIR 1988 1037; *Leander* v. *Sweden* Series A, Vol. 116 (1987); *Gaskin* v. *United Kingdom* Series A, Vol. 160 (1989), which although not based on environmental facts, established the legitimacy of a right to access of information. See further, S. Weber, 'Environmental Information and the European Convention on Human Rights', 12 *Human Rights Law Journal* (1991) 177.
93.   Article 25 ICCPR; Article 13(1) Banjul Charter; Rio Declaration on Environment and Development (Principle 10); OAU Charter for Popular Participation in Development and Transformation 1990; Convention on Access to Information, Public Participation and Access to Justice in Environmental Matters.
94.   See Article 13 ECHR; Rio Declaration on Environment and Development (Principles 10 and 13); Convention on Access to Information, Public Participation and Access to Justice in Environmental Matters.
95.   Articles 5, 6, 13 and 16 of the Basel Convention. The Basel Convention seeks to ensure effective compliance through a supervisory body, the Secretariat. Its powers are not extensive but it can assist in the identification of illegal traffic, Birnie and Boyle, note 1 *supra*, p. 341. In 1992 the Secretariat intervened in the planned export of hazardous waste from some European countries to Somalia and was successful in putting a halt to such exports, UN Doc. E/CN.4/1993/ 119. See also Articles 5, 6, 13 and 16 of the Bamako Convention; Shearer, note 13 *supra*, pp. 166, 67. The lack of adequate information has been identified by the OAU as one of the main problems facing African countries and calls have therefore been made for a database, UN Commission on Human Rights,

Adverse effects of the illicit movement and dumping of toxic and dangerous products and wastes on the enjoyment of human rights, Report of the Special Rapporteur, UN Doc. E/CN.4/1998/10/Add.2, paras. 45, 58.

96. Article 5(4).

97. UN Commission on Human Rights, Adverse effects of the illicit movement and dumping of toxic and dangerous products and wastes on the enjoyment of human rights, Report of the Special Rapporteur, UN Doc. E/CN.4/1998/10/Add.2, para. 45.

98. Principles 10 and 11, the latter of which requires States to enact effective environmental legislation. See further, UN General Assembly Resolution A/RES/S-19/2, paras. 107–10. However, it is instructive to note that the EC is committed to environmental policies at the supranational level, see Articles 3(l) and 174 EC Treaty.

99. The Environmental Protection (Prevention of Dumping) Act 1988, 1 *RADIC* (1989) 178.

100. UN Doc. E/CN.4/Sub.2/1997/27, para. 12. See further Eguh, note 28 *supra*, pp. 145–51.

101. Environment Protection Act 1994, 20 *CLB* (1994) 785.

102. UN Doc. CCPR/C/75/Add.2, para. 74(b).

103. Environmental Protection and Pollution Control Act 1990, 17 *CLB* (1991) 1152.

104. In 1988 the National Agency for the Protection of the Environment was established with responsibility for combating all forms of pollution, monitoring pollutant waste and processing facilities and instituting legal proceedings to obtain compensation for damage caused to the environment. Decree No. 90–2273 of 25 December 1990 requires impact studies to be made before the erection of any industrial, agricultural or commercial body whose activities may be a source of environmental damage or pollution.

105. Act No. 89/027 of 29 December 1989, UN Doc. CCPR/C/63/Add.1, para. 49.

106. UN Doc. E/CN.4/1998/SR.16, p. 8; see further, UN Commission on Human Rights, Adverse effects of the illicit movement and dumping of toxic and dangerous products and wastes on the enjoyment of human rights, Report of the Special Rapporteur, UN Doc. E/CN.4/1998/10/Add.2, paras. 8–33.

107. Ibid., paras. 34–40.

108. See the recommendations of the Special Rapporteur, UN Commission on Human Rights, Adverse effects of the illicit movement and dumping of toxic and dangerous products and wastes on the enjoyment of human rights, Progress Report of the Special Rapporteur, UN Docs. E/CN.4/1997/19, pp. 17–20; E/CN.4/1998/10, pp. 21–3; E/CN.4/1998/10/Add.2, pp. 14, 15.

109. It appears that many NGOs in Africa lack the necessary means to play an effective role in monitoring the traffic in waste, UN Commission on Human Rights, Adverse effects of the illicit movement and dumping of toxic and dangerous wastes on the enjoyment of human rights, Progress Report of the Special Rapporteur, UN Doc. E/CN.4/1998/10/Add.2, paras. 50, 51.

110. The Special Rapporteur has reported that the monitoring mechanisms under the Basel Convention are being patchily observed, UN Commission on Human Rights, Adverse effects of the illicit movement and dumping of toxic and dangerous wastes on the enjoyment of human rights, Progress Report of the Special Rapporteur, UN Docs. E/CN.4/1997/19, para. 88.

6

The African Economic Community

Since independence the economies of most African States have been dominated by a series of financial crises and largely characterized by sluggish performance. A combination of internal and external factors have been responsible for this state of affairs. The former include the pursuit of ill-advised economic policies, lack of financial resources, deficiencies in institutional and physical infrastructures, insufficient managerial/administrative capacity, often leading to rampant corruption, inadequate human resource development, political instability, disparities in urban and rural development aggravated by ecologically unfriendly agricultural policies and exacerbated by a population boom. External factors include adverse terms of trade, a decline in financial flows, a decrease in commodity prices and high debt and debt-servicing obligations.[1] Although the international community is attempting to adopt co-ordinated programmes towards Africa aimed at ensuring economic growth,[2] the African States have come to the conclusion that indigenous solutions are also possible and even preferable. The founding of an African Economic Community under the auspices of the OAU is the most significant development to date in this field.

It should be recalled that economic development is one of the principal concerns of the OAU and hence finds expression in the OAU Charter. Article 2(1)(b) thereof proclaims the need of African States to 'co-ordinate and intensify ... co-operation efforts to achieve a better life for the peoples of Africa', while Article 20 makes provision for specialized commissions to accomplish these functions.

Background

As part of the UN Development Decade the OAU and the ECA convened a colloquium in Monrovia, Liberia, in February 1979 on Perspectives of Development and Economic Growth in Africa Up to the Year 2000. The resulting document was subsequently adopted by the OAU Assembly in Resolution AHG/ST.3 (XVI) Rev.1 as the Monrovia Declaration of Commitment of the

Heads of State and Government of the Organization of African Unity on Guidelines and Measures for National and Collective Self-Reliance in Social and Economic Development for the Establishment of a New International Economic Order. Under this Declaration African States committed themselves, *inter alia*, to promoting the economic and social development and integration of their economies with a view towards achieving self-sufficiency; to promoting the economic integration of Africa; and to establishing national and regional institutions to realize these objectives.[3] This programme was to pave the way for an African Economic Community. The OAU Assembly consequently held a Special Economic Summit in Lagos, Nigeria, in April 1980 to advance these aims.

The Lagos Plan of Action

The Lagos Plan of Action was the outcome of a joint OAU/ECA venture to elaborate a successful regional strategy for development in Africa.[4] It aimed to create conditions to encourage economic growth in African States, particularly in the sectors of food and agriculture, industry and energy, and at protecting the environment. But perhaps its most ambitious proposal was for an African Economic Community by the year 2000.

The preamble to the Lagos Plan of Action recognized the general economic decline of African States and the obvious importance of reversing this trend. It reaffirmed the Monrovia Declaration and declared its commitment to the goal of African collective economic self-reliance.

The objective of establishing an African Economic Community in gradual steps by the millennium was to 'ensure the economic, social and cultural integration' of Africa. To this end the Lagos Plan of Action recommended that the OAU should initially 'strengthen existing regional economic communities and establish other economic groupings in the other regions of Africa, so as to cover the continent as a whole';[5] strengthen sectoral integration at the continental level, particularly in the fields of agriculture, food, transport and communications, industry and energy; promote co-ordination and harmonization among the existing and future economic groupings for a gradual establishment of an African Common Market. Once these objectives had been achieved further sectoral integration would lead to the creation of an African Economic Community.

Progress was slow on the implementation of the Lagos Plan of Action and various initiatives were taken to relaunch the project. Africa's Priority Programme for Economic Recovery 1986–1990 (APPER), adopted by the Twenty-First Summit in 1985, outlined conditions for integration. But much more significant was the programme of action adopted by the UN designed to halt Africa's economic decline. Under the UN Programme of Action for African Economic Recovery and Development 1986–1990 (UN PAAERD), the international community undertook to support the initiatives of the OAU under APPER to, *inter alia*, promote food production and develop agro-industries and human resources.[6] One of the principal follow-up sessions of UN PAAERD was the conference, The Challenge of Economic Recovery and Accelerated Development, held in Abuja, Nigeria in June 1987 with the purpose of conducting an in-depth review of Africa's recovery process and prospects for long-term development.[7] The Conference put economic integration back on the agenda and urged African States to embark on a comprehensive approach to the issue, including the pursuit of measures for the close co-ordination of economic and social policies.

The AEC Treaty

The AEC Treaty was adopted at Abuja on 3 June 1991 and entered into force on 12 May 1994, behind the time schedule envisaged by the Lagos Plan of Action.[8] By virtue of Article 2 an African Economic Community is established.[9] Its objectives are: to promote economic, social and cultural development and the integration of African economies in order to increase economic self-reliance and promote development; to harness and develop Africa's human and material resources; and to promote co-operation so as to raise the standard of living and enhance economic stability, foster peaceful relations among Member States and contribute to the progress, development and economic integration of Africa.[10] These aims are to be achieved by, *inter alia*, the liberalization of trade through the abolition of customs duties on imports and exports and non-tariff barriers in order to establish a free trade area, the adoption of a common trade policy *vis-à-vis* third States, the harmonization of national policies in agriculture, industry, transport and communications, energy, trade, money and finance and science and technology, the establishment of a common external tariff, the removal of obstacles to the free movement of persons, goods, services and capital and the right of residence and establishment, and the establishment of a common market.[11] Not unlike the European Union, the AEC foresees a role beyond the economic sphere, in the social and political worlds, leading eventually to political union.[12]

However, as is common with regional economic integration organizations, this is to be achieved progressively in six stages over a transitional period not exceeding forty years.[13] The first stage, reflecting the Lagos Plan recommendations, requires the strengthening of existing regional economic communities, including the creation of new ones where they do not exist.[14] The second stage involves the gradual removal of tariff and non-tariff barriers and the gradual harmonization of customs duties in relation to third States. The third and fourth stages are the establishment of a free trade area and a customs union, while the next stage is the establishment of an African Common Market. The final stage envisages: (a) the consolidation and strengthening of the African Common Market through the inclusion of the free movement of persons, goods, capital and services, as well as rights of residence and establishment; (b) the integration of all economic, political, social and cultural sectors, establishment of a single domestic market and a Pan-African Economic and Monetary Union; (c) the setting up of an African Monetary Union, including a single African Central Bank and a single African currency; (d) harmonizing and co-ordinating the activities of regional economic communities;[15] (e) setting up the structures of African multinational enterprises in all sectors; and (f) setting up the structures of the AEC organs.

The Organs of the AEC

Article 7(1) establishes the organs of the AEC. These are: (a) the Assembly; (b) the Council of Ministers; (c) the Pan-African Parliament; (d) the Economic and Social Commission; (e) the Court of Justice; (f) the General Secretariat; and (g) the Specialized Technical Committees.[16]

The Assembly

The Assembly, which is the supreme organ of the AEC,[17] has legislative and supervisory functions and is responsible for implementing the objectives of the AEC and to that end it has the power to, *inter alia*, determine the general policy of the AEC and harmonize the sectoral policies of the Member States, approve the AEC's programme of activity and budget, on the recommendation of the Council, refer matters to the Court of Justice, and take any action to attain the objectives of the AEC.[18]

The Council

The Council is responsible for the functioning and development of the AEC and to that end it has the capacity, *inter alia*, to make recommendations and submit proposals to the Assembly concerning programmes of activity and budget of the AEC, request advisory opinions from the Court of Justice, and guide the activities of the subordinate organs of the AEC.[19]

The Parliament

The Pan-African Parliament is established with a view to ensuring the participation of the peoples of Africa in the running of the AEC. However, its composition, functions and powers are undefined, the details simply left to a later protocol.[20] There is therefore no indication whatsoever how the people are to be involved nor whether the Parliament is meant to exercise any democratic accountability over the AEC. Neither is there any intimation as to whether it will have legislative or supervisory powers. The Treaty's framework suggests that the answer should be in the negative since all legislation is, directly or indirectly, adopted by either the Assembly or the Council and the supervision of the activities of the AEC organs has been entrusted to the Court of Justice. The European Parliament obviously provides a model[21] but whether the political will exists to set up a democratically elected supranational body, over which the Member States can exercise little or no control, must be open to question.

The Commission

The Economic and Social Commission is composed of the ministers responsible for economic development, planning and integration of the Member States.[22] The Commission, which has not been granted any decision-making power, is expected to, *inter alia*, prepare policies and strategies for co-operation in the fields of economic and social development among African countries, and between Africa and the international community, and make recommendations to the Assembly, through the Council; to make recommendations to the Assembly, through the Council, on the co-ordination and harmonization of the activities of the regional economic communities; to co-ordinate, harmonize and supervise the activities of the Secretariat and the Committees; to examine and assess the reports and recommendations of the Committees and forward them to the Assembly, through the Council; and supervise the preparation of international negotiations and report to the Assembly, through the Council.[23]

The Secretariat

The Secretary-General directs the activities of the Secretariat and is charged with securing the implementation of the Assembly's decisions and the application of the Council's regulations; promoting development programmes and drafting studies with the aim of attaining the objectives of the AEC; draft proposals on the programme of activity and budget and secure their implementation upon approval by the Assembly; and submit a report on the activities of the AEC to the meetings of the Assembly, the Council and the Commission.[24] The Secretary-General is a full participant in the meetings and deliberations of the regional economic communities.[25]

The Committees

Provision is made for seven specialized technical committees, on Rural Economy and Agricultural Matters, on Monetary and Financial Matters, for instance, composed of representatives from the Member States.[26] Their function is, *inter alia*, to prepare projects and programmes for submission to the Commission, to co-ordinate and harmonize the projects and programmes of the AEC, to report to the Commission on the implementation of the Treaty, and to ensure the supervision, follow-up and the evaluation of the decisions of the organs of the AEC.[27] It seems that the term 'decisions' in this context refers to secondary legislation only, i.e., Council decisions and Commission regulations.

The Court of Justice

A matter of some importance is the creation of a Court of Justice assigned with the task of ensuring adherence to the law in the interpretation and application of the Treaty and deciding on disputes submitted to it under the Treaty.[28] The Court, the independence of which is guaranteed,[29] is endowed with jurisdiction over actions brought by a Member State or the Assembly on grounds of a violation of the Treaty or of a legislative measure, or on grounds of lack of competence or abuse of powers by an organ or a Member State.[30] Furthermore, it should be observed that the Assembly may refer any dispute concerning the Protocol on the Relationship between the African Economic Community and the Regional Economic Communities to the Court as a measure of 'last resort'.[31] The Court can also issue advisory opinions at the request of the Assembly or the Council.[32] The Assembly may additionally confer on the Court of Justice jurisdiction over any dispute other than those referred to in Article 18(3)(a).[33] The judgments of the Court are binding on Member States and organs of the AEC.[34] They are final and not subject to appeal.[35]

The wording of Article 18(3)(a) is problematic and it is not apparent whether the Court is empowered to annul Community, or possibly even municipal, legislation. The absence of judicial review enabling the Court to annul Community legislation would undermine the rule of law and marginalize the Court to the point of irrelevancy. Such a power must be implied. Alternatively, the provision can also be understood to mean that the Assembly or a Member State could institute proceedings against another Member State's municipal legislation for lack of competence or abuse of powers. A capacity to annul municipal legislation would be a radical development.[36]

It is especially worthy of comment to observe that no other organ, such as the Council or the Commission, can institute contentious proceedings before the Court even though it may be a defendant to an action before the

Court. These organs will have to rely on the parties with *locus standi* to defend their interests before the Court[37] or on the Council invoking the advisory jurisdiction of the Court to obtain, in effect, a declaratory judgment.

In addition to the Court's jurisdiction under Article 18, the AEC Treaty stipulates the further involvement of the Court in the 'procedure for the settlement of disputes'. Hence Article 87 envisages that all disputes regarding the interpretation and application of the AEC Treaty are to be settled initially through amicable agreement by the parties concerned. Should this attempt fail, either party may refer the matter to the Court within the next twelve months, the decisions of which are to be final and not subject to appeal.

The relationship between these two provisions appears problematic, however. For example, a dispute may fall within the ambit of both provisions. In which case, which method of settlement governs the dispute?

It remains to be seen how the Court will operate in practice and the provisions of the AEC Treaty relating to the Court raise many questions. An obvious omission is a procedure for obtaining a preliminary ruling on the interpretation of AEC law comparable to that available under Article 234 (ex Art 177) EC Treaty.[38] Moreover, there is no provision on whether the Court may issue interim measures of protection,[39] and it is unclear whether the Court will be allowed to determine its own jurisdiction. For instance, Article 18(3) states that the Court *shall* give advisory opinions. Does this mean that the Court is compelled to do so even if it considers the question frivolous or without merit? In addition, the very limited number of parties with *locus standi* has been criticized as unduly restrictive.[40] The different legal traditions in Africa may make agreement on these issues difficult but their adoption would advance the rule of law and would allow the indirect involvement of private individuals in ensuring that Community law is observed in the domestic legal systems.[41]

Furthermore, unlike the African Commission on Human Rights[42] and the African Court of Human Rights[43] no guidance is provided as to whether the Court can draw inspiration from general principles of international or other law as developed by other organs such as the ECJ.[44] It is submitted that the Court must be given the freedom to be guided by persuasive authorities from other jurisdictions and thus benefit from their experience.

Although the judgments of the Court are binding on Member States and AEC organs there is no express reference to the enforcement of judicial decisions and an expectation that Member States will simply abide by the Court's decisions may be naive.[45] However, Article 5(1), (2) requires Member States to take all necessary measures to fulfil their obligations and paragraph (3) thereof does allow for sanctions against a Member State which persistently fails to honour its undertakings under the Treaty and it may be that this provision can be used against a State which flouts the Court's decisions.

It has already been observed elsewhere that African States have traditionally been wary of binding adjudication and past experience therefore suggests that the Court may be underused. However, it is submitted that the Court has a central role to play in the development of the AEC and it must be permitted to contribute fully to that growth. One can only anticipate that the Court will assume effective powers. The experience of the EC has amply demonstrated that without an active, dynamic and forceful court the objectives of the EC would have been thwarted.[46] Neither should the ECJ's salient role in making the EC Treaty and secondary legislation effective and in evolving general principles of EC law be overlooked.[47] The EC experience provides a role model for the AEC but whether the African States are prepared to follow that path must be open to serious doubt.[48]

Sources of Law

The AEC Treaty provides for various sources of law. First and foremost, there is the Treaty itself, which may be termed the primary source. By virtue of Article 18(3)(a) the Treaty is given priority over conflicting legal obligations contained in what may be classified as secondary sources of law, i.e., decisions and regulations.

Both the Assembly and the Council are empowered under the Treaty to adopt subordinate legislative measures. However, it is important to note that the Treaty establishes a hierarchy of secondary sources. The Assembly acts by decisions, the principal enactment, which are binding on Member States and AEC organs as well as regional economic communities.[49] Decisions are automatically enforceable thirty days after their signing by the Chairman of the Assembly.[50]

Regulations are issued by the Council and are similarly binding on Member States, AEC organs and regional economic communities after their approval by the Assembly.[51] However, no prior permission is necessary where the Council is acting under powers delegated by the Assembly.[52] Regulations are likewise automatically enforceable thirty days after their date of signature by the Chairman of the Assembly.[53]

It is not apparent whether decisions and regulations are meant to take effect without further legislative enactment on the part of Member States.[54] This then begs the question whether the Court of Justice will take the giant step of adopting the concept of direct effect, i.e., measures which give rise to rights or obligations which individuals can invoke before their national courts.

In this context attention must be drawn to Article 5 of the AEC Treaty which requires Member States to take all necessary measures to fulfil their obligations. This provision is similarly worded to Article 10 (ex Art 5) of the EC Treaty from which the ECJ has derived the principle of indirect effect, i.e., that all the organs of state are obliged to achieve the result stated in the EC legislation, and the duty of interpretation, i.e., that Member States must interpret domestic law in the light of EC law.[55] An activist Court of Justice may follow a path similar to that cleared by the ECJ.

Under Article 8(3)(a) the Assembly can additionally issue directives. These seem to be 'guiding principles' rather than legislative measures and may therefore allow States a measure of discretion.[56] The Council, the Commission and Specialized Technical Committees are authorized to make recommendations and submit reports[57] which are not legally binding.[58]

It is important to observe that the Assembly has expressly been granted broad general powers, which must necessarily include residual legislative powers, under Article 8(3)(b) to attain the objectives of the AEC.[59] This provision is limited by the requirement to act *intra vires* but otherwise the Assembly hardly seems to be placed under any severe restraint, with the exception that it may not effect changes akin to treaty amendments by relying on this provision.[60]

Finally, attention has already been drawn above to the fact that the decisions of the Court of Justice are binding, giving it a central role in the evolution of the AEC legal system. It is anticipated that the Court will develop a substantial body of case law.

General Principles of Law

The development of general principles of law by the jurisprudence of the Court of Justice must be contemplated. One of the fundamental principles enshrined in the AEC Treaty is the observance of the Community's legal system and the protection of human rights.[61] Moreover, as has been observed above, Member States undertake to further, and refrain from hindering, the objectives of the AEC.[62] There is therefore an explicit commitment on the part of the Member States to the rule of law.[63] In addition, it should be recalled that under Article 18(3)(a) the Court can annul legislation on the grounds of, *inter alia*, abuse of powers.

It does not seem unreasonable to assert therefore that the Court may find legislative measures to be in violation of human rights norms, e.g., the principle of non-discrimination on grounds of nationality and sex,[64] or the principles of legal certainty,[65] legitimate expectations[66] and proportionality,[67] which have been such distinctive features of the jurisprudence of the ECJ.

Supremacy of AEC Law

As the States of Africa proceed towards economic integration and beyond, a fundamental question that must be addressed is that of supremacy. Economic integration implies and demands transfer of sovereignty from Member States to the Community.[68] Furthermore, if the Community's objectives are to be achieved and disparities between Member States avoided, including the harmonization of differing national legal codes, a uniform approach to the incorporation, application and interpretation of Community law seems necessary. As the ECJ has stated, the EC 'would be quite meaningless if a state could unilaterally nullify its effects by means of a legislative measure which could prevail over Community law'.[69] However, as has already been seen, the traditional emphasis on sovereignty and domestic jurisdiction by African States is bound to be problematic.[70]

In terms of international law the AEC Treaty is an international agreement entered into by sovereign states. Ratification of the AEC Treaty takes place in accordance with the constitutional procedures of participating States.[71] Once incorporated the AEC Treaty will take effect. The AEC has the features of a supranational organization with all that that implies.[72] While the AEC Treaty is silent on the issues of 'sovereignty' or 'domestic jurisdiction'[73] the AEC is about the division of competence between it and the Member States.[74] In addition, the AEC Treaty requires the co-ordination and harmonization of laws and policies across a spectrum of activity.[75]

The AEC is unlikely to function effectively unless and until it is accorded supremacy in its areas of competence. How can its objectives ever hope to be achieved if conflicting national laws are given precedence over AEC law? Logic dictates that AEC law must have priority over national laws. Article 5 of the AEC Treaty does seem to lend support to the principle of supremacy of AEC law over national law.[76] It thus follows from the precedent provided by EC law that AEC law must not be invalidated by national law,[77] it must not be annulled by a national court,[78] conflicting national legislation must be disapplied,[79] or even set aside,[80] and national law must be interpreted in light of AEC law.[81] In this context the principle of direct effect of AEC law will be an essential element in securing the harmonization of national laws.

The Regulation of Substantive Law in the AEC Treaty

The AEC Treaty seeks to regulate various areas of economic activity at both the regional and continental levels.

Customs Union and Liberalization of Trade

Article 29 requires the progressive establishment of a customs union involving the elimination of customs duties, quota restrictions, other restrictions or prohibitions and administrative trade barriers, as well as all other non-tariff barriers, and the adoption of a common external customs tariff.[82] Subsequent provisions set out how these objectives are to be achieved and include: a prohibition on the imposition of any new customs duties and on the increase of existing customs duties;[83] the progressive reduction and eventual elimination of customs duties;[84] the progressive relaxation, ultimate removal and prohibition of quota restrictions and other non-tariff barriers and prohibi-tions;[85] the gradual establishment of a common external customs tariff applicable to goods originating from third States imported into Member States;[86] a prohibition on customs duties on goods originating in one Member State and imported into another and on goods originating from third States in free circulation in Member States and imported from one into another;[87] a prohibition on national legislation implying direct or indirect discrimination against identical or similar products originating from another Member State;[88] a prohibition on internal taxes in excess of those levied on similar domestic products on goods originating from a Member State and imported into another;[89] and the progressive elimination of internal taxes levied for the protection of domestic products.[90]

The experience of the EC demonstrates that States are ingenious in erecting all sorts of new barriers obstructing the free movement of goods and it may therefore have been sensible to insert the phrase 'and measures of equivalent effect' where appropriate in the relevant provisions of the AEC Treaty.[91]

Article 35 allows for derogations in a number of circumstances, none of which can be used as a means of arbitrary discrimination or a disguised restriction on trade.[92] It is not clear whether the derogations are subject to the principle of proportionality.[93] The grounds of derogation, which appear to be exhaustive, include national security, the control of arms and military equipment, protection of health and life of humans, animals and plants, public morality, protection of national treasures of artistic or archaeological value, protection of industrial, commercial and intellectual property, exports of strategic minerals and precious stones, the protection of infant industries, the control of hazardous and radioactive wastes and products and nuclear materials, the control of strategic products, balance of payment difficulties, and serious economic difficulties arising from imports from a Member State.[94]

Other areas of co-operation include re-export of goods and intra-com-munity transit facilities,[95] harmonization and standardization of customs regulations and procedures,[96] simplification and harmonization of trade documents and procedures,[97] corrective measures in respect of substantial diversion of trade arising from barter or compensatory exchange agreements with third States,[98] and trade promotion.[99]

In relation to intra-community trade, Article 37 requires Member States to accord one another most-favoured-nation treatment and in no case must tariff concessions granted to a third State be more favourable than those applicable under the AEC Treaty. Clearly, Member States must never be put at a disadvantage *vis-à-vis* third States.

Free Movement of Persons

Pursuant to Article 43 Member States undertake progressively to secure for their nationals the free movement of persons and the rights of residence and establishment within the AEC.[100] The details have been left to a protocol. The free movement of persons is an essential element of economic integration.[101] By analogy with the EC experience, the issues that will need to be addressed in the protocol include rights of entry and residence, the right to take up offers of employment, the right to look for employment,[102] employment and associated rights, including equality in employment, unemployment and incapacity to work, the right to remain after employment, family rights, including schooling for dependants, the rights of non-AEC national dependants, entitlement to social security,[103] public service employment, access to the professions, including the mutual recognition of qualifications, the rights of legal persons, and derogations on grounds of public policy, public security or public health, and the appropriate safeguards for persons whose rights of free movement may be restricted on such grounds.

Money, Finance and Payment Policies

Another crucial area is that of money and finance. Member States are to harmonize their monetary, financial and payment policies, including the fields of insurance and banking, with the eventual aim of establishing an African Monetary Union.[104] Furthermore, the free movement of capital is to be achieved through the elimination of restrictions on the transfer of capital funds between Member States. This should facilitate the opening of bank accounts or the obtaining of loans from a financial institution in another Member State. If the free movement of persons is to be properly secured then restrictions on the movement of capital belonging to persons resident in other Member States must be reduced. However, the risk exists that the liberalization of monetary controls, particularly exchange controls, could lead to the flight of funds to economically and politically stable countries.

Other Areas of Co-operation

Other areas of co-operation covered by the AEC Treaty are: (i) agricultural development and food production;[105] (ii) industrial development, science and technology, energy and natural resources, and the environment;[106] (iii) transport and communications (post, telecommunications and broadcasting), including an integrated network;[107] (iv) tourism;[108] (v) education, training and culture;[109] and (vi) human resources, social affairs, health and population.[110]

Conclusion

The AEC Treaty is an ambitious, perhaps overambitious, project which reflects the global trend towards regional economic integration. In addition, it is an indication of the readiness of African States to confront and solve their economic problems through indigenous solutions and turn themselves away from a reliance on aid and economic policies foisted upon them by external bodies. However, there cannot be any doubt that this will be a long-term proposition as many obstacles still need to be overcome and even the lengthy period set by the AEC Treaty may come to be seen as unduly optimistic. The success of the AEC will depend to a large measure on the political attitude of the Member States, particularly whether they will be willing to surrender some control over their financial and economic affairs. Enmities and rivalries will have to be set aside. The weakness and misman-agement of many African economies are obvious difficulties. But neither should legal problems be underestimated. The diversity of legal systems and the different national commercial and company law codes will not facilitate co-operation and harmonization.[111] Moreover, it would seem that many such laws, including conflict of laws rules, are so antiquated that they will be unable to meet the challenges ahead.[112] Law reform, usually a painfully slow process, on a vast scale appears necessary as a condition precedent for the success of the AEC. Nevertheless, these difficulties should not be exagger-ated since the States of the EC have faced similar hurdles which have been overcome and that Community continues to evolve towards a longer term project. In principle the AEC Treaty seems sound enough to fulfil its objectives but whether it will function in practice remains to be seen and much will depend on the various protocols forthcoming and the creativity of the Court of Justice. Certainly the Protocol on the jurisdiction of the Court is a priority. The success of the AEC will depend in large measure on the political will of the Member States to put aside their differences, suppress the national interest, and co-operate through the Assembly and Council to attain the AEC's objectives.[113]

Notes

1. *Africa's Submission to the Special Session of the United Nations General Assembly on Africa's Economic and Social Crisis* (1986). See further, T.M. Callaghy and J. Ravenhill (eds.), *Hemmed In: Responses to Africa's Economic Decline* (1993); J.A. Widner (ed.), *Economic Change and Political Liberalization in Sub-Saharan Africa* (1994); C. Clapham, *Africa and the International System* (1996) Chapter 7.
2. See, e.g., the joint IMF/World Bank Highly Indebted Poor Countries (HIPC) initiative of 1996 which aims to provide debt relief in return for economic reform and liberalization. In addition, according to the terms of the Mauritius Mandate, launched by Commonwealth finance ministers in 1997, the inter-

national community is called upon to ensure that eligible countries are embarked on the process of securing a sustainable release from the debt burden by 2000. The economic outlook for Africa has improved in recent years with sub-Saharan Africa experiencing three successive years of strong economic growth which appears capable of being maintained for the foreseeable future.

3. R.M. D'Sa, 'The Lagos Plan of Action – Legal Mechanisms for Co-operation between the Organisation of African Unity and the United Nations Economic Commission for Africa', 27 *JAL* (1983) 4 at pp. 11, 12.

4. D'Sa, note 3 *supra*, pp. 12–21. The Lagos Plan of Action has been described as 'economically illiterate', Clapham, note 1 *supra*, p. 176.

5. Probably the most important African regional economic organizations are: ECOWAS, 14 *ILM* 1200 (1975), revised treaty in 35 *ILM* 35 (1996); COMESA, 33 *ILM* 1072 (1994); and SADC, 5 *RADIC* (1993) 415. See K.K. Mwenda, 'Legal Aspects of Regional Integration: COMESA and SADC on the Regulation of Foreign Investment in Southern and Eastern Africa', 9 *RADIC* (1997) 324.

6. General Assembly Resolution S-13/2 (1986). This special session of the General Assembly was convened at the request of the OAU and was the first such conference ever held by the UN to consider the economic plight of a specific geographic region.

7. The Abuja Statement, ECA/CERAD/87/75.

8. Text in *Naldi*, pp. 203–43. The AEC was inaugurated at the Thirty-third OAU Summit held in Harare in 1997, *Keesing's*, Vol. 43, 1997, p. 41674. It has been ratified by forty-two Member States. The fears of some that the AEC Treaty would remain unratified for a lengthy period of time simply did not materialise, see B. Thompson and R.S. Mukisa, 'Legal Integration as a Key Component of African Economic Integration: A Study of Potential Legal Obstacles to the Implementation of the Abuja Treaty', 20 *CLB* (1994) 1446 at pp. 1448–9. For analysis, see further N.L. Lumu, 'De la Nature de la Communauté Economique Africaine', 8 *RADIC* (1996) 51; M. Ndulo, 'Harmonisation of Trade Laws in the African Economic Community', 42 *ICLQ* (1993) 101; B. Thompson, 'Economic Integration Efforts in Africa', 5 *RADIC* (1993) 743.

9. According to the preamble and Article 98(1), the AEC forms an integral part of the OAU. Furthermore, Article 99 provides that the Treaty and Protocols are integral parts of the OAU Charter. Thompson and Mukisa are of the view that this language is not conclusive of the AEC's legal personality and predict trouble ahead, note 8 *supra*, p. 1452. However, since the OAU has legal personality, see Chapter 1, p. 18, *supra*, it would seem to follow that the same holds true for the AEC. Cf. Article 281 (ex Art 210) EC Treaty and see Case 43/59 *Lachmuller* v. *Commission* [1960] ECR 463.

10. Article 4(1); and see further, Thompson, note 8 *supra*, p. 747.

11. Article 4(2); Thompson, note 8 *supra*, pp. 747, 748.

12. Ndulo, note 8 *supra*, p. 102; Y. Omorogbe, 'Economic Integration and African National Development', *ASICL Proc.* 7 (1995) 279 at p. 286; Thompson, note 8 *supra*, pp. 765–77.

13. Article 6. See Thompson, note 8 *supra*, pp. 750 751; Omorogbe, note 12 *supra*, pp. 284, 285.

14. This stage, which has already commenced, should be completed by May 1999. See further, Article 3 of the Protocol on the Relationship between the African Economic Community and the Regional Economic Communities 1998, 10 *RADIC* (1998) 157. See also, S.B. Ajulo, 'Temporal Scope of ECOWAS and AEC Treaties: A Case for African Economic Integration', 8 *RADIC* (1996) 111.

15. See the Protocol on the Relationship between the African Economic Community and the Regional Economic Communities, note 14 *supra*.

16. It should be observed that the Assembly, the Council and the General Secretariat are the same as those of the OAU, see Article 1(h),(i), (n).
17. Article 8(1).
18. Article 8(2), (3). The Assembly has been given a dispute resolution function under Article 30 of the Protocol on the Relationship between the African Economic Community and the Regional Economic Communities, note 14 *supra*. Ordinarily, the Assembly meets once a year, Article 9(1).
19. Article 11(2), (3). Ordinarily the Council meets twice a year, Article 12(1).
20. Article 14; and see Thompson, note 8 *supra*, p. 757.
21. See Case 138/79 *Roquette Frères* v. *Council* [1980] ECR 3333, para. 33, where the ECJ referred to 'that fundamental democratic principle that the peoples should take part in the exercise of power through the intermediary of a representative assembly'.
22. Article 15(2). Representatives of regional economic communities have the right to take part in its meetings, Article 15(3). The Commission meets at least once a year but can meet in emergency session on its own initiative or at the request of the Assembly or the Council, Article 17.
23. Article 16. Thompson views the Commission's functions as central to the objectives of the AEC, note 8 *supra*, p. 762.
24. Article 22. Thompson sees the General Secretariat as the 'nerve centre' of the AEC, note 8 *supra*, p. 761.
25. Articles 20(1) and 23 of the Protocol on the Relationship between the African Economic Community and the Regional Economic Communities, note 14 *supra*.
26. Article 25. The Committees can meet as often as necessary, Article 27.
27. Article 26. See also the co-ordination organs established under Articles 6–10 of the Protocol on the Relationship between the African Economic Community and the Regional Economic Communities, note 14 *supra*.
28. Article 18(1), (2). Under Article 87(1) parties to a dispute regarding the interpretation or application of the Treaty may, failing amicable settlement, refer the matter to the Court. The Court's statute and procedures have been left to be determined by the Assembly in a subsequent protocol, Article 20. See generally, C.M. Peter, 'The Proposed African Court of Justice-Jurisprudential, Procedural, Enforcement Problems and Beyond', 1 *East African Journal of Peace & Human Rights* (1993) 117.
29. Article 18(5). See further, Peter, note 28 *supra*, p. 120.
30. Article 18(3)(a). See also Article 8(3)(k) which specifies an absolute majority vote in the Assembly to refer a matter to the Court. It is generally accepted that the ground of lack of competence is equivalent to the doctrine of *ultra vires* in English law. It has similarities with the power of judicial review in US constitutional law. Consequently institutions can act only when empowered to do so by law, for an example in EC Law, see Case 22/70 *Commission* v. *Council (ERTA)* [1971] ECR 274. Abuse of power refers to the use of power for the wrong purpose or not for the purpose originally intended, Case C-156/93 *Parliament* v. *Commission* [1995] ECR I-2019. It is interesting to note that no express provision is made for finding a Member State or organ in breach of a general principle of law, see further p. 248 *supra*.
31. Article 30 of the Protocol on the Relationship between the African Economic Community and the Regional Economic Communities, note 14 *supra*.
32. Article 18(3)(b). See also Articles 8(3)(l) and 11(3)(f).
33. Article 18(4). Peter is sceptical of the worth of this provision given that the Assembly meets so infrequently. In his view the Court should have been given inherent jurisdiction to entertain any justiciable dispute concerning the AEC, note 28 *supra*.
34. Article 19. See also Article 5.

35. Article 87(2). The question whether the Court will have the power to revise its own judgments is not addressed at this stage; cf. Article 40 of the Statute of the ECJ and Article 102 of the Rules of Procedure.

36. Although the European Court of Justice can require that a national statute be set aside on the ground of incompatibility with EC law it cannot invalidate municipal law, see C-213/89 R v. *Secretary of State for Transport, ex parte Factortame Ltd (No. 2)* [1990] ECR I-2433.

37. Note that this has occurred in the EC. See the ruling of the European Court of Justice in relation to the European Parliament in the 'Comitology' case (Case 302/87 *European Parliament* v. *Council* [1988] ECR 5616), subsequently reversed as inadequate in the 'Chernobyl' case (Case C-70/88 *European Parliament* v. *Council* [1990] ECR 2041).

38. See G. Bebr, 'Preliminary Rulings of the Court of Justice: Their Authority and Temporal Effect', 18 *CMLRev* (1981) 475.

39. Cf. Article 243 (ex Art 186) EC Treaty and Article 83(2) of the ECJ's Rules of Procedure; and see, G. Borchardt, 'The Award of Interim Measures by the ECJ', 22 *CMLRev* (1985) 203.

40. Ndulo, note 8 *supra*, ibid., notwithstanding the possibility under Article 18(4) that the Assembly may refer to the Court disputes between natural or legal persons and Member States concerning the latter's compliance with Treaty obligations or Community legislation. Staff disputes may also be included. As Ndulo points out, natural and legal persons have proved effective guardians of the EC legal order and have contributed enormously to the evolution of EC Law, see, e.g., C. Harding, 'The Private Interest in Challenging Community Action', 5 *ELRev* (1980) 354; C. Harlow, 'Towards a Theory of Access for the European Court of Justice', 12 *YEL* (1992) 213.

41. Ndulo, note 8 *supra*, p. 107. This contrasts with the EC where new Member States must accept the *acquis communautaire*, see Articles 2 and 3 (ex Art B) Treaty on European Union. Issues where disagreement is likely to arise concern the style of the Court's judgments, collegiate versus individual, and the doctrine of precedent. See generally, A. Arnull, 'Owning up to Fallibility: Precedent and the Court of Justice', 30 *CMLRev* (1993) 247.

42. Cf. Articles 60 and 61 Banjul Charter. See further p. 147 *supra*.

43. Cf. Article 7 of the Protocol to the African Charter on Human and Peoples' Rights on the Establishment of an African Court on Human and Peoples' Rights, see Chapter 4, p. 154 *supra*.

44. See generally, P. Craig and G. de Burca, *EC Law: Text, Cases and Materials* (1996) Chapters 7 and 8.

45. Note Article 3(e) and Article 5. See the scepticism expressed by Thompson and Mukisa, note 8 *supra* p. 1454; Ndulo, note 8 *supra*, ibid.

46. F. Jacobs, 'Is the Court of Justice of the European Communities a Constitutional Court?' in D. Curtin and D. O'Keeffe, (eds.), *Constitutional Adjudication in European Community and National Law* (1992) 25.

47. The literature on these subjects is enormous but see, P.P. Craig, 'Once upon a Time in the West: Direct Effect and the Federalization of EEC Law 12', *Oxford Journal of Legal Studies* (1992) 453; L. Krogsgaard, 'Fundamental Rights in the EC after Maastricht' [1993] *Legal Issues of European Integration* 99; A. Arnull, *General Principles of EEC Law and the Individual* (1990).

48. Thompson, note 8 *supra*, p. 762.

49. Article 10(1), (2). Decisions are adopted by consensus, or failing that, by a two-thirds majority, Article 10(4). However, no quorum is specified.

50. Article 10(3).

51. Article 13(1), (2). Regulations are adopted by consensus, or failing which, a

two-thirds majority of Member States, Article 13(4). Again, no quorum is specified.

52. Article 13(2) in conjunction with Article 8(3)(j).

53. Article 13(3).

54. See Thompson, note 8 *supra*, pp. 763, 764, who is uncertain whether regulations are self-executing, or directly applicable in terms of EC law, see Article 249 (ex Art 189) EC Treaty, and see further, T. Winter, 'Direct Applicability and Direct Effects', 9 *CMLRev* (1972) 425.

55. Case 14/83 *Von Colson and Kamann* v. *Land Nordrhein-Westfalen* [1984] ECR 1891; Case C-106/89 *Marleasing SA* v. *La Comercial Internacional de Alimentación SA* [1990] ECR I-4135; Case C-91/92 *Faccini Dori* v. *Recreb* [1994] ECR I-3235.

56. Under Article 21(1), (2) of the Protocol on the Relationship between the African Economic Community and the Regional Economic Communities, note 14 *supra*, both the Assembly and the Council can address directives to regional economic communities and their member states.

57. Articles 11(3)(a), 16 and 26 respectively.

58. Thompson, note 8 *supra*, p. 764. However, it is interesting to note that the ECJ has held that hortatory measures are not necessarily without legal significance, see Case C-322/88 *Grimaldi* v. *Fonds des Maladies Professionelles* [1989] ECR 4407.

59. Cf. Article 308 (ex Art 235) EC Treaty and Case 22/70 *Commission* v. *Council (ERTA)* [1971] ECR 274; and see J. Weiler, 'The Transformation of Europe', 100 *Yale Law Journal* (1991) 2403. On the principle of implied powers generally, see *Reparation for Injuries Suffered in the Service of the United Nations* ICJ Reports 1949, p. 174, at p. 182; *Certain Expenses of the United Nations* ICJ Reports 1962, p. 151, at p. 168.

60. See Article 103.

61. Article 3(e) and (g).

62. Article 5(1), (2). It should be observed that further to Article 5(3) any Member State persistently failing to honour its general undertakings or abiding by Community measures may be subjected to sanctions by the Assembly at the recommendation of the Council, including the suspension of membership rights and privileges.

63. Although not as explicit as that contained in Article 6 (ex Art F) Treaty on European Union. Thompson and Mukisa see the 'chronic disregard for the principle of legality' on the part of many African governments as one of the most formidable obstacles to economic integration, note 8 *supra*, p. 1454.

64. In relation to EC law, see generally Article 13 (ex Art 6(a)), and further Articles 12 (ex Art 6), 39(2) (ex Art 48(2)), 43 (ex Art 52), 49 (ex Art 59) and 50 (ex Art 60) EC Treaty (nationality), and Article 141 (ex Art 119) EC Treaty (sex), and C. Docksey, 'The Principle of Equality between Men and Women as a Fundamental Right under Community Law', 20 *Industrial Law Journal* (1991) 258.

65. Case 98/78 *Firma A. Racke* v. *Hauptzollamt Mainz* [1979] ECR 69; Case 63/83 *R* v. *Kirk* [1984] ECR 2689.

66. Case 120/86 *Mulder* v. *Minister van Landbouw en Visserij* [1988] ECR 2321; E. Sharpston, 'Legitimate Expectations and Economic Reality', 15 *ELRev* (1990) 103.

67. Case C-331/88 *R* v. *Minister for Agriculture, Fisheries and Food, ex parte Fedesa* [1990] ECR 4023; G. de Burca, 'The Principle of Proportionality and its Application in EC Law', 13 *YEL* (1993) 105.

68. Case 26/62 *Van Gend en Loos* v. *Nederlandse Administratie der Belastingen* [1963] ECR 1; Case 6/64 *Costa* v. *ENEL* [1964] ECR 585.

69. Case 6/64 *Costa* v. *ENEL* [1964] ECR 585.

70. Thompson and Mukisa see the issue as national sovereignty versus supranationality, note 8 *supra*, pp. 1449–51.

71. Article 100. For some general problems in relation to the ratification process, see Thompson and Mukisa, note 8 *supra*, pp. 1448, 1449.
72. See note 68 *supra*.
73. Thompson and Mukisa, note 8 *supra*, p. 1450.
74. It should be observed that the question of the EC's exclusive competence remains controversial in EC law because the EC Treaty does not make this distinction clear, see Article 5 (ex Art 3b) EC Treaty (subsidiarity clause), and *Brunner* v. *The European Union Treaty* [1994] 1 CMLR 57 (Federal Constitutional Court of Germany). It seems that the areas that fall within the EC's exclusive competence are those relating to the internal market, Craig and de Burca, note 44 *supra*, pp. 113, 114.
75. For example, Article 39 on customs co-operation and administration, and Article 40 on trade documents and procedures.
76. Thompson, note 8 *supra*, p. 749.
77. Case 11/70 *International Handelsgesellschaft GmbH* v. *EVGF* [1970] ECR 1125.
78. Case 314/85 *Firma Foto-Frost* v. *Hauptzollamt Lübeck-Ost* [1987] ECR 4199.
79. Case 106/77 *Amministrazione delle Finanze dello Stato* v. *Simmenthal SpA* [1978] ECR 629.
80. Case C-213/89 *R* v. *Secretary of State for Transport, ex parte Factortame* (No. 2) [1990] ECR I-2433.
81. Case C-106/89 *Marleasing SA* v. *La Comercial Internacional de Alimentación SA* [1992] ECR I-4135.
82. It should be observed that all these measures are to be taken at the level of regional economic communities, see Articles 13 and 14 of the Protocol on the Relationship between the African Economic Community and the Regional Economic Communities, note 14 *supra*.
83. Articles 30(1), (2), and 33(1).
84. Article 30(2), reinforced by Article 33(1).
85. Article 31(1).
86. Article 32(1).
87. Article 33(1). According to paragraph (3) thereof goods from third States are considered to be in free circulation in a Member State where the import formalities have been complied with, where customs duties have been paid in the Member State, and where the goods have not benefited from any exemption from custom duties.
88. Article 33(4).
89. Article 34(1).
90. Article 34(2).
91. Cf. Articles 28 and 29 (ex Art 30, 34) EC Treaty. See R. Barents, 'Charges of Equivalent Effect to Customs Duties', 15 *CMLRev* (1978) 415; and 'New Developments in Measures Having Equivalent Effects', 18 *CMLRev* (1981) 271.
92. Cf. Article 30 (ex Art 36) EC Treaty.
93. Cf. Case 145/88 *Torfaen Borough Council* v. *B & Q plc* [1989] ECR 3851. Under Article 35(6) the Council oversees the operations of such restrictions and prohibitions and is authorized to take appropriate action in this regard. This could include seeking an advisory opinion from the Court on whether national measures are compatible with AEC law.
94. Cf. Articles 30 and 134 (ex Art 36 and 115) EC Treaty.
95. Article 38.
96. Article 39.
97. Article 40.
98. Article 41.
99. Article 42.
100. The AEC Treaty seems broader in scope than the corresponding provisions of

the EC Treaty (Title III) and appears to envisage a general movement of population. No express provision is made for the freedom to provide services, cf. Article 50 (ex Art 60) EC Treaty, although the scope of the provision seems broad enough to encompass this freedom.

101. See also Article 71(2)(a). Thompson laments the lack of reference to 'Community citizenship', unlike the experience of ECOWAS, since he regards a common position on this issue as imperative for the accomplishment of the AEC's goals, note 8 *supra*, pp. 753, 754. Cf. Articles 17, 18 (ex Art 8) EC Treaty. The free movement of persons is described as one of the 'fundamental freedoms' of EC Law, see, e.g., Case 53/81 *Levin* v. *Staatssecretaris van Justicie* [1982] ECR 1035.

102. See also Article 71(2)(b), (e).

103. See also Article 72(2)(b).

104. Article 44.

105. Articles 46 and 47.

106. Articles 48–60.

107. Articles 61–4.

108. Article 65.

109. Articles 68–70.

110. Articles 71–6.

111. Ndulo, note 8 *supra*, pp. 107–1; Thompson and Mukisa, note 8 *supra*, pp. 1452, 1453.

112. Thompson and Mukisa, note 8 *supra*, pp. 1453, 1454.

113. Thompson, note 8 *supra*, p. 762.

Index

Abuja Statement 242, 253
Abuja Statement on Southern Africa 47
AEC (African Economic Community) 19, 20, 21, 22, 29, 149, 209, 218, 240–58
  Assembly 243, 244, 245, 247, 254, 256
  Council 243, 244, 245, 246, 247, 254, 256, 257
  Commission 243, 244, 245, 254
  Committees 243, 245
  Court of Justice 15, 32, 149, 209, 243, 244, 245–7, 248, 252, 254, 257
  General principles of law 248
  Parliament 243–4
  Protocol on the Relationship between the AEC and Regional Economic Communities 245, 253, 254, 256, 257
  Secretariat 243, 244, 254
  Substantive law 249–51, 257
  Supremacy 248–9, 256
African (Banjul) Charter on Human and Peoples' Rights 40, 80, 90, 99, 109–212, 222
  adoption and entry into force 109, 112–13
  African values 40, 111–12, 113, 114, 130, 131, 132, 138, 147
  amendment 23–4
  application of 115–17
    incorporation 115–16, 161–2

    non-discrimination 80, 116–17, 162, 163, 164, 165, 166, 167
  background 109–13
  basic principles 80, 113–14
    African conception of human rights 114
  civil and political rights 111, 113, 117–27
    assembly, right of 124, 188–9
    association, right to 115, 124, 187–8
    dignity and integrity of the individual 118–21, 171–7
    equality and non-discrimination 117, 162–7
    liberty and security of person, right to 121, 177–9
    fair trial, right to 118, 121–2, 179–83
    free movement, right to 83, 84, 85, 88, 124–6, 189–90
    freedom of conscience and religion 122–3, 183–5
    freedom of information and opinion 123–4, 185–7
    life, right to 117–18, 167–71
    participation in government, right to 126, 190, 238
    property, right to 105, 126–7, 190–2
  distinctive features 114–15
    lack of derogation clause 115
    lack of judicial body 114–15

African (Banjul) Charter on Human
and Peoples' Rights (*continued*)
second and third generation rights
113, 114, 127–8, 131–2
drafting of 110–13
duties of individual 138–9, 205
economic, social and cultural rights
111, 113, 127–30
children's rights 130, 199–200
education, right to 129–30, 195–6
equal pay, right to 128, 193
family, right to 130, 196–8
health, right to 128–9, 193–5
work, right to 128, 192–3
and OAU Charter 3, 4, 15, 19, 20,
110, 112, 113
omissions
marry, right to 130, 196–7
found a family, right to 130, 197
minority rights 138, 204–5
privacy, right to 127, 192
peoples' rights 111, 113, 131–8
common heritage of mankind
137, 204
development, right to 136–7,
202–204
environment, right to 138, 204,
220, 237, 238
peace and security, right to 105,
137–8, 204
self-determination, right to 46–7,
132–6, 200–2
preamble 113–14
ratification 23, 113, 158
African Charter on the Rights and
Welfare of the Child 117, 119,
149, 162, 165, 171, 172, 173, 183,
199
African Commission on Human and
Peoples' Rights 19–20, 23, 44,
86, 105, 108, 113, 117, 120, 121,
122, 124, 126, 133, 139–47, 159,
161, 162, 167, 182, 246
and African Court on Human and
Peoples' Rights 148–52, 153,
156, 246
individual communications 144–6
inter-state communications 143–4
mandate 141–2

African Court on Human and Peoples'
Rights 15, 20, 21, 115, 147–56
jurisdiction 149–53
African Development Bank 29
Africa's Priority Programme for
Economic Recovery 241, 242
Algeria 14, 38, 39, 42, 101, 102, 159,
161, 167, 168, 169, 170, 174, 183,
186, 191, 194, 195, 199
see also Western Sahara
American Convention on Human
Rights 109, 121, 125, 127, 147,
149, 152, 153, 154, 158, 159, 162,
164, 169, 170, 171, 179, 183, 187,
188, 189, 190, 191, 192, 196, 197,
199, 205, 206, 207, 208, 209, 210,
211, 212
Protocol on Economic, Social and
Cultural Rights (Protocol of San
Salvador) 128, 188, 193, 194,
196, 199, 220
Angola 6, 8, 9, 33, 39, 42, 101, 102,
159, 168, 169, 172, 185, 227
UNITA 6, 9, 11, 41

Benin 31, 38, 39, 42, 101, 102, 159, 161,
199, 221, 224, 228, 230
Biafra *see* Nigeria
Botswana 6, 7, 39, 101, 102, 106, 167,
171, 174, 176, 177, 178, 179, 182,
183, 184, 186, 187, 188, 189, 191,
192, 194, 200
Brazzaville Group 2, 38
Burkina Faso 39, 42, 101, 102, 161,
171, 172, 176, 197, 199, 221, 223,
230
frontier dispute with Mali 12–13
Burundi 6, 7, 11, 14, 33, 36, 38, 39, 40,
60, 84, 86, 87, 96, 101, 102, 103,
105, 107, 108, 158, 159, 167, 168,
173, 228

Cameroon 15, 31, 33, 38, 39, 42, 101,
102, 119, 159, 161, 170, 171, 173,
174, 175, 177, 179, 181, 182, 188,
197, 224, 230
Cape Verde 39, 101, 102, 159, 169, 173,
194, 199, 221
Casablanca Group 2, 17, 38

Central African Republic 9, 10, 38, 39, 41, 101, 102, 159, 170, 230
    Bokassa 40, 109
Chad 14, 38, 39, 101, 102, 159, 161, 168, 169, 170, 171, 173, 174, 185, 192, 195, 199, 230
    OAU peace-keeping *see under* Organization of African Unity: Charter
Commonwealth 51
    see also under Human Rights
Comoros 11, 16, 39, 43, 228
    purported secession of Anjouan 14, 33, 39, 45
Congo 6, 33, 38, 39, 40, 42, 43, 101, 102, 159, 161, 221, 223, 224, 230
Congress of Berlin 1, 12
Convention to Suppress Slavery, and Supplementary Convention on the Abolition of Slavery 118
Côte d'Ivoire 38, 39, 61, 101, 102, 159, 169, 170, 172, 173, 228, 230

Democratic Republic of the Congo 8, 39, 40, 42, 43, 96, 101, 102, 103, 159, 167, 173, 228, 230
Djibouti 39, 101, 174, 198, 230

Economic Commission for Africa (ECA) 29, 88
Economic Community of West African States (ECOWAS) 7, 10, 33, 49, 149, 209, 253, 258
ECOMOG 10, 41, 42
ECOSOC 95, 127
Egypt 1, 38, 39, 42, 101, 102, 159, 160, 162, 167, 168, 169, 170, 171, 172, 173, 174, 176, 184, 187, 191, 192, 193, 194, 196, 198, 199, 221, 228, 229, 230
Environment 213–39
    Agenda 21, 221, 228, 238
    Basel Convention 215–6, 217, 219, 223, 224, 229, 230, 231, 233, 238–9
    Bamako Convention 138, 217–20, 223, 224, 231, 232, 238
    Buenos Aires Plan of Action 225, 227

Convention on Access to Information, Public Participation in Decision-Making and Access to Justice in Environmental Matters 221, 236, 238
Convention on Biological Diversity 225
Convention on Prior Informed Consent Procedure for Certain Hazardous Chemicals 233
European Convention on Civil Liability for Damage Resulting from Activities Dangerous to the Environment 231, 232, 233, 236
European Convention on the Protection of the Environment Through Criminal Law 229, 233, 236
Geneva Convention on Long-Range Transboundary Air Pollution 204
human rights 220–3
IMO Convention on Liability and Compensation for Damage in Connection with the Carriage of Hazardous and Noxious Substances by Sea 231–2
Kyoto Protocol 225, 227
London Convention on the Prevention of Marine Pollution 231
Montreal Convention on Substances that Deplete the Ozone Layer 204
Oslo Convention for the Prevention of Marine Pollution 231
Protocol to the Barcelona Convention on the Prevention of Pollution of the Mediterranean Sea 230, 231
Rio Declaration 204, 213, 221, 223, 225, 232, 234, 237, 238
Stockholm Declaration 204, 213, 221, 234
UN Convention to Combat Desertification 204, 226

Environment (*continued*)
  UN Environment Program (UNEP)
    215, 223
  UN Framework Convention on
    Climate Change 225
  Vienna Convention for the
    Protection of the Ozone Layer
    204
  Waigani Convention to Ban the
    Importation into Forum Island
    Countries of Hazardous and
    Radioactive Wastes 230
Equatorial Guinea 39, 40, 76, 101, 102,
    109, 157, 159, 165, 171, 179–80,
    185, 188, 195
Eritrea 6, 39, 79, 86, 158, 171, 226
  border dispute with Ethiopia 15, 44
  independence 14, 45
Estrada Doctrine 36
Ethiopia 1, 14, 38, 39, 42, 45, 79, 101,
    102, 103, 119, 158, 159, 168, 171,
    172, 173, 183, 184, 205, 221, 224,
    226
  border dispute with Eritrea 15, 44
  dispute with Somalia 14
European Charter for Regional or
    Minority Languages 165
European Commission on Human
    Rights 139, 206
European Community/Union (EC/
    EU) 29, 39, 100, 128, 230, 242,
    247, 248, 250, 251, 252, 254, 255
  EC Directives 162, 193, 231, 232,
    233, 234, 237
  EC Treaty 49, 126, 162, 164, 165,
    166, 193, 204, 212, 220, 232, 234,
    237, 238, 239, 246, 247, 253, 255,
    256, 257, 258
European Convention for the
    Prevention of Torture and
    Inhuman or Degrading
    Treatment or Punishment 119
European Convention on Human
    Rights 20, 106, 109, 112, 121,
    147, 149, 150, 152, 154, 159, 160,
    162, 163, 176, 179, 180, 181, 184,
    185, 186, 187, 188, 190, 192, 196,
    197, 199, 206, 207, 209, 210, 211,
    212, 238

First Protocol 127, 190, 191, 192,
    195, 196, 202
  Fourth Protocol 125, 189
  Seventh Protocol 125, 180, 183,
    197
  Eleventh Protocol 139, 211
  Committee of Ministers 20, 185
European Convention on Human
    Rights and Biomedicine 171
European Convention on the Legal
    Status of Children Born Out of
    Wedlock 165
European Court of Human Rights
    147, 151, 159–60, 191, 205, 209,
    211, 212
European Framework Convention for
    the Protection of National
    Minorities 165
European Social Charter (Revised)
    128, 164, 188, 192, 193, 194, 195,
    196, 237, 238
  First Protocol 192, 193, 194

France 7, 8, 39–40
Front-Line States 3, 16, 43

Gabon 31, 38, 39, 59, 60, 101, 102, 159,
    161, 169, 171, 173, 174, 179, 180,
    196
Gambia 39, 101, 102, 126, 159, 169,
    171, 173, 195, 196, 205, 224, 228
Genocide 7, 79, 87, 100, 103, 107, 138,
    204–5
Geneva Conventions (1949) and
    Additional Protocols (1977) 42,
    43, 47, 89, 102, 201–2
Ghana 1, 38, 39, 42, 101, 102, 106, 161,
    171, 196, 221, 227
Guinea 31, 38, 39, 42, 61, 63, 101, 102,
    159, 161, 173, 176, 183, 221, 228,
    230
Guinea-Bissau 37, 39, 76, 101, 102,
    159, 169, 171, 230

Hague Convention IV 43
Homelands 104, 201
Human Rights 6, 40, 41, 103, 107, 109,
    157
  Commonwealth 7, 40, 47, 126

Human Rights Committee 145, 147, 167, 169, 170, 172, 173, 174, 175, 177, 178, 180, 181, 184, 185, 186, 190, 197, 199, 200, 237

ILO Convention Concerning Forced or Compulsory Labour 176
ILO Convention Concerning the Abolition of Forced Labour 176
ILO Convention on Association and Protection of the Right to Organize 187
ILO Convention on the Right to Organize and Bargain Collectively 187
ILO Equal Remuneration Convention 193
Inter-American Commission on Human Rights 139, 205, 237
Inter-American Convention on Forced Disappearances of Persons 168
Inter-American Convention on the Granting of Political Rights to Women 164
Inter-American Convention to Prevent and Punish Torture 119
Inter-American Convention on the Prevention and Eradication of Violence Against Women 198
Inter-American Court of Human Rights 152, 153, 154, 158, 161, 209, 210, 211, 212
International Court of Justice 12, 13, 30, 31, 35, 46, 54, 151, 153, 237
    Statute 15, 25, 26, 28, 46, 49, 51, 210, 212
International Covenant on Civil and Political Rights 82, 105, 106, 109, 113, 121, 125, 128, 136, 154, 159, 162, 164, 166, 171, 180, 182, 183, 184, 185, 186, 187, 188, 189, 190, 192, 196, 197, 199, 200, 202, 237, 238
    Optional Protocol 157, 159, 206, 207
    Second Optional Protocol 169
International Covenant on Economic, Social and Cultural Rights 82, 109, 113, 127, 128, 136, 159, 166,

188, 192, 193, 194, 195, 196, 199, 200, 202, 237, 238
International Law Commission, Draft Articles on State Responsibility 75, 205, 225, 228, 235
International Monetary Fund 203, 252

Katanga 13, 144
Kenya 39, 63, 67, 101, 102, 103, 159, 171, 172, 185, 187, 188, 190, 191, 193, 195, 237

Lagos Conference on the Rule of Law 110
Lagos Plan of Action 241–2, 253
Lesotho 6, 7, 39, 42, 101, 102, 106, 159, 161, 163, 174, 175, 178, 179, 183, 195, 199, 221, 230
Liberia 1, 10, 33, 38, 39, 42, 49, 61, 78, 101, 102, 119, 159, 168
Libya 38, 39, 67, 102, 159, 162, 169, 170, 173, 175, 185, 192, 193, 194, 195, 196, 197, 198, 199, 230
Limburg Principles 128
Lome Conventions 29, 218

Madagascar 16, 38, 39, 60, 101, 102, 159, 161, 169, 203, 221
Malawi 6, 39, 101, 102, 106, 159, 162, 164, 165, 166, 167, 170, 171, 172, 173, 174, 175, 176, 177, 178, 179, 180, 181, 182, 183, 185, 187, 188, 189, 190, 191, 192, 194, 195, 196, 197, 198, 199, 221, 228, 238
Mali 38, 39, 42, 61, 63, 101, 102, 159, 161, 168, 170, 171, 173, 174, 192, 195, 199, 221, 230
    dispute with Burkina Faso 12–13
Mauritania 38, 39, 42, 101, 102, 118, 167, 173, 190, 198
    Western Sahara see Western Sahara
Mauritius 16, 39, 58, 102, 159, 169, 172, 173, 174, 177, 183, 184, 191, 194, 196, 199, 204, 228, 230
Mercenarism 11, 42, 200
MINURCA 41
MINURSO
    see under Western Sahara
MISAB 10

Monrovia Group 2, 3,
MONUA 9
Morocco 12, 14, 38, 39, 42, 87, 103,
    159, 174, 228
  Western Sahara *see under* Western
    Sahara
  withdrawal from OAU 3, 34, 35, 36,
    39,
Mozambique 8, 9, 39, 78, 86, 101, 102,
    118, 119, 159, 169, 171, 221, 228

Namibia 6, 16, 63, 76, 93, 101, 159,
    162, 164, 165, 169, 171, 172, 173,
    174, 176, 177, 178, 179, 180, 181,
    182, 183, 186, 187, 188, 189, 190,
    191, 192, 193, 194, 195, 196, 197,
    202, 221, 228
National liberation movements, and
    wars of 17, 47, 59, 85, 132–5,
    201–2
Niger 38, 39, 42, 101, 102, 159, 170,
    171, 176, 195, 198, 199, 221, 224,
    230
Nigeria 7, 15, 31, 38, 39, 40, 42, 45, 51,
    61, 63, 69, 101, 102, 117–18, 126,
    147, 151, 159, 167, 168, 169, 170,
    172, 173, 180, 186, 188, 193, 195,
    196, 197, 224, 227, 228
  Biafra 13
Nkrumah, Kwame 1, 2, 5, 29
Non-Aligned Movement 18, 66, 114
Non-Governmental Organizations 88,
    91, 92, 94, 95, 142, 144, 149, 151,
    152, 181, 225, 239
Nuclear Test Ban Treaty 204
Nyerere, Julius 7, 14, 61

Organization of African Unity Charter
    2, 3, 12, 15, 16, 18, 25, 26, 28, 29,
    30, 46, 48, 51, 56, 57, 59, 66, 67,
    70, 72–3, 76, 82, 85, 110, 125, 240
  African Nuclear-Weapon-Free Zone
    Treaty (Treaty of Pelindaba) 18,
    158
  Assembly of Heads of State and
    Government 19–20, 22, 28, 27,
    33, 35, 37, 38, 60, 61, 62, 65, 66,
    67, 68, 69, 70, 82, 91, 97, 111, 112
  see also under AEC

budget 21, 22, 23, 34, 50
Charter for Popular Participation in
    Development and
    Transformation 238
colonialism and neo-colonialism 2,
    12, 15, 110, 113, 134
Commission of Mediation,
    Conciliation and Arbitration
    14, 24–9
Convention on a Cultural Charter
    for Africa 39
Convention on the Elimination of
    Mercenarism in Africa 11
Convention on the Conservation of
    Nature and Natural Resources
    226
Council of Ministers 20–1, 28, 30,
    58, 59, 60, 67, 68, 82, 97, 214
    see also under AEC
Declaration on the Problem of
    Subversion 11, 85
dispute settlement 5, 14, 15, 46,
    75
domestic jurisdiction 5–10, 11–12
expulsion 36–7
founding 1–2
General Convention on Privileges
    and Immunities, and Protocol
    23, 48
General Secretariat/Secretary 21–4,
    29, 33, 34–5, 61, 62, 67, 97
    see also under AEC
human rights 15
    see also African (Banjul) Charter
    on Human and Peoples' Rights
    independence 1, 2, 3, 11
Mechanism for Conflict Prevention,
    Management and Resolution 5,
    14, 32–3, 36, 38, 50, 51
membership 2, 22, 34–7, 67, 70
non-alignment 17, 18
non-intervention/non-interference
    5, 6, 11, 32–3, 51
objectives 2–18
peace-keeping 7, 29, 30–2, 33, 50,
    63, 64, 65
racial discrimination (apartheid) 2,
    6, 16
recognition 35–6, 39

Organization of African Unity Charter (*continued*)
  Rules of Procedure 19, 21, 22, 30, 48, 49, 50, 51, 59, 60, 67
  secession 3, 13, 14, 45, 145
  self-determination 16, 45–6, 60, 73, 110
  sovereignty 4, 5, 11, 32, 33, 57
  Specialized Commissions 29–32, 49
  subversion 11, 125
  territorial integrity 3, 4, 5, 11, 32, 45, 57
  uti possidetis 3, 12, 13, 16, 38, 43, 44, 73
  refugees *see* Refugees
  Resolution on the Intangibility of Frontiers 12, 57
  Western Sahara *see* Western Sahara

Refugees 78–108
  Addis Ababa Recommendations 93–5
  Arusha Conference 88–91, 95, 98
  asylum 80, 83, 88, 89, 90, 104, 106
  Bureau for Refugees 97–8
  Caracas Convention on Diplomatic Asylum 104
  Caracas Convention on Territorial Asylum 104
  Cartagena Declaration 101
  customary international law 80, 81
  definition of 79–80, 83, 89, 100
  domestic law 81, 91, 94, 100, 106
  expulsion 90, 104
  Geneva Convention on Refugees 79, 81, 82, 85, 88, 90, 91, 95, 100, 101–2, 104, 110
    Protocol 81, 82, 101–2, 110
  human rights 78, 81–2, 86, 99, 104, 107
  ICARA 91–2
  internally displaced persons 78, 79, 101, 108
  non-refoulement 80, 81, 83, 84, 88–9, 90, 101, 104, 125
  OAU Commission for Refugees 97, 102
  OAU Convention on Refugees 79,

  80, 81, 82–8, 89, 90, 91, 94, 102, 103, 104, 110, 125, 149
  SARRED 92–3
  subversion 42, 85, 86, 91
  UN Declaration on Territorial Asylum 83, 104
  UN Draft Convention on Territoriarial Asylum 104
  UNHCR 64, 81, 85, 86, 87, 88, 89, 91, 93, 94, 95–6, 97, 98, 99, 102, 103–4, 105, 106, 107, 108
  voluntary repatriation 86, 87, 89, 91, 105
Rwanda 6, 7–8, 33, 39, 40, 42, 50, 78, 83, 85, 86, 87, 96, 101, 102, 103, 104, 105, 107, 119, 159, 167, 168, 169, 170, 171, 198, 230
  International Criminal Tribunal on Rwanda 40, 100, 103–4, 169, 204

Saharan Arab Democratic Republic (SADR) *see* Western Sahara
São Tomé e Príncipe 39, 101, 102, 159, 169, 171, 221
Sea, Law of
  Geneva Convention on the High Seas 204
  UN Convention on the Law of the Sea 204
Self-determination 44–5, 46–7, 54, 56, 58, 60, 61, 63, 65, 66, 73, 74, 75, 103
  see also African Charter on Human and Peoples' Rights; General Assembly Resolutions; Organization of African Unity: Charter
Senegal 31, 38, 39, 42, 59, 101, 102, 159, 161, 167, 168, 173, 176, 177, 178, 191, 193, 197, 204, 228, 230
Seychelles 39, 42, 101, 102, 159, 169, 173, 199, 221, 224, 228
Sierra Leone 38, 39, 41, 43, 46, 63, 66, 101, 102, 159, 167, 168, 170, 173, 175
Somalia 8, 12, 14, 38, 39, 41, 45, 78, 101, 102, 159, 168, 169, 171, 173, 198, 226, 230

Somaliland, Republic of 3, 13, 14, 39, 45

South Africa 1, 6, 7, 39, 47, 86, 101, 102, 104, 106, 118, 159, 160, 162, 164, 165, 166, 167, 168, 169, 170, 171, 172, 173, 174, 175, 176, 177, 178, 179, 180, 181, 182, 183, 184, 185, 186, 187, 188, 189, 190, 191, 192, 194, 195, 199, 201, 202, 204, 221, 224, 228, 229, 238

Sudan 39, 40, 42, 43, 45, 60, 61, 63, 78, 79, 83, 86, 101, 102, 103, 119, 121, 151, 159, 167, 169, 170, 171, 173, 176, 179, 183, 184, 185, 188, 189, 196, 197, 199, 201, 224, 226, 230

Swaziland 39, 101, 102, 157, 171, 183, 198, 230

Tanzania 39, 40, 42, 63, 96, 102, 104–5, 158, 159, 161, 162, 163, 166, 172, 174, 177, 183, 184, 185, 187, 190, 191, 192, 193, 194, 195, 201, 204, 205, 221, 228, 230

Togo 38, 39, 42, 60, 76, 102, 158, 159, 161, 162, 168, 169, 171, 172, 173, 174, 175, 177, 180, 186, 188, 192, 196, 197, 199, 221, 230

Treaties, Law of 18, 57, 115
  see also Vienna Convention on the Law of Treaties; Vienna Convention on the Law of Treaties between States and International Organizations

Tunisia 39, 42, 102, 159, 161, 169, 170, 173, 178, 179, 180, 181, 182, 183, 185, 186, 187, 195, 197, 198, 199, 228, 230

Uganda 7, 39, 40, 102, 103, 105, 119, 125, 157, 159, 161, 163, 173, 199, 203, 205, 221
  Idi Amin 109, 125

United Nations 5, 14, 50, 62, 77
  Charter 4, 5, 11, 15, 18, 25, 26, 28, 45, 49, 50, 51, 53, 70, 74, 77, 106, 109, 110, 132, 204
    decolonization 53, 55–6
    domestic jurisdiction 6, 7
    good faith 69, 76
    human rights 40, 41, 110
    implied powers 30
    peace-keeping 7, 49, 63, 64, 65
    prohibition on the threat or use of force 11, 45, 56, 74
    regional bodies 4, 30, 60
    self-defence 30
    settlement of disputes 14, 45, 50
  membership 35
  recognition 35

UN-OAU Co-operation Agreement 39

UN Convention against the Recruitment, Use, Financing and Training of Mercenaries 42

UN Convention Against Torture and Other Cruel, Inhuman or Degrading Treatment or Punishment 119, 173, 175

UN Convention on the Elimination of All Forms of Discrimination against Women 164, 197–8

UN Convention on the Elimination of All Forms of Intolerance and Discrimination Based on Religion or Belief 183

UN Convention on the Elimination of All Forms of Racial Discrimination 163, 164, 187

UN Convention on the Suppression and Punishment of the Crime of Apartheid 163

UN Convention on the Rights of the Child 166, 169, 171, 172, 173, 183, 199

UNAMIR 7, 8, 50

UNAVEM 9

UNESCO Convention Against Discrimination in Education 195

UNECO Convention for the Protection of the World Cultural and Natural Heritage 204

UNESCO Convention on the Means of Prohibiting and Preventing the Illicit Import, Export and Transfer of Ownership of Cultural Property 204

UNHCR *see* Refugees
UNOSOM 8
UNITAF 8
UNOMIL 10, 42, 49
UNOMSA 10
UN General Assembly Resolutions 40,
    47, 53, 54, 57, 74, 77, 86, 91, 99,
    101, 106, 107, 108, 136, 170, 200,
    201, 202, 214, 226, 228, 231, 233,
    237, 239, 253
  Basic Principles of the Legal Status
    of Combatants 47, 74, 201
  Charter of Economic Rights and
    Duties 191, 202
  Declaration on Development 136,
    137, 203, 204, 237–8
  Declaration of Mentally Retarded
    Persons 193
  Declaration on the Elimination of
    All Forms of Intolerance and of
    Discrimination Based on
    Religion or Belief 165
  Declaration on the Establishment of
    a New International Economic
    Order 202
  Declaration on the Granting of
    Independence to Colonial
    Countries and Peoples 38, 46,
    53, 200
  Declaration on the Inadmissibility of
    Intervention in the Domestic
    Affairs of States 39, 42, 47, 74
  Declaration on the Peaceful
    Settlement of Disputes 45
  Declaration of Principles Governing
    the Sea-Bed and the Ocean
    Floor 204
  Declaration on Principles of
    International Law Concerning
    Friendly Relations and Co-
    operation Among States 39, 42,
    46, 47, 74, 138, 200, 201
  Declaration on the Protection of All
    Persons from Enforced
    Disappearance 168
  Declaration on the Protection of All
    Persons from Torture and
    Other Cruel, Inhuman or

    Degrading Treatment or
    Punishment 119
  Declaration on the Rights of Persons
    Belonging to Ethnic, Religious
    and Linguistic Minorities 165
  Definition of Aggression 42, 47, 74
  Principles for Older Persons 194
  Proclamation on Ageing 194
  Resolution on Permanent
    Sovereignty over Natural
    Resources 202
  Safeguards Guaranteeing Protection
    of the Rights of Those Facing
    the Death Penalty 169–70
UN High Commission/er for Human
    Rights 95, 99, 104, 105, 107, 108
UN Secretary-General 10, 50, 59, 70,
    71, 72, 77, 99
UN Security Council and resolutions
    7, 8, 9, 10, 11, 31, 37, 39, 40, 41,
    42, 43, 47, 49, 50, 54, 71, 72, 73,
    74, 76, 77, 105, 108, 204
Universal Declaration of Human
    Rights 82, 83, 106, 109, 110,
    113, 147, 154, 158, 188, 189, 190,
    192, 193, 199
Upper Volta *see* Burkina Faso

Vienna Convention on the Law of
    Treaties 36–7, 47, 48, 75, 102–3,
    112, 160
Vienna Convention on the Law of
    Treaties between States and
    International Organizations 48,
    51, 75
Vienna Convention on the
    Representation of States in
    Their Relations with
    International Organizations of a
    Universal Character 58–9
Vienna Declaration and Programme of
    Action 44–5, 74–5, 99, 101, 105,
    106, 108, 114, 119, 128, 137, 158,
    159, 162, 163, 164, 165, 167, 168,
    171, 200, 201, 202, 203, 220, 238

Western Sahara 52–77, 198, 199
  Algeria 54, 56, 59, 61
  history 52–6

ICJ Advisory Opinion 54, 58
Mauritania 53, 54, 55, 58, 59, 60, 61,
    62, 69
MINURSO 71, 72, 73
Morocco 52, 53, 54, 55, 56, 58, 59,
    60, 61, 62, 63, 64, 65, 66, 69, 70,
    71, 72, 75, 76, 87
OAU 55, 56–67, 68, 71, 72, 73
  Ad Hoc Committee 61–2
  admission to 3, 22, 55, 56, 65–7,
    70
  Implementation Committee 63–5,
    69, 75
  membership 68, 70
  Polisario Front 17, 53, 54, 55, 56,
    58, 59, 60, 62, 63, 65, 68, 70, 71,
    72, 75, 76, 87
SADR 39, 58, 62, 66, 68, 69, 70, 76,
    103
  criteria of statehood and
    recognition 66, 69, 70, 76
  declaration of independence 54,
    76
Spain 52, 53, 55, 56, 57, 58, 61

United Nations 53, 55, 56, 70, 71,
    72, 73
Settlement Plan 71
World Bank 203, 252
World Conference on Women (Beijing
    Platform for Action) 120, 137,
    177, 194, 197, 198, 200

Zaïre 6, 11, 39, 40, 70, 84, 85, 103, 104,
    105, 108, 144, 168, 174, 185, 195
  Mobutu 6, 11, 40, 85, 103, 174
  see also under Democratic Republic
    of the Congo
Zambia 6, 39, 42, 102, 159, 160, 161,
    163, 165, 168, 169, 170, 171, 172,
    174, 175, 176, 177, 178, 179, 180,
    181, 182, 183, 184, 185, 186, 187,
    188, 189, 190, 191, 192, 228
Zimbabwe 6, 16, 39, 42, 64, 102, 106,
    159, 163, 164, 165, 166, 168, 170,
    171, 172, 174, 176, 177, 178, 179,
    180, 181, 182, 183, 185, 186, 187,
    188, 189, 190, 191, 192, 194, 196,
    198, 199, 204, 230